Musorgsky

Eight Essays and an Epilogue

Musorgsky

Eight Essays and an Epilogue

By

RICHARD
TARUSKIN

PRINCETON UNIVERSITY

PRESS

Chapter 2 of this volume, "Handel, Shakespeare, and
Musorgsky: The Sources and Limits of Russian
Musical Realism," is reproduced from *Studies in the
History of Music*, vol. 1: *Music and Language*.
Copyright © 1983 by Broude Brothers Limited
Reproduced by permission of Broude Brothers Limited

Library of Congress Cataloging-in-Publication Data

Taruskin, Richard.
Musorgsky : eight essays and an epilogue /
Richard Taruskin.
p. cm.
Includes bibliographical references and index.
ISBN 0-691-09147-1
1. Mussorgsky, Modest Petrovich, 1839–1881—
Criticism and interpretation. I. Title.
ML410.M97T37   1992
780'.92—dc20   92-12124

This book has been composed in Linotron Palatino
Designed by Jan Lilly

Princeton University Press books are printed on
acid-free paper and meet the guidelines for permanence
and durability of the Committee on Production
Guidelines for Book Longevity of the
Council on Library Resources

Printed in the United States of America

2 4 6 8 10 9 7 5 3 1

GERALD ABRAHAM

in memoriam

Искусство есть средство для беседы с людьми,
а не цель.

Art is a means of human exchange, not an end.

Modest Petrovich Musorgsky, Autobiographical Note
(June 1880)

CONTENTS

FOREWORD

By
Caryl Emerson

———■———

IN 1839, the year of Musorgsky's birth, the Marquis de Custine made a three-month journey through the Russian Empire. The travel account he published four years later, *La Russie en 1839*, became an international bestseller; to this day, it is read as a key to that country's most grimly persistent cultural traits.[1] Astolphe de Custine was an aristocrat from a family ravaged by the French Revolution. Nevertheless, he came to view the Russian absolute autocracy (and the cunning, imitative, servile subjects it engendered) as far more deceitful and potentially dangerous than the more straightforward instability he had known at home. As chief historical culprit Custine named Peter the Great, who, "paying no respect to time," had thrust Western forms so precipitously onto his barbaric homeland that organic maturation had become almost impossible.

And yet the Russian sense of time fascinated him. Contemplating the austerity and earnestness of Tsar Peter, Custine wrote: "In Russia at that time, everything was sacrificed to the future; every one was employed in building the palaces of their yet unborn masters . . . There is certainly a greatness of mind evidenced in this care which a chieftain and his people take for the power, and even the vanity, of the generations that are yet to come. . . . It is a disinterested and poetical sentiment, far loftier than the respect which men and nations are accustomed to entertain for their ancestors."

The Marquis de Custine was unjust in many of his judgments, but on this point he was right. Imperial Russia—and especially its capital,

---

[1] See the recent reprint edition of the first (anonymously translated) English version of 1843, the Marquis de Custine, *Empire of the Czar: A Journey through Eternal Russia* (New York: Anchor-Doubleday, 1989). Quotations in this essay occur on pp. 600, 109, and 206 respectively. George Kennan has called *La Russie en 1839* "not a very good book about Russia in 1839" but "an excellent book, probably in fact the best of books, about the Russia of Joseph Stalin" (George F. Kennan, *The Marquis de Custine and His Russia in 1839* [Princeton: Princeton University Press, 1971], p. 124).

St. Petersburg—was heavily mortgaged to future glory. This appetite
was reflected in all the arts. In the 1840s and 1850s, sentimentally
optimistic historical drama was extremely popular on the Russian
stage; from the 1860s on, in a flush of patriotic feeling occasioned by
the Great Reforms and later fed by emergent Pan-Slavism, Rimsky-
Korsakov and many lesser talents were turning these dramas into
historical operas inspired by both socially progressive and statist-ex-
pansionist historiography. Even that small band of gifted, conten-
tious amateurs who made up the "New Russian School of Music"
was not immune to the call for a great and forward-looking Russia.
The patriotic ideology of Serov's 1865 opera *Rogneda* had much in
common with Glinka's founding text of thirty years before, *A Life for
the Tsar*.

One member of the Nationalist School, however, remained consistently outside this understanding of empire and historical progress.
Where other composers of his generation celebrated integration and
grandeur, he was at his best breaking things down, isolating Russian
leaders from the people they aspired to lead and denying historical
effectiveness to both sides. He invited his audience to laugh as well
as to weep at the broken parts; and his special talent, it seemed, was
to juxtapose estranged social classes so that maximal confrontation
produced minimal communication. Because his creative personality
underwent major (but usually well-masked) shifts throughout his
short life, the most painstaking scholarly energy and insider's knowledge is required to reconstruct the musical and extramusical context
for his works. It is this fully illuminated story that Richard Taruskin,
in the path-breaking essays collected here, unfolds around Modest
Musorgsky, Russia's greatest national composer.

Musorgsky's vision was neither populist nor imperial. He granted
the people no special virtues, and doubted that the passing of time
could itself assure to any nation victory. In 1872, several weeks into
the gala celebrations marking the bicentennial of Peter the Great's
birth, he wrote to Vladimir Stasov, "The power of the black earth will
make itself manifest when you plow it to the very bottom. . . . And
at the end of the seventeenth century they plowed Mother Russia
with just *such* [alien] tools . . . And she, our beloved, received the
various state bureaucrats, who never gave her, the long-suffering
one, time to collect herself and to think, '*Where are you pushing me?*'
. . . '*We've gone forward*'—you lie. '*We haven't moved!*' Paper, books
have gone forward—we *haven't moved*. . . . The people groan, and so

as not to groan they drink like the devil, and groan worse than ever: *haven't moved!*"[2]

Anyone familiar with Musorgsky scholarship will sense how embarrassing this piece of epistolary evidence is for the received image of the composer, both in Russia and abroad. Musorgsky the *narodnik* or radical populist, Musorgsky the rebellious antiestablishment figure and singer of the Russian folk—these were obligatory epithets in the civic-minded 1860s and 1870s as well as during the Soviet era. Along with this political correctness came the image of Musorgsky as a latter-day holy fool: the tragic and seedy figure in Repin's famous portrait, an amateur of genius who was also, alas, an alcoholic, a man who in his lucid moments jotted down raw, unconsidered masterpieces—in short, a creator not in control of his own significance. At the base of both images is the same assumption: that Musorgsky remained, throughout his life, a contrary child. Thus the composer is not perceived as having developed through his own disciplined, consciously creative choice; he is explained as naively spontaneous or as politically "oppressed," and everywhere he is seen as a man in opposition to the institutions and traditions that surrounded him (rarely an integral part of them). The most enduring virtue of Taruskin's work, perhaps, is its reconquest of a wider, healthier, more complexly intelligent image of Musorgsky. As a musician Musorgsky was indeed deficient in some areas of technique, and he was clearly a man of unappealing prejudices. He was also, however, a fastidious craftsman open to multiple influences, flexible on occasion but equally distinguished by a principled stubbornness.

The chapters that follow are the product of two decades' work by an American scholar who, it is fair to say, has almost single-handedly revised and set right the nineteenth-century Russian operatic canon. For sheer density of information per page—considering also the footnotes, which often amount to miniature essays—Richard Taruskin is without peer; what is remarkable, however, is his ability to shape this vast bulk of data into sharply articulated theses. Where others might inundate, Taruskin pursues an argument. This dual accomplishment is of the utmost importance. For until quite recently in Anglophone countries, the objective research base that is presumed for the masters of French, German, and Italian music has not been in place in Russian opera. Arguments in the realm of Russian music are fre-

[2] Letter from Musorgsky to Vladimir Stasov, 16/22 June 1872.

quently based on conventional truths and falsehoods that have migrated effortlessly from rumor into memoir and from there into academic discourse. For whatever reason—perhaps the language and alphabet barrier, or perhaps Soviet ideological constraints—scholarly discussion has all too often remained at the level of unexamined cliché.

As the reader will realize, Taruskin leaves absolutely no convention or cliché unexamined. But he does more: he sucks the reader into an eddy of facts all moving in a particular, and usually controversial, direction. The very pull of his thesis occasionally prods us to protest and strike out on our own. (As Taruskin invites us to do: "let me conclude by forswearing any claim of privilege for the authorial conceptions and purposes I have tried to tease out of the scores and documents," he demurs in his Epilogue. "In no sense do they set boundaries to legitimate reading.") No methodology could better serve a scholarly field.

The organization of the present book deserves comment. In plan it is a fat core of previously published (but not easily available) essays, flanked on either end by new and provocatively polemical pieces. Chapters 1 through 7, several of which are already classics, are arranged here not in order of their writing but rather to accord with Musorgsky's own biographical development. The outer frame, however, is more sensitive to contemporary events: it owes its punch and coherence to *glasnost'* and to the de-ideologization of Russian cultural heroes that got under way in the late 1980s.

Some words first on the core. By daring to open the body of his text not on the big known operas but on tiny, more peripheral matters (the dating of two versions of an early, relatively unfamiliar song; the grounding of Musorgsky's maiden experiment in realistic recitative, a setting of Gogol's *Marriage*, in neoclassical mimetic theories of art; the composer's relationship with the then-celebrated, now-forgotten Alexander Serov), Taruskin in effect liberates both his hero and his reader from the anachronistic temptations of a later fame and places Musorgsky back into the thick of the 1860s, where he was a minor and eccentric figure still very much in search of his own voice. Chapters 4 through 7, the book's inner core as it were, give us the Musorgsky corpus we know best and love most, *Boris Godunov* and *Khovanshchina*. But beware: Taruskin's revisions of received wisdom are many and profound. Among the most significant are his insistence on the integrity and autonomy of the two authorial versions of *Boris*; his refusal to endorse the image of Musorgsky as martyr and its concomitant "myth of the malign directorate [of the Imperial Theaters]"; his uncovering of historiographical subtexts for the Kromy scene in *Boris* that detach it ideologically from mass scenes in other contemporaneous operas; his account of the weirdly complex, counterintuitive origins of the folk songs in *Boris*, in particular the famous *Slava!*; and a reading of *Khovanshchina* that is boldly contrary to the reformist spirit of the sixties, which is to say, a reading that defines this second historical opera, despite its subtitle, as precisely the opposite of a progressive "musical folk drama." Heretically (and quite persuasively), Taruskin classifies it as an "aristocratic tragedy informed by pessimistic historiography." One wishes that the Marquis de Custine could have seen a performance of the opera thus construed; he would have rejoiced.

As Taruskin's chapters progress, fussy detail diminishes, literary and cultural background comes into play in a more focused way, and arguments become increasingly lapidary and robust. Chapter 8 on *Sorochintsï Fair*, new for this volume, takes as its starting point the ambivalent moral and political message underlying Nikolai Gogol's contribution to Russian opera. Taruskin suggests that Gogol's Ukrainian tales, massively popular as sources for potential libretti, were permeated by the same retrograde, nonprogressive, implicitly imperialist brand of folklore that came powerfully back into vogue in the 1860s, through the efforts of opera composers such as Alexander Serov.[3] En route to *Sorochintsï Fair*, Musorgsky's talent evolved from extremist-realist recitative to so-called rationally justified melody of the *Khovanshchina* sort, where folk melody marked the identity not of persons but of groups and moods—in short, a return to the world of romantic *narodnost'*. Did this conservative turn in Musorgsky's musical thinking bespeak a larger and less attractive conservatism in other realms?

Taruskin devotes some space to the Byzantine refinements of Musorgsky's anti-Semitism, but that is just the beginning. His tour de force comes with a frontal attack on all the Soviet-bred truisms that for a century have been refashioning Musorgsky into a dissident populist, militant realist, and radical democrat from what the evidence in fact suggests he was: an aristocrat with an early clinical interest in

[3] For more extensive development of Serov's role in Russian musical culture, see Taruskin's massive *Opera and Drama in Russia as Preached and Practiced in the 1860s* (Ann Arbor: UMI Research Press, 1981), especially chapters 2–4.

true-to-life musical portraiture and a later penchant for drinking partners who were both folklore buffs and political reactionaries. Taruskin concludes that at the time of his death Musorgsky, along with
what was left of his early maverick circle, was on the brink of being
absorbed, and most willingly, into the Establishment—much as happened with Ilya Repin and his breakaway band of artists. Professional at last.

This revisionist biography is set off nicely by the book's outer
frame, where the politics of Modest Musorgsky are deftly pre- and
postfigured. We note a satisfying symmetry. The Introduction fo-
cuses on what we might call, echoing Musorgsky's second historical
opera, "Stasovshchina"—the -shchina suffix referring to distortions,
however well-meant, brought on by the pervasive, possessive meddling of Vladimir Stasov both during and after the composer's life.
Stasov's grim rectitude is contrasted with the more aristocratic and
"decadent" intimacy Musorgsky achieved with Count Arseny
Golenishchev-Kutuzov, poet for several of Musorgsky's most inspired songs and later a high-ranking official at the imperial court.
The tension between the composer's "aristocratic inclinations and
kuchkist pose" is thus set up from the start, not to be resolved until
the end of the eighth chapter.[4]

But does Taruskin resolve this tension? In the Epilogue, he notes
with deep pleasure the fact that Musorgsky, whose jubilee decade
(1981–89) loosely overlapped the glasnost' years, is now no longer
routinely "Stasovized." To be sure, in the Russian context this has
not meant that he was depoliticized, or that his image was released
to seek its own free-wheeling, contradictory stability. "So far from
the proto-Soviet populist of old," Taruskin writes of this era that so
eagerly dethroned precursors to communism, "he was now to be
consecrated as the grim prophet of the Soviet tyranny." This inver-
sion has occasioned some peculiar and quite fanciful inventions,
most noticeably the Christianization of Musorgsky's operas and
worldview. But in that, too, Taruskin sees the healthy first steps toward genuine cultural pluralism. Of course, Musorgsky's own artistic intent should be recuperated under conditions of optimal schol-

___

[4] It is worth noting that the animus against Golenishchev-Kutuzov, and a defensive
dismissal of his memoirs of Musorgsky, is still alive and well among Soviet-trained
musicologists, even those publishing in the West. See the quite intemperate preface in
Alexandra Orlova, ed. and compiler, Musorgsky Remembered (Bloomington: Indiana
University Press, 1991), pp. x–xii.

arly freedom. But those documented intentions need not constrain later competing interpretations of the work.

The Russian literary scholar Mikhail Bakhtin put this point well in his discussion of the artistic potential of great works. "Neither Shakespeare himself nor his contemporaries knew that 'great Shakespeare' whom we know now," Bakhtin wrote. "There is no possibility of squeezing our Shakespeare into the Elizabethan epoch. . . . The author is captive of his epoch, of his own present. Subsequent times liberate him from this capitivity."[5] Taruskin concurs: "The works are ours now, not Musorgsky's." And thus we have Taruskin's goal in this collection of essays, one he has vigorously pursued in other forums where questions of musical authenticity are debated: "to inform choice, not delimit it."

To return, in closing, to the Marquis de Custine. In 1839 he was negatively impressed by the imitativeness, regimentation, and frivolity of Russian efforts in the realm of culture. "The Russians have not yet reached the point of civilization at which there is real enjoyment of the arts," he wrote from St. Petersburg. "At present their enthusiasm on these subjects is pure vanity; it is a pretense, like their passion for classic architecture. Let these people look within themselves, let them listen to their primitive genius, and, if they have received from Heaven a perception of the beauties of art, they will give up copying, in order to produce what God and nature expect from them." Whatever complex image we eventually construct of Modest Musorgsky, he was indisputably a titan of that generation that Custine so hoped would arrive, to reveal to Russia her own intensifying and protean self.

[5] "Response to a Question from the Novy Mir Editorial Staff" [1970], in M. M. Bakhtin, *Speech Genres and Other Late Essays*, trans. Vern W. McGee (Austin: University of Texas Press, 1986), pp. 4–5.

A NOTE ON
TRANSLITERATION

——————■——————

AFTER MUCH thought and experiment, it was decided to adopt with modifications the system for transliterating Russian vowels that was worked out by Gerald Abraham for the *New Grove Dictionary of Music and Musicians*. For a complete account of it, see the *New Grove* 1.xvi–xvii.

The chief merit of the system is that it assigns Roman characters to Cyrillic ones with consistency, so that adjectival endings may be rendered faithfully. The Russian letter ы, pronounced as a thick short *i*, is represented by the character *ï*, while the Russian й, signifying iotation, is represented by *y*. The palatalizing vowels я and ю are represented by *ya* and *yu*. The Cyrillic E is usually transliterated by its Roman cognate, but in initial position and after vowels or hard/soft signs it is rendered as *ye*. Where *e* is found in such positions, it signifies the Russian э.

Modifications are introduced for the sake of clarity, based on the pronunciation habits of English-speaking readers. Thus the dipthong "АЙ" (which rhymes with "high" as in Nikolai) is rendered as *ai*, since *ay* would suggest to English readers a rhyme with "day." When the vowels А and И are conjoined, each receiving its full phonetic value, this is signified by the use of an accent, thus: Mikhaíl (pronounced Mi-kha-EEL). When one of a pair of и's receives an accent, the pair is represented by *-iyi-*, as in "Mariyinsky Theater." When the pair occurs at the end of a plural or a genitive, neither member taking an accent, *-ii* is the form adopted in transliteration.

Like the *New Grove*, this book respects standard renderings where they have become firmly established and where a more faithful transliteration would therefore be distracting. Thus the usual spelling *-sky* is retained for the suffix СКИЙ in names like Rimsky or Musorgsky. Such other customary Roman spellings as Prokofiev and Koussevitzky are likewise retained. Many such spellings not sanctioned by the *New Grove*, such as Diaghilev and Chaliapin, are also kept. On the other hand, owing to a confessed quirk on the part of the author, who is possibly oversensitive to reminders of the onetime musical provincialism of the English-speaking peoples, "Tchaikovsky" is rejected in favor of the more literal "Chaikovsky," which is perfectly regular for English, though not for French or German.

In bibliographical citations, transliteration is strictly according to the rules, letter by letter, not according to customary usage or phonetics. г is always g, even in genitive endings where Russians now pronounce it v. Those for whom the citations are useful are precisely the ones who would find sound-based modifications annoying in this case.

A NOTE ON DATES

THE Julian calendar (known as the "Old Style," abbreviated O.S.) was used in Russia until 1 February 1918, and is still the calendar of the Russian Orthodox Church. In the nineteenth century Russian dates were twelve days behind those of the Gregorian calendar ("New Style," or N.S.), used elsewhere in Europe and in America. The year 1900 being a leap year according to the Julian calendar but not the Gregorian, from 29 February 1900 to 1 February 1918 the two "styles" were thirteen days apart.

In this book dates for events taking place in Russia will always be given according to the calendar in use in Russia. Whenever there is a possibility of confusion, or where Russian dates must be synchronized with Western ones, double dating will be employed unless O.S. or N.S. is specified.

TABLE OF
ABBREVIATIONS

—■—

AsIT   Akademik Boris Vladimirovich Asafyev, *Izbrannïye trudï* [Selected papers]. 5 vols. Moscow: Akademiya nauk SSSR, 1952–57.

BalStasP   M. A. Balakirev and V. V. Stasov, *Perepiska* [Correspondence]. Ed. Anastasya Sergeyevna Lyapunova. 2 vols. Moscow: Muzïka, 1970–71.

BorP   Sergey Alexandrovich Dianin, ed., *Pis'ma A. P. Borodina* [Letters of A. P. Borodin]. 4 vols. Moscow: Muzgiz, 1928–50.

CuilP   César Antonovich Cui, *Izbrannïye pis'ma* [Selected letters]. Leningrad: Muzgiz, 1955.

CuilS   César Antonovich Cui, *Izbrannïye stat'i* [Selected articles]. Leningrad: Muzgiz, 1952.

FridMPM   Emiliya Lazarevna Frid, *M. P. Musorgskiy: Problemï tvorchestva: issledovaniya* [Musorgsky: research problems involving the works]. Leningrad: Muzïka, 1981.

GozROT   Abram Akimovich Gozenpud, *Russkiy opernïy teatr* [The Russian operatic theater]. 5 vols.:

   GozROTI: *Russkiy opernïy teatr XIX veka (1836–1856)*. Leningrad: Muzïka, 1969.

   GozROTII: *Russkiy opernïy teatr XIX veka (1857–1872)*. Leningrad: Muzïka, 1971.

   GozROTIII: *Russkiy opernïy teatr XIX veka (1873–1889)*. Leningrad: Muzïka, 1973.

   GozROTIV: *Russkiy opernïy teatr i Shalyapin 1890–1904*. Leningrad: Muzïka, 1974.

   GozROTV: *Russkiy opernïy teatr mezhdu dvukh revolyutsiy 1905–1917*. Leningrad: Muzïka, 1975.

JAMS   *Journal of the American Musicological Society* (periodical).

MR   Jay Leyda and Sergey Bertensson, eds. and trans., *The Musorgsky Reader: A Life of Modeste Petrovich Musorgsky in Letters and Documents*. New York: W. W. Norton, 1947.

MusCW   Modest Musorgsky, *Complete Works* (reordered reprint of MusPSS). 23 vols. (26 installments). New York: Edwin F. Kalmus, 1969.

TABLE OF ABBREVIATIONS

MusIM   Malcolm Hamrick Brown, ed., *Musorgsky: In Memoriam 1881–1981*. Ann Arbor: UMI Research Press, 1982.

MusLN   Modest Petrovich Musorgsky, *Literaturnoye naslediye* [Literary legacy]. Ed. Mikhail Pekelis and Alexandra Orlova. 2 vols. Moscow: Muzïka, 1971–72.

MusPD   Andrey Nikolayevich Rimsky-Korsakov, ed., *M. P. Musorgskiy: Pis'ma i dokumentï* [M. P. Musorgsky: letters and documents]. (Moscow and Leningrad: Muzgiz, 1932).

MusPSS   M. P. Musorgsky, *Polnoye sobraniye sochineniy* [Complete collected works]. Ed. Pavel Alexandrovich Lamm. 8 vols. (26 installments). Moscow: Muzgiz; and Vienna: Universal, 1928–39).

MuzN   Mikhaíl Vladimirovich Ivanov-Boretsky, ed., *Muzïkal'noye nasledstvo: Sbornik materialov po istorii muzïkal'noy kul'turï v Rossii* [Musical heritage: an anthology of archival materials on the history of art music in Russia]. Moscow: Ogiz and Muzgiz (joint publication), 1935.

MZh   *Muzïkal'naya zhizn'* [Musical life] (periodical).

NasMPM   Yevgeniy Mikhailovich Levashov, ed., *Naslediye M. P. Musorgskogo* [The legacy of M. P. Musorgsky]. Moscow: Muzïka, 1989.

OldBGC   Robert William Oldani, "*Boris Godunov* and the Censor." *19th-Century Music* 2 (1978–79): 245–53.

OrTD   Alexandra Anatolyevna Orlova, *Trudï i dni M. P. Musorgskogo: letopis' zhizni i tvorchestva* [M. P. Musorgsky's works and days: a chronicle of his life and works]. Moscow: Muzgiz, 1963.

R-KMusL   Nikolai Rimsky-Korsakov, *My Musical Life*. Trans. Judah A. Joffe. London: Eulenberg Books, 1974.

RMusMus   Edward R. Reilly, *The Music of Musorgsky: A Guide to the Editions*. New York: The Musical Newsletter, 1980.

SerIS   Alexander Nikolayevich Serov, *Izbrannïye stat'i* [Selected articles]. 2 vols. Moscow: Muzgiz, 1950–57.

SovM   *Sovetskaya muzïka* [Soviet music] (periodical).

StasIS   Vladimir Vasilyevich Stasov, *Izbrannïye sochineniya* [Selected works]. 3 vols. Moscow: Iskusstvo, 1952.

StasPR   V. V. Stasov, *Pis'ma k rodnïm* [Family correspondence]. Ed. Yelena Dmitriyevna Stasova. 3 vols. (vols. 1 and 3 in two parts each). Moscow: Muzgiz, 1953–62.

StasSEM   Vladimir Stasov, *Selected Essays on Music*. Trans. Florence Jonas. New York: Frederick A. Praeger, 1968.

StasSM   V. V. Stasov, *Stat'i o muzïke* [Articles on music]. 5 vols. Moscow: Muzïka, 1974–80.

TarODR   R. Taruskin, *Opera and Drama in Russia*. Ann Arbor: UMI Research Press, 1981.

YasVR-K   Vasiliy Vasilyevich Yastrebtsev, *Nikolai Andreyevich Rimskiy-Korsakov: Vospominaniya* [Memoirs of N. A. Rimsky-Korsakov]. Ed. Alexander Vyacheslavovich Ossovsky. 2 vols. Leningrad: Muzgiz, 1959–60.

PRONOUNCING
THE NAME

———■———

IT IS always a shock for an Anglophone to hear a Russian pronounce
the name MOO-sor'-sky for the first time, especially if one knows that
the Russian word *músor*, which the dictionary translates decorously
as "sweepings," means "garbage" (including, in slang usage, the
kind that is expelled from the nose). Mu-SORG-sky, seemingly a Polish variant (but the only way of salvaging the *g* for sound), has become so well entrenched in the West (reinforced by accommodating
émigrés like Chaliapin) that a plea for authenticity seems quite futile.

———————

THAT much, until recently, would have been a sufficient note on pronunciation. But there has lately been a move afoot in Russia to adopt
the second-syllable stress, abetted by no less a personage than Ti-
khon Khrennikov, the Stalin-appointed tsar of Soviet music, who
made a point of accenting the *o* in a televised speech. The concomitant debate, largely carried on in the television column of the newspaper *Sovetskaya kul'tura*, demands attention.

The question was first broached in 1975 by Alexey Kuzmich Yugov,
a novelist and amateur etymologist, in a book called *Thoughts on the
Russian Word*. "Frankly," he began, "it somehow pains me to hear an
announcer say, 'The great Russian composer Snotsky.' " Fixing on
the soundless *g*, he traced the name back to the Church Slavonic *mu-
sórg*, from the Greek *musúgr* or *musúrgos*, meaning artist, poet, or—
musician! "In short," he concluded, "there is no doubt that the surname of the great composer must be pronounced *Musór(g)sky!*"[1]

A charming folk etymology, this, but very easily disproved. Musorgsky's family name, it turns out, did not sport that crucial *g* until
the composer's generation. Family documents, going back as far as
the seventeenth century, give a wide range of spellings: Muserskoy,
Musirskoy, Musarsky, Musersky, Musursky, and Musorsky.[2] The

---

[1] *Dumï o russkom slove* (Moscow: Sovremennik, 1975), pp. 211–12.

[2] Nikolai Novikov, "Ego rodoslovnaya," SovM, no. 3 (1989): 32. Also see idem, *U
istokov velikoy muzïki* (Leningrad: Lenizdat, 1989), pp. 94–102. These documents were

aristocratic suffix *-skoy*, where it appears, suggests an accent on that syllable (cf. the writers Tolstóy and Shakhovskóy, the painter Kramskóy, etc.). In the other variants, the mutability of the second-syllable vowel is conclusive evidence that that syllable did not carry an accent; since *-sky* never takes an accent, only the first syllable, with its constant vowel, remains eligible. The composer's baptismal record reads "Musersky."[3] His own letters and manuscripts are signed "Musorsky" through 1862.[4] Even after that year, he used the older, *g*-less spelling in business documents and letters to his country relatives.[5] Indeed, his name was indubitably "Snotsky" by traditional pronunciation, if not etymologically.

But how did *he* pronounce it (or prefer it), and how did the *g* get there? These questions have been complicated by some intriguing testimony from the last of the Musorgskys, Tatyana Georgiyevna *Musórgskaya*, granddaughter of the composer's elder brother Filaret (1836–89), squire of the family estate near Pskov. Tatyana, who lived in Ryazan and died childless in 1984 (thus extinguishing the line), maintained that her father Georgiy Filaretovich and her aunt Tatyana Filaretovna pronounced the name *Musórgsky*, with the *ó* "more sonorous [than in Russian], in the Polish fashion."[6] According to Yugov's literary executor, moreover, Tatyana Georgiyevna alleged explicitly that the composer followed his brother's example.[7]

One cannot doubt Tatyana's contentions with respect to her parents and her grandfather, but there are two facts militating against her assertion with respect to her famous great-uncle. Modest Petrovich himself played on the *músor* connection, signing his letters to Vladimir Stasov (and other members of the Stasov clan) with the nickname Musoryanin—"garbage dweller"—beginning in 1870. Oc-

---

first described in print by Vyacheslav Karatïgin, who constructed the composer's family tree for the special Musorgsky issue of Andrey Rimsky-Korsakov's music magazine: "Rodoslovnaya M. P. Musorgskogo po muzhskoy i zhenskoy liniyam," *Muzïkal'nïy sovremennik*, nos. 5–6 (1917): insert between pp. 14 and 15.

[3] "Telegid," *Sovetskaya kul'tura* (13 July 1989), p. 8. My thanks to Laurel Fay, of all Americans the most au courant with Soviet musical affairs, for copies of the TV column.

[4] The first appearance of "Musorgsky" in his correspondence is a letter to Balakirev dated 14 March 1863 (MusLN 1.64; cf. Chapter 1 of the present book, where an important argument depends on this fact). Since he had been signing his letters to Balakirev "Modest" since June 1858, the use of the altered surname seems calculated and demonstrative.

[5] Novikov, "Ego rodoslovnaya," p. 32.

[6] Ibid.

[7] V. Serebrovsky, letter to "Telegid," *Sovetskaya kul'tura* (13 July 1989).

casionally he would even sign his letters to Stasov with the unmodified noun itself: "Your *Musor*."[8] Yugov had a ready answer for this— "Anything can be said in friendly jest!"[9]—though it might seem to take a bit of forcing to derive all these *músor* jokes from a name in which the dominating syllable was "sorg," especially when an equally homely Russian word, *sórgo* (sorghum), was available for friendly jesting.

Harder to counter is the evidence of an unpublished verse by Count Golenishchev-Kutuzov (who met Musorgsky in 1872), where the composer's name is embedded in an iambic meter that decisively fixes its accentuation:

> Skazhí mne, Músorgsky, zachém
> Poróy tomyát menyá somnén'ya,
> I v chas schastlívïy vdokhnovén'ya
> Ya ostayús' unïl i nem?[10]

> [Tell me, Musorgsky, why
> Doubts at times torment me,
> And in the happy hour of inspiration
> I remain gloomy and mute?]

If Musorgsky's closest friend had been used to hearing the name accented on the second syllable, he could easily have written "*Skazhí, Musórgsky, pochemú*," using an alternate (even, in this context, slightly preferable) form of the word "why." Obviously, then, in and after 1872 the composer had gone back to saying his name exactly as he had done before adding the *g*.

So why the *g*? An answer to this question, as well as a means of reconciling the evidence from all sides, can be deduced by juxtaposing two writings by Stasov—one public, the other private. In his biographical essay, published the year of Musorgsky's death, Stasov drew on a great deal of family lore, some of it obtained directly from Filaret. Thus we learn that after his father's death in 1853, Musorgsky lived with his mother and elder brother in St. Petersburg, and that after his mother went back to the ancestral estate in 1862, he stayed on with Filaret (by then married) until the fall of 1863, when he moved with some friends into a communal flat.[11] The period during

---

[8] See the letter of 12 February 1876; MusLN 1.213; MR, 327–28.
[9] *Dumï o russkom slove*, p. 211.
[10] Quoted in FridMPM, 131.
[11] StasIS 2.173.

which the younger brother was living as the virtual ward of the elder was exactly the period in which the *g* was introduced into the family name. Evidently it was Filaret's idea, which comports well with his granddaughter's recollections.

But where did Filaret get the idea? Modern genealogists have confirmed that a fifteenth- or sixteenth-century ancestor of the Musorgskys, Roman Vasilyevich Monastïryov, went by the sobriquet *Musorga*, from which the family name was eventually derived.[12] Possibly owing to Yugov's influence, it has been surmised that this nickname identified Roman Vasilyevich as a monastic singer.[13] But family traditions were different. In a very late letter (24 January 1903) to the Moscow impresario Arkady Kerzin, Stasov finally explained how Musorgsky got to be called Musoryanin: "So I called him to his face during our interminable chats," he wrote, "and so I called him ever *in jest*, stubbornly proving to him, with laughter, that he did not descend from some Tatar named 'Musorga,' as he insisted, but simply from our plain old Russian 'músor.' "[14]

To sum up, then: In 1862–63, at the age of twenty-three, Modest Petrovich *Músorsky*, impelled by his elder brother Filaret, the head of the family, inserted a *g* into his name and affected a new accentuation, *Musórgsky* (fancifully derived from family traditions), so as to obscure a resemblance to a lowly Russian word that Filaret, a snooty landowner, resented. Filaret used the new pronunciation to the end of his days and passed it on to his descendents. The composer, however, could not get his friends to take it seriously, and eventually (by 1870 at the latest) he gave it up, retaining the *g* in writing but reverting to, or at least tolerating, the earlier pronunciation: *Músorgsky*. It would seem pedantic now to follow the composer's halfhearted and temporary caprice whereas those who addressed him every day did not. However one might wish to accentuate it, his name was in fact stressed on the first syllable, as it is among Russian speakers today— even in his home village, Karevo (Pskov district), where the inhabitants still speak of the *"Músorgskaya gorá"* (the Musorgsky hill), the *"Músorgskoye polye"* (the Musorgsky field), and the *"Músorgskaya*

[12] He is mentioned in the *Barkhatnaya kniga*, the sixteenth-century genealogy of the boyars (which traces the composer's ancestry straight back to Ryurik, the fabled ninth-century founder of the Russian state) as grandfather of the first actual Musor(g)sky. See Karatïgin, "Rodoslovnaya."

[13] Novikov, "Ego rodoslovnaya," p. 33.

[14] "17 pisem V. V. Stasova k A. M. Kerzinu," *Muzïkal'nïy sovremennik*, no. 2 (1916): 19.

roshcha" (the Musorgsky grove).[15] "What Alexey Yugov happens to think," wrote Gavriyil Yakovlevich Yudin, a veteran composer and conductor, "completely contradicts what St. Petersburg thought and Leningrad thinks."[16] On the other hand, those comfortable with the common Western mispronunciation have Filaret, Tatyana, and (from 1863 to 1870) the composer on their side.

[15] Novikov, "Ego rodoslovnaya," p. 33.

[16] Letter to "Telegid," *Sovetskaya kul'tura* (13 July 1989), p. 8. Yudin offered his own account of the stress shift: "The conductor N[ikolai Semyonovich] Golovanov [1891–1958, longtime head of the Moscow Philharmonic and the All-Union Radio Orchestra] did not like the fact that Musorgsky's surname was reminiscent of garbage, and he did not hesitate to demand that on the radio everyone pronounce the name with the accent on the second syllable. I endured this for four years and finally turned to the Academician B[oris] Asafyev and the corresponding member [of the Academy of Sciences] A[lexander] Ossovsky. They launched the appropriate démarche and categorically demanded a halt to this atrocious distortion of the great Russian composer's name, which was done. This happened, if I am not mistaken, immediately after the War."

A Pronouncing Glossary of Selected Russian Names and Titles

Balákirev
Borís Godunóv
Borodín
Filíppov
Goleníshchev-Kutúzov
Gurilyóv
Kamárinskaya
Karamzín
Karmálina
Khovánshchina
Khudyakóv
Kostomárov

Missaíl
mogúchaya kúchka
Petróv
Seróv
Shestakóva
Solovyóv
Soróchintsï
Stasyulévich
Tsïganóv
Varlámov
Vorobyóva

WHAT IS A *KUCHKA*?

——■——

First, what is a *kucha*? A heap. A *kuchka*, therefore, is a little heap: a contradiction in terms. Or else a heap of beloved things (in which case they would not be in a heap: another contradiction in terms). Most often the word *kuchka* is used, with affectionate irony, to denote a small group of people toward whom one's attitude is positive. So Vladimir Stasov used it in the typically megaphoned and sloppily written peroration to an article describing a concert conducted by Miliy Balakirev on 12 May 1867 before an audience of Serbian, Croatian, and Bohemian delegates to a Slavonic ethnographic congress. The program had contained music by Rimsky-Korsakov (*Serbian Fantasy*), Balakirev (*In Bohemia* and the Oriental romance "Song of the Golden Fish"), Glinka (*Kamarinskaya* and the Napoleonic ballad "The Midnight Review"), Dargomïzhsky (*Little-Russian Kazachok*), A. F. L'vov (the overture to *Undina*), Moniuszko (an aria from *Halka*), Liszt (*Hungarian Fantasy*—Stasov insisted it was really Slovak), and Berlioz (the march from *La Damnation de Faust*). Stasov ended his tribute "with a wish: God grant that our Slavonic guests never forget today's concert; God grant that they always remember how much poetry, feeling, talent, and skill there is in the small but already *mighty little heap* of Russian musicians."[1]

Moguchaya kuchka was really too much. Doubly an oxymoron, it sounds much more ridiculous than Stasov could have meant. It was an irresistible target for those (and there were many) whom Stasov annoyed with his tub-thumping journalism. First to pick it up was Alexander Serov, Stasov's archenemy (naturally, they had once been best friends), whose music had been conspicuously snubbed on this occasion. He made merry over the *moguchaya kuchka* in his own journal, *Muzïka i teatr* (see Chapter 3), and succeeded at first in turning both the term and its referents into a laughingstock. Even Musorgsky (see Chapter 8) used the term this way, opprobriously.

But its very ridiculousness made the phrase ultimately endearing, and it attached itself benignly to the group of maverick composers

[1] V. V. Stasov, "Slavyanskiy kontsert g. Balakireva," *Sanktpeterburgskiye vedomosti*, no. 130 (13 May 1867); StasIS 1.173 (italics added).

gathered around Balakirev (known in its day, through the journalistic activity of César Cui, as the "New Russian School"). That was not how Stasov had originally meant it, for the Russian composers on the "Slavonic concert" had included a few members of an older generation, and only two members of the Balakirev circle (Musorgsky not among them). Later, the purview was narrowed further still, until the term referred, quite neutrally, to the composers otherwise known as "The Five" (in Russian, *pyatero*): Balakirev, Cui, Borodin, Musorgsky, and Rimsky-Korsakov, in order of seniority. The English phrase "Mighty Five" thus conflates two separate Russian sobriquets.

The standard English renderings of Stasov's original phrase—"The Mighty Handful" or "The Mighty Band"—altogether miss the special nuance of *kuchka*. To coin a new English ersatz like "The Mighty Little Heap" seems especially pointless, since English does not normally heap people (living ones, anyway). Therefore, in this book the group to which Musorgsky belonged in his youth will be called the "mighty kuchka," or simply the kuchka. This will enable the retention of such useful forms, well established in Russian musicography, as the adjective "kuchkist," denoting the members or the characteristics of the group, and the abstract noun "kuchkism," denoting its Davidsbündlerish (rather than simply nationalistic) attitudes.

Musorgsky

*Eight Essays and an
Epilogue*

———■———

Introduction

WHO SPEAKS FOR
MUSORGSKY?

THE ONLY exception the Russian crown ever made to its nineteenth-century monopoly on theaters was for the sake of operetta, deemed a useful public diversion at a time of mounting civic strife. During the 1870s, two private establishments were set up to regale St. Petersburgers with the latest amusements from Paris. The larger of them, the so-called Teatr-buff (*Théâtre bouffe*) was able to import productions of Offenbach and Lecocq with the original casts. So it was that in March 1875, the composer of *Boris Godunov*, freshly dubbed "a thinking realist in Russian opera," happened in on *Madame l'Archiduc*, Offenbach's latest (it had opened at the *Bouffes-Parisiens* not five months before) and heard Mlle Annie Judic, the Boulevard King's latest discovery, singing lines like these:

> Oh! yes splendid l'Italie, London y préfer,
> Oh! yes moi comme vous y préfer Birmingham and Manchester.
> Oh! Venise elle est jolie, Very beautiful,
> Y préfer Dublin oh! Liverpool! Very nice Liverpool . . .
> Oh! d'houdou you dou.

He loved it. He came back a second time, bringing his singer friend Osip Petrov along so that Petrov too could enjoy Mlle Judic's charms. He then sent an enthusiastic description of the performances to his poet friend, Count Golenishchev-Kutuzov, and went back to work on *Khovanshchina*.[1] He never mentioned his trip to the Bouffe to his librarian friend Vladimir Stasov, his collaborator on *Khovanshchina* and his "lifelong adviser, preceptor, helpmeet and inspirer," as one insistent Soviet commentator has put it.[2] Stasov would not have understood.

There were many things about Musorgsky that Stasov—for all that

---

[1] Letter of 18 March 1875; MusLN 1.187–88; English translation in MR, 292–94.
[2] P. T. Shchipunov, commentary to StasIS 2.748.

he knew the composer from the age of seventeen and rendered him incalulable assistance—refused to understand. He could not understand why Musorgsky did not muster up a decent hatred for *Judith*, an opera by Stasov's archenemy Serov ("I think he's a complete idiot," Stasov shrieked in a letter to Balakirev).[3] He could not understand why Musorgsky was "so cowardly, so shallow and small" as to allow Nápravník, who conducted the première production of *Boris*, to make cuts—and even thank him for it.[4] He could not understand why Musorgsky chose to turn *Khovanshchina* into "an opera of princely *spawn*?!!"[5] And he could not understand how Musorgsky could choose the likes of Arseniy Arkadyevich Golenishchev-Kutuzov for a friend. In his essay "Perov and Musorgsky," in which Stasov compared Russia's outstanding musical realist with Vasiliy Grigoryevich Perov (1833–82), Musorgsky's near-exact contemporary and, as Stasov saw it, his closest counterpart among painters, Stasov went out of his way to deplore the composer's relationship with the poet:

> Turning to thoughts of Perov's and Musorgsky's ends, I again find a striking resemblance: both died without finishing their true work, and even, in their last years, forfeited a significant portion of their creative energy and their talent because both of them were deflected into new and alien directions. Perov did pictures on religious and allegorical or mythological subjects that did not suit his nature at all; . . . Musorgsky did a series of romances on words by Count A[lexey] K[onstantinovich] Tolstoy and Count A. A. Golenishchev-Kutuzov, on lyrical subjects that were not at all appropriate for him—"Troubadours," "Commanders" (from the [*Songs and*] *Dances of Death*) and so on. Both of them did a lot of things in an idealized vein, devoid in their very roots of that national character and that concreteness in which their whole strength lay, Perov's and Musorgsky's alike.[6]

"Perov and Musorgsky" was only one of a whole series of biographical essays and critical squibs that Stasov unleashed during the years immediately following the composer's awful death from alcoholism on 16 March 1881, one week past his forty-second birthday.[7]

---

[3] 17 May 1863; BalStasP 1.203.

[4] Letter to his daughter Sofiya, 2 February 1874; StasPR 1/2.209.

[5] Letter to Musorgsky from Vienna, 15/27 August 1873; MR, 244.

[6] "Perov i Musorgskiy" (1883), in StasIS 2.152.

[7] They included, in chronological order: 1) an obituary ("Nekrolog M. P. Musorgskogo," *Golos* [17 March 1881]; reprint, StasIS 2.117–18; StasSM 3.45–46; trans. R. Hoops in MusIM, 315–17); 2) a brief unsigned description of the composer's burial

It was a valorous campaign to achieve recognition for an artist who had perished—it is hard now to remember this—in virtual obscurity. The one opera Musorgsky had managed to finish had had only fifteen (incomplete) performances in one theater over a span of four seasons. (Rimsky-Korsakov's *Pskovityanka* and Chaikovsky's *Vakula the Smith* had both done better as of 1881, and their careers would continue.) Besides its vocal and piano scores (St. Petersburg: Bessel, 1874), he had published only two song cycles (*The Nursery* and *Sunless*), eighteen individual songs, one chorus, and seven insignificant piano pieces at the time of his death.[8] Stasov told the world of the

---

(*Golos* [19 March 1881]; reprint, StasSM 3.47); 3) an account of the unveiling of Ilya Repin's famous portrait of the composer ("Portret Musorgskogo," *Golos* [26 March 1881]; reprint, StasIS 2.119–21; StasSM 3.48–56; trans. MusIM, 318–19); 4) an extended biographical essay that remains a fundamental source on the composer to this day ("Modest Petrovich Musorgskiy: Biograficheskiy ocherk," *Vestnik Yevropï*, no. 5 [1881]: 285–316, and no. 6 [1881]: 506–45; reprint, StasIS 2.161–213; StasSM 3.51–112); 5) a description of a concert organized in Musorgsky's memory by the St. Petersburg Circle of Musical Amateurs ("Kontsert v pamyat' Musorgskogo," *Poryadok* [10 November 1881]; reprint, StasSM 3.113–14, trans. MusIM, 320–21); 6) "Perov i Musorgskiy," originally published in the journal *Russkaya starina* (May 1883): 433–58; (reprint, StasIS 2.133–52; StasSM 3.120–42); 7) *Pamyati Musorgskogo* (St. Petersburg, 1885), a brochure on Musorgsky's monument in the Alexander Nevsky cemetery (reprint, StasSM:3.267–76; reworked into an article for the journal *Istoricheskiy vestnik* [March 1886]: 644–56; reprint, StasIS: 3.31–43); plus several articles concerning the completion and first performances of *Khovanshchina* (1883–86); in addition, there was a glowing tribute to Musorgsky in the musical section of Stasov's survey, "Dvadtsat' pyat' let russkogo iskusstva" [Twenty-five years of russian art], *Vestnik Yevropï*, no. 10 (1883): 561–623; trans. Florence Jonas in StasSEM, 66–116.

[8] The songs: "Gopak," "Hebrew Song" (*Yevreyskaya pesnya*), "The Feast" (*Pirushka*), "Gathering Mushrooms" (*Po gribï*), "Lovely Savishna" (*Svetik Savishna*), "A Society Tale" (*Svetskaya skazochka*)—usually called by Stasov's title, "The Goat" (*Kozyol*)—and "Tell Me Why" (*Otchego skazhi*), published by Iogansen (Johansen) in 1867–68; "The Classicist" (*Klassik*), published by E. Arngold at the composer's expense in 1870; *Seminarist*, printed in Leipzig by W. Benicke in 1870 at the composer's expense, but confiscated at the border by the Russian censor; "Jeremy's Lullaby" (*Kolïbel'naya Yeryomushki*) after Nekrasov, "The Peepshow" (*Rayok*), "The Orphan Girl" (*Sirotka*), "Magpie Whitesides" (*Strekotun'ya-Beloboka*), "King Saul" (*Tsar Saul*), "Night" (*Noch'*), "Go to Sleep, Peasant Lad" (*Spi, usni krest'yanskiy sïn*) from Ostrovsky's *Voyevoda*, and "The Urchin" (*Ozornik*), published by Bessel in 1871. In the ten years remaining to the composer he published only two more songs (both with Bessel): "The Song of the Schismatic Marfa" (*Pesnya raskol'nitsï Marfï*) from act 3 of *Khovanshchina* (1873), i.e., an arrangement of the folk song "The Maiden Went Walking" (*Iskhodila mladen'ka vse luga da bolota*); and "The Forgotten One" (*Zabïtïy*), to words by Golenishchev-Kutuzov (1874). The chorus was "The Rout of Sennacherib" (*Porazheniye Sennakheriba*), issued in vocal score by A. Bitner in 1871. The piano pieces were the juvenile *Porte-Enseigne Polka*, published by Bernard in 1852 at Musorgsky's father's expense; "Ein Kinderscherz" and *Intermezzo in modo classico*, issued by Bitner in a collection called *Frühlingsblüten-Album* (1873), and four pieces printed in the publisher Bernard's journal *Nuvellist*: "The Seamstress" (*Shveya*), subtitled "Scherzino" (1872); *Méditation* (*Razdum'ye*, subtitled *Listok is al'boma* [*Albumblatt*]) (1880); and two picturesque souvenirs of his 1879

existence of *Khovanshchina*, of *Sorochintsï Fair*, of the *Songs and Dances of Death*, of *Night on Bald Mountain* and the *Pictures at an Exhibition*. He made a huge noise about *Khovanshchina*, in which he had an enormous stake, at the time of its publication and early performances, though he did not live to see it staged by the Imperial Theaters (1911, in a production co-directed by Chaliapin and conducted by Albert Coates). He continued to propagandize for Musorgsky to the end of his long life, affirming his faith resoundingly, even in the midst of forlorn jeremiads at contemporary "decadence," in his huge retrospective survey, "Art in the Nineteenth Century" (1901): "Without doubt Musorgsky's time will yet come, as it comes to all that is full of truth and talent. Not all times will be drab, dark and deteriorated for music. Not forever will everyone rejoice in rottenness, stupidity and perversion."[9] To whatever extent Musorgsky's time arrived, Stasov deserves huge credit and loud plaudits for bringing it about. Along with Rimsky-Korsakov, Stasov was one of Musorgsky's heroic rescuers.

But both rescuers were also mediators. Both presented the world with the Musorgsky they wanted, not necessarily the Musorgsky that was, or even the one they knew. Stasov and Rimsky-Korsakov did not always want the same Musorgsky (though in the case of *Khovanshchina* their purposes certainly meshed). Stasov in fact condemned some of Rimsky's editorial emendations, though he did so implicitly, without naming the editor's name.[10] But the images of

---

concert tour with the contralto Darya Leonova—"Near the Southern Shore of the Crimea" (*Bliz yuzhnogo berega Krïma*), subtitled "Baidarki"; and "On the Southern Shore of the Crimea" (*Na yuzhnom beregu Krïma*), subtitled "Gurzuf at Ayu-Dagh"—both published in 1880.

[9] "Iskusstvo XIX veka," StasIS 3.731.

[10] The relevant passage, from "Art in the Nineteenth Century," is an oddly reasoned forerunner of countless comparable fulminations: "In my opinion, beyond that which the author himself admitted, there must not be admitted any changes or corrections in Musorgsky's creations. That would be altogether illicit and indecent. There is no author in literature, in poetry or in art in whom one could not find reason for making improvements. Fétis even found it necessary to correct the Third Symphony of Beethoven. Many have wished to correct the finale of the Ninth. Once you allow corrections, there can be no limit to the caprices or the personal tastes of correctors. Even if we take just painting for example, you would have to correct thousands of pictures, sometimes the work of great talents, you would have to correct every museum in the world. It would turn out that this was wrong, and that was wrong, hundreds and thousands of things would be wrong. In music, even more so. But corrections have never led to any profitable result. Mozart corrected Handel, Richard Wagner Gluck, and completely in vain. Nothing good has ever issued from outsiders' work. Perhaps it, too, will need correction! No, let every author remain what he actually was, and let each answer for his own sins" (StasIS 3.732).

Musorgsky they advanced were equally one-sided, each distorted, as Tolstoy might have said, in its own way.

There is no need to rehearse the case of Rimsky-Korsakov. His redactions have been the subject of debate, and of often wildly exaggerated censure, ever since Musorgsky became a modernist cult object in the wake of Diaghilev's phenomenal Paris productions. Diaghilev himself, who at first enthusiastically espoused Rimsky-Korsakov's redactions, even commissioning additional embroidery on *Boris Godunov* for his Paris spectacle of 1908, later provoked and exploited the anti-Rimskian backlash as a way of generating publicity for his production of *Khovanshchina* in 1913. M.-D. Calvocoressi, who perhaps did more in his time than anyone else to denigrate the Rimsky-Korsakov redactions, was at the time of those productions Diaghilev's paid publicist.[11] While it would be too much to say that the matter has been settled in favor of the original texts (the Bolshoy, for one, will likely remain faithful to Rimsky-Korsakov until kingdom come or the market economy, whichever arrives first), it has been aired at length and in detail, the relationship between the original and revised redactions has been clarified, and no one today is likely to confuse Rimsky's versions with Musorgsky's, or accept them as representing Musorgsky's true intentions (i.e., what he would have done had he known how).

It is different with the other mediator. Stasov's authority with respect to Musorgsky and the other members of the mighty kuchka—a group Stasov, after all, had named—has rarely been questioned. In the Soviet Union his writings were literally unquestionable, virtual canon law until the Gorbachev-inspired *glasnost'* of the late 1980s. In the West they have hardly been any the less monumentalized. The earliest writers on Musorgsky in English, including Calvocoressi, were Stasov's confessed disciples. Rosa Newmarch made this quite explicit in her ground-breaking volume *The Russian Opera*, which con-

[11] See any of Calvocoressi's three biographies—*Moussorgsky* (Paris: Alcan, 1908; English trans. [by A. Eaglefield Hull], London: Kegan, Paul, Trench, Trubner, 1919), *Mussorgsky* (London: J. M. Dent, 1946; with Gerald Abraham), *Modest Mussorgsky: His Life and Works* (London: Rockliff, 1956)—but especially *Le vrai 'Boris Godounof' de Moussorgsky* (London: Oxford University Press, 1928), a brochure issued in connection with the Oxford University Press reissue of the original Bessel vocal score of 1874 (it had first been serialized in translation under the title "Boris Godunov as Moussorgsky Wrote It," in *Musical Times* 69 [1920]: 318–20, 408–12, 506–8). Undoubtedly the distinction of reaching highest dudgeon on matters of fidelity to Musorgsky's texts belongs to Robert Godet, in his legendarily ill-informed and intemperate *En marge de Boris Godounof* (Paris: Alcan; London: J. and W. Chester, 1926).

tains an account of her pilgrimages to the kuchkist patriarch ("the godfather of Russian music"), and what she learned at his feet.[12] Gerald Abraham, long the most influential of all writers on Musorgsky in English, while highly critical of Newmarch, was the disciple of Calvocoressi, hence indirectly Stasov's all the same, and never deviated from Stasovian orthodoxy either with respect to the overall shape of Musorgsky's career or when it came to evaluating specific works. As recently as 1983, Yuri Olkhovsky characterized Musorgsky's downfall more dramatically than Stasov ever did, as a ruin he had brought upon himself by obstinately rejecting Stasov's control.[13]

In fact, Stasov's Musorgsky *was* Stasov's creation—in more ways than one. He manufactured not only Musorgsky's historiographical image but also, to a considerable extent and for a considerable time, the actual historical person.

VLADIMIR Vasilyevich Stasov (1824–1906), though nominally a civil servant attached to the Imperial Public Library in St. Petersburg, was in fact the most prolific and polymorphic arts journalist Russia has ever known. Not quite a critic, more than a publicist but less than a historian or chronicler, and certainly no aesthete, Stasov was an indefatigable *deystvovatel' v khudozhestve* [functionary in art], to fall back on the whimsical mock-bureaucratic title he invented for himself. To numbers of Russian writers, painters, and musicians he acted as idea-man, tribune, confidant, and factotum, and wrote graphomaniacally about them all.[14] His tone was ear-splitting, his style at once hectoring and prolix, gratuitously redundant, supererogatory. His arguments gave new meaning to the word tendentious. Though his works are an inexhaustible mine—of gold, pyrites, and sheer dirt— and exert the inevitable fascination of eyewitness reportage, he is about the most annoying writer in the Russian language. Yet he must be given his due: with apologies to Gogol, he had a nose. And he

[12] See *The Russian Opera* (New York: E. P. Dutton [1914]), pp. 212–17, 248–49.

[13] *Vladimir Stasov and Russian National Culture* (Ann Arbor: UMI Research Press, 1983), pp. 68–74.

[14] His "suggestions to artists," as he listed them shortly before his death in a letter to his niece and biographer, include (in the musical sphere) *La Meunière de Marly* and *Rogneda* by Serov, Balakirev's *King Lear* music, Cui's *Angelo*, Borodin's *Prince Igor*, Rimsky-Korsakov's *Tsar Saltan* (as well as "significant portions" of his *Sadko* and *Pskovityanka*), and Chaikovsky's *The Tempest* (to Varvara Komarova-Stasova, 10 August 1906; StasPR 3/2.323–24). Stasov also took full credit for the idea behind *Khovanshchina* ("the consequence of my reading, while still a boy, Konstantin Masalsky's novel *The Streltsy*"); but this is doubtful (see Chapter 7).

was undeniably the first to take the true measure of Musorgsky's genius. But then, a famous browbeater, Stasov projected onto the very impressionable younger man—and, at first, onto the even younger Rimsky-Korsakov—all his hopes for Russian music, and (what is more) all that he demanded of it. His description of their early relationship, written decades later and much mellowed by nostalgia, still shows how far Stasov cast himself in loco parentis:

> I'll never forget that time, when they, still youngsters, lived together in one room, and I used to come to them early in the morning, find them still asleep, wake them, get them out of bed, help them wash, give them their stockings, their trousers, their robes or jackets, their slippers, how we used to drink tea together, munching sandwiches with Swiss cheese, which we loved so much that our friends even used to call Rimsky and me "the cheese-eaters." And right after tea we would get down to our main, our favorite, business, music, the singing would start up, and the piano, and they would show me with rapture and the greatest excitement what they had composed and accomplished in the last few days, yesterday or the day before. How fine it all was, but how long ago![15]

The blessed time to which Stasov refers in this letter was the winter of 1871–72, when the two youngsters in question were respectively thirty-two and twenty-seven years old. Stasov was filling the gap left in their lives by Balakirev's sudden estrangement from all his erstwhile colleagues and activities. Yet all he could offer was meddlesome encouragement, not musical guidance. Before long Rimsky-Korsakov, too, left the scene. His marriage in 1872, at first much resented by Musorgsky, took him out of their shared domestic quarters. He was also embarking on his epic feat of self-education, following on his surprise appointment to the staff of the St. Petersburg Conservatory. This, too, was much resented, not only by Musorgsky but by Stasov as well, since with Rimsky's acquisition of professional technique came the possibility of living a real musician's life, which liberated him from his former dependence on Stasov's praise.

Musorgsky remained singularly dependent on that praise, since unlike chemist Borodin and military engineer Cui he did not have a real profession outside of music and no other outlet for his creative energies save composition. Stasov kept the praise coming, knowing

[15] To Arkadiy Mikhailovich Kerzin, 20 April 1905; *Muzïkal'nïy sovremennik* 2 (1916): 24.

how essential it was both to his friend's self-confidence and to his own hold on him. Not that he did not mean every word. Looking back on his two closest artistic collaborators after their deaths, he wrote, "Well, anyhow Musoryanin and Borodin were the best of the lot. I managed to tell them so, both of them, a thousand times during their lifetimes. How awful it would have been if such a pair had expired never having heard from anyone what kind of people they were!"[16]

Writing with primary reference to Borodin, Tamara Livanova has observed that "Stasov knew many artists in *the moment of creation*, and this was given to him simply because he himself was necessary and close to them precisely at that moment."[17] But that need arose out of not altogether healthy circumstances. Unstinting praise can infantilize, and it does not seem to be a coincidence that the two artists Stasov praised the most were the two who may have realized the least of their potential, leaving between them three unfinished operas (two of them on Stasovian scenarios, and *Prince Igor* still an elephantine embryo after an eighteen-year gestation) to the Rimsky-Korsakov completion mill. "It is not because I need you that you are dear to me," wrote Musorgsky to Stasov in the first letter to hint at *Khovanshchina*, "but because you demand much."[18] Those demands stopped short of ordinary training, though; and this is where Stasov's praise could be dangerous. "Maybe I'm afraid of technique because I'm bad at it?" Musorgsky wrote with unusual candor a month later. But then he allowed himself to shake off the thought: "However, there are those who will stand up for me as an artist even on that score."[19] First among them was his "demanding" collaborator.

From about 1870, when "Musoryanin" began addressing him in letters as "my dear general" (later "généralissime"), until 1873, when Golenishchev-Kutuzov entered the picture, Stasov was the unrivaled dominator of Musorgsky's creative life, the one from whom he took his marching orders (such as composing "The Peepshow"—see Chapter 3). It was a brief but critical period, encompassing the revision of *Boris Godunov*, the composition of most of *The Nursery*, and the beginning of work on *Khovanshchina*. Thus it represented the highest achievements of Musorgsky's realist phase and also the peak of his commitment to civic themes. Both of these (related) strains re-

[16] To Dmitry Stasov, 18 January 1893; StasPR 2.371.
[17] *Stasov i russkaya klassicheskaya opera* (Moscow: Muzgiz, 1956), p. 278.
[18] Letter of 16/22 June 1872; MusLN 1.132; MR, 186.
[19] To Stasov, 13 July 1872; MusLN 1.136; MR, 192.

flected Stasov's direct creative input. For Stasov was at the time still faithful to the aesthetic creed he had imbibed during his school days from the frenzied writings of Vissarion Belinsky (1811–48), the "father of Russian criticism," who had issued the first call in Russia for an *art engagé* and who thereby defined what it would mean to be an *intelligent* (hard *g*!), a member of the "intelligentsia." (Stasov's later migration from this position to one of jingoism was typical of his generation.) It was a view that radically dichotomized form and content, inevitably subordinating the former to the latter, and denigrated subjectivity. Belinsky's watchword was *mïshleniye v obraztsakh* [thinking in types], characters that would be highly particular and specific, but nevertheless embody "universal" themes and melioristic social tendencies. It is only too easy to associate such a view with *Boris Godunov*, but extremely difficult to do so with any of Musorgsky's other operatic fragments or torsos. The way the task has been accomplished—by editors, by critics, by historians, and—not least—by regisseurs (see Chapters 7 and 8)—is the essential history of Musorgsky reception, and the cardinal measure of Stasov's success in controlling perceptions of the composer.

He accomplished this feat by portraying Musorgsky's career, in his biographical essay of 1881 and in the two great synoptic essays that followed, as a pertinacious ascent to the period of greatest intimacy and ideological congruence with Stasov himself, and an inexorable decline therefrom unto death.[20] The story carried conviction by reason of its shapeliness (the climax comes just where it ought to, at the Golden Section), and also by reason of the fact that the one fully realized masterpiece of Musorgsky's maturity, *Boris Godunov*, was located precisely at the Stasovian zenith. "Later," wrote Stasov, "under the influence of weakening health and a broken organism, his talent

[20] In his biographical essay, following the Beethovenian convention, Stasov described this trajectory in terms of three creative periods: "The first, lasting from 1858 to 1864, was the period of musical study, gathering strength; the second, lasting from 1865 to 1874–75, was the period of the full flowering of Musorgsky's musical personality and creative independence [!]; the third period—from 1874–75 to the end of 1880—is the time of incipient diminution and weakening of Musorgsky's creative activity" (StasIS 2.170). The reason for equivocation as to the border between the second and third periods must be the the fact that *Sunless*, a "weak" work owing to the influence of Golenishchev-Kutuzov, appeared in 1874, but concentrated work on *Khovanshchina*, Musorgsky's closest collaboration with Stasov (including the successful completion of the first act in vocal score), went on into 1875. Stasov also singled out the *Songs and Dances of Death*, written precisely in the winter of 1874–75, for praise; they escaped the Golenishchev-Kutuzov curse because, although the hated interloper wrote the actual words, the idea for the cycle had been Stasov's.

began to weaken and, it seems, change. His compositions started to become obscure, contrived, at times even incoherent and insipid."

Yet ironically enough, in view of his pronouncements on Musorgsky's latter-day incoherence and obscurity (which were precisely the qualities he reviled in the "decadent" art he came to know in his old age), Stasov was in large part the author of Musorgsky's modernist appeal. For it was Stasov who made the most insistent claim—a claim no doubt motivated in part by self-justification—that Musorgsky's supposed technical shortcomings were not a limitation but a liberation. His assertions along this line were actually quite various and contradictory. Here are three of them, arranged to show a characteristically nimble rhetorical progression:

> If Musorgsky had many deficiencies of technique, if he was not sufficiently drilled in classroom lore, if he was not a gifted orchestrator—one may indeed regret it. Any such deficiencies prevented him, of course, from reaching an even higher rung than the one he reached in his lifetime; but from such imperfections it is a far cry to the "ignorance" and "worthlessness" in which his enemies and opponents have so eagerly sought to bury him. Grammatical mistakes or transgressions of syntax will not dim that great spirit, that great creativity that resides in the breasts of true poets and artists. Mistakes and transgressions against the rulebooks—what schoolteacher could not point them out or even correct them! But how far yet is this scholastic shackling from lofty poetic creation![21]

> Critics have spoken of Musorgsky's musical ignorance and musical solecisms, of his impudent infractions of all kinds of school habits and norms, of his indecorous realism, the "monstrosity" of his construction; in a word, they have displayed all their incapacity to understand Musorgsky's talented innovations, the novelty of his aims and the profundity of his musical expression. They have stopped at grammar.[22]

> Musorgsky, despite all his imperfections, was a great poet and artist. He has irresistibly affected the spirit and emotions of those of his listeners who have not yet been spoiled by school, by classrooms, Italian habits and vapid traditions.[23]

First Musorgsky's technical shortcomings are acknowledged, even regretted. One is merely asked to keep them in perspective. Next—a typical Stasov maneuver—criticism of Musorgsky is turned against

[21] "Iskusstvo XIX veka," StasIS 3.730.
[22] "Dvadtsat' pyat' let russkogo iskusstva," StasIS 2.556–57.
[23] "Iskusstvo XIX veka," StasIS 3.730.

the critics, until, finally, "schools and classrooms" have in themselves become as evil as "Italian habits." Here in fact is the seed of the French cult of Musorgsky, epitomized by Debussy, who saw in the Russian composer an artist "spontaneous and free from arid formulas," and therefore "something of a god in music . . . [who] will give us a new motivation to rid ourselves of ridiculous constraints."[24] Those are easy affirmations for a composer who spent ten years at the Conservatoire (Debussy, to Ernest Guiraud: "True enough, I feel free because I have been through the mill, and I don't write in the fugal style because I know it").[25] Musorgsky did not write in the fugal style because he couldn't (cf. the "Revolutionary chorus" in *Boris*, where he tried). His unfinished scores stand in minatory witness against those who aspire to his "freedom."

But nothing could be more futile or less relevant than polemics at this late date against Musorgsky's Stasovian persona. Musorgsky the myth has had a cultural significance in the twentieth century as vast as Musorgsky the composer's impact on his own times was nil. If the myth gave Debussy the courage of his convictions, that is already sufficient justification for its construction. Nor does one wish to level charges at Stasov for his defensive tactics, though they included such things as the personal suppression of the operatic fragment *Marriage* (later so influential on Ravel) even as he touted it in print (see Chapter 2). A rescue mission, even one that entailed wholesale chicanery, deserves gratitude for its success.

Still, when composers become causes they tend to disappear. Cause becomes orthodoxy, ready-made interpretation narrows perspective, and their work is correspondingly diminished. Therefore one hastens to report on a contemporary polemic with Stasov that for various reasons has never received due consideration; for it will bring us closer than Stasov alone ever will to the man who wrote the works we love, and will help us recover from them meanings the Stasovian propaganda mill has been shouting down for more than a century.

COUNT Arseniy Arkadyevich Golenishchev-Kutuzov (1848–1913), to whom Musorgsky was distantly related on his mother's side, met the

---

[24] Claude Debussy, *Monseiur Croche, Dilettante Hater*, trans. Lawrence Gilman (New York, 1928), p. 41; idem., "La Musique russe et les Compositeurs français," *Excelsior* (9 March 1911); both quoted in Malcolm H. Brown, introductory article to MusIM, pp. 7, 4.

[25] Edward Lockspeiser, *Debussy: His Life and Mind* (London: Cassell, 1962), p. 208.

composer at the home of Vladimir Stasov's brother Dmitry, a jurist and arts patron who kept a distinguished salon, in 1872. The twenty-five-year-old poet and the thirty-four-year-old composer became *tutoyer* friends the next summer, and—just as Musorgsky and Rimsky-Korsakov had done three years earlier—shared bachelor quarters for about fourteen months, beginning at the end of March 1874.[26] The reason for the breakup of their domesticity was again a replay of the earlier one: the poet decided to get married, leaving the composer so wounded that one has to wonder about the nature of their "most intimate friendship," as Golenishchev-Kutuzov called it in his memoirs.[27] If there was an incident that precipitated Musorgsky's ruinous heavy drinking, this was surely it.

In the spring of 1877, Golenishchev-Kutuzov came into possession of his ancestral estate near Tver and moved thither, where he became a justice of the peace; while cordial letters continued, the friends no longer saw each other regularly until 1879 when, leaving his family in Tver, Golenishchev-Kutuzov took an apartment in the capital for business reasons, dividing his time thereafter between his two residences. Although he was frequently absent, he nonetheless records that "when I was in St. Petersburg, it was a rare day that Musorgsky did not come to see me; he would spend whole evenings playing [the piano] in my flat." Golenishchev-Kutuzov was among those who tended the composer during his final illness.[28]

Stasov suffered Golenishchev-Kutuzov's presence in his circle for Musorgsky's sake, even made him one of his famous "suggestions": a long poem called *Hashish: A Tale of Turkestan*, dedicated to Stasov, with which the young poet broke into print in 1875. (Much later it would inspire a tone poem by Lyapunov.) They kept up outwardly polite relations until 1902, when they finally fell out for good over a

[26] The date is given here following OrTD, 390; in his memoir, Golenishchev-Kutuzov dates their living arrangement from the fall.

[27] A. A. Golenishchev-Kutuzov, "Vospominaniya o M. P. Musorgskom" (1881–88), in MuzN, 13. For Musorgsky's anguished reaction to Golenishchev-Kutuzov's marriage see his letter to Stasov, written during the night of 29–30 December 1875 (MusLN 1.210–11; MR, 322–23) and especially the postscript ("10–11 December [1875]—night again") to a somewhat earlier letter to Golenishchev-Kutuzov himself (MusLN 1.209; MR, 321). By the spring of 1876 Musorgsky had reconciled himself to his friend's marriage, and as a (somewhat equivocal) peace offering to the seventeen-year-old bride, dedicated to her the Dances of the Persian Slave Girls from *Khovanshchina* (letter to Olga Andreyevna Golenishcheva-Kutuzova [*née* Gulevich], 9 April 1876; MusLN 1.216; MR, 329).

[28] MuzN, 28–29.

scandal concerning Maxim Gorky's being named and then (at the tsar's insistence) unnamed to the St. Petersburg Academy of Sciences, of which both Stasov and Kutuzov were members.[29] But, as his many frosty references to *Sunless* make clear, Stasov was suspicious of Golenishchev-Kutuzov and resented the young usurper's meteoric advent in Musorgsky's life.

It was not simply a matter of jealousy. A member of the titled nobility, Golenishchev-Kutuzov retained an aristocratic—which is to say, aestheticist—outlook on art that in the 1870s appeared retrograde (though it would make a powerful comeback, known as the "Silver Age," in the nineties). We have seen that Stasov, while a member of the upper bourgeoisie, entertained typically "mixed-caste" (*raznochinets*) liberal views on art and politics. As long as he was able to maintain his tutelage over Musorgsky (a scion of the impoverished gentry), Stasov was able to impose on him a *raznochinets* mentality that is fairly epitomized in the libretto of *Boris Godunov*, particularly the revised version that the composer worked out with Stasov's help (see Chapters 4 and 5). Golenishchev-Kutuzov threatened that precarious commitment—and *Khovanshchina* gives evidence that he actually overturned it (see Chapter 7). That opera's eventual pessimism, as well as its focus on the nobility—both of them aspects tendentiously modified by the opera's various editors and denied by seven decades of Soviet criticism—were plain enough to Stasov, and account for his disingenuous description of the work in the biographical essay ("obscure, contrived," etc.).

Count Golenishchev-Kutuzov's career in the decades following Musorgsky's demise abundantly confirmed whatever suspicions Stasov may have entertained of a pernicious influence on the composer, and casts a suggestive retrospective light on the works of Musorgsky's final years. In the 1880s the count embarked on a career as a banker, moving back with his family to St. Petersburg. Noticed by Tsar Alexander III, whom he hero-worshiped, he was appointed to a high position in the Ministry of Finance and became a court familiar. In 1895, the year following Alexander's death, Golenishchev-Kutuzov was appointed personal secretary to the dowager empress, Maria Fyodorovna, with the title *Ober-gofmeyster Vïsochaishego Dvora* [senior

[29] Golenishchev-Kutuzov upheld the move, Stasov opposed it (though, unlike Chekhov, he did not resign); see his letter to Dmitry Stasov, 12 March 1902, in StasPR 3/2.114–16. The correspondence between Stasov and Golenishchev-Kutuzov (1874–1902) was published in the *Russkaya muzïkal'naya gazeta* in 1916 (nos. 41–43).

dignitary of the royal court], a post he retained for eighteen years, until his death. He maintained a distinguished collection of Renaissance art, presided over a salon of aging court poets and "Pushkinists"—Apollon Maikov, Afansiy Fet, Yakov Polonsky, and Nikolai Strakhov were among the regulars—and founded the notoriously reactionary "Society of Defenders of Russian Historical Enlightenment in Memory of Emperor Alexander III" (*Obshchestvo revniteley russkogo istoricheskogo prosveshcheniya v pamyat' Imperatora Aleksandra III*) during the period of official mourning for the deceased emperor. The enlightenment he defended was in fact a latter-day brand of Russian "official nationalism," as reactionary a position as one could espouse in the 1890s. In letters to another Defender he wrote: "Cosmopolitanism deceitfully and hypocritically upholds a banner of freedom to seduce the masses, a freedom whose illusive character is exposed everywhere in contemporary Europe; on the contrary, the triumph and realization of the Russian statist idea of Autocracy (*samoderzhaviye*), as the reign of Alexander III so brilliantly proved, is the only thing that can secure the maximum freedom, peace, and well-being for the people, both collectively and individually"; and, "Russia is an integral, self-sufficient world, which must stand firm on the border between West and East, and not incline this way and that depending on circumstances; the inner meaning of Russia is contained in her Orthodox religion [*Pravoslaviye*]."[30] In his cultural politics and in his creative work, Count Golenishchev-Kutuzov ardently opposed every manifestation of the "spirit of the sixties" (the nineteenth century had one too), which he characterized in the title of an article as "The attack of the barbarians on Russian literature" (*Nashestviye varvarov na russkuyu literaturu*). This spirit, of course, is the very one of which Musorgsky is conventionally deemed the principal musical representative—and in an opera based on Pushkin![31]

Golenishchev-Kutuzov, finally, was an aesthete among aesthetes. "In the opinion of critics in the eighties," read one of his obituaries, "form predominated over content in his work, rendering it known to few and loved by even fewer."[32] Among his admirers, however, was

[30] Letters of 5 March 1895 and 5 February 1896, quoted in "G.S.T.," "Graf A. A. Golenishchev-Kutuzov: Vospominaniya," *Russkiy arkhiv*, no. 3 (1914): 306.

[31] Biographical data otherwise uncredited follows N. Zverev, "Graf Arseniy Arkad'yevich Golenishchev-Kutuzov (26 maya 1848 g.–28 yanvarya 1913 g.)," introductory article to *Sochineniya Grafa A. Golenishcheva-Kutuzova* (St. Petersburg: tip. Tovarishchestva A. S. Suvorina—Novoye vremya, 1914), vol. 1, iii–xxviii.

[32] "Pochotnïy akademik K. R.," "Pamyati grafa A. A. Golenishcheva-Kutuzova," *Iz-*

Valeriy Bryusov, a leading symbolist, and a veritable vogue for the old courtier's Pushkinesque lyrics arose among the minor composers of the Silver Age.[33] To Vladimir Solovyov, the religious philosopher, he was the poet of "death and nirvana."[34] "The elegant, serene muse of Golenishchev-Kutuzov," wrote the literary historian Semyon Vengerov, "which knows nothing of restless quests, is so far removed from the evils of the day, that without any biographical data it would be hard to tell what period his work belonged to."[35] Compare Musorgsky, whose career is commonly described as one great restless quest "toward new shores" (*k novïm beregam*), and whose topicality is often cited as his principal virtue.[36]

In other ways the poet was only too well aware of the evils of the day. Remaining a highly placed bureaucrat into the time of Nikolai II, he became involved in government repressions, most heavily so in the revolutionary year 1905. The writer Vladimir Korolenko (1853–1921), who served alongside Golenishchev-Kutuzov on the so-called Kobeko Commission, which met to consider questions of press freedom and censorship, recalled that "Count Golenishchev-Kutuzov remained where he always was, in the reactionary arrière garde, voting without exception against all the most important 'emancipation' proposals of the other members of the commission."[37] How could such

---

vestiya otdeleniya russkogo yazïka i slovesnosti Imperatorskoy akademii nauk 18, no. 4 (1913): 2.

[33] Settings by no fewer than forty-three composers, all of them composed after Musorgsky's death, are recorded in Georgiy Ivanov's invaluable catalog, *Russkaya poèziya v otechestvennoy muzïke* (vol. 2 [Moscow: Muzïka, 1966], pp. 99–102). The authors include a scattering of big or biggish names—Balakirev, Cui, Rachmaninoff, Arensky, Ippolitov-Ivanov—but are mainly representatives of the "Belyayev" generation (Cherepnin, Alferaki, Blumenfeld) or younger (Ivan Pokrovsky, Stravinsky's early friend and mentor, and Myaskovsky).

[34] "Pamyati grafa A. A. Golenishcheva-Kutuzova," p. 3.

[35] *Ocherki po istorii russkoy literaturï* (St. Petersburg: Tipografiya tovarishchestva "Obshch est vennaya pol'za," 1907), p. 171.

[36] The Lermontovesque motto became a Musorgskian emblem by degrees. It first appears in Musorgsky's letter to Stasov of 18 October 1872 (MusLN 1.141; MR, 199); Stasov's sister-in-law Polixena had a ribbon with the motto attached to a wreath for presentation at the first performance of (excerpts from) *Boris Godunov* in February 1873; finally, Nikolai Kompaneysky used it as the title of an extended memoir: "K novïm beregam: Modest Petrovich Musorgskiy (1839–1881)," *Russkaya muzïkal'naya gazeta*, nos. 11–12 (1906): 14–18. James Billington, for whom Musorgsky was "the consummate 'man of the sixties,'" appropriated the phrase as the emblem of the whole era; see *The Icon and the Axe: An Interpretive History of Russian Culture* (New York: Knopf, 1966), part 5: "On to New Shores" (pp. 359–472; the characterization of Musorgsky is on p. 407).

[37] Quoted in FridMPM, 125–26.

a man have been friends with a composer known in his day as an "immature liberal" and a nihilist who, holding nothing dear, could say with Molière's Sganarelle, *"nous avons changé tout cela"*?[38]

Evidently he was not. Which is not to say that he and Musorgsky were not friends, but that, according to Golenishchev-Kutuzov, the composer was not as he was commonly depicted and perceived. The poet's memoir, written in direct answer to Stasov's and therefore comparably tendentious, portrays an aristocratic artist of idealistic, subjective and pessimistic bent, who, having spent the larger part of his career under the warping influence of strong-willed associates, finally found his true path . . . but alas, too late.

Golenishchev-Kutuzov made no bones about his motives in setting down his portrait. Immediately after the composer's death, he relates, he began filling up a notebook with recollections so that when his immediate bereavement had passed, and with it the impulse to divulge too much of a purely personal nature, he could properly memorialize his friend's genius.

> Meanwhile, at first in the newspapers, but then also in the thick journals, there began to appear articles on Musorgsky with biographical information as well as critical verdicts on his achievements. In one of the latter, the largest in bulk, which appeared in the two most recent issues of the *Vestnik Yevropï* over the signature of Mr. Stasov, even the most intimate aspects of his life and works were laid bare. For the first time Musorgsky appeared before the public not only as a composer but as a person, but arbitrarily illuminated from one side only, and perhaps the side that corresponded least to his artistic mission; at the very least it did not enable the reader to see in their totality all the traits that made up his distinctive, original character. In Mr. Stasov's article Musorgsky appeared exclusively as the member of a certain group, a certain musical sect—to which he did belong, but only for a certain rather limited time—whose theories weighed down his native gifts and inclinations like a heavy yoke; but from which he at last managed to extricate himself completely in the period of the full flowering of his talent.[39]

Golenishchev-Kutuzov therefore decided to write the memoirs quickly and publish them immediately as an antidote to Stasov's. He did not do this however; the memoirs as we have them were only

[38] Hermann Laroche, "Mïslyashchiy realist v russkoy opere," *Golos*, no. 44 (13 February 1874); and "Russkaya muzïkal'naya kompozitsiya nashikh dney," in ibid., no. 18 (18 January 1874).

[39] MuzN, 14.

finished in 1888. Though he had them professionally copied, he still did not publish them (owing, it seems likely, to his new-won position at the court of Alexander III, where—thanks, ironically, to the very Stasovian image Golenishchev-Kutuzov sought to supplant—Musorgsky was regarded as a tainted "sixties" artist). They lay in his archive at the Historical Museum in Moscow for almost half a century, until they were discovered in 1935 (along with a batch of correspondence) by a Moscow Conservatory student named Pyotr Vasilyevich Aravin, and published with an extensive commentary by Aravin's "chef," the distinguished Soviet musicologist Yuriy Keldïsh, then a lecturer (*docent*) at the Conservatory.

In Golenishchev-Kutuzov's description, Musorgsky, "a *barin* [patrician] to the marrow of his bones, who had grown up and been raised in a fine old landowning family," had given himself up, briefly but decisively, to the "fanaticism" (*izuverstva*) of the sixties, and as a result had "striven with all his strength, and, unfortunately, not without occasional success, to fashion for himself a stance of crudeness, rudeness, and vulgarity, being convinced (by the words of others, of course) that these were the traits of inner strength and genius."[40] It was only with Golenishchev-Kutuzov that Musorgsky, to his vast relief, could be himself.

The central anecdote that establishes the pressures Musorgsky was under, his relief, and the immediate context of his burgeoning intimacy with his young admirer, concerns "The Peepshow" (*Rayok*), the "musical pamphlet" Musorgsky had written as a direct contribution to "kuchkist" politics.

On the way home alone with Musorgsky, I decided to ask him, not without some diffidence, whether he himself thought his "Peepshow" a work of art.

"You, it seems, are pleased to be displeased, Mr. Poet?" Musorgsky grinned good-naturedly.

"Oh no, no," I hastened to object, "not at all! It just seems to me that 'The Peepshow' is a joke; witty, wicked, ingenious, but still just a joke, a prank . . ."

"But why are you so mad at me for this joke?" Musorgsky interrupted. "At the concert you greeted me, pinned me to the wall as if to

---

[40] MuzN, 16. The context leaves no doubt that the "words of others" were Stasov's; in giving these points anecdotal support, Golenishchev-Kutuzov quotes words of approbation with which the composer's preceptors egged him on, including one—*Tuzovo!* [Ace!]—that many other sources cite as Stasov's patented property.

complement me, shouting that you recognized yourself. Look at him—
he laughs, and all the while he's quivering with rage."

We reached our house.

"I'm not at all sleepy," said Musorgsky. "Let's go to your room and
I'll show you something else."

We went in, lit the candles, and he sat down at the piano.

"I know what you need," he said and he played the "Lullaby" from
Ostrovsky's *Voyevoda* [*Spi, usni, krest'yanskiy sïn*]—a beautiful work, musical, straightforward, and full of feeling. It sent me into an unfeigned,
heartfelt rapture.

"Now that's no 'Peepshow'!" I couldn't help exclaiming. Musorgsky
grinned again. "That is dedicated to the memory of my late mother," he
said.

"And 'The Peepshow,' who's it dedicated to?" I asked. We both
laughed out loud.[41]

"The Peepshow," of course, is dedicated to Vladimir Vasilyevich
Stasov.

At this point Musorgsky and Golenishchev-Kutuzov, not quite
roommates yet, occupied two apartments in one building. They
spent their evenings together, Musorgsky improvising at the piano
the music he would write down the next day for *Khovanshchina*. If
Golenishchev-Kutuzov's recollections are correct, they offer a rare insight into the difference between what he called Musorgsky's native
inclinations and his kuchkist pose.[42] "Almost always," he wrote,
"the *first form* in which his thought flowed out in the course of im-
provisation, was better, in my opinion, more beautiful and even
grander, than what followed after the development of the themes,
their harmonization and all the finishing touches had been applied.
The fact is, it was Musorgsky the artist who improvised, while the
one who did the writing-down was Musorgsky the group-member,
the musical innovator, who above all took into account the reactions
of the group leaders, whose tastes he knew and whose approval he
sought."[43]

When it came to the first production of *Boris Godunov*, Goleni-

[41] MuzN, 16–17.

[42] And they resonate intriguingly with some recent controversial testimony about
the creative habits of Charles Ives, a composer with whom Musorgsky is often compared: see Elliott Carter's memoir in Vivian Perlis, *Charles Ives Remembered* (New Haven: Yale University Press, 1974), p. 138; or, for a general discussion that has bearing
on Musorgsky as well, Maynard Solomon, "Charles Ives: Some Questions of Veracity," JAMS 40 (1987): 443–70.

[43] MuzN, 17.

shchev-Kutuzov reports, as it were from the other side, Musorgsky's reactions to the preparations and, in particular, to Nápravník's interventions. This, too, was a direct jab at Stasov, who had allowed himself, in his very public biographical essay, a derogatory general lament—"O inscrutable Russian spinelessness!"—at Musorgsky's compliance.[44]

> The rehearsals . . . went quickly and well. Musorgsky attended every one and always came back happy and full of hopes for success. He could not sufficiently praise the attitudes of all concerned, but especially that of Napravnik, the conductor, who, Musorgsky said, gave him a great deal of good advice at these rehearsals, and at whose insistence many longueurs were removed, digressions and mediocre spots that spoiled the overall scenic effect. . . . Musorgsky completely and sincerely concurred with Napravnik's opinion and hotly contended with those who reproached him for his weakness of character and his submissiveness.
>
> "All of that is totally impossible on the stage," he often said to me after these arguments, "but these gentlemen do not want to know it. They don't care about the quality of the impression, they care only about quantity. They say that I am weak-willed, but they don't understand that the author himself can never judge the impression his opera will make on the public before it is finally produced. Meyerbeer threw whole pages out without pity—he knew what he was doing, and he was right!"[45]

So total has been the dominance of the Stasovian line concerning the relationship of Musorgsky to the theaters directorate and with Eduard Nápravník personally, that even Stravinsky succumbed to it, refusing a request from Nápravník's son to contribute a centenary testimonial to the Mariyinsky conductor because of the latter's purported hostility toward the composer of *Boris Godunov*. Stravinsky went out of his way, in fact, to dismiss the existing documentary evidence of Musorgsky's gratitude to the man who "created" *Boris*:[46] "That letter," he wrote, "changes nothing, since it is a completely natural gesture of thanks from Musorgsky to Eduard Frantsevich, whose performance, like all his performances, was doubtless first

---

[44] StasIS 2.199.

[45] MuzN, 19.

[46] Letter of 6 February 1873, following the preliminary presentation of three scenes; the concluding sentence: "I tell you openly, I bless your name for giving me the opportunity to go on learning" (MusLN 1.145; MR, 206).

class."[47] Meanwhile, Nápravník's own very interesting memoir of *Boris Godunov*, elicited by the same son, Vladimir, in the year of the conductor's death (1916), while it is written from the point of view of an *homme de métier* and maintains certain conventional judgments, was far from hostile. An excerpt:

> Musorgsky . . . was a sort of precious ore, who recognized no body of learning, who was practically *a musical illiterate*, a realist and a musical revolutionary, but always and everywhere with his own personal stamp. Like Dargomïzhsky, the text and the music with him formed one indivisible whole, such as you rarely find in other operatic composers . . . If he had followed Rimsky-Korsakov's example and had enthusiastically studied elementary theory, harmony, counterpoint, instrumentation and so on, what marvelous things he might have contributed to operatic literature. But he was prevented from doing this mainly by his improper and careless way of living and his disinclination to persevere in his work. This aberrant behavior cut his time short. He died in his forty-second year, in 1881, in the Nikolayevsky military hospital. . . . I and the singer Ivan Melnikov, then an excellent peformer [actually the creator] of the role of Tsar Boris, visited him there more than once. . . . I often used to meet him at the home of that artistic couple, the Petrovs [see Chapter 8] . . . [where] Musorgsky would play all of his vocal compositions and sing the voice parts masterfully, with a strong voice.[48]

It is also worth recalling that at the time of *Boris Godunov*'s notorious rejection by the repertoire committee of the Imperial Theaters, Nápravník had cast the one white ball.

In what has become the most controversial passage in the memoirs, Golenishchev-Kutuzov reports Musorgsky's reaction to the Mariyinsky Theater's decision, beginning in October 1876, to drop the final (Kromy Forest) scene of the opera. This cut had called forth a choice journalistic blast from Stasov, for whom it meant the "castration" of the entire work. "They'll come back at me, if you please, 'But of course we have the author's consent, he himself approved the cut,' " Stasov scoffed:

[47] Letter to Vladimir Eduardovich Nápravník, 15 November 1932; L. S. Dyachkova, ed., *I. F. Stravinskiy: Stat'i i materialï* (Moscow: Sovetskiy kompozitor, 1973), p. 493. It is possible that Stravinsky's attitude toward Nápravník had been colored by that of his teacher, Rimsky-Korsakov, whose relations with the conductor were indeed distinctly rancorous, stemming originally from a very haughty review that the twenty-five-year-old Rimsky-Korsakov, standing in for César Cui, had written of Nápravník's first opera, *Nizhegorodtsï* [The men of Nizhny-Novgorod] in 1869.

[48] E. F. Nápravník, *Avtobiograficheskiye, tvorcheskiye materialï, dokumentï, pis'ma* (Leningrad: Muzgiz, 1959), pp. 47–48.

Now don't you talk to me about "consent"! What does the author's consent mean to us! You've got every author in your clutches. He's in your power, he'll agree to anything you want, he is defenseless, he can't protest. And so willy-nilly you agree, when otherwise they might simply throw out your whole opera and all its performances. Not everyone has it in them to be as manly as Beethoven or Franz Schubert, and take their creation back rather than agree to the mutilation of their work.[49]

Stasov gave the impression of having stepped in to defend the hamstrung author. In the obituary essay he would claim that the removal of the Kromy scene mortally offended and embittered Musorgsky, even hastened his death. Meanwhile, the other memoirist reports, "Musorgsky not only approved this cut, he was particularly pleased with it." When Golenishchev-Kutuzov (so he writes) argued the point, the composer "heatedly asserted that its complete omission was demanded not only by the plot of the drama and the demands of the stage but also by his author's conscience."

> I was amazed at this and asked for an explanation.
> "In this act," Musorgsky answered me, "and for the only time in my life, I lied about the Russian people. The people's mockery of the boyar [Khrushchov]—that's untrue, that is an un-Russian trait. An infuriated people may kill, may execute, but they do not mock their victim."
> I had to agree.
> "Now that is really there, sweet friend," he added, all serious and stern, "an artist must never trifle with such things. In *Khovanshchina* there will be nothing of that, unlike *Boris*."[50]

On this point Golenishchev-Kutuzov felt it particularly needful to rebuke Stasov's obituary essay. "The author of that article heard it from Musorgsky more than once that he fully approved the abbreviation of *Boris*, and although he never agreed with Musorgsky on this score, he still had no right, as I see it, to ascribe to the deceased composer those feelings he (the author of the article) would have liked to see in him during his life, but never saw."

The height of Musorgsky's relationship with Golenishchev-Kutuzov came in the winter of 1874–75, the time of their domestic intimacy. Predictably enough, that juncture emerges in the poet's memoirs as a watershed, ushering in what should have been Musorgsky's

---

[49] "Urezki v 'Borise Godunove' Musorgskogo (Pis'mo v redaktsiyu)," *Novoye vremya* 239 (27 October 1876); reprint, StasIS 1.278–79; StasSM 2.308–10; trans. R. Hoops in MusIM, 313–15.

[50] MuzN, 20.

best creative period: "The formerly obedient executor of *orders from outside* began assigning his own themes and projects, which answered better to his own nature and his own specific gifts." The works Musorgsky produced that winter and the next (before Golenishchev-Kutuzov's departure for Tver) included *Sunless* and *The Forgotten One* (both to texts by Golenishchev-Kutuzov) and many items for *Khovanshchina*, including Shaklovitïy's big act 3 aria. These, of course, are precisely the ones in which the lyrical and subjective aspects Stasov deplored (the poet-memoirist calls them "Fet-like") came to the fore.[51] There is a hint of polemic with Stasov in a reported remark of Musorgsky's: "Many say that my only good points are my picturesqueness and my humor. Well sir, let's see what they say when I bring them your poems—here there's only feeling and nothing else, and it seems to have come out all right." *Khovanshchina*, Golenishchev-Kutuzov notes with satisfaction, "started to take on a completely different look from what was planned at first. . . . And all these departures from the first conception of *Khovanshchina*—from 'nationalism' and 'realism' and 'critical ideas'—in all these inserted songs and arias that so clutter up the development of the plot in every act—therein lies all the enjoyment, all the excellence in *Khovanshchina*."[52] The crux of his polemic with Stasov is reached with the observation that "those who regarded 'The Peepshow' as a chef d'oeuvre of talent, brilliance, and picturesqueness, and all those 'Goats,' 'Beetles,' 'Crabs' and so on as if they were a string of pearls and gems, creations 'worth whole symphonies and operas'—they, of course, not only could not rejoice, they could not even understand the arias of Shaklovitïy or Marfa, the *Sunless* cycle, the piano pieces without program [i.e., not the *Pictures at an Exhibition*], to which Musorgsky turned once more at the end of his life."[53]

[51] Afanasy Afanasiyevich Fet (1820–92) was a lyric poet who had remained true to aestheticist principles all through the realist age, and whose name therefore had become by the 1880s a polemical rallying point. His verses were much set by Chaikovsky.

[52] From Golenishchev-Kutuzov—and from him alone—we learn of a pair of "picturesque and humorous" episodes that were excluded from *Khovanshchina* to make room for the lyrical interpolations: a lottery wheel in the act 1 crowd scene, and a whole scene in the German quarter that would have contained "a parody of German music in a regressive Mozartean style" (MuzN, 27).

[53] Quotations in this paragraph from MuzN, 26–27. "The Goat" was Stasov's name for the song Musorgsky published as "A Society Tale" (see n. 8); "The Beetle" is the third song in *The Nursery*. "The Crab," another Stasov-inspired satirical essay like "The Peepshow," was one of a pair of projected songs—the other to be entitled "The Hill of Nettles"—planned in the summer of 1874 as an answer to critics of *Boris Godunov*. Omitted from Golenishchev-Kutuzov's account of it is that he was to have been the

Musorgsky's deathbed wish, according to the memoirist, was to "take a rest from history, and especially from every kind of *'prosiness,'* which even in life itself gives you no breathing room." He requested of his poet friend "something major," a "fantastic drama" that he promised to set without changing a word. From the perspective of that wish, and from the form *Khovanshchina* eventually took, Golenishchev-Kutuzov ends his memoir of Musorgsky by insisting that "the period of his activity which Mr. Stasov considers the most brilliant, was actually a transitional period." From his perspective as an intimate friend and collaborator he insists that "Musorgsky's nature constantly drew him, notwithstanding the convictions that were foisted upon him, toward pure, ideal poetry and beauty, to the higher, spiritual world in which alone an artist may find true solace and satisfaction." Musorgsky's tragedy, he concludes, was the tragedy of the sixties: "in his formative period he could not find, either in the spirit of the times or in the milieu that happened to surround him, that guidance and support a young talent needs. . . . Had Musorgsky been born twenty years earlier—or perhaps even twenty years later—his name might now be on a level with the most celebrated names among European composers."[54]

WHAT shall we make of these memoirs, which so perfectly invert the long-accepted view of the composer? Soviet writers have never had any doubt. Golenishchev-Kutuzov has been consistently dismissed on the tautological grounds that as a representative of "monarchism and Black-Hundreds reaction," he cannot speak for a "populist" like Musorgsky.[55] "A courtly dignitary and aristocrat like Count Kutuzov, closed off in his proud secluded sphere," wrote Keldïsh, "in the final analysis did not and could not understand a great artist-democrat and humanist like Musorgsky, who burned with bitter pain on behalf

---

author of the text. A draft (of "The Hill of Nettles"), together with an unsent note to Stasov, was discovered in Golenishchev-Kutuzov's archive and published by Keldïsh in the commentary to the memoirs (MuzN, 47; the letter is translated in MR, 274).

[54] Quotations in this paragraph from MuzN, 29.

[55] Pyotr Aravin, contribution to symposium "Stsena 'pod Kromami' v dramaturgii 'Borisa Godunova,' " SovM 3 (1970): 108. The official Soviet line on Golenishchev-Kutuzov is disappointingly maintained by Alexandra Orlova in her annotations to the first English translation of the memoirs: see A. Orlova, comp. and ed., *Musorgsky Remembered*, trans. Véronique Zaytseff and Frederick Morrison (Bloomington and Indianapolis: Indiana University Press, 1991), pp. 81–99 (translation), 171–75 (commentary).

of all oppressed, suffering and deprived humanity."[56] That his memoirs were published at all in Soviet times, and as late as 1935, seems miraculous—as, in a way, it was. (A scant year later, after the final ideological clampdown signaled by the denunciation of Shostakovich's *Lady Macbeth of the Mtsensk District*, their publication would surely have been impossible.) But their ticket of admission, so to speak, was an enormous sanitizing apparatus. Keldïsh's introduction and commentary take up far more space than the memoirs themselves, and (in a fashion typical of Soviet source publications of the period) keep up something of a running feud with the object they ostensibly illuminate.[57]

The main strategy was to question at every point the closeness of the poet's relationship to the composer, and to cast their break in ideological terms. One especially intransigent Soviet specialist, absolutely unwilling to let Musorgsky off the Stasovian hook, has actually tried to debunk the relationship from start to finish—"and did it even exist, this closeness, or was it just the influence of Musorgsky's mighty personality on a youthful, not yet fully formed friend (?), and did not Musorgsky passionately, painfully exaggerate the degree of his rapport with the co-author of the *Songs and Dances of Death* out of craving for spiritual support and emotional warmth?"—but some two dozen surviving letters from composer to poet, written over a period of six years, full of many moods but consistently warm and confiding, contradict her.[58] The first thing they show is how far Golenishchev-Kutuzov had replaced Stasov as Musorgsky's primary confidant; and among the ways they show this is one that should have been obvious to a Russian: in contrast to all surviving communications with Stasov (or even with his fellow kuchkists, his near-contemporaries), Musorgsky's letters to Golenishchev-Kutuzov use

[56] Introduction to M. P. Musorgsky, *Pis'ma k A. A. Golenishchevu-Kutuzovu* (Moscow and Leningrad: Muzgiz, 1939), p. 20.

[57] Four years later, in his introduction to the first publication of Musorgsky's letters to the count, Keldïsh was back with an explanation of why the memoirs would not be republished with them—or ever. It was a kind of cancellation, no doubt under pressure: "To reprint them a second time was not thought advisable. Written in a blatantly tendentious fashion, abounding in crude straining of the evidence or in plain distortions, these memoirs have a rather limited interest and are more revealing of their author's ideological path than they are of Musorgsky's person. The specialist researcher can always turn to the original publication, but the general reader can only be led into error" (Introduction to *Pis'ma k A. A. Golenishchevu-Kutuzovu*, p. 5).

[58] Emiliya Frid, in "Stsena 'pod Kromami' v dramaturgii 'Borisa Godunova' " (see n. 55), p. 98.

the familiar second-person pronoun. Still, if the memoirs could be shown to reflect changed attitudes, at variance with those entertained at the time of the purported friendship they describe, this could be claimed as evidence to discredit them.

The "hardest" bit of evidence cited against Golenishchev-Kutuzov's authority—not only by Keldïsh but also by Yevgeniya Gordeyeva in her commentary to the memoirs on their republication as recently as 1989[59]—consists of an undated poem, "To M. P. Musorgsky" (M. P. Musorgskomu), first published in 1884, three years after the composer's death:

Dorógoy nevznachai, mï vstretilis' s toboy;
Ostanovilisya, okliknuli drug druga,
Kak stranniki v nochí, kogda bushuyet v'yuga,
Kogda ves' mir ob'yat i kholodom i t'moy.
Odin pred nami put' lezhal v stepi bezbrezhnoy,   5
I vmeste mï poshli. —Ya molod bïl togda;
Tï bodro shol vperyod, uzh gordïy i myatezhnïy;
Ya robko brel vosled... Promchalisya goda.
Plodï glubokikh dum, zavetnïye sozdan'ya
Tï lyudyam v dar prinyos; khvalu, rukopleskan'ya   10
Vostorzhennoy tolpï c ulïbkoyu vnimal,
Venchalsya slavoyu i lavrï pozhinal.
Zateryannïy v tolpe, toboy ya lyubovalsya;
Dalyokiy dlya drugikh, tï blizok mne yavlyalsya;
Tebya ya ne teryal: ya znal—nastanet chas,   15
I bleskom suyetnïm, i shumom utomyas',
Vernyosh'sya tï ko mne v moyo uyedinen'ye,
Chtobï delit' so mnoy mechtï i vdokhnoven'ye.
Bïvalo, v pozdnïy chas vecherney tishinï,
Ko mne sletalisya videniya i snï,   20
To polnïye toski, somneniya i muki,
To svetlookiye, s ulïbkoy na ustakh...
Mechtan'ya izlival v pravdivïkh ya strofakh,
A tï ikh oblekal v taínstvennïye zvuki,
Kak v rizï chudnïye—i, spetïye toboy,   25
Oni nezhdannoyu sverkali krasotoy!
Bïvalo... No k chemu budit' vospominan'ya,
Kogda v dushe gorit nadezhdï tyoplïy svet?

[59] Ye. M. Gordeyeva, ed., M. P. Musorgskiy v vospominaniyakh sovremennikov (Moscow: Muzïka, 1989), pp. 132–52, with characteristically outsized commentary on pp. 252–60; this omnibus of memoirs and reminiscences by Musorgsky's contemporaries was one of several official observances of his sesquicentenary.

Pust' budet pesn' moya ne pesneyu proshchan'ya,
Pust' luchshe v ney zvuchit gryadushchemu privet.   30
Tuman volshebnïkh gryoz, taínstvennïkh stremleniy
Bezumnoy yunosti samolyubivïy vzdor
Prognal ya ot sebya—i novïkh vdokhnoveniy
Otkrïlsya predo mnoy nevedomïy prostor.
"Bez solntsa" tyazhelo bluzhdat' mne v mire stalo,   35
Vo mrake slïshalsya mne smerti lish' yazïk;
No utra chas nastal, i solntse zablistalo,
I novoy krasotï predstal mne svetlïy lik.
Dusha moya polna schastlivogo dover'ya,
Umu somnen'ya dan' spolna ya zaplatil,   40
Khram tvorchestva otkrït, i groznogo preddver'ya
I, osenyas' krestom, porog perestupil.
Ya veryu, v khrame tom mï vstretimsya s toboyu,
S zhivïm sochuvstviyem drug k drugu podoydyom,
Mï vdokhnovimsya vnov',—no krasotoy inoyu,   45
I pesnyu novuyu soglasno zapoyom![60]

[Somewhere along the way by chance we met;
We stopped, called out to one another,
Like wanderers at night, when storm blows up,
When all the world is wrapped in cold and dark.
One path before us stood in that uncaring steppe,   5
And together we set out. —I was young then;
You went boldly forward, already proud and stubborn;
I toiled timidly behind... The years went by.
The fruits of thoughts profound, hallowed works
You bestowed on people as a gift; praise, applause   10
You, with a smile, acknowledged from the eager crowd,
Covered yourself in glory, reaped your laurels.
Lost in the crowd, I admired you;
Remote to others, to me you still were close;
I never lost you: I knew—the hour would come,   15
And, tired of vain noise and glitter,
You would return to me in my seclusion,
To share with me your thoughts and inspirations.
It used to be that, late in evening's quiet,

---

[60] *Stikhotvoreniya grafa A. A. Golenishcheva-Kutuzova* (St. Petersburg: tip. A. S. Suvorina, 1884), p. 38; the poem was reprinted once during the poet's lifetime: *Sochineniya grafa A. Golenishcheva-Kutuzova* (St. Petersburg: tip. Golike and Vilborg, 1904), p. 38; and was included in the posthumous collection of his works: *Sochineniya Grafa A. Golenishcheva-Kutuzova* (St. Petersburg: tip. Tovarishchestva A. S. Suvorina—Novoye vremya, 1914), vol. 1, pp. 115–16.

Visions and dreams came flying to me,   20
Some full of woe, doubt and torment,
Others bright-eyed, with smiling lips...
I poured out my thoughts in truthful lines,
And you would clothe them in mysterious sounds,
As if in wondrous priestly vestments—and, sung by you,   25
They sparkled in undreamt of beauty!
It used to be... But why arouse these recollections,
When the warm light of hope burns in my soul?
Let my song not be a song of parting,
Better let it ring with future greeting.   30
The mist of magic reveries, of secret strivings,
The narcissistic folly of mad youth
I have put away—and of new inspirations
An untold vastness has opened up before me.
"Sunless," I had to grope about me clumsy in the world,   35
The only tongue I heard amid the dark was death's;
But the morning hour has come, and out has come the sun,
And a bright face of beauty new now stood before me.
My soul is full of happy trust,
I have paid full tribute to my doubting mind,   40
The temple of art stands open, and the threatening gate,
Under cover of the cross, I have gone through.
I believe that in that temple you and I will meet,
In glad fellowship we'll come together,
We'll inspire one another anew,—but with a different beauty,   45
And in a new song our voices we will blend!]

The interest of commentators has focused, of course, on the second half of the poem, with its talk of time past and time present. Keldïsh, who knew the poem only from Golenishchev-Kutuzov's posthumous collected works, assumed—possibly because of its companion piece, a poem composed in memoriam[61]—that it was "probably written rather a long time afterward, following [Musorgsky's] death." He goes on to observe that "Kutuzov does not hide his break with the ideals and enthusiasms that they both shared in the period of their

---

[61] "Pamyati M. P. Musorgskogo (Posle predstavleniya 'Borisa Godunova')" [In memory of M. P. Musorgsky (after a performance of *Boris Godunov*)], 1884 ed., pp. 41–42; collected works, vol. 1, pp. 117–18. This is a lament, in which the poet, coming from the theater and recalling his absent friend amid the audience's plaudits, goes to his grave and weeps. The performance that inspired the poem must have been that of 8 October 1882, the only one to take place in St. Petersburg between the composer's death and the première of Rimsky-Korsakov's first redaction of the opera in 1896.

friendship." Gordeyeva, who prints the whole poem, explains it as follows: "If at first Golenishchev-Kutuzov, under the impact of Musorgsky's ideas [cf. lines 6–8] paid tribute to democratic ideals and answered to them creatively, as time went on, freed from this influence, he became more and more firmly committed to the tenets of so-called pure art . . . Golenishchev-Kutuzov clearly saw the reason for his break with Musorgsky; he consciously insisted on his idealistic position in his later poetical works, and laid out the history of his relationship with the great composer in [this] poem."[62]

These assumptions and conclusions are all unfounded. There is no reason to assume that this poem, like its companion, was written after Musorgsky's death; on the contrary, the poet looks forward to future collaborations. There is no reference to a break with shared principles (still less to "democratic ideals," which were never a part of the Musorgsky physiognomy as Golenishchev-Kutuzov described it); there is only vague reference to a break in their personal relationship (lines 27–30). The poet does not renounce former ideals; he speaks only of immaturity overcome (lines 31–34) and a spiritual crisis weathered (lines 35–43).

The most reasonable interpretation, overall, seems to be that Golenishchev-Kutuzov intended the poem as a maximally flattering peace offering to the composer after renouncing their unwholesome intimacy in favor of marriage. Alexandra Orlova has discovered and published a sketch of its first half; her proposed date, "the beginning of the year [1876]," accords with this reading.[63] Many details support it: Golenishchev-Kutuzov's bride makes an appearance in line 38; line 42 alludes to the wedding sacrament (strange that no Soviet commentator has exorcised that cross!); and the mysterious references to secret wishes, narcissism, and dementia in lines 31–32 may be a clue to the homoerotic nature of the former relationship.[64]

[62] M. P. Musorgskiy v vospominaniyakh sovremennikov, pp. 253–54.

[63] OrTD, 456–57.

[64] This surmise arises not only out of the present context but out of a cluster of oft-noted if seldom interrelated circumstances: Musorgsky's many intimate male relationships; his lack of interest in women (as attested most forcefully by the case of Alexandra Purgold-Molas, Rimsky-Korsakov's sister-in-law, who tried hard to arouse it—see the extracts from Nadezhda Purgold translated in MR, 154–55); the absence of a prima donna role in Boris until the Imperial Theaters forced it; the surprising fact (attested by Stasov) that Musorgsky had indeed sketched the Fountain scene before submitting the opera, but shelved it; the lack of a love duet in Khovanshchina, either between Andrey and Emma or between him and Marfa (save a few ecstatic lines—the so-called Love Requiem—as they leap into flames at the end, which seem far more a death ecstasy

But the really tough nut for Soviet scholars in Golenishchev-Kutu-zov's memoir has always been Musorgsky's reported rejection of the Revolutionary scene in *Boris*. Confronting it, Keldïsh fell back on Sta-sov's argument of last resort, "inscrutable Russian spinelessness."

> It is hard to verify whether such words were ever spoken by Musorg-sky; but even if they were, they do not furnish proof of the author's true attitude toward the scene in question. From reports of Goleni-shchev-Kutuzov, and others as well, we are familiar with Musorgsky's mildness and changeability, and his way of submitting to the influence of his interlocutors, to whom he was often inclined to give in. Casually, under the influence of a passing mood, he might throw out a phrase for which he himself might not vouch afterward. But in the given instance, taking the general polemical tendency of Golenishchev-Kutuzov's "Reminiscences" into account, the faithfulness of his transmission of Musorgsky's words inspires involuntary [!] doubt, since they all too plainly contradict Stasov's opinion.[65]

Only two Soviet scholars have professed belief in this story. Boris Asafyev (1884–1949), who started his career as a Stasov protégé, was able to report that "at the end of his life even Stasov considered Go-lenishchev-Kutuzov to be among those friends of Musorgsky who had evaluated his work justly" (but of course Stasov did not know the unpublished "Reminiscences"!). The agreement between Goleni-shchev-Kutuzov's account, the firsthand survivors' reports that Asa-fyev had heard of many crucial and often misrepresented episodes, plus his own early observations—concerning Musorgsky's relations with Nápravník, the behavior of the audience at the *Boris* première, Balakirev's hostility toward his former pupil's work, Stasov's one-sided preference for Musorgsky's "naturalistic buffoonery," and

---

than a love ecstasy); the extreme rarity of love lyrics in his songs, save the necrophiliac variety; one could go on. (One who does, very far indeed, is Jane Turner, in an article innocently titled "Musorgsky" [*Music Review* 47 (1986–87): 153–75]; in her view, Mu-sorgsky's homosexuality was a symptom of a more general sadomasochism.)

[65] MuzN, 39. This one passage from Keldïsh's commentary even found its way into *The Musorgsky Reader*, an American publication (p. 350), showing that the Stasov line could be held sacrosanct even outside the boundaries of Russia. Interestingly enough, another Soviet researcher, Emiliya Frid, dismissed the veracity of the same passage on equally if oppositely tautological grounds, because they did not conform to her image of Musorgsky as "the most stubborn member of his circle, who was first to break with the despotic Balakirev" ("Stsena 'pod Kromami' v dramaturgii 'Borisa Godunova,'" p. 98). It is hardly necessary to point out that Musorgsky's tone in the cited passage is indeed stubborn, not submissive, for all that he speaks of having made his original mistake by heeding suggestions from others (Stasov? Nikolsky? Kostomarov?—see Chapter 4) rather than his inner dictates.

much else—had convinced him that the disputed memoirs were in the main "undeniably authentic, and, I would say, trustworthy as well."[66] Accepting, then, Musorgsky's judgment of the Kromy scene as "untrue and un-Russian," Asafyev went on to draw a conclusion much more damaging than anything Golenishchev-Kutuzov himself had implied: "And so, *knowing this untruth*, Musorgsky had undertaken to write the Kromy scene. What could have impelled him to do this? One can only suppose that precisely in the Kromy scene Musorgsky saw the figurative culmination and the dramatic apex of *Boris Godunov*—a popular drama, which he had understood before writing the Kromy scene."[67] Which is hardly the modus operandi of a "realist."

The essay containing these avowals was a very late work of Asafyev's, written right after the Patriotic War, which was a time of relative relaxation in Soviet artistic and historiographic controls. It was not published, however, owing to the ideological clampdown of 1948, which lasted until the death of Stalin.[68] It finally saw print in 1954, at the very beginning of the post-Stalinist "thaw," another brief period when anti-Stasovian sentiments could find public voice in the pre-*glasnost'* USSR.

Yuriy Tyulin (1893–1978), a distinguished music theorist associated with the Leningrad Conservatory, published his endorsement of Golenishchev-Kutuzov's memoir in 1970, at the height of what is now known as the "Brezhnevite stagnation." The testimony of Musorgsky's friend played only an incidental role in the case Tyulin was

[66] " 'Boris Godunov' Musorgskogo kak muzïkal'nïy spektakl' iz Pushkina," in AsIT 3.133.

[67] Ibid., p. 134; italics added.

[68] See the publication note in AsIT 3.317, where it is stated that the essay had been designated "for a volume of 'Learned Papers of the Moscow State Conservatory,' scheduled for publication in 1949; the publication did not take place." Around the same time as Asafyev wrote, in 1946, the Bolshoy Theater staged the opera without Kromy; the reason given was squeamishness, so soon after the Patriotic War, at the triumph of what looked like foreign invaders. "A principled Party critique helped the production staff get over its errors, and Kromy was reinstated as the culminating scene of the show" (A. Menkov, "Zhizn' spektaklya prodolzhayetsya," SovM, no. 5 [1983]: 45). Even so, Varlaam and Missaïl were replaced, as leaders of insurrection, by the Muscovite crowd and the pilgrims from scene 1, and they "remained silent" in the face of the Pretender, following the famous last stage direction in Pushkin's drama. Not only that, but the crowd stood in place after the Pretender's exit and listened to the Holy Fool's lament, so as to leave no doubt that they sided with Russia against the Poles and Jesuits. Even today, the Bolshoy's staging attempts to hide the fact that the Kromy crowd actually believes in the Pretender's assumed identity and supports his claim to the throne.

building against the Kromy scene, which he attacked from an independent—and fully Soviet-compatible—perspective as a "topsy-
turvy" slander of the gullible (as opposed to the spiteful) peasantry.
Nevertheless, extraordinary measures had to be taken to insulate his
article for publication in *Sovetskaya muzïka*, the official organ of the
Union of Soviet Composers. It was preceded by an editorial apologia
that started right off with a quote from Lenin ("Science is a *circle of
circles* . . ."), and it was followed by no fewer than four commissioned rebuttals —all of them sharp, lengthy, and directed particularly against Golenishchev-Kutuzov's veracity—by Soviet scholars of
equal seniority to Tyulin, including Boris Yarustovsky, the uncrowned political commissar of Soviet musicology; Emiliya Frid,
whose strained but contemptuous dismissal of Golenishchev-Kutuzov's authority has already been cited; Alexey Kandinsky, the head
of the department of Russian music history at the Moscow Conservatory; and—inevitably—Pyotr Aravin, the original discoverer of the
document, who after 1939 had written on nothing but Kazakh music,
and whose command performance here has all the ugly earmarks of
a public recantation.[69]

IF ONE of the parties to a debate remains silent for fifty years and is
only allowed to speak thereafter in the presence of spin doctors, it is
hardly to be wondered that his voice has grown faint. But, as the one
fully articulated portrait of Musorgsky from the pen of a dissenting
eyewitness, Golenishchev-Kutuzov's testimony is precious. It is not
any more to be relied on as an authority than anyone else's memoirs.
But it offers a general corroboration to the revisionist picture of Musorgsky that emerges inexorably over the course of this book. The
essays collected here were written over a period of about a dozen
years beginning in 1980 (though some of the preparatory research
went back to the time of my doctoral dissertation, completed in 1974)
and are presented not in the order of writing but according to the
chronology of Musorgsky's works. It seemed appropriate, when
gathering them together, to preface the lot with a detailed account of
Golenishchev-Kutuzov, his relationship to Musorgsky, his debate
with Stasov, and the debates to which his work gave rise in turn, so

[69] "Stsena 'pod Kromami' v dramaturgii 'Borisa Godunova,' " SovM, no. 3 (1970):
90–114.

as to equip the reader with what I now regard as a very necessary subtext.

But no more than a subtext. The reader will notice that Golenishchev-Kutuzov's memoirs are never cited as an authority or even as a source in the pages that follow. Partly that is because I read him late. I, too, had been spoon-fed the Stasovian line at the outset of my work on Musorgsky. While an exchange student at the Moscow Conservatory in 1971–72, I was assigned as *nauchnïy rukovoditel'* [something a bit more than an adviser] one of the scholars who engaged in the polemic with Yuriy Tyulin, described above. I was of course assured that Golenishchev-Kutuzov's testimony was of no value and I allowed myself to be dissuaded from consulting him, the more so as my project at the time did not cover the time frame of Golenischev-Kutuzov's eyewitness testimony. All of the conclusions and evaluations I arrived at in the course of composing these essays, then, were arrived at independently. It was only when writing Chapter 8, published here for the first time, that I realized my own work was taking me in an inexorably anti-Stasovian direction, and I finally engaged with my natural preceptor.

In the end I am glad he was not my guide but my substantiator. I was free, for one thing, to consider the Kromy scene (in Chapter 5) on what seemed to be its own terms as of 1871–72, the time of its composition; for what it is worth, I emphatically disagree that the scene should be omitted, no matter what the composer may have thought or said about it in 1876. (Besides, the behavior of the crowd, as soon as it became clear that the three-day Soviet coup of August 1991 had failed, showed that Musorgsky had not lied after all.) My late encounter with Golenishchev-Kutuzov enabled independent formulation of theses I might not have developed so elaborately had I been able to cite a ready authority: this applies above all to the matter of comic versus tragic tone in *Boris Godunov* (Chapter 5) and to the characterization of *Khovanshchina* as an aristocratic tragedy informed by pessimistic historiography (Chapter 7). My independence also enables the claim—as important for the personally implicated Golenishchev-Kutuzov, in a sense, as for me—that nonpartisan investigation of Musorgsky's late work (that is, beginning with the revision of *Boris Godunov*) may indeed lead to conclusions completely at variance with the received Stasovian doctrine. And, say I, if they are truly nonpartisan—not to use a word as hopelessly tainted as "objective"—they must inevitably lead there.

Two of the amplest essays in this book, Chapters 4 and 8, were originally envisioned, some two decades ago, as the unwritten concluding chapters of my doctoral dissertation.[70] They are surveys— weighted somewhat, in keeping with their present purpose, in favor of the subject of this book—of the two dominant genres of Russian opera in the 1870s, the decade in which the composers responsible for the bulk of the standard performing repertory (*russkaya opernaya klassika*, as they call it at home) were first becoming active. Chaikovsky, Rimsky-Korsakov, and Musorgsky each wrote historical costume dramas dealing with the period of or preceding the so-called Time of Troubles, the crisis of succession following the death of Ivan the Terrible. This genre is the subject of Chapter 4, and the chapter's present incarnation is not all that different from what it might have been had I written it up for the dissertation in the early seventies.

The same three composers each wrote (or began) peasant comedies based on "Little-Russian" (Ukrainian) tales by Gogol. This genre is the subject of Chapter 8, a chapter that is utterly unlike what it would have been in the dissertation. The dramatic way this was driven home to me, in 1986, gave me the initial impetus to collect these essays for publication. I had been invited to address the Royal Musical Association, meeting that year at Kings College, Cambridge, on the subject of national opera. My old dissertation notes on *Sorochintsï Fair* seemed to be a natural source for such a paper, and so I dashed off an abstract that reflected all the received ideas I had imbibed, as it were, at their fount during my stint on the academic exchange fifteen years previously. Then I sketched the paper, the nucleus of Chapter 8, and found I had to mount the podium in Cambridge and explicitly disavow my abstract, devoting my time, in fact, to its systematic rebuttal. I made light of my embarrassing plight at the time (what choice did I have?), comparing myself with New York's mayor Robert Wagner, who had successfully campaigned for reelection in 1961 by running as a reform candidate against his own record. (I further excused my change of heart by citing the seven-year cycle of anatomical cell replacement: my dissertation notes, I suggested, had after all

---

[70] Published in revised form as *Opera and Drama in Russia as Preached and Practiced in the 1860s* (Ann Arbor: UMI Research Press, 1981).

been assembled "two Taruskins ago.") But I was shaken, and this book is the result. My thanks, then, to Dr. Jan Smaczny, who was behind my invitation to address the RMA, for giving me an unintended shock and leading my research in unforeseen directions.

Hearty thanks are also due to the indefatigable Malcolm H. Brown, selfless instigator and editor of no fewer than three hefty Festschriften—in honor of Gerald Abraham, Boris Schwarz, and Musorgsky himself—published between 1982 and 1985. He kindly asked me to contribute to all three, and thus stood midwife to Chapters 1, 3, and 4. He even let me get away with a deliberate misquotation of Musorgsky in the title of Chapter 4: the composer's famous slogan, enunciated with respect to *Khovanshchina*, had been "The past within the present—there's my task" (*Proshedsheye v nastoyashchem—vot moya zadacha*).[71] My transposition was inadvertent; but when queried on it (by Caryl Emerson), I decided that I was right after all: "The present in the past" conveys better than the original formulation the quality of implicit contemporary relevance Musorgsky sought in his historical dramas.

Though it languished a long time in the clutches of a dilatory publisher, Chapter 2 was the earliest of the essays to be written. A record of Musorgsky's peak involvement with theories of realism and his early "scientistic" predilections, it resonates strongly with the main themes of *Opera and Drama in Russia*, and can be regarded as a spinoff from the earlier project. I am grateful to Piero Weiss, with whom I shared an office in 1979–80, for helping me rewrite it.

Chapter 5, the product of a dozen years of musing on my best beloved opera, came out too long for an article and too short for a book. I thus owe a great debt to Joseph Kerman, who rescued it from limbo by allowing its serial publication in *19th-Century Music*, which he then oversaw. Chapter 6 owes its existence to Patrick J. Smith, editor of *Opera News*, who kindly commissioned it and gave me an outlet for a quantity of curiosa I had filed away.

Chapter 7, the most recent essay and the most impressionistic (though it sports a little trophy of positivism at the end), was commissioned by Deutsche Grammophon as notes to a "restorative" recording of *Khovanshchina* (Vienna State Opera, Claudio Abbado conducting). Its conceptual basis, though obviously congruent with the general tendency in evidence throughout the latter portion of the

[71] To Stasov, 13/22 June 1872; MusLN 1.132; MR, 186.

book, owes a great deal to the writing and the conversation of Caryl Emerson. Her essay, "Musorgsky's Libretti on Historical Themes: From the Two *Borises* to *Khovanshchina*," in Arthur Groos and Roger Parker, eds., *Reading Opera* (Princeton: Princeton University Press, 1988), is a useful complement to mine, as is (for background) another effort of my own—"Christian Themes in Russian Opera: A Millennial Essay," in the *Cambridge Opera Journal* 2, no. 1 (March 1990): 83–91. Having mentioned her name twice now, I should confess that Professor Emerson is my anything-but-hypothetical Other when it comes to writing about classical Russian opera, and that there is no living person to whom I owe a greater general debt for whatever merits my work in the field may claim. The epilogue to this book, too, could not have been written without her help, as the citations attest. I am more beholden to her than ever for consenting to grace this volume at the other end as well, with a foreword.

The greatest of all my debts, however, is to one unfortunately no longer living. Gerald Abraham was the first serious writer on Russian music whose first language was English, and his work led him for over half a century into byways no Anglophone writer had visited before. He lit them up and passed on. The rest of us who work in the field have been following in the wake of this phenomenal path-breaker, adding our little tensor beams alongside his great torches. I have drawn inspiration from him since high-school days, and many of my central professional concerns have had their origin in thought he stimulated. Every one of the essays in this book (except, of course, the last) has its counterpart in Professor Abraham's published work and can be thought of as a counterpoint to it. If the frequency of disagreement with him seems rather high in a book dedicated to his memory, all disputation and attempted corrective should be understood in the light of my overriding debt: had it not been for Gerald Abraham, not one word that follows would have been written.

1

"LITTLE STAR"

An Etude in the Folk Style

IF THERE was a musical idiom that more than any other distinguished and epitomized the "early kuchkist" period, when the Balakirev circle was indeed a unified "mighty little bunch" and Chaikovsky a friendly fellow-traveler, it was the "intonation" of the melismatic peasant song, the so-called *protyazhnaya*. The most florid, musically complex, and, so to speak, aesthetically autonomous genre of Russian folk music, it continues to enjoy a special status among musicians and ethnographers alike as "the summit of the development of the Russian peasant lyric tradition."[1] As a preliminary example, to define the genre and to serve as point of reference and comparison in the subsequent discussion, Examples 1a and 1b present two variants of an especially popular and widely disseminated *protyazhnaya*, "Little Path" (*Dorozhen'ka*), sometimes classified as a "coachman's song."

The supermelismatic style and the concomitant "artistic" distension of the text are self-evident. The greater floridity of the second version is due no doubt in part to more modern (phonographic) methods of transcription but nonetheless demonstrates the degree to which the melismata are a variable function of performance style and spontaneous decision. No two performances of a *protyazhnaya* are identical. "Little Path" belongs to a modal type that for the sake of

---

[1] Izaliy Zemtsovsky, *Russkaya protyazhnaya pesnya: opït issledovaniya* (Leningrad: Muzïka, 1967), p. 20. Zemtovsky, the foremost Soviet authority, draws a careful distinction between *protyazhnïye* and the more inclusive category of *liricheskiye pesni* [lyrical songs], on the basis of what he calls the former's "intrasyllabic melodic expansion" (*vnutrislogvaya raspevnost'*), that is, the presentation of the most characteristic and structurally important melodic turns in the guise of decorative melismata (often quite hopelessly disfiguring the text). This is the reason I have chosen to translate the word *protyazhnaya* as "melismatic," rather than the more usual "protracted" or "drawn-out."

EXAMPLE 1a. N. M Lopatin and V. P. Prokunin, *Russkiy narodnïye liricheskiye pesni* (1889). Reissued with an introduction by Victor Belyayev (Moscow: Muzgiz, 1956), no. 22

EXAMPLE 1b. Yevgeniya Eduardovna Linyova, *Velikorusskiye pesni v narodnoy garmonizatsii*, vol. 2 (St. Petersburg: Akademiya nauk, 1909), no. 7, p. 16a

There's more than one little path across the field . . .

EXAMPLE 2. N. P Kolpakova et al., *Russkiye narodnïye pesni povolozh'ya, vïpusk pervïy: pesni, zapisannïye v Kuybïshevskoy oblasti* (Moscow and Leningrad: Izdatel'stvo Akademii nauk SSSR, 1959), no. 27

O mountains of Zhiguli, you have begotten nothing.

convenience we may as well call natural minor. It exhibits two highly pertinent and characteristic structural features. First, we may note the opening ornamental falling fifth to the tonic (it is often preceded by an initial upward leap), which becomes a kind of model for further variation or development (Zemtsovsky calls this trademark of the *protyazhnaya* the "intonational thesis"; Glinka, more simply, called it the "soul of Russian music"). Second, we may observe a propensity to make one or more cadential approaches to the lower neighbor of the tonic. If one such approach is made, as in "Little Path," its position is usually the penultimate phrase. If the approach is made repeatedly, the effect of equilibrium or "stalemate" between two tonics can be created, as in Example 2, "O Mountains of Zhiguli" (*Uzh vï, gorï Zhigulevskiye*). This tonal ambiguity or oscillation is generally referred to in the analytical literature as *peremennost'*, "mutability."

The rhythm of the *protyazhnaya* is fitful, capricious, rubato, the opposite of regular or pulselike. These songs have nothing to do with dance, with work, or with ceremony. Indeed the lyrical song is a highly exceptional genre within the spectrum of Slavic folk music in that it is unattached to any specific social, ritual, or seasonal context at all. As Zemtsovsky puts it, it is not "subject in daily life to any, so to speak, functional application; its performance is devoid of 'extramusical ties.' Therefore its musical language, as a rule, depends neither on dance rhythms nor on directly reflected intonations of speech. . . . Music itself, melodic line takes on a dominating significance in it."[2]

Protyazhnïye are in fact "art songs" by any meaningful standard, just as their texts are artful lyric poems, full of subtle imagery and rhetoric. Their lyric impulse is personal, not collective. They are what Chernïshevsky had chiefly in mind when he formulated his notorious concept, so influential for a time, of "natural singing as the expression of emotion," the spontaneous sublimation of personal "joy and sorrow" (but chiefly sorrow), the empirical model that forms the basis in reality of all "artificial singing," that is, cultivated music.[3]

Though Chernïshevsky wrote as a militant realist and as an advocate of a sternly positivist, utilitarian aesthetic, his ideas on music were neither original nor "progressive." Poorly integrated into his overall thesis, they preserved a healthy residue of romantic subjectivity. And it was in the heyday of Russian romanticism, from the 1820s to the 1850s, that the *protyazhnaya* had been "discovered" by the educated urban classes and made the focal point of an intense national enthusiasm. The craze for literary imitations of peasant lyrical songs coincided with and contributed to the golden age of Russian lyric poetry. The chief practitioners included Pushkin (it goes without saying, though "Russian songs" formed only the merest fraction of that supreme stylist's wildly variegated output), but more characteristically Pushkin's best friend, Baron Anton Delvig (1798–1831), along with the serf actor Nikolai Tsïganov (1797–1831), and above all, Alexey Vasilyevich Koltsov (1809–42), whose widely admired "artificial folk songs," as Prince Mirsky calls them,[4] made the rhetoric and imagery of the *protyazhnaya* a permanent resource of cultivated lyric poetry in Russia.

There was a parallel development in music, to which both Glinka and Dargomïzhsky made minor contributions, but whose real leaders were a trio of Alexanders: Alyabyev (1787–1851), Varlamov (1801–48),

---

[2] Ibid., pp. 7–8.

[3] Nikolai Chernïshevsky, "Aesthetic Relations of Art to Reality" (1855), in *Selected Philosophical Essays* (Moscow: Foreign Languages Publishing House, 1953), pp. 346–47; quoted and glossed in my "Realism as Preached and Practiced: The Russian Opéra Dialogué," *Musical Quarterly* 56, no. 3 (July 1970): 436.

[4] D. S. Mirsky, *History of Russian Literature* (New York: E. P. Dutton, 1949), p. 124.

and Gurilyov (1803–58). Their work, however, did not attain the authenticity of the poets', for they lacked comparable access to authentic prototypes. Far less care was taken by the early collectors of folk songs with the music than with the texts, when indeed the music was included at all.[5] When it was, the intended audience was the amateur aristocratic or bourgeois singer, not the scholar, and every compromise was made so as to render the style of the "simple Russian songs" palatable to tastes formed on the fashionable Italianate salon music of the day. Where folk poetry was deemed acceptable to cultivated tastes, undoctored folk music was not.

The melodically unruly and rhythmically elusive *protyazhnaya* suffered the most from this attitude. It was more or less ignored by the early collectors, who were far more interested in dance songs, and when it was included, its melismata were pruned and trimmed to conform with Italianate coloratura formulas.[6] Varlamov and Gurilyov were vocal pedagogues who taught fashionable ladies by Italian methods, and their "Russian songs," both to genuine folk texts and to poems by Delvig, Tsïganov, Koltsov, and others, were modeled on the folk prototype not directly, but as mediated through the early published collections. A comparison of "Little Path" as transcribed by Ivan Rupin (alias Rupini, 1831) and as arranged more freely by Varlamov (1834) will illustrate (Examples 3a and 3b).

The most distinctive style characteristics of the *protyazhnaya* have been all but ironed out. Rhythm and phrase structure have been made as placid and regular as possible. Where Rupin had left a whiff of the waywardness of the original in his mixture of note values, Varlamov, the suave professional, has limited his note values to four, and these are deployed in recurring and fairly predictable patterns. Varlamov shows greater restraint in the matter of range, as well. Where Rupin had counted on a highly trained, operatic voice (a range of a thirteenth, a climactic A♭), Varlamov limits his setting to a

[5] The most important early collections to contain music were those of Vasily Trutovsky (*Sobraniye russkikh prostïkh pesen s notami*, 4 vols., 1776–95), Nikolai Lvov (*Sobraniye narodnïkh russkikh pesen s ikh golosami. Na muzïku plolzhil Ivan Pratsch*, 2 vols., 1806–15), Ivan Rupin (or Rupini [!]) (*Narodnïye russkiye pesni, aranzhirovannïye dlya golosa s akkompanementom fortepyano i khora*, 1831), and Daniyil Kashin (*Russkiye narodnïye pesni, sobrannïye i izdannïye dlya peniya i fortepyano*, 2 vols., 1833–34).

[6] Not that masterpieces could not arise from such an adulterated style: the Italianized *protyazhnaya* formed the basis for the roles of Antonida and Lyudmila in Glinka's operas, and one of Chaikovsky's greatest songs, *Ya li v pole da ne travushka bïla?* (1880), op. 47, no. 7, text by I. Surikov, is a very late, supreme example of the kind of "Russian song" typified by the work of the "Alexanders."

EXAMPLE 3a. Ivan Rupin, *Narodnïye russkiye pesni* (1831), reprinted in Semyon Ginzburg, ed., *Istoriya russkoy muzïki v notnïkh obraztsakh*, vol. 2 (Moscow: Muzïka, 1969)

modest octave (narrower, in fact, than the ranges of either of the transcriptions in Example 1) for his intended amateur performer. Even without the accompaniment it is obvious that the harmonic minor has replaced the natural. Leading tones are borrowed not only for the dominant of the main key but for secondary dominants as well. The latter is explicit in Rupin's melody in measure 4, but occurs in Varlamov's accompaniment even more frequently (V of iv in bars 3–4, V of VII at the end of bar 4). Both composers harmonize the cadential fall to the lower neighbor with a VII leading as a dominant

EXAMPLE 3b. Alexander Varlamov, *Romansï i pesni*, vol. 4 (Moscow, 1976), p. 57

to III (Varlamov) or through a chromatic bass progression to i (Rupin). Either way the sense of tonal mutability (*peremennost*) is forfeited, as the lower neighbor is deprived of cadential stability. And both composers seek out pretexts for ascending leaps of a sixth, the trademark of the salon romance (and entirely absent from the more "scientific" field transcription, Example 1b), though Varlamov is nowhere nearly as blatant as Rupin, with his downright embarrassing treatment of the final word.

Varlamov's setting is paired with another (*Ne budite menya, molodu*), marked "quickly, animated" in a contrast of tempi that was a stereotypical feature of "Russian songs" of this vintage. It has been suggested that this reflects the pairing of Italian aria and cabaletta.[7] But it seems at least as likely to be a reflection of the habits of Gypsy singers (recall Liszt's *lassu* and *friss*) who were enjoying a tremendous vogue in Russia at the time, and further adulterating the style of the Russian songs they performed. Their manner of performance was taken by many connoisseurs as exemplary, however. "Their true virtuosity," wrote one, "consisted in the faithful understanding and artistic expression of our national Russian and Little-Russian tunes. Preserving the true folk character of mournfulness or playfulness that was endemic to Russian or Little-Russian song, the Gypsies knew how to *modulate from one to the other* in their own way, and, without betraying their essential naiveté, expressed all the poetry of these melodies with uncommon artistry."[8] This encomium was echoed by many other urban lovers of Russian song, particularly literary men like Apollon Grigoryev, who know Varlamov well and furnished him with a number of texts to set.

Though, for all these reasons, Varlamov's setting of "Little Path" might not bear much resemblance to a peasant song, it is the work of a skilled and sensitive composer. The craftsmanship is rationalistic, even schematic. Note, for example, how the final melisma reproduces the opening "intonational thesis" in diminution. Such endearing details and hidden relationships, worked in, one feels, "für die Kenner," are even more pronounced in his independently conceived "Russian songs" than in his folk song arrangements. Songs like "Akh, tï vremya, vremyachko" (1837) or, above all, "Krasnïy sarafan" (1833), both to poems by Tsïganov, have become so popular in

---

[7] Natalia Listova, *Aleksandr Varlamov* (Moscow: Muzïka 1968), p. 162.

[8] A. V. Meshchersky, "Iz moyey starinï," *Russkiy arkhiv* 1, (1901): 113. Quoted by Listova, p. 181. Italics added.

EXAMPLE 4. Alexander Gurilyov, *Grust' devushki* ("Otchego skazhi
. . ."). In Semyon Ginzburg, ed., *Istoriya russkoy muzïki v notnïkh obraztsakh*, vol. 3 (Moscow: Muzïka, 1970), pp. 321–22. Piano accompaniment
omitted

Ot - che - go, ska - zhi, moy lyu - bi - mïy serp, po - cher -

nel tï ves', chto ko - sa moya? Il'____ o - brïz - gan tï

v sku-ke - go-re-sti po-mi - lom druzh-ke____ slyo-zoy de-vi-ch'yey?

Tell me why, my beloved sickle, have you turned all black, my scythe? Is it because you
have been spattered with a maiden's tears, in longing and in sorrow for her sweet love?

Russia that only musicologists seem to know that they are not folk
songs. The trained eye, however, easily spots the symmetries and
the clever manipulations that give the hand of the urban professional
away.

Varlamov's work represents at its best and most characteristic the
kind of "Russian song" that grew up around the work of Delvig, Tsïganov, and Koltsov. But a good many settings of the work of these
poets, including some of the most famous, never even made an attempt to capture the musical style of the folk model. A good example
is Gurilyov's still-popular setting of Koltsov's "A Maiden's Sorrow"
(*Grust' devushki*, ca. 1848). It is a strophic "salon romance" (*bïtovoy
romans*), whose echoes of the ballroom in waltz time (the polonaise
was another favorite) and sentimental melodic style (*sekstovïy*—"six-
thy"—in Russian critical parlance) are completely at variance with
the peasant language and imagery of the poem (Example 4).

Only when more elevated ideas on the significance of peasant culture for the culture of the nation began to win adherents in Russia[9]

[9] The ideas were derived from the German and English romantics, as adopted and
propagated by early Slavophiles such as Khomyakov and the Kireyevsky brothers.
See, for example, Yury Sokolov's interesting account of the "Historiography of Folk-
loristics" in his *Russian Folklore* (Hatboro, Pa.: Folklore Associates, 1966), esp. pp. 45–
65.

was the attempt made to achieve in the presentation of the music of folk songs an authenticity to match that of the texts. It is noteworthy that the earliest Russian folk song anthologies to present *protyazhnïye* in a guise modern ethnographers feel they can rely on[10] were the work of the *pochvenniki* [men of the soil], representatives of the quasi-Slavophile literary movement that had its apogee in the early plays of Ostrovsky, who incorporated many folk songs (including *protyazh-nïye*) into their dramatic fabric in a newly "organic" way.[11]

The collection that really put the *protyazhnaya* on the map, so to speak, was that of the youthful Balakirev (St. Petersburg: Johansen, 1866), who, fired with enthusiasm by the work of the *pochvennik* collectors, made his own Volga collecting trip in the summer of 1860, when he was just twenty-three years old. Balakirev was the first Russian musician of the front rank to engage personally in folk song collecting, and the first collector to be interested in folk songs more from the musical than from the textual standpoint.[12] Unlike previous collectors, moreover, his interest was not ethnographic or archaeological; he was, rather, in active search of what Russians call "*tvorcheskiy material*"—material for creative use. And unlike previous arrangers, he was not interested in furnishing music to fashionable homes and salons but was motivated by lofty romantic ideals.

Since he approached his material as one who intended not simply to display it but to use it, Balakirev was naturally on the lookout for what seemed freshest and least spoiled in the music he encountered. So he was especially drawn to the *protyazhnaya*. And he was far less inclined than his predecessors to distort it. But for the same reason he was not content merely to transcribe the melody faithfully and present it unadorned (as would later Russian ethnographers begin-

[10] Cf. Zemtsovsky, p. 23.

[11] For a consideration of these collections, i.e., those of Mikhail Stakhovich (3 vols., 1851–54) and Konstantin Villebois (2 collections, both issued in 1860), and their significance as background to the new treatment of folk song in art music (particularly as embodied in Alexander Serov's *Power of the Fiend* [*Vrazhya sila*, 1871]), see TarODR, Chapter 4. Villebois's was a particularly significant collaborative effort; it was the result of a collecting expedition along the Volga in which Ostrovsky took part, and its texts were edited by Apollon Grigoryev, *pochvennik* par excellence.

[12] Villebois, who went on the Volga expedition of 1856 on the initiative, and as the employee, of the journal *Morskoy sbornik* [Maritime miscellany], cannot be considered a collector in the same sense as Balakirev. The latter's comparative neglect of the texts (which he left largely to a collaborator, the poet Nikolai Shcherbina) has been documented by Yevgeniy Gippius ("M. Balakirev—sobiratel' russkikh narodnïkh pesen," SovM, no. 4 [1953]: 75).

ning in the 1890s, with the Istomin-Dyutsh and Istomin-Lyapunov collections sponsored by the Imperial Geographical Society). Balakirev was much concerned—one might even say primarily concerned—with the problem of harmonization as the first step toward the fruitful assimilation of folk music into the music of the high culture. Therefore, every item in his collection is presented in the form of an exquisite little art song, its melody reverently rendered "from life," as it were, but fitted out with an imaginative, elaborate and figurative, individualized accompaniment of Balakirev's devising, harmonically colorful yet appropriate to the idiom of the folk song.[13]

Appropriateness can only be judged subjectively, of course, but Balakirev's criteria are plain from the consistency of his practice. The main objective was not to compromise the diatonic purity of the melodies.[14] The main technical task, therefore, was to avoid the harmonic minor and to let the tonal ambiguity of many of the melodies (their *peremennost'*) emerge by eschewing such modulatory harmonies as secondary dominants. This "pure diatonic" harmonic style is best observed in the *protyazhnïye*, which are far better represented in Balakirev's collection than in any previous one.[15]

---

[13] His method was taken over by his disciple Rimsky-Korsakov (two collections, 1877 and 1882) and the latter's pupil Lyadov (four collections, 1898–1901). Chaikovsky, too, employed Balakirev's methods when harmonizing the songs collected by Prokunin (1872).

[14] Yet here, too, Balakirev's motives were aesthetic and artistic, not scholarly. He had, for instance, no use for Stasov's preposterous theories on the survival of the "church modes" in Russian folklore, and refused to be guided by them when Stasov tried to meddle in his work (though he did recognize the existence in Russian folklore of the Dorian mode, calling it the "Russian minor"). "Do not give yourself up excessively to archaeological investigations," he warned Stasov. "That is dry work; it narrows the mind and dries up the aesthetic sense. I know this from my own experience" (letter of 20 June 1861, BalStasP 1.139–40). Accordingly, where Balakirev saw fit he did not hesitate to introduce decorative chromaticism into the accompaniments, particularly of the dance songs, where Glinka's *Kamarinskaya* had set a perhaps ineluctable example. In short, Balakirev had a scholar's conscience only with respect to the melodies. In harmony he followed only his own taste and was quite pleased when an unnamed German professor at the Prague Conservatory pronounced his harmonizations "ganz falsch" (letter to Musorgsky, 11 January 1867, quoted in Edward Garden, *Balakirev* [New York: St. Martin's Press, 1967], pp. 57–58). For this reason, along with many others, Balakirev's folk song anthology ranks as a kind of manifesto of early kuchkism.

[15] Two of the *protyazhnaya* melodies are set to the same text, so the total may be given as either ten out of thirty-six songs (there are three other instances of two tunes for one text) or eleven out of forty melodies. Either way it is more than a quarter of the whole. One of the *protyazhnïye* (given in Example 5b) seems to have been taken over from Villebois, though reharmonized in Balakirev's inimitable fashion.

Example 5 gives two of them. The first is in the natural minor, the second in what Balakirev called the "Russian minor" (the equivalent of what is popularly known as the Dorian mode). In neither is a sharp or flat anywhere to be found, whether in the melody or in the accompaniment.

Several features of the harmonizations deserve comment. First and foremost is the total avoidance of the leading tone and, consequently, of dominant harmony. Besides the solutions shown here (plain "minor V" in no. 36, the same with a deceptive progression leading to a plagal cadence in no. 4), Balakirev also used a special form of plagal cadence, in which the subdominant harmony is employed under the second scale degree, yielding a half-diminished chord color. Two factors favor the untrammeled emergence of *peremennost'*: first, the very wayward harmonic rhythm (characteristically very slow at the outset, and then a surprising burst of chord changes on the half-beat), which creates a static, undirected effect; second, the habit of sustaining common tones, which contributes further to a sense of tonal stasis, as harmonies seem to change not all at once but a little at a time. (The use of sustained tones in this way may be an attempt to capture something of the flavor of *podgoloski*, the Russian brand of improvised folk polyphony.) Not only do these devices impede the "Western" sense of onward harmonic progression, they quite faithfully mirror the "fitful, capricious" rhythm of the *protyazhnaya*, one of its chief stylistic traits as noted above. Precisely this had always been the first element to go when the *protyazhnaya* was forced into the Procrustean bed of the early nineteenth-century "Russian song."

Balakirev's folk song collection was one of the great watersheds of nineteenth-century Russian music. And it would be hard to say which of its features was the most influential: its faithful transcription principles or the novel harmonic idiom of the accompaniments. It was mined avidly for thematic material from the start: at least twenty-five out of the forty songs in it found their way into more than that many compositions by Balakirev himself, his then most faithful follower Rimsky-Korsakov, Musorgsky, Chaikovsky, and even Serov (who used the song given as Example 5b in *The Power of the Fiend*), along with various composers of a later generation.[16] But

[16] See Nina Bachinskaya, *Narodnïye pesni v tvorchestve russkikh kompozitorov* (Moscow: Muzgiz, 1962).

EXAMPLE 5a. No. 4: *Protyazhnaya*, Simbirsk province, village of Pramzin. *Sbornik russkikh narodnïkh pesen sostavlennïy M. Balakirevïm* (St. Petersburg: Johansen, 1866).

EXAMPLE 5a, *continued*

За дворомъ, дворомъ за батюшкинымъ,
Какъ за горенкой, за матушкиной,
За моимъ ли за высокимъ теремомъ,
Выростала трава шелковая,
Разцвѣли цвѣты лазоревые,
Понесли духи малиновы.
Невеличка птичка пташечка,
Сине море перелетывала,
Чисто поле перепархивала
Садилася птичка пташечка
Ко дѣвушкѣ на окошечко
Она слушала ея голосу,
Какъ красная дѣвка плакала,
За стараго замужъ идучи,
За ровнюшкой небываючи:
„Ужъ ты старый мужъ, погубитель мой,
„Погубилъ мою головушку,
„Головушку - красну дѣвушку,
„Красоту мою невестушкину.“

EXAMPLE 5b. No. 36: *Protyazhnaya*, Nizhny-Novgorod province and district. *Sbornik russkikh narodnïkh pesen sostavlennïy M. Balakirevïm* (St. Petersburg, 1866)

EXAMPLE 5b, *continued*

да - -етъ, здѣсь въ не-счаст-ной сто - ро - нѣ.

Что на свѣтѣ прежестокомъ
Прежестокая любовь!
Оставляетъ, покидаетъ,
Здѣсь въ несчастной сторонѣ,
Не несчастной сторонѣ.
Здѣсь травынька не ростетъ,
Кавыль травинька не ростетъ,
Здѣсь цвѣточки не цвѣтутъ.
Говорила я милому,
Любезному своему
„Если я тебѣ по нраву,
„Возьми замужъ за себя.
„Если тебѣ не по нраву,
„Сошли на сву (свою) сторону.
„Возьми въ ручки пистолетикъ,
„Прострѣли ты грудь мою.
„Я навѣки буду спать
„Отъ любови отъ твоей.
„Приходи на гробъ проститься,
„Ты съ любовію моей.
„Напиши на гробѣ надпись,
„Что любила я тебя,
„И любя не оставляла
„По гробъ сердца моего. "

that is the least of it: following Balakirev's example, the lyrical strains of melismatic peasant songs harmonized in a "pure diatonic manner" sounded forth everywhere, not only in operas where they often represented themselves, as it were, but increasingly in instrumental contexts. Actual *protyazhnïye* can be found in Chaikovsky's First and Second Symphonies (not to mention the Andante cantabile from the First String Quartet) and in Rimsky-Korsakov's early Symphony in E♭ minor. And imitations were legion: the orchestral preludes to both *Boris Godunov* and *Khovanshchina*, the second movement of Chaikovsky's First Symphony, and any number of works by Borodin, who appears never to have appropriated a genuine *protyazhnaya* but imitated them better than anyone else.[17] From the publication of Balakirev's anthology to, say, the death of Borodin two decades later, the sound of the *protyazhnaya*, along with the ostinato dance tune, formed the very basis of the Russian "nationalist" style. Thereafter its use became more and more a sign of epigonism, whether of the "Belyayevets" variety (e.g., Glazunov's symphonies) or of the latter-day Balakirev school. Balakirev's own latest works—for example, the Piano Sonata or the song "The Rock" (*Utyos*) after Lermontov (1909)—though of excellent quality, are strangely anomalous and anachronistic, and his continued reliance on the "intonations" of the *protyazhnaya* was one of the chief symptoms of his arrested stylistic development. Not that the use of folk song was dead in Russia by any means. But "progressive" interest had shifted to the short-breathed "calendar song" (a shift best traced in Rimsky-Korsakov's operas), and Stravinsky, for example, who based his whole "Russian period" style on the calendar song, imitated the *protyazhnaya* only once—Ivan Tsarevich's theme in *The Firebird*.

LENGTHY though it is, the foregoing historical introduction is necessary if we are properly to evaluate Musorgsky's earliest song, "Where art thou, little star?" (*Gde tï, zvyozdochka?*), and sort out its complicated history. It remained unknown to the world[18] until May

---

[17] It has been suggested (Bachinskaya, pp. 142–43) that the first theme of *In the Steppes of Central Asia* was adapted from the famous "Little Path" melody (cf. Example 1), but the only published variant of the tune that resembles Borodin's theme (that of Lopatin and Prokunin, Example 1a) appeared two years after Borodin died. The Peasants' chorus (*khor poselyan*) in the last act of *Prince Igor* is a locus classicus both of *protyazhnaya* stylization and of imitation folk polyphony.

[18] And even to Stasov, who discussed a number of Musorgsky's early and unpublished works in his big memorial biography, including the *Souvenir d'Enfance* for piano

1909, when Charles Malherbe and Louis Laloy published a startling article in the *Bulletin français* of the International Music Society announcing that Malherbe had come into possession of an autograph containing no fewer than eighteen songs by Musorgsky composed between 1857 and 1866, of which only five had been published.[19] The composer himself had bound the manuscript and given it a title page, *Yunïye godï,* or "Youthful Years." Four of the thirteen new songs were printed as an appendix to the article, with French text only, and with the customary free alterations to Musorgsky's music. "Little Star," which aroused particular interest as it bore the earliest date, was one of these. The group was republished by Bessel, with Russian text restored and with Vyacheslav Karatïgin named as editor, in 1911. Twelve years later the rest of the collection, except for the last piece, an Italian vocal duet that remained unpublished until 1931, was issued by Bessel (now located in Paris).

The exceptional quality of "Little Star" was evident from the start.[20] Oskar von Riesemann, the first biographer of Musorgsky to deal with the "Youthful years" songs, judged that "of the six [*recte*: five] songs written [before 1860] the palm must be awarded to this one."[21] Indeed, one could go further and claim that "Little Star" surpasses all the songs in the manuscript except those Bessel published within Musorgsky's lifetime,[22] and even these only in their published, heavily revised form. For "Little Star" is at once a perfect paradigm of Balakirevesque *protyazhnaya* stylization, and an art song of

and the student pieces of the first Balakirev year, but who wrote that of the earliest group of songs, "he published only one: 'Tell Me Why, Fair Maiden'; the rest are lost" (StasIS 2:167).

[19] This manuscript now belongs to the Library of the Paris Conservatoire housed at the Bibliotèque Nationale (MS 6966). See Pavel Lamm, "Ot redaktora," in MusPSS 5/1–2 (*Yunïye godï: sbornik romansov i pesen* [Moscow, 1931]), p. iv.

[20] It has since become the most popular of the "Youthful Years" songs, to judge by its inclusion in anthologies and recordings. As early as 1917 it was chosen by Kurt Schindler for his collection *Masters of Russian Song* (New York: G. Schirmer). The earliest recording seems to have been that of Vladimir Rosing (1938, for the British Moussorgsky Song Society). Subsequent recording artists have included Igor Gorin, Boris Christoff, Jennie Tourel, Galina Vishnevskaya, Benjamin Luxon, Kim Borg, and Igor Navoloshnikov (winner of an "All-Union Musorgsky Song Conpetition" held in the USSR in 1970). "Little Star" was one of six Musorgsky songs orchestrated by Igor Markevitch as a suite (Milan: Suvini Zerboni, 1950).

[21] Oskar von Reisemann, *Moussorgsky,* trans. Paul Englund (New York: Alfred A. Knopf, 1929; reprint, New York: Dover Books, 1971), p. 46.

[22] These were "King Saul," "Night," and "Go to sleep, peasant lad," from Ostrovsky's *The Voyevoda* (*Spi, usni, krest'yanskiy sïn*), published by Bessel in 1871 along with five others composed in 1867 and 1868. The versions published by Bessel differ markedly from those in the "Youthful Years" manuscript.

great subtlety and refinement. Neither aspect compromises the other; their relationship is superbly symbiotic. Of its type, "Little Star" is unexcelled in the whole repertoire of Russian music. (See Figure 1, in which the autograph, signed and dated "1857. St. Petersburg," is reproduced.[23])

The text, by Nikolai Grekov, is a "Russian song" à la Koltsov, cast, like "A Maiden's Sorrow," in the 5 + 5–syllables-per-line meter that Koltsov had abstracted from the Russian wedding song, and that bears his name (*kol'tsovskiy stikh*):[24]

> Gde tï, zvyozdochka, gde ti, yasnaya?
> Il' zatmilasya tuchey chornoyu,
> Tuchey chornoyu, tuchey mrachnoyu?[25]
>
> Gde tï, devitsa, gde tï, krasnaya?
> Il' pokinula druga milova,
> Druga milova, nenaglyadnogo?
>
> [I ya s goresti, so lyutoy toski
> Poydu vo polye, polye chistoye;
> Ne uvizhu li yasnoy zvyozdochki,
> Ne povstrechu li krasnoy devitsï?][26]
>
> Tucha chornaya skrïla zvyozdochku,
> Zemlya khladnaya vzyala devitsu.[27]

[23] Comparison with MusPSS 5/1–2.1–3 reveals a number of errors in the texting of the melismata. In addition, Lamm silently adopted from Karatïgin's edition a number of questionable interpretations of Musorgsky's ambiguous rhythmic notation.

[24] Nikolai Porfiryevich Grekov (1810–66) was, in the estimation of the *Bol'shaya sovetskaya entsiklopediya* (edition of 1930—he is dropped from later editions), a "second-rate eclectic poet" who earned his living as a versatile translator of Shakespeare from English, Goethe and Heine from German, Musset and Gautier from French, and Calderon from Spanish. He was surprisingly popular with composers of songs. Georgy Ivanov's catalog, *Russkaya poeziya v otechestvennoy muzïke* (Part 1, Moscow: Muzïka, 1966), lists no fewer than forty-four poems by Grekov set (some more than once) by a large group of composers including the "three Alexanders," Dargomïzhsky, Rubinstein, and Chaikovsky. "Little Star" was set by four other composers, including Varlamov. The latter's setting, however, is a salon romance in "couplet" (i.e., strophic) style, and bears no significant comparison to Musorgsky's. Musorgsky does not name Grekov in his manuscript; the identification was first made by Lamm, evidently on the basis of the other settings. Varlamov's setting may even have been Musorgsky's source for the text, since the book of poems by Grekov in which "Little Star" first appeared was published after Musorgsky had already composed his song.

[25] In place of *mrachnoyu* (gloomy, somber) Musorgsky has *groznoyu* (menacing, threatening).

[26] This stanza is omitted by Musorgsky.

[27] *Stikhotvoreniya N. Grekova* (Moscow, 1860), p. 31.

[Where art thou, little star, where art thou, so bright?
Hast thou gone behind a dark cloud,
A dark cloud, a lowering cloud?

Where art thou, maiden, where art thou, so fair?
Hast thou forsaken thy beloved,
Thy beloved, thy darling?

And I with sorrow, with cruel pain,
Will go out into the field, the open field;
Will I never see my bright star,
Will I never meet my fair maid?

The dark cloud has hidden my little star,
The cold earth has taken my fair maid.]

With a boldness that seems uncommon in a composer so young, Musorgsky omitted four lines so that he might cast his song in an elegantly varied ternary form. The relationship between this form and the truncated poem is masterly. The A and B sections contrast (rather conventionally, it is true) in theme and key, apostrophizing star and maiden in turn. But when the second theme comes back in the tonic major in unexpected support of the final cadence, and at the last mention of the departed maiden, the symbolic effect is magical. One is reminded of the way Schumann often poignantly transformed his texts by his settings.

Now the extraordinary thing is that this very sophisticated art song is written in a pseudo-folk idiom pure enough to bear comparison with Balakirev's songbook. Let us, in fact, make the comparison, by juxtaposing Musorgsky's song with the Balakirev setting given as Example 5a, in the same key. The style of the melismata has the same pliant flexibility in both; in fact, the two songs have some actual figures in common. The "intonational thesis," as presented in the introductory unaccompanied piano phrase and then restated by the voice in Musorgsky's song, is as authentic not only as Balakirev's but as those of the field-collected *protyazhnïye* in Examples 1 and 2.[28] Musorgsky's voice part is in just as pure a natural minor as Balakirev's:

[28] The opening is labeled *dudka* (reed pipe) in the autograph, which rightly reminded von Reisemann of Gritsko's "Duma" in *Sorochintsï Fair*, composed some twenty years later. This number, written as it were at the other end of Musorgsky's career, is in fact his only other full-fledged *protyazhnaya* stylization. The genre sandwiches his output. One might add that the "dudka" solo in "Little Star," with its fussy, self-conscious cancellation of the leading tone, seems the one naive or immature detail in the song.

FIGURE 1. "Gde ty zvezdochka?" (*Iunye gody* [Youthful years], no. 1). Paris, Bibliothèque nationale (ancien fonds du Conservatoire national de musique, MS 6966)

it contains not a single chromatic alteration. And while the harmony does include C♯-major chords, they are handled very circumspectly. The only authentic cadence to F♯ occurs with the voice silent, in the little piano interlude that introduces the last section of the song (a harmonization of the opening "intonational thesis"). In the final cadence of the song, the use of the D♯ resulting from the reminiscence of the second theme creates a deceptive progression very close to the one that ends Example 5a. The only other C♯-major chord occurs in the middle section (nominally in A major). It is not allowed to resolve to F♯. Instead, the progression in which it occurs is interrupted and reiterated (iv–V/iv–V in F♯ minor), and on a second iteration the C♯-major chord is evaded altogether; it is replaced by F♯ major (V of ii in A major), which is then pushed down the circle of fifths until a cadence to A is reached. But it is a plagal, not an authentic, cadence. (Note, in fact, how the authentic progression from E major to A major on the way is prevented by the typically wayward harmonic rhythm from sounding cadential.)

Other chromatic touches are either expressive or conventionally ornamental in ways that had by Musorgsky's time a tradition in Russian music. The diminished chord at the cadence of the first section is common word painting (the word is *groznoyu*, "threatening"). But note that the D♯ persists after the resolution, giving a hint of Balakirev's "Russian minor." The F♮ in the interlude introducing the second section is a device (chromatic alteration in passing between the fifth and sixth degrees in either direction) so common in Glinka and Dargomïzhsky as to be a "style russe" cliché. Another altered sixth degree evoking the "Russian minor" comes with the B-major chord that prepares the closing cadence in the voice part.

Consider now the matter of tonal mutability (*peremennost'*). As already implied, the middle section is in the relative major to the tonic key. But A major is very weakly and ambiguously expressed. Cadences are plagal, and the main theme of the section is contrived so that the first A in the bass comes under an F♯ in the melody, creating maximum degree ambiguity and a maximum identification of A with the actual tonic of the song. (The C♯ major chords in the middle section, already mentioned, also adumbrate F♯, of course.) Such ambiguity is the very essence of *peremennost'*. The beautiful final cadence of the second section is a small masterstroke: the note melodically emphasized is not A but its dominant E, which is also the lower neighbor to the main tonic, the traditional *peremennost'* tone of minor-mode *protyazhnïye* (cf. Examples 1, 2, and 5). Best of all is the magnificently ambiguous cadential unison, approached in a three-part counterpoint that is "ganz falsch" from the point of view of harmonic rhythm and of voice leading, but which reproduces to perfection a cadence typical of authentic *podgoloski*. The tied note in the upper voice is mainly responsible for the finality of the approach to E. It is uncannily stable, not at all felt as the dominant of A. A comparable cadence was not written until Borodin's famous Peasants' chorus (also in F♯ minor with *peremennost'* mutations to E), a quarter of a century later. Even more uncanny is the fact that the voice part makes this wonderful cadence through a figure note for note (if not quite rhythm for rhythm) identical to the voice part in Example 5a, measures 6–7.

And now the rub. Can we believe that this brilliant essay in the folk style was composed by an untutored eighteen-year-old who had not yet met Balakirev,[29] some three years before the latter made his Volga expedition and some nine years before his epoch-making anthology was published? In 1857 there was absolutely no precedent for a song like "Little Star," and yet it is no groping attempt but a minor masterpiece.

The problem gets worse. In the course of preparing his critical edition of Musorgsky's songs, Pavel Lamm discovered in the library of the Leningrad Conservatory a manuscript orchestral score of "Little Star," headed "My little song, arranged for orchestra by myself," signed, and dated very precisely: "Begun on June 3 at one o'clock in the morning, finished June 4 at six in the afternoon, 1858."[30] Its many divergences from the "Youthful Years" manuscript demanded its publication as a "second version." Comparison dismays, for the "second version" is so clearly inferior to the "first." None of the excellent qualities noted above seem to have survived the revising process; in particular, the wonderful purity of the *protyazhnaya* stylization is totally lost. The melismas are skimpy and primitive. The harmony is often clumsy and ineffective (e.g., measure 8). The vocal phrases are

[29] Alexandra Orlova interprets the earliest surviving letter from Musorgsky to Balakirev (15 December 1857) to mean that the two had met in the early part of the month (OrTD, 64).

[30] The "second version" is printed in piano-vocal reduction in MusPSS 5/1–2.4–6, to which the reader is referred. The full score was announced for inclusion in a subsequent volume, but never appeared. It is announced for publication in the new Academic edition of Musorgsky's complete works under the general editorship of Yevgeniy Levashov (see NasMPM, 59).

rhythmically monotonous, and the overall shape of the piece is unrelieved, lacking the piano interludes that divided the other version into well-defined sections. The melody has lost its diatonic purity, and the use of the harmonic minor at times painfully obtrudes, especially at the very end, where instead of the unforgettable cadence of the first version there is only a lamely conventional authentic close. Nor are secondary dominants absent: the baldest V of V makes a sudden and unwelcome cadential appearance nine bars before the end. Most disappointing of all is the cadence of the second stanza. Instead of the *peremennost'* mutation to E that was at once so authentically folklike and so beautifully expressive in its restrained way, there is now a sentimental ascent to a high A through a Gurilyov-like minor sixth, and then a melodramatic arpeggiation of a half-diminished chord, with a final plunge to a low D♯ approached by a tritone that would have made old "Rupini" blush.

Faced with these two versions, both explicitly dated, commentators have been understandably perplexed.[31] Calvocoressi, for one, complains that the second version

> is less attractive, less subtle, less sensitive. Not one of the changes seems to have been dictated by considerations of orchestral needs or possibilities (of which Musorgsky, in 1858, must have known practically nothing); nor are these changes of a kind which might have been suggested by an adviser. One is almost tempted to wonder whether Musorgsky did not, when composing, occasionally lack decision and consistency, whether he did not remain very much at the mercy of the inspiration, or whim, or chance of the moment. The doubts are formidable ones even when one remembers that in the music of his maturity he showed purpose enough; they are doubts certainly not to be dealt with casually.[32]

Calvocoressi should not have given in so easily to temptation. His assumption—essentially, that Musorgsky did not know what he was doing—shows how thoroughly we have all, even the most sympa-

[31] Lamm himself did not comment, beyond his general remark that "for performance, preference must always be given to the latest version." In the case of "Little Star" this advice has never been followed to my knowledge, at least by those who have recorded the song. Of course, the fact that Lamm's "second version" is an orchestral reduction provides performers with an easy out.

[32] M. D. Calvocoressi, *Mussorgsky* (London: J. M. Dent, 1946; reissue, New York: Collier Books, 1962), p. 86. Calvocoressi's "doubts" are echoed by Edward Reilly when he writes, "The composer's versions are sometimes of equal interest, but in a few cases the earliest of the two is substantially fresher than the later (one wonders if Musorgsky at times doubted his own distinctive voice)" (RMusMus, 29).

thetic among us, been conditioned to patronize the composer as a kind of idiot savant. Is there another among the "world classics" about whom comparable "doubts" could be entertained? No, not even Bruckner. It is time to shelve them. And once we have shelved them, it is inconceivable that the differences between the versions of "Little Star" presented by Lamm were the result of a deliberate process of revision—*unless we reverse their order*. If we assume, dates notwithstanding, that the first version is in fact a revision of the second, we may now observe a sure-handed artist at work: the focus is sharpened, the style purified, the structure reinforced. In short, the second version is just what one might expect from an eager but unresourceful beginner, and the first exhibits precisely the kinds of improvement a young master, who knew Balakirev's songbook (and particularly setting no. 4 therein), might have made.

Alongside these judgment calls, open by nature to dispute on grounds of subjectivity or circularity, we may set one telling fact: the "second version" of the song incorporates the full text. Calvocoressi interprets this to mean that "in the orchestral version a middle section has been added."[33] But that is inaccurate. In place of the tripartite structure of the first version, the second is in a weakly articulated binary form, with two stanzas of the poem on either side of an abrupt dominant chord that serves all too blatantly to mark the great divide. The third stanza, that is, the "new" material, is thus the beginning of the second section, and is in fact a kind of varied reprise of the opening of the song. This stanza, moreover, contains some really glaring errors of declamation, which again it would be scarcely possible to imagine Musorgsky deliberately introducing in the process of revision.

It is perfectly easy, on the other hand, to imagine the composer sacrificing a portion of the text so as to improve the form of the song. And that the section sacrificed contained some embarrassing lapses in declamation would only have made it that much easier for a composer whose concern with declamation came to be the very foundation of his style to delete it. What on first acquaintance with the song seemed unusual in Musorgsky's approach to the text becomes far easier to understand as the result of a revision. There are precedents, one from within the "Youthful Years" group: the song "Night" (*Noch'*, 1864), after a poem by Pushkin. It was published in

---

[33] Calvocoressi, *Mussorgsky*, p. 86.

1871, set to a free prose paraphrase that scandalized lovers of the Pushkin original. The indubitably earlier version in the "Youthful Years" manuscript follows Pushkin faithfully. In this case, as evidently in "Little Star," the integrity of the text was sacrificed to musical values on revision.[34]

But if these arguments are still judged insufficient, consider one final piece of evidence: the autograph of the piano-vocal original of the second version, entitled "Rustic Song" (*Sel'skaya pesnya*) and dated 18 April 1857 (Figure 2). Only known since Lamm's death, it was published in 1963, but inconspicuously, and has been little noticed since.[35] It corresponds in every significant detail with Lamm's edition of the second version in orchestral reduction, and should therefore settle once and for all which of the versions is the original and which the revision.

What, then, of the date 1857, entered so clearly in black and white in the Paris autograph? Now that we have the securely dated "Rustic Song" it will, I think, be easy to demonstrate that the date in the Paris source is the date of the original song, not the revision, which in fact was certainly made at least six, and probably as many as nine years later. First, and perhaps in itself conclusive, we have the two signatures. On the manuscript of the "Rustic Song" (Figure 2), the composer spells his name "Musorsky," without the *g*. This is the spelling one finds in the signatures of all the early letters to Balakirev (1857–58).[36] The Paris manuscript of the song (Figure 1) shows the standard spelling, which makes its first securely dated appearance in the surviving autograph documents in a letter of March 1863.[37] This date, then, may be regarded as a provisional *terminus post quem* for the Paris holograph of "Little Star." Looking further into the physical evidence of the "Youthful Years" collection, we note that it is not a

[34] The most famous instance of textual mutilation upon musical revision is, of course, the second act of *Boris*, particularly the title character's great monologue, whose text was turned to prose on its being transformed into an "aria" (see Chapter 5).

[35] The facsimile faces OrTD, 65 from which it is reproduced here. Orlova's caption gives no hint of its relationship to "Little Star." Very oddly, Orlova lists the song under the correct month and date, but the wrong year (1858), although the date on the manuscript is perfectly legible in the facsimile.

[36] See letters nos. 1–6 in MusLN 1.35–37.

[37] MusLN 1.64. The date of a possibly older letter with the standard spelling, given by Andrey Rimsky-Korsakov as "1861" in MusPD, 75 (letter no. 36), is purely conjectural. On the matter of the composer's surname and its variants, see "Pronouncing the Name" (pp. xxvii–xxx).

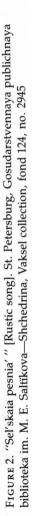

FIGURE 2. "Sel'skaia pesnia'" [Rustic song]. St. Petersburg, Gosudarstvennaya publichnaya biblioteka im. M. E. Saltíkova—Shchedrína, Vaksel collection, fond 124, no. 2945

miscellany of manuscripts on various papers, as one might expect in a privately bound group of songs dated over a seven-year span, but a fair copy whose uniformity of paper type suggests that the date of all the manuscripts contained therein must postdate the composition of the latest song in the manuscript, which happens to be no. 10, *Malyutka* [Little one], dated 7 January 1866.[38] If this is now accepted as the *terminus post quem* for the copying of the "Youthful Years" manuscript, then Musorgsky's revision of "Little Star" would very likely have dated precisely from the time Balakirev was hardest at work on his folk song anthology,[39] and the revised version of the song would thus indeed reflect what the internal evidence already so strongly suggested—namely, the direct influence of Balakirev's arrangements on its style, and even on one or two of its actual details. The revised version would also thus have been composed later than *Kalistrat* (after Nekrasov, dated 22 May 1864), the "étude in the folk style" in which Musorgsky first manifested the principle of *peremennost'* in the cadential oscillations between F♯ and E (Example 6). The song happens to be in the same key as "Little Star," and Musorgsky may well have been moved to revise the earlier song in the course of work on the later one.

Finally, let us recall the numerous instances in which revised manuscripts by Musorgsky carry the date not of the revision but of the original composition. Four are to be found in "Youthful Years": the three songs published by Bessel in 1871, and "Kalistrat," published posthumously (in a further revision by Rimsky-Korsakov) in 1883. All of them were published in versions that postdate the assemblage of the "Youthful Years" manuscript, but the dates on the revised manuscripts in all cases agree with those in the Paris source.

So let us now attempt to reconstruct the creative history of "Little

[38] Actually, two papers were used. One, sixteen-staff oblong, is used for all but four songs. The latter group, which includes "Little Star," is written on an eighteen-staff paper, also oblong in format. Since the group also contains one of the latest songs (*Molitva* [A prayer], 1865), as well as one of the earliest songs (*Vesyolïy chas* [A merry time], 1858), which, like "Little Star," exists in a more primitive version in a manuscript located in Russia that carries a paradoxical later date, we may venture the guess that the eighteen-staff paper was used when the sixteen-staff paper ran out, and represents the later layer of the "Youthful Years" manuscript. The revision of "Little Star," then, probably took place at a late stage in the compilation of the manuscript, in the spring of 1866.

[39] In his autobiography, Rimsky-Korsakov recalls that in the spring of 1866 Balakirev "was then harmonizing the Russian folk songs he had collected, was tinkering a great deal with them and making many changes. I gained a thorough knowledge of the song material collected by him and his method of transcribing it" (R-KMusL, 62–63).

EXAMPLE 6. *Peremennost'* in "Kalistrat" (1864)

Over me my mother used to sing me a lullaby as she rocked me . . .

Star." The song, entitled "Rustic Song," was completed on 18 April 1857 and orchestrated on 3–4 June of the following year.[40] Some time after 22 May 1864 (the date of *Kalistrat*) Musorgsky decided to revise a song to bring it into line with the style of Balakirev's *protyazhnaya* settings, which, though not yet published, were of course well known to him as a member of Balakirev's circle. This revision was copied out for inclusion in the "Youthful Years" collection sometime after 7 January 1866 (the date of *Malyutka*, the latest song in the collection). In keeping with what was by now his habit, Musorgsky retained the original date on the revised fair copy.

Can we also postulate a *terminus ante quem*? It seems we can, simply by observing the date of Musorgsky's next song: "The Wish" (*Zhelaniye*, after Heine), composed, according to the date on the earliest autograph, "from the 15th to the 16th of April, 1866 (at two o'clock in the morning)." By this date "Youthful Years" must have been all copied and bound, or this song would have been included, too; for, with one insignificant exception, the anthology contains every song Musorgsky had composed to date.[41] He then presumably submitted the lot to Johansen, who was just then publishing his mentor's folk song anthology, and with whom Musorgsky therefore

[40] This first attempt at an orchestral score was a symbolic turning point for Musorgsky. The very next day, 5 June 1858, O.S., he received his release from the Preobrazhensky Guards, which he had requested in May for "family reasons" (but really so as to be able to devote himself entirely to music). This fatal decision determined the entire tragic course of his career.

[41] The exception is "Meines Herzens Sehnsucht," composed in 1858 to a German text as a wedding present to Malvina Bamberg, César Cui's bride. Having given his present, Musorgsky no longer possessed the manuscript, which has since been lost. See Lamm's critical report in MusPSS 5/3.xii. The song was reprinted in MusPSS 5/3 (MusCW 9) from a Kiev music magazine, where it had appeared with Cui's cooperation in 1907.

EXAMPLE 7. Musorgsky, "Otchego skazhi, dusha devitsa" (1858), opening section. Piano accompaniment omitted

Ot-che-go___ ska - zhi, du - sha de - vi - tsa, tï si -

dish' te-per___ pri-go-ryu - ni - las' i bez - molv - na - ya na do-

ro - zhen' - ku tï vzdokh - nuv glya - dish' ne na - smot - rish' - sya?

Tell me why, fair maiden, do you sit sad and silent by the way, why, sighing, you gaze longingly?

had an entrée. His disappointment must have been great when Johansen took only one of them, and the "safest" one at that: the utterly conventional salon romance, "Tell me why, fair maiden" (*Otchego skazhi, dusha devitsa*, 1858). In waltz time, it is Musorgsky's answer to Gurilyov's "A Maiden's Sorrow," whose text actually begins with the same words (cf. Example 4). Its style is one Musorgsky had long since outgrown, and he could scarcely have been very proud to see it in print in 1867. A glance at this song vis-à-vis "Little Star" will show not only how far Musorgsky had come but how far Russian music was in the process of transforming itself in the 1860s (Example 7).

One more guess: early in 1870, after the satisfaction of placing two songs with Bessel, the most prestigious music publisher in St. Petersburg,[42] Musorgsky was emboldened to dust off the "Youthful Years" volume and try again. As we know, Bessel picked three songs, which Musorgsky, with several years' more experience now behind him, spruced up for publication sometime later that year. They came out in the fall of 1871,[43] after which Musorgsky did nothing more with his youthful anthology. How, sometime between 1871 and 1909, the manuscript found its way to Paris, remains a mystery. It could not have been among Musorgsky's papers at his death, or else Stasov would have reported its existence, and Rimsky-Korsakov would very

[42] Cf. OrTD, 185.
[43] Ibid., p. 223–24.

likely have edited some or all of it for publication. Maybe Musorgsky had given it back to Johansen, whose holdings were acquired in 1895 by the ten-year-old Belyayev firm (through an intermediate copyright holder, one Khavanov).[44] Since the Belyayev offices and printing facilities were located in Western Europe, this might help account for the manuscript's "emigration." (But if Belyayev acquired it, surely Rimsky-Korsakov, as head of the firm's editorial board, would have been informed.)[45]

To sum up, our investigation of Musorgsky's "Little Star" has illustrated with unusual clarity the way in which Balakirev's innovations in the transcription and harmonization of folk songs were consciously and deliberately adopted by the other composers of his generation as a means of refreshing their style and giving it greater authenticity. Although the Balakirevesque melodic and harmonic turns in the revised version of "Little Star" did become for him a permanent stylistic resource, Musorgsky was far less interested than Balakirev in folklorism per se; consequently, he left far fewer "études in the folk style." Another tendency claimed him, that of realism and speech-song (see the next chapter), and to a great extent he parted aesthetic company with Balakirev quite shortly after the "Youthful Years" period. The imitation *protyazhnaya* was above all a culminating reflection of Russian romanticism, and it was the pair of kuchkists who remained essentially romantics at heart—Balakirev and Borodin—who contributed the most to the genre. Nor is it surprising that the stylistic retrenchment Musorgsky made in the closing years of his short career should have brought him back to the *protyazhnaya* at the very end, in the *Dumï* he wrote for *The Fair at Sorochintsï*. His early and extremely successful flirtation with the genre gives us a sense of the composer he would have been had he hewn closer to Balakirev's line, and enhances our sense of his versatility. Above all—and even allowing possibly for direct meddling on the part of Balakirev—one cannot come away from the revised "Little Star" without a perhaps

[44] See Boris Volman, *Russkiye notnïye izdaniya XIX-nachala XX veka* (Leningrad: Muzïka, 1970), pp. 128, 138.

[45] For the record, there is one more not-too-promising lead. In his autobiographical sketch of 1880, Musorgsky writes of a shadowy friend named von Madeweiss, who had sent a few of his songs to the Strasbourg Library for safekeeping (MusLN 1.269–70). The songs are named, however, and they are not those in the "Youthful Years" manuscript. Until further data surface, there will always be the outside chance that the composer had forgotten both the contents of the "Youthful Years" manuscript and its actual destination.

unaccustomed admiration for the young Musorgsky's craftsmanship. He was, all the myths and legends notwithstanding, a painstaking artist. Let us begin to remember him less as the unkempt, red-nosed subject of Repin's all-too-famous portrait, and more in terms of the elegant, lapidary calligraphy of his manuscripts. The former may appeal to our imagination in its evocation of Musorgsky's tragic fate. But there can be no question that the latter is a truer reflection of the creative artist.

2

HANDEL, SHAKESPEARE,
AND MUSORGSKY

The Sources and Limits of
Russian Musical Realism

———■———

"MUSORGSKY'S *Boris Godunov*," writes Carl Dahlhaus in an influential recent essay, "is a major work, yet the musical realism of which it is the outstanding document is so isolated a phenomenon that it can hardly be called a style—for one of the characteristics of style is recurrence in more than one work."[1] Musorgsky's great opera was not quite as isolated as that. While it is the only major musical document of Russian realism that has become an enduring part of the standard repertoire, it was not without precedent and issue. In the guise in which it is best known—the second version (1872)—it even marked something of a retreat from the hard-line aesthetic tendencies of the 1860s. During that remarkable decade musicians were easily as deeply involved as painters and writers in the realist ferment that gripped Russian art, and for a time it looked as though the genres of song and opera were undergoing as drastic and lasting a change as were those of short story and novel. The real musical monument of this fascinating moment in Russian intellectual history was not *Boris* but a far less well known work by the same composer—*Marriage* (*Zhenit'ba*), after Gogol, which Musorgsky, in a typically "scientistic" affectation, subtitled "an experiment in dramatic music

THIS chapter is reproduced from *Studies in the History of Music*, vol. 1: *Music and Language*. Copyright © 1983 by Broude Brothers Limited. Reproduced by permission of Broude Brothers Limited.

[1] "Neo-Romanticism," *Between Romanticism and Modernism: Four Studies in the Music of the Later Nineteenth Century*, trans. Mary Whittall. (Berkeley and Los Angeles: University of California Press, 1980), p. 7.

in prose" (in 1868 a remarkably early use of the term "experiment" in reference to a work of art).

This opera is often treated as a kind of appendage to Dargomïzhsky's *The Stone Guest*, the work with which the older composer thought to slash the Gordian knot of "operatic form" by throwing out the whole idea of *dramma per musica* and setting a preexistent stage play to music verbatim, in a style César Cui dubbed "melodic recitative"—a kind of flexible, madrigalian, continuous arioso. Elsewhere I have tried to show that among the philosophical antecedents to Dargomïzhsky's experiment was that Bible of Russian realism, Chernïshevsky's *Esteticheskiye otnosheniya iskusstva k deystvitel'nosti* [Aesthetic relations of art to reality, 1855], with its radical opposition of emotion and form, and its curious dichotomy of music into "natural and artificial singing."[2] But, while Musorgsky's aesthetic and even stylistic debt to Dargomïzhsky is real enough (as Musorgsky openly, indeed gratefully, acknowledged[3]), and though the suggestion that Musorgsky attempt a "dialogue opera" of his own on the text of Gogol's comedy seems to have come from Dargomïzhky himself,[4] the differences between *The Stone Guest* and *Marriage* are no less noteworthy than the similarities.

They begin with the literary sources. Where Pushkin's *Stone Guest*, a retelling of the Don Juan legend from the "Little Tragedies" of 1830, was a work of elegant lyric poetry and lofty romantic theme, Gogol's "altogether improbable occurrence in three acts" entitled *Marriage* (1833) must rank with the most "unmusical" prose ever penned. The play's literary idiom is naturalistic colloquialism exaggerated to absurd hyperbole. Its themes are paltry, its humor the silliest sort of caricature. Not even Vladimir Nabokov could summon up much admiration for the artistic qualities of this "rather slipshod comedy

[2] R. Taruskin, "Realism as Preached and Practiced: The Russian *Opéra Dialogué*," *Musical Quarterly* 56 (1970): 434–37. For a somewhat divergent view of Dargomïzhsky's masterpiece, see Jennifer Baker, "Dargomïzhsky, Realism, and *The Stone Guest*," *Music Review* 37, no. 3 (August 1976), especially pp. 206–7. A translation of Chernïshevsky's book may be found in N. G. Chernïshevsky, *Selected Philosophical Essays* (Moscow: Foreign Languages Publishing House, 1953).

[3] Two of Musorgsky's naturalistic songs of the late sixties—*Kolïbel'naya Yeryomushki* ["Jeremy's Cradle Song," 1867] and *S nyaney* ["With Nanny," the first of the *Detskaya* (*Nursery*) cycle, 1868]—bear a dedication to Dargomïzhsky, the "great teacher of musical truth."

[4] "It was suggested by Dargomïzhsky (in jest) and seconded by Cui (not in jest)," wrote Musorgsky to Stasov on 2 January 1873. MusLN 1.144.

about the hesitations of a man who has made up his mind to marry, has a swallowtail suit made, is provided with a fiancée—but at the last moment makes a fenestral exit."[5] Its roughness, its bluntness and, above all, its total lack of "poetry" were just what made *Marriage* attractive to "the thinking realist of the Russian operatic stage." Such a literary ambience was absolutely uncharted terrain for music; here was a chance to widen the art's horizons, to free it from the shackles of the lyric and the beautiful, truly to live up to the kuchkist slogan "Toward new shores!"

It was in his faith in laconic prose texts and in naturalistic declamation as the key to truth of emotional expression in music that Musorgsky went beyond even Dargomïzhsky's most advanced thinking and parted company with Chernïshevsky altogether. Chernïshevsky's model of "natural singing" was the Russian *protyazhnaya* (see Chapter 1), which the philosopher viewed as a natural artifact in that it was an unmediated, untutored and spontaneous "expression of joy or sorrow."[6] Chernïshevsky's unwontedly nonempirical citation of these vaguely defined emotions as music's natural source and model can in any case be construed as leading back to the aesthetic of the *Affektenlehre*, and hence, paradoxically enough for a critic to whom "emotion and form are opposites," to the acceptance and justification of rounded forms in dramatic music. Chernïshevsky in fact speaks of the aria, not the recitative, as the artful imitation of "natural singing." And the "melodic recitative" in *The Stone Guest*, though avowedly realist in its "formlessness," is not particularly naturalistic as regards declamation. Musorgsky, on the other hand, gave repeated expression to an aesthetic wholly founded on imitation of speech as bona fide empirical model for his music. Here is a sample, from a letter written during his period of work on *Marriage*:

> This is what I would like: for my characters to speak onstage as living people speak, but in such a way that their essential nature and force of intonation, supported by an orchestra that forms a musical canvas for their speech, shall hit the target squarely. That is, my music must be the artistic reproduction of human speech in all its subtlest twistings; that is, the sounds of human speech, as the exterior manifestation of thought and feeling, must, without exaggeration or strain, become mu-

[5] *Nikolai Gogol* (New York: New Directions, 1959), p. 158.
[6] For the relevant passage in Chernïshevsky, see *Selected Philosophical Essays*, p. 346. On this passage, see Taruskin, "Realism as Preached and Practiced," p. 436.

sic—truthful, accurate, *but* (read: which means) artistic, in the highest sense artistic.[7]

Striking and somewhat unexpected in this context is the neoclassical tint. In his call for the mimesis of speech, which in its turn is itself a mimesis—"the exterior manifestation of thought and feeling"—Musorgsky sounds like a regular Aristotelian, even a latter-day Galilei. Where could the Russian composer have encountered such ideas? Or is this merely one more independent formulation of an obvious and endlessly recurring reformist slogan, one more case of ontogeny recapitulating phylogeny in the history of operatic reform?

Though many writers have reasonably assumed the latter to be the case, Musorgsky left a strong clue to the particular sources of his aesthetic outlook and, in particular, his view of the relationship between music and speech. In the autobiographical sketch he prepared in 1880 at the request of Hugo Riemann for inclusion in the first edition of the latter's *Musik-Lexicon*, Musorgsky followed the factual information with this self-styled *profession de foi*: "Proceeding from the conviction that human speech is strictly regulated by musical laws (Virchow, Gervinus) he [Musorgsky] views the aim of musical art as the reproduction in musical sounds not only of modes of feeling [*nastroeniya chuvstva*] but mainly of the reproduction of modes of human speech [*nastroeniya rechi chelovecheskoy*]."[8]

Given the context, there was certainly a pro forma aspect to the citation of the two German names. The composer seems to have wanted to show the eminent German *Musikwissenschaftler* that he, too, was up on his *Wissenschaft* (and not only musical).[9] Rudolf Virchow (1821–1902), cellular pathologist, anthropologist, and political activist, was a standard hero of positivists and progressives: a "scientific luminary" (as Chernïshevsky called him) who sought active participation in governmental and social reform and hence exercised an enormous appeal on the progressive intelligentsia in Russia, where more than anyplace else the arts and sciences were assumed to be *engagés*.

[7] To Lyudmila Shestakova, 30 July 1868. MusLN 1.100.

[8] Ibid., 270.

[9] Musorgsky may have also intended a nod in Chernïshevsky's direction. Both Virchow and Gervinus are mentioned in Chernïshevsky's "nihilistic" novel *What Is to Be Done?* of 1862 (see the Vintage edition, trans. Benjamin Tucker [New York, 1961], pp. 176–77, 223).

To the literary historian and Shakespearean scholar Georg Gott-fried Gervinus (1805–71), on the other hand, the proposition with which Musorgsky associates his name may be directly attributed. Einstein calls Gervinus the "dry German pope of letters,"[10] and sees in Musorgsky's invocation of his name only a general reflection of the Russian composer's antiromanticism. But Gervinus was vitally interested in music and music aesthetics, and his writings on the sub-ject provide the link between Musorgsky and the neoclassical think-ing his letters reflect. Gervinus's great passion was Handel. In 1856 he was one of the founders—along with Chrysander, Hauptmann, and Dehn—of the Deutsche Händelgesellschaft, and contributed many German translations of the oratorio texts that remain in use to this day. His essays in the *Niederrheinische Musikzeitung* and later in the *Deutsche Musikzeitung* earned him a reputation as a leading prac-titioner of musical hermeneutics, and during the 1860s that reputa-tion spread to Russia. Some oblique testimony to Gervinus's status as interpreter of music is given by Cui, sarcastically reviewing the public final examinations for pianists being graduated from Rubin-stein's conservatory in 1866:

> These ladies are utterly finished pianists; each of them possesses all the attributes of a performing artist: calm self-assurance, excellent tech-nique, stamina, scrupulousness and understanding. But the reader must not forget that one had to judge these qualities in performances of nothing but a repertory of study pieces—and what pieces? Concerti by Mozart, Beethoven, Chopin, Mendelssohn! These concerti have been performed for hundreds of years by hundreds of pianists; the expres-sive content of every little note in them has been explicated practically by Gervinus himself; nothing in their interpretation is up to the inspi-ration of the artist.[11]

Gervinus's major contribution to musical aesthetics was his last book, *Händel und Shakespeare: Zur Aesthetik der Tonkunst* (Leipzig, 1868), dedicated to Chrysander. It came out, significantly enough, in the very year Musorgsky went to work on *Marriage*. As its title indi-cates, the book is devoted to establishing parallels between music and literature through a comparison of the two arts' greatest—to Ger-vinus, paradigmatic—exponents. Its thrust is against the newfangled

[10] *Music in the Romantic Era* (New York: W. W. Norton, 1947), p. 314. Einstein prob-ably refers to Gervinus's magnum opus, the five-volume *Geschichte der poetischen Na-tional-Literatur der Deutschen* (Leipzig: W. Engelmann, 1835–42).

[11] *Sanktpeterburgskiye vedomosti*, 31 January 1867. Quoted from CuiIS, 83.

formalism of Herbart, Dehn, and an unnamed Hanslick, in favor of
"the three thousand–year-old, ever constant, never contested notion
of the nature and essence of music," namely, that it is an art of "feeling and expression."[12] In defining musical expression, Gervinus
reaches back beyond the various aesthetic theories of the preceding
hundred years and attempts, from his very first sentence, to resurrect
the imitation theory à la Aristotle in all its glory.[13] The latest authority
Gervinus cites with complete approval is Rousseau, and the earliest
roots of his idea are sought among the pre-Socratics. The whole three
thousand–year history of musical expression is set out with Germanic
thoroughness in a series of chapters tracing the development of music from the Greeks, through the Renaissance humanists and the
early opera composers (with Peri at their head rather than Monte-
verdi, who is for Gervinus a madrigalist), up to the Handelian pin-
nacle. The story is told with all the traditional embellishments: the
misguided deviance of "der polyphone Gesang des Mittelalters"; Palestrina's heroic rescue;[14] the salutary influence of folk song; the new
deviance in the form of "die reine Instrumentalmusik."

But Gervinus's book is far more than a historical panoply. The author attempts to construct a coherent theory of musical expression in
which the rationalistic *Affektenlehre* of Handel's time could be made
consistent with more modern psychology[15] and with nineteenth-century scientific empiricism, so as to support the positivistic thesis that
the composer objectifies through his work his own and his hearers'
subjective, personal feelings. Like Wagner, whom he in most other
respects opposes, Gervinus sees the greatest opportunities in the hy-
bridization of the arts: "The range, strength, value and effect [of mu-
sic] increase with the objectivity of the individual work and with the
ever-expanding assemblage of means—instruments [combined] with
voices, vocal expression with the sense of the words, words with dramatic action" (244).

[12] *Händel und Shakespeare* (Leipzig: W. Engelmann, 1868), pp. 201–2. Subsequent page references to this work will be given in the text.

[13] "Der älteste Erforcher der Kunstgesetze hat den Satz aufgestellt, dass alle Künste, und so auch die Musik, dem Wesen nach auf Nachahmung beruhen" (ibid., p. 3).

[14] This, too, may have found echo in Musorgsky's autobiographical sketch, where Palestrina is listed among the "artist-reformers," who alone have the right to "lay down laws for art." (MusLN 1.270).

[15] A major portion of Gervinus's book is given over to a consideration of "Die Forderungen an eine geistig begründete musikalische Kunstlehre," with subsidiary headings embodying an exhaustive classification of feelings and emotional states (pp. 203–44).

No matter how grand or complex, however, a work of musical art can ultimately derive its validity only from imitation, that is, by taking as its point of departure the reproduction of the sounds of animate and inanimate nature. But since real expression of emotion can be effected only by the human organs that make direct appeal to other human organs—that is, by facial muscles and the speaking voice as received by eyes and ears—music must take speech as its model, and in particular, the aspect of speech that effects expression in real life: stress or accent (*Betonung*). "Accent is the mother of music [*Betonung ist die Mutter der Musik*]," proclaims Gervinus at the outset of his study, and by way of emphasizing the point and its classical pedigree, he immediately restates the maxim in Latin: *accentus mater musices*. Three varieties of *Betonung* are distinguished: grammatical or syllabic stress, rhetorical emphasis, and finally, "infinitely rich (by comparison with the other two), ruling a whole musical world, which alone will occupy us henceforth—the pathetic or affective accent [*der patetische oder Empfindungsaccent*], which through the subtlest shading of the voice endows the speaker's feelings with a special language of their own" (17). The first two kinds of accent are often indicated in writing, but "if one wanted to show *Empfindungsaccente* in written form, one could do it only by means of notes" (18). It is precisely at this point that spoken language passes over into music.

Thus the special relationship between speech and music lies in the wide range of emotional communication that a speaker can convey over and above the lexical meaning of the uttered words, and it is precisely where expression and communication are concerned that speech appears to follow a system that Gervinus describes as "ruling a whole musical world," or that Musorgsky, paraphrasing him, describes as speech "governed by musical laws." If music itself were to act in harmony with these laws, objective and definite communication of meaning through the medium of musical sounds might become a real possibility. One can easily imagine the effect on Musorgsky's creative imagination of a passage in Gervinus such as this one:

> *Empfindungsaccent* introduces, behind the language of logic, a new language, by means of which ordinary speech is transformed by the raising and lowering of pitch, increase and decrease of volume, rushing and lingering, intensification and weakening, or by the muffling or amplification of the vowels of those words which are to be set apart by means of emotional accentuation. This makes possible not only the understanding of speech but also empathy with that which is being said. It

often happens that inner nervous stresses, which arise in the soul under the influence of external vivid impression, seek a keener outlet [than is provided by the verbal content of the utterance]. The resonator of emotion in such cases becomes not the given strictly delimited substance of the word, but the elastically pulsing and limitlessly flexible musical tone. (p. 19)

Gervinus speaks here not of literal music but of those paralexical attributes of speech—contour, pitch level, volume, tempo—that often convey more emotion than words. When speech passes over into music, according to the workings of Gervinus's *Betonung* theory, the first type encountered is recitative, and thus Gervinus becomes the single nineteenth-century aesthetic theorist to see the most potent manifestation of music in what for so many was its lowliest form. His description of Peri's achievement could also be a description of Musorgsky's, and it provides a genuine point of contact between the seventeenth-century Florentine and the nineteenth-century Russian: "Through the observance of the natural accents of the emotions in joy and sorrow, and through attending to the delivery of such words in correctly enunciated speech, he was able to base a melody[16] on their intonation" (25).

In an especially characteristic passage, Gervinus observes that recitative as handled by Peri corresponds to the ideal of poetry as set forth by such classicistic writers as Martianus Capella: a genre lying midway between speech and music, which transcends their individual powers by uniting them (26). We need not consider further Gervinus's application of his theory to actual music (chiefly Handelian recitative) in the second half of his book, for Musorgsky made his own application "in the field," which took him much farther than anything Gervinus imagined in his armchair (though he employs such prophetic terms as *Sprechgesang*). It will suffice to compare the foregoing quotations with one more passage from the letters Musorgsky wrote during the time of his work on *Marriage*, to perceive the extent of the impression Gervinus's book made on him: "In my *opéra dialogué* I am trying to underscore as vividly as possible those abrupt changes of intonation that crop up in the characters during their dialogue, seemingly for the most trivial of reasons, and on the most

[16] *Eine Harmonie*, after the Greek 'αϱμονία, a usage one finds in the writings and prefaces of the early Baroque monodists, Peri himself included.

insignificant words, in which is concealed, it seems to me, the power of Gogol's humor."[17]

It is almost a paraphrase. And, as a matter of fact, Musorgsky cites Gervinus directly in the autobiographical sketch quoted above, where he refers clumsily to "modes [or moods] of feeling" (*nastroeniya chuvstva*). This is a translation of Gervinus's term *Gefühlsstimmungen*,[18] one of the categories through which the German writer sought to rationalize the effects and the content of instrumental music.

What Musorgsky got from Gervinus, then, and patently not from Dargomïzhsky, was his overriding preoccupation with speech. Dargomïzhsky's professed preoccupation was with the expression of the *word*.[19] But Musorgsky, following Gervinus, recognized that words do not possess immutable meaning.[20] For emotional expression in music to qualify as "truthful" there must be an empirically real natural model, and such a model cannot be provided by words in themselves. Dargomïzhsky's aims and methods had been empathic and subjective.[21] Musorgsky, in the spirit of nineteenth-century science, wished to go beyond that. If speech is the exterior form given to the emotions, one must reproduce the former with the greatest objective accuracy if one is to capture the latter in tones. Musorgsky's letters of 1868 are full of such quasi-mechanistic thinking, which we may now confidently, with reference to Gervinus, call Aristotelian (at least as Aristotle's nineteenth-century interpreters understood him). Another example:

> On nature's scale man is the highest organism (at least on earth), and this highest organism possesses the gift of word and voice without equal among terrestrial organisms. If one admits the reproduction by artistic means of human speech in all its subtlest and most capricious shades—to depict it naturally, as life and human nature demand— would this not amount to the deification of the human gift of words?

[17] To Cui, 3 July 1868. *Literaturnoe nasledie* 1.98.

[18] Carefully distinguished, be it noted, from the more active *Stimmungsgefühle*; see *Händel und Shakespeare*, pp. 225–34.

[19] E.g., his oft-cited letter to the singer Lyubov Karmalina (19 December 1857): "I want the note to express the word. I want truth." *A. S. Dargomïzhskiy: Avtobiografiya, pis'ma, vospominaniya sovremennikov*, ed. Nikolai Findeyzen (Peterburg: Gosudarstvennoye izdatel'stvo, 1921), p. 55.

[20] Cf. Gervinus on interjections: "Das O zur Interjection geworden, empfängt wie A und Ach von dem Empfindungsaccente jeden Ausdruck der Freude wie des Schmerzes" (*Händel und Shakespeare*, p. 19).

[21] See Taruskin, "Realism as Preached and Practiced," pp. 445–46.

And if by this simplest of means, simply submitting strictly to artistic instinct in catching human vocal intonations, it becomes possible to capture the heart, then is it not a worthy enterprise? And if one could, along with that, catch the thinking faculties in a vise, then would it not be worthwhile to devote oneself to such an occupation?[22]

The musical mirroring of speech became a veritable obsession. "Whatever speech I hear, whoever is speaking (or, the main thing, no matter what he is saying), my brain is already churning out the musical embodiment of such speech."[23] In language far more explicit and deliberate than any expression of Dargomïzhsky's, Musorgsky cast himself in the actor's, interpreter's role vis-à-vis his text: "The success of Gogolian speech depends upon the actor and his correct intonation. Well, I want to fix Gogol's place and the actor's, too; that is, to say it musically in such a way as it could never be said otherwise, and say it as Gogol's characters would wish to speak."[24]

It is doubtful whether Musorgsky ever intended *Marriage* seriously for public performance. He meant his scientistic subtitle literally, and constantly referred to *Marriage* in his letters as "an étude for chamber trial" and his "crossing of the Rubicon." Speaking on behalf of the Balakirev circle, Rimsky-Korsakov wrote to Musorgsky that "your work is terribly interesting, and not only because it undoubtedly contains excellent things; besides that, it ought to clear up a great deal."[25]

Carried away in his experimental zeal, Musorgsky worked on the opera with great urgency and with unprecedented speed. He carefully entered the date of completion of each scene in his manuscript, and so we learn that, having begun the project on 11 June 1868, Musorgsky had the first scene (up to the matchmaker Fyokla's entrance) completed by the twentieth. The second scene (up to Kochkaryov's arrival) was done by 2 July; the third and shortest (up to Fyokla's exit) was completed in a mere four days (finished 6 July), and the whole act was complete in vocal score by the eighth.[26] Then followed a long period of rest, reflection, and the intense epistolary activity we have been sampling. Musorgsky jocularly credited his rapid work to the

[22] To V. V. Nikolsky, 15 August 1868. MusLN 1.102–3.
[23] To Rimsky-Korsakov, 30 July 1868. Ibid., p. 102.
[24] To Shestakova, 30 July 1868. Ibid., 100.
[25] 17 August 1868. MusPD, 464.
[26] See the description of the manuscripts in Pavel Lamm's foreword to MusPSS 4/2 (MusCW 23), p. xii.

inclement weather at his country estate (Shilovo), which kept him indoors. Another explanation for it lies in the way the formal freedom of the *opéra dialogué* technique, in which the composer follows a ready-made text moment by moment, worked to the advantage of the autodidact. What is rather extraordinary, in view of the empirical method Musorgsky adopted, is that he worked (by force of circumstance) without a piano.

Musorgsky treated Gogol's text with greater freedom than Dargomïzhsky had treated Pushkin's. Lines were often shortened and changed slightly, but never in such a way as to affect meaning. The composer's most conspicuous contribution was a plethora of extra, hyper-Gogolian exclamations and expletives. Clearly, he wanted to reduce the formal lexical content of the play to the barest minimum, leaving the greater room for paralexical play—that is, for the "musical" qualities of speech. Thanks to Gogol's prose medium, he was able to do this without much harm to the original. Further in keeping with these aims is the abundance of expression marks and directions, most of them Musorgsky's own, with which he attempted to "fix the actor's place" by imparting a special, individual character to almost every line.

The music with which Musorgsky clothed Gogol's prose, for all that it is usually lumped together with Dargomïzhsky's, is in fact utterly different and in some ways opposed to it in style and aim. It *is* recitative; there is no discernible lyric impulse, not the slightest kinship to the art song or romance. The rhythm and melodic contour of the vocal parts are so completely formed by the patterns of speech that they lose all significance, indeed all coherence, when divorced from the lines upon which they were modeled. There are no vocal melodies as such in *Marriage*, only terse, laconic musical "statements" that certainly do justice to Musorgsky's description of his work as the "exercise of a musician, or rather a nonmusician, desirous of studying and mastering the flexes of human speech, and giving it the same immediate, truthful exposition as is transmitted by that greatest of geniuses, Gogol."[27] To observe Musorgsky's procedure at its most characteristic, we need only examine the very opening of the play, the little monologue of the bachelor antihero, Podkolyosin (Example 1).

[27] To Arseniy Golenishchev-Kutuzov, 15 August 1877. MusLN 1.232.

EXAMPLE 1. *Marriage* (MusPSS 4/2), pp. 1–3

Well, when you begin thus, alone, and at leisure to think about it, you see that you positively have to get married. What do you find? You live your life, but in the end, finally, what a horror it becomes. Again I've let the winter go by, and all the while, it seems, everything is ready: the matchmaker has been coming three months already. Really! You get to feeling ashamed of yourself. Hey! Stepan!

The primary essential attribute of Russian speech that informs the setting of these lines is the even distribution of accents, the tempo varying according to affect. Podkolyosin is lying on a divan, smoking his pipe. Accented syllables fall regularly on the half-note in "rather slow" tempo, as befits his lethargic state. Unaccented syllables are arranged in formations of short equal values between the accented ones. Two peculiarities of the treatment of accent in relation to rhythm and meter set Musorgsky's naturalistic declamation apart from all previous Russian recitative. First, an unaccented syllable is never allowed to occupy the beginning of a beat, lest it introduce an un-Russian secondary accent. Where the beat is the quarter-note and the accents fall on the half-note, as here, this means that the intervening quarter-note pulses will be occupied by rests, as is uniformly the case in the present example up to the words "nádo zhenít'sya." The resultant strings of little notes, evenly crowded into the duration of one beat and interrupted by a rest at the beginning of the next, is instantly recognizable as "Musorgskian," and remained a permanent feature of his style. Later in the scene, when Podkolyosin becomes more agitated, the accents fall on the quarter-notes, and so the necessity for rests is obviated except at normal points of punctuation.

The other typically Musorgskian peculiarity is the utter fastidiousness with which note values are assigned. Musorgsky's ear for the tempo of Russian speech was superbly refined. The rhythm of "na dosúge," for example, decelerates (triplets followed by eighths), while the next word, "podúmïvat'," reverses the order of note values and accelerates. These rhythms are not arbitrary or subjective; Musorgsky is drawing from life. Similarly, the lengths of upbeats vary according to the natural model. The first syllable of "odín" and the unaccented word "chto" are set as sixteenth-notes, while the word "tak," even when unaccented, is usually drawled in spoken Russian, and hence is entitled to an eighth-note.

Naturalism notwithstanding, Musorgsky exercises a careful control ("in the highest sense artistic") over the shape of the line, directing all tension to release on the explosive "nádo zhenít'sya." This phrase is the first since the initial word, "vót," in which the first syllable is an accented one, and hence unpreceded by an upbeat. It therefore gives the impression of being delayed, and this reinforces the sense of climax. It is precisely here that the accents begin falling on the quarter notes, suggesting the anxiety that the thought of marriage has aroused in a confirmed old bachelor.[28]

[28] Gogol had the word "nakonets" (finally) before the last three words of the first sentence: "chto nakonets tochno nado zhenit'sya!" Musorgsky omitted it, apparently for the reason that if he had included it, the word "tochno" would have had to be set as an accented syllable after a rest, not preceded by an upbeat. This would have paralleled, and hence mitigated, the effect of the climax ("nado zhenit'sya"). The change is typical of Musorgsky's procedures in setting Gogol's text. Many other minor variants from the standard version of Gogol's play are the result of Musorgsky's having worked either from the first edition of the play (*Sochineniya Nikolaya Gogolya* [St. Petersburg: Izdatel'stvo Glazunova, 1842], vol. 4)—the only edition to appear in print during the author's lifetime—or else from the first posthumous edition (*Sochineniya i pis'ma N. V. Gogolya* [St. Petersburg, 1857], vol. 2), neither of which incorporated the final manuscript fair copy that has become the basis of what is now the standard

Melodic contour is also handled naturalistically, but with artistic control. The climactic "nádo zhenít'sya" is exceeded, as melodic high point, only by "takáya skvérnost' " [what a horror]. These affective climaxes stand out all the more because Musorgsky has surrounded them with neutral utterances that reproduce the characteristic Russian monotone quite accurately. Podkolyosin's initial turbid deliberations are deftly transmitted by singsong oscillation between a "reciting tone" of sorts (E–E♭), which takes the strings of unaccented syllables, and a higher pitch area (A–A♭) that divides the accented syllables alternately with the lower pitch. Where irony is called for ("zhivyosh', zhivyosh' "), the contour of this oscillation is widened to grotesque sevenths. The intonational model is always provided by the spoken language, and melodic contour is dictated throughout *Marriage* by the type of utterance—declarative, interrogative, exclamatory, and so on—that the music is called upon to reflect.

One of the most fascinating of Musorgsky's antimusicalisms in *Marriage* is the harmonic ambience. In this musical prose, tonal motion is kept purposefully static and ambiguous for long stretches, Musorgsky being highly sensitive to the tendency of functional harmony to periodize phrase structure. From beginning to end, there are no key signatures. In the vocal parts this tonal ambiguity is reflected in an unprecedented reliance on augmented and diminished intervals, with chords of corresponding intervallic content in the accompaniment. These, of course, are the "unsingable" intervals shunned by conventional vocal composers, and hence all the more desirable if lyric atmosphere is to be avoided and the illusion of speech maintained in the presence of fixed pitch. Occasionally Musorgsky even manages a witty conflict between the general tonal stasis and firm tonal resolution, as in Podkolyosin's first exchange with his manservant, Stepan. Podkolyosin's queries end on suitably "interrogatory" tritones. Stepan's monosyllabic responses resolve the tritones abruptly by interpreting the last note of the question as a leading tone (Example 2).

As we have seen, Musorgsky attached special importance to his role as "actor" and to the quest for renderings of Gogol's lines that were original and characteristic even as they conformed to the normative patterns governing all Russian speech. His letters are full of

---

text. See the critical notes to N. V. Gogol, *Polnoye sobraniye sochineniy* (Moscow: Izdatel'stvo Akademii nauk SSSR, 1949), vol. 5, pp. 395, 447.

EXAMPLE 2. *Marriage*, p. 3

—Has the matchmaker come?—No.—And have you been to the tailor's?—Yes.

enthusiastic references to "fortunate acquisitions" of this sort. The composer was particularly proud of the way he had managed the "sudden change from laziness to exasperation" in Stepan's responses to his master's idiotic questioning.[29] This change is not indicated by Gogol; Musorgsky invented a stage direction for Stepan—"at the threshold, looking back at Podkolyosin with irritation"—and has him say the perfectly innocuous line "He didn't say anything," to the music in Example 3.

Here the affective communication is entirely on the paralexical level, completely at variance with the surface content of the words, and yet in context both appropriate and true to life. The rhythm (par-

[29] Letter to Cui, 3 July 1868. MusLN 1.98.

EXAMPLE 3. *Marriage*, p. 14

Ni - che - go ne go - vo - ril!

ticularly the enormous elongation of the unaccented second syllable of "nichegó" and the rapid explosion that follows) and the contour spanning an entire octave (and including the highest note in all of Stepan's small part) reproduce the Russian intonation pattern associated with the specified affect. Later in the act, Musorgsky gave special attention to the words "grey hair" and to Podkolyosin's "bearlike agitation" at the mention of it (Example 4).[30] Here the operative factors are the complex rhythm Musorgsky devised to reproduce the pronunciation of the words "sedóy vólos" in a state of agitation, and the way he keeps returning to it (and to the progression A–E♭) upon Podkolyosin's obsessive repetitions. The composer must have been pleased with the "acquisition" of the dissonant secundal harmony as well.

Musorgsky was leery of literal repetition of music even where there was repetition of text. Verbal repetitions must have a reason, after all, and the reason is usually one of emphasis. So, when lines are repeated in *Marriage*, the music attempts to convey an intensification through changing "nuances of speech," as Gervinus might have said. An example is Stepan's repetition of the line "He's already begun the buttonholes," when Podkolyosin fails to hear him the first time. There could scarcely be a less "affective" line than this, so any affective illustration must relate beyond the line to Stepan's attitude toward his master. This we hear (the beginnings of his irritation) in the drawling rhythm and the really weird intervallic structure of the repetition (Example 5). One readily understands the advantages for Musorgsky in the affective neutrality and "unmusicalness" of lines such as this. All the affect in the setting has to come from the music. From this point of view the composer has an even greater responsibility in setting prose dialogue than he would in a more normal, lyric context.

The only "purely musical" shaping in the score occurs in the orchestra (or rather piano: Musorgsky never got around to the instru-

[30] Ibid., p. 97.

EXAMPLE 4. *Marriage*, p. 34

And since when do I have grey hair? Where? Where's the grey hair?

mentation), and it is minimal. There are signature tunes for each character (Podkolyosin in fact has two), which crop up at entrances and at points where the characters mention or indicate one another.[31] But these never provide a frame for musical elaboration or development even to the extent that, say, the Statue's music does in *The Stone Guest*. There is only one spot in all of *Marriage* where the accompaniment performs even a nominally unifying or generalizing role, and that is in the matchmaker Fyokla's description of the bride's dowry. Musorgsky set this longest speech in the act as a sort of *moto perpetuo*. The "orchestra" rips along in steady, rapid triplets, while Fyokla maintains a characteristic *parlando* declamation above it. Her part is cast wherever possible in triplets to match the orchestra's, but this is not always possible, lest fidelity to speech rhythm be disturbed. Thus, her part is actually in a rather complex rhythmic relationship to the accompaniment, with frequent two-against-three and four-against-three superimpositions. During this little number, the only "detachable" one in the opera, Musorgsky seems to have been at

[31] This applies chiefly to the revised score of the work (see Chapter 5).

EXAMPLE 5. *Marriage*, p. 4

—*He's already begun the buttonholes.—What's that you say?—I'm saying, he's already
begun the buttonholes!*

special pains not to let the regularity of the accompaniment impose itself upon the vocal part; Fyokla's phrase lengths are irregularity itself.

For the rest, the independent role of the accompaniment is limited to an occasional ironic comment on the text. When the matchmaker describes the bride, the orchestra plays a sickly-sweet little phrase (Fyokla never sings it, though; nor does she sing her signature tune, the only folk-style melody in the score). When Kochkaryov describes the joys of wedded life to Podkolyosin, we hear another tritely sentimental snatch. At mention of children, the orchestra breaks into what Nadezhda Purgold (the later Mme Rimsky-Korsakov), who accompanied the early run-throughs, described in a memoir as some "amusing curlicues."[32] When Kochkaryov mentions a washtub we hear a splash; when he mentions boots we hear them thump (even though the pair he refers to are lying on the floor); mention of snuff calls forth an orchestral sneeze; and so on.

Apart from such trivia, Musorgsky appeared determined to frustrate and stifle "purely musical" invention to an extent that disconcerted even his fellow kuchkists. What his experiment seemed to

---

[32] She further recalled that Dargomïzhsky, when singing the part of Kochkaryov at a kuchkist soirée, at this place "was always obliged to stop, he was so overcome with laughter, and he said to me, 'You're playing some sort of symphony there, you're getting in my way' " (MR, 124).

"clear up" most conclusively was that realism, after all, had its limits. When evening gatherings at Dargomïzhsky's resumed after the summer of 1868, *Marriage* received the "chamber trial" Musorgsky awaited. According to Rimsky-Korsakov, who was present, it was read concurrently with *The Stone Guest* and by the same ".cast"; Musorgsky himself as Podkolyosin, Alexandra Purgold as Fyokla, General Velyaminov as Stepan, and Dargomïzhsky himself, who, "interested in the highest degree, . . . copied out the part of Kochkaryov in his own hand and performed it with enthusiasm."[33] But Dargomïzhsky was heard to mutter at times that "the composer had gone too far," and for the seniors of the group, Balakirev and Cui, "*Marriage* [was] only a curiosity with some interesting moments of declamation."[34] Borodin, only recently involved in the Balakirev circle, wrote to his wife that Musorgsky's work was "an extraordinarily curious and paradoxical thing, full of innovation and at times of great humor, but as a whole—*une chose manquée*—impossible to perform.[35]

Borodin alone raised the question of practicability, but it is a fair point. Musorgsky at times allowed himself to get so carried away with his quest for accuracy in the transcription of speech patterns that his writing became quite unrealistically complex.[36] Notations like the following pair from Fyokla's part (Examples 6a and 6b, overleaf) hardly admit of accuracy in rendition at the indicated tempi.

These passages are actually written at the speed of the spoken language (at least!), and this, of course, was a cardinal difference between Musorgsky's objective naturalism and the subjective lyricism of *The Stone Guest*, where the tempo "is all moderato, adagio, lento, occasionally andantino."[37] But finding the correct pitches (and the examples will show that these are not always easy to find) inevitably slows the singer down. In recordings of the score[38] the singers fail to

[33] R-KMusL, 89. Dargomïzhsky's copy survives in the Saltïkov-Shchedrin Public Library in St. Petersburg, and was collated by Lamm in the critical edition (cf. Lamm's preface, MusPSS 4/2.xii).

[34] Ibid., pp. 90–91.

[35] 25 September 1868. BorP 1.109.

[36] This had been a matter of concern, apparently, from the very beginning, for Musorgsky wrote to Cui from the country (3 July 1868) that "guided by your comments and Dargomïzhsky's, I . . . have considerably simplified what I showed you." Reference is to the first scene, which had been begun in St. Petersburg before Musorgsky's departure.

[37] Laroche, in *Muzïkal'nïy svet*, quoted from GozROTII, 291.

[38] Oceanic OCS 36 (orchestrated by Duhamel, conducted by Leibowitz; reissued on Olympic 9105), Westminster OPW 1202 (completed and orchestrated by Ippolitov-Iva-

EXAMPLE 6a. *Marriage*, p. 29

Ta - ka - ya uzh na to vol - ya bo - zhi - ya!

Such is God's will.

EXAMPLE 6b. *Marriage*, p. 37

Da, ved', sam zhe pri-stal: zhe - ni ba-bush-ka da i tol'-ko!

You yourself insisted: Find me a wife, good woman, that's all I ask!

maintain Musorgsky's tempi, nor do they even come close to the difficult rhythm of Example 6b. What they do is actually deliver the line "as it comes" in speech, which may, it could be argued, have been precisely Musorgsky's intention. But if so, then his finicky descriptive notation is merely an impediment. And did he not declare, after all, that his aim was to "fix" and control?

In any case, the kuchkist consensus was that Musorgsky's excessive naturalism not only limited but distorted musical values. When Rimsky-Korsakov issued his edition of *Marriage* in 1908, he referred in his foreword not only to the "harmonic excesses" about which one is accustomed to hearing complaints in Musorgsky's case but also to "melodic and rhythmic monstrosities." But these were not the result of arbitrary novelty seeking, nor even of unfinished technique (to cite the usual explanations where Musorgsky is concerned). They lie at the very heart of the composer's ruling asthetic aim. One cannot agree with Rimsky when he protests that "the author obviously did much that went against his own excellent ear" in his "youthful and understandable impulse for progress." No, it was in fact that excellent, indeed far *too* scrupulous ear that dictated them. But then Rimsky-Korsakov adds that "in general, the whole piece should be performed as if *a piacere*, to which I, who heard the author's own

nov, conducted by Kovalyov), Melodiya A10 00039 007 (orchestrated and conducted by Rozhdestvensky).

interpretation many times, . . . can testify with authority."[39] Why then Musorgsky's fiendish exactitude of notation on the one hand, or Rimsky's complaints (and corrections) on the other?

What *Marriage* "cleared up" for Cui was that prose was not a suitable musical medium. He had suggested that it was—for comedy—in an 1868 article on *The Stone Guest*.[40] But later, he attempted to show the opposite, using *Marriage* as his prize exhibit.

> For us [Russians], with our tonic prosody, this question [of prose in musical setting] is one of the first importance, and a libretto written entirely in prose would have to be considered a liability for music. Of course, in vocal music the structure of the text determines and explains the given structure of the musical discourse. But even in vocal music one should not ignore the finish and symmetry of musico-architectonic forms. This finish is dependent to a large degree upon the definite and sustained meter of these musico-architectonic lines. Sustained meter in music written to prose is unthinkable; can one imagine, after all, that the music be an entity entire unto itself, and the text likewise, or that the text be applied to music written without regard for it?
>
> Musorgsky attempted to write *Marriage* to Gogol's prose without adaptation. He wrote the first scene of the first act [*sic*] and saw that this was a thankless and inartistic task. So the opera has remained unfinished. And bear in mind that in this case the task was considerably lightened by the fact that Musorgsky was a man of remarkable talent and a skillful versifier. Our tonic verses not only allow but demand sustained meter—that is their chief significance for music. But from this it does not necessarily follow that individual brief phrases of recitative must necessarily be turned into verse. On the contrary, they will sound truer in prose. Thus the use of prose in libretti is altogether possible and permissible, but only as an exception.[41]

Cui's assumptions about Musorgsky's attitude toward his own work seem a tendentious extrapolation, for Musorgsky's letters are full of plans for the opera's completion. But the cool reception given *Marriage* by the rest of the kuchka undoubtedly played a part in Musorgsky's decision not to pursue the experiment beyond the one act written. It is true that he had chafed a bit in a letter to Shestakova about the limitations his task had set upon his musical imagination—

[39] All quotations in this paragraph from Rimsky-Korsakov's introduction to his edition of *Marriage*, as reprinted in the Ippolitov-Ivanov version of the vocal score (Moscow: Muzgiz, 1934).

[40] " 'Kamennïy gost' ' Pushkina i Dargomïzhskogo," CuiIS, 143–47.

[41] Ibid., 427.

"*Marriage* is a cage in which I am imprisoned until tamed, and then on to freedom."[42] And it was right at the time of the first act's trial readings that Vladimir Nikolsky suggested that the composer look into Pushkin's *Boris Godunov*. Musorgsky needed no second hint.[43]

But, Cui and Rimsky-Korsakov notwithstanding, Musorgsky never renounced his early work. Quite the contrary, not only did he remain convinced of his experiment's essential validity but he thought of it as the key to his dramatic style. On Stasov's forty-ninth birthday (2 January 1873), Musorgsky presented his friend with the manuscript, adding in his inscription: "I cannot abide obscurity and think that for one sympathetic *Marriage* will reveal much with regard to my musical audacities. You know how *dearly* I value it, this *Marriage*."[44]

Musorgsky chose his recipient well—the single noncomposer in the mighty kuchka. Stasov alone "went into ecstasies" when *Marriage* was tried out chez Dargomïzhsky,[45] and no wonder. He had no reason to keep account of the price Musorgsky had to pay as composer for his achievements. For Stasov the *opéra dialogué* was an idea whose time had come, the irresistible wave of the future. "*Zukunfts-musik* is not Wagner," he wrote to his brother Dmitri, "but Dargomïzhsky and Musorgsky."[46] And Stasov gave strident, even intolerant, expression to this one-sided view at every opportunity, most

[42] MusLN 1.100.

[43] After the publication of *Marriage* (ed. Rimsky-Korsakov [St. Petersburg: Bessel, 1908]) and its first performance in that year under Arkady Kerzin's auspices (Moscow), there were several orchestrations of Musorgsky's act, and at least two completions of the score. Ippolitov-Ivanov's completion was commissioned in 1931 by the USSR radio in commemoration of the fiftieth anniversary of the composer's death. Alexander Tcherepnin's completed version followed in 1935 and was first performed in Essen two years later as *Die Heirat* (vocal score, Vienna: Universal, 1938). Musorgsky's act has been orchestrated by Alexander Gauk (1917), by Antoine Duhamel, by M. Béclart d'Harcourt, and by Gennadiy Rozhdestvensky (ca. 1984). Both Lamm (preface to the critical edition, p. xi) and Loewenberg (*Annals of Opera*, 3d ed. [Totowa, N.J.: Rowman and Littlefield, 1978], col. 1292) refer to an orchestration by Ravel (ca. 1923), but this appears to be an error. In 1946, Alexander Grechaninov, commissioned by Koussevitzky, made his own setting of the entire three-act play, in a style very different from Musorgsky's. This was first performed at the Berkshire Festival under Goldovsky (third act only) and premièred officially in Paris in 1950. For the record, operas based on Gogol's play have been written by two Czech composers: Jaroslav Jiránek and Bohuslav Martinu (1953). Ironically, Cui became interested late in life in the prospect of completing *Marriage*, following his completion of *Sorochintsï Fair*, but decided that the task was "utterly unthinkable; I don't even want to try" (letter to M. S. Kerzina, 12 December 1916; CuiIP, 471).

[44] MusLN 1.144.

[45] R-KMusL, 90.

[46] 29 July 1870. Quoted from Vladimir Karenin (pseudonym for Varvara Kamorova-Stasova), *Vladimir Stasov* (Leningrad: Mïsl', 1927), p. 395.

particularly, where *Marriage* was concerned, in his biography-necrology of 1881:

> This "experiment in dramatic music in prose" is as yet insufficiently appreciated. It seems to me that it will not remain without consequence and followers. The time will come to throw off prejudices as to the inevitable necessity of a "text in verse" for libretti, and when opera, like all future art, will become more and more realistic in the hands of Musorgsky's heirs, *Marriage* will receive its due place and evaluation. . . . At every step one encounters that astounding truth of expression, that closeness to ordinary everyday human speech which can only be considered a great step forward in the affairs of art, even when compared with Musorgsky's own highly original songs of 1866–68. Musorgsky here has come upon a completely new terrain: he has thrown off to one side all conventions of form and all artistic formalism. He has pursued only the expression of his text and in this he went even further than Dargomïzhsky, who even in his *Stone Guest* retained "conventional, rounded forms" in a few instances. Fidelity to the text cannot go further than this. There is no convolution of thought, feeling, transient mood, mimetic movement, spiritual or even purely physical expression that Musorgsky's music has not here reproduced.[47]

But what Stasov did not reveal is that if *Marriage* was "insufficiently appreciated," it was mainly because he was sitting jealously on the manuscript the composer had given him. In fact, once in possession of the score, Stasov went to great lengths to keep it under wraps. He would show it to no one, and when, in 1893, he presented his great collection of manuscripts and letters to the Imperial Public Library, he wrote upon the title page of Musorgsky's work, in his own hand, that "I earnestly request that it not be given or shown to anyone during my lifetime."[48] And he lived until 1906. Despite his published assurances that Musorgsky's opera was "endlessly talented, true and original," then, Stasov took every measure to suppress the work and leave the reputation he created for it unchallenged by actual performance or publication. As late as 1901, when A. M. Kerzin, a Moscow impresario who was considering producing *Marriage* (doubtless after reading Stasov's exuberant encomia), wrote to the aging custodian of the work requesting the score, he received an astonishingly worded refusal: "It is an unsuccessful thing, an ex-

---

[47] StasIS 2.194.

[48] See the description of the manuscript in Lamm's foreword to the critical edition, p. xii.

aggeration, a monstrosity and a blunder on Musorgsky's part, and to facilitate a new public and popular 'failure' for Musorgsky when our poor Modest already has such a host of enemies—this is something we cannot do."[49]

One can hardly doubt that these were Stasov's true feelings, and his public encomia a propagandist's pose. After *Marriage*, disillusion with its whole tendency was complete within the kuchka. "Enough of *The Stone Guest!*" was Rimsky-Korsakov's exasperated exclamation in 1898, as recorded by his son. "Music, too, is needed!"[50] And Cui, when he set about packaging kuchkism for export in 1878, wrote of *The Stone Guest*—which he nonetheless continued to tout as "the capital work, the keystone of the New Russian Operatic School"—that

> as a general rule, it is better to avoid such texts by great poets, seductive though their intrinsic beauty may render them in the eyes of musicians, because they are not made for music. Moreover, one must take care to avoid as much as possible both philosophical excursions and the familiar language of everyday speech. A truly *lyric* text, lending itself favorably to the development of vocal melody, is, in sum, that which should be sought above all in a libretto.[51]

Yet be that as it may, a study of *Marriage* and its theoretical backgrounds does, in the words of Rimsky-Korsakov, "clear up a great deal" for us about the sources of Russian musical realism. Nor was Musorgsky's experiment completely fruitless. The earlier 1869 version of *Boris* was virtually identical to it in approach. And when Musorgsky's "*chose manquée*" was finally given a public hearing in St. Petersburg in February 1909, at one of Karatïgin and Krizhanovsky's "Evenings of Contemporary Music," in the audience was the seventeen-year-old Serge Prokofiev, whose early operatic outlook was strongly shaped by the experience of hearing it.[52] Stravinsky heard *Marriage* even earlier, at a private performance at Rimsky-Korsakov's home on 4 January 1906.[53] A trace of the impression it made upon

[49] "17 pisem V. V. Stasova k A. M. Kerzinu," *Muzïkal'nïy sovremmenik*, no. 2 (1916): 14.

[50] Andrey Rimsky-Korsakov, *N. A. Rimskiy-Korsakov: Zhizn' i tvorchestvo* (Moscow: Muzgiz, 1933), vol. 5, p. 190.

[51] Cui, *La musique en Russie* (Paris: Fischbacher, 1880), p. 108. The contents of this book had appeared two years earlier as a series of articles in the *Revue et Gazette Musicale*.

[52] See R. Taruskin, "Tone, Style, and Form in Prokofiev's Soviet Operas: Some Preliminary Observations," *Studies in the History of Music* 2 (1988): 215–39.

[53] See YasVR-K 2.370–71. Some evidence that Stravinsky contemplated orchestrat-

him may be found on certain pages in *Le Rossignol*. As a matter of fact, he recalled having written himself a note while at work on his first opera: "Why should I be following Debussy so closely, when the real originator of this operatic style was Musorgsky?"[54] The influence of the published score spread even beyond the borders of Russia. It prompted Ravel to set Franc-Nohain's farce *L'Heure espagnole* to music in a similar idiom of naturalistic recitative. (The composer referred to Musorgsky's work as his opera's "only direct ancestor" in a manifesto published in *Le Figaro* in 1911.[55]) Thus, though down to a trickle, and by now at fourth hand, the "Aristotelian" current flowed into the twentieth century, and continued (*pace* Dahlhaus) to recur "in more than one work."

---

ing *Marriage* in 1920 is presented by Vera Stravinsky and Robert Craft in *Stravinsky in Pictures and Documents* (New York: Simon and Schuster, 1978), p. 32.

[54] Igor Stravinsky and Robert Craft, *Memories and Commentaries* (Garden City, N.Y.: Doubleday, 1960), p. 125.

[55] Cited in Arbie Orenstein, *Ravel: Man and Musician* (New York: Columbia University Press, 1975), p. 55.

3

SEROV AND MUSORGSKY

By the end of the 1860s the warring camps of Russian music—Rubinstein-Conservatory, Balakirev-Free Music School, the Serovian "opposition"—had become so firmly entrenched in their respective positions and mutual hatreds that one tends to forget the atmosphere of sweet camaraderie that prevailed a decade earlier, when the musical profession was just getting on its feet in Russia.[1] In Stasov's memoir on César Cui (written in 1894 to mark the silver anniversary of *William Ratcliff*), right before launching into a typically hysterical attack on the memory of his former friend Serov, the kuchkist tribune recalled this pleasant time with real nostalgia:

> Serov himself, the most noteworthy writer on music and critic of the fifties, who was then still forward-looking and who then had a great influence on the better members of our public, made Cui's acquaintance with pleasure, delighted in his interesting and talented nature, his first experiments in composition, and, in turn, was an object of great affection, even adoration on the part of Cui. Nor is this hard to understand. Serov was such an animated, diverting conversationalist, especially when it came to music; he in those days so passionately loved all that was highest and best in music, especially Beethoven and Glinka; he was so enthusiastic, and so gifted in enthusing others; his nature contained so many truly artistic, warm, and lively traits! So one can see why God only knows how pleasant it was for Cui and Balakirev to be in close contact with such a nature. And they all three got together very often (and I, too, belonged to that company though I was not a musician, but a long-standing friend and comrade of Serov's who in fact grew up with him, but was now very close to these *newly*

[1] For an introduction to the tumultuous world of St. Petersburg musical politics, see Robert C. Ridenour, *Nationalism, Modernism and Personal Rivalry in Nineteenth-Century Russian Music* (Ann Arbor: UMI Research Press, 1981). Ridenour places a healthy emphasis upon the last element in his triad, and this should be held in mind cantus firmus–like when considering relations between Serov and the "elder" members of the mighty kuchka, Balakirev and Cui.

arrived, talented Russian musicians). But starting in 1858-59, things changed.[2]

That is when things changed for Stasov, to be sure, for that is when the furious press controversy between him and Serov got under way.[3] But cordial relations between Serov and the "newly arrived" composers, whose circle by now included Musorgsky as well, persisted for a while. They reached their peak during the 1859–60 concert season, when Rubinstein's Russian Musical Society made its long-awaited bow. The precarious Era of Good Feeling in Russian music was epitomized when both Cui and Musorgsky made their debuts as serious composers at Society concerts under Rubinstein's baton during this inaugural season—and were greeted with warm reviews by Serov, who gladly wielded his considerable power as St. Petersburg's critic of record on their behalf. Both of them were represented by orchestral scherzos composed under Balakirev's tutelage. Of Cui's, performed at the fourth concert of the series (14 December 1859), Serov had this to say:

> In conclusion—greetings to a Russian composer who made his first appearance before the public with an extremely remarkable work. The scherzo of César Antonovich Cui, a student of Stanislaw Moniuszko, is, in its individual way, closely related to Schumann's symphonic works with shades of something Chopinesque as well. There are hardly any vivid "effects," whether of invention or of orchestral combination, but

[2] StasIS 3.396.

[3] For the details of this war of words, see my "Glinka's Ambiguous Legacy and the Birth Pangs of Russian Opera," *19th-Century Music* 1, no. 2 (November 1977): 142–62. (Relations between Stasov and Serov were also severely complicated by the former's affair with the latter's sister, Sophie DuTour; see the introductory article by A. A. Gozenpud and V. A. Obram to the voluminous Stasov-Serov correspondence in *Muzïkal'noye nasledstvo*, vol. 1 [Moscow: Muzgiz, 1961], p. 77.) In 1858–59 Stasov interfered strenuously with the continued development of good relations between Serov and the "newly arrived" Balakirev and Cui, as can easily be seen in the fourteen letters from Serov to Balakirev published by A. S. Lyapunova in SovM, no. 5 (1953): 68–75. The correspondence is regular and extremely cordial through 1856 and 1857; then it suddenly breaks off after 9 February 1858. The only letter to follow, dated 1 March 1859, begins thus: "If *Monsieur Cui bono* cannot attend my lectures [i.e., Serov's ill-starred venture of 1858–59 at St. Petersburg University on "Music from the Technical, Aesthetic, and Historical Points of View"] because the Stasovs [i.e., the brothers Vladimir and Dmitry] have forbidden him, that certainly doesn't surprise me (Poles [!] love to submit)." And it ends even more ominously: "How can I persuade you that it is neither wise nor right to make an enemy for oneself out of someone who could be a strong ally?" Little need be added to account for the break between Serov and the mighty kuchka. Stasov's meddling accounts for it all. It is all the more remarkable, then, how long Serov strove to maintain good relations with Balakirev and Cui, e.g., in his critiques of the early sixties.

all the ideas inhabit the noblest spheres, are combined and developed effortlessly and with a profound internal logic. In the technical workmanship of the rhythm, harmony, and orchestration, one can see knowledge and subtle planning, such as one very rarely encounters in debutantes. From one who begins *thus*, one can expect *much* that is uncommonly good. Make way, make way for *Russian* musicians. There will be the most unexpected, the most heartening results.[4]

Musorgsky's scherzo was premièred at the seventh and last concert of the season (11 January 1860), on a program that also included Meyerbeer's incidental music to his brother's tragedy *Struensee* (1846). Serov's review compared the two works in a curious—but to Musorgsky no doubt exceptionally gratifying—fashion.

About the *Struensee* music I can't give a report this time, for I chanced to arrive late, and only caught the last two numbers from this big score. . . . Both numbers, to my taste, were very bad. And what I found especially pleasant to notice was that the antimusicality of this work of Meyerbeer's was frankly perceived by the audience. Applause, which accompanied practically every piece on the program, was almost entirely absent here.

And it was even more pleasant to encounter the audience's warm sympathy toward the Russian composer M. P. Musorgsky, who made his debut with an extremely good—only, unfortunately rather too short—orchestral scherzo.

This scherzo is not as interesting, in my view, as the scherzo of C. A. Cui, which was performed at the fourth concert, but it also revealed decided talent in a young musician embarking upon a creative career.

It was remarkable that this symphonic fragment by a composer as yet unknown, placed alongside the music of a "celebrated" maestro, not only lost nothing but actually gained a great deal by comparison.[5]

Serov had also had nothing but good to say of Balakirev's creative debut with a movement of a never-to-be-finished piano concerto in 1856. His review of the collection of songs Balakirev published in 1859 was nothing short of ecstatic. And as late as 1867 he greeted Rimsky-Korsakov's appearance on the musical firmament (with the *Serbian Fantasy*) in terms equally cordial. His opposition to the kuchka is a Stasovian myth, based on invective directed at Balakirev and at

---

[4] SerIS 2.612–13.
[5] Ibid., pp. 616–17.

Cui only after huge provocation, mainly engineered by Stasov himself.[6]

How, then, did Musorgsky feel toward Serov? That seems an easy enough question to answer, since Musorgsky's letters are full of condescension toward the older composer, and in "The Peepshow"

[6] Serov's review of Balakirev's debut is reprinted in ibid., pp. 542–43 (the conclusion: "Mr. Balakirev's talent is a rich find for our nation's music"); his review of Balakirev's collection of songs is in SerIS 1.339–42. The latter concluded on an avuncular note that may have rankled a bit: "It remains to wish Mr. Balakirev the maximum possible ardor and strength of will in embarking on a career as difficult as that of a composer of music! A Russian musician must remember at all times that fame, esteem, and money are not for him. For all these things to materialize as in a dream, one needs, besides talent (which hardly matters), first of all not to be Russian, even if born in Russia." These lines were written out of bitter personal frustration, and mainly vent the writer's anti-Semitic envy of Rubinstein. Anti-Semitism is even closer to the surface of Serov's review the same year of Balakirev's first Overture on Russian Themes, where he commiserates with the composer because his name is not Balakirstein. Such remarks could only have gratified Balakirev, whose anti-Semitism, if anything, surpassed Serov's. But the avuncular note was also intensified in this review, where Serov complained of Balakirev's inability to sustain the sonata form: "His overture . . . is not yet a complete work of art; the general impression the piece makes is unsatisfactory, it seems to lack wholeness of form, roundedness; . . . in the overall sequence of events one wants something a bit different, and the central development section (the *Mittelsatz*, to speak technically) is not clearly enough carried through" (SerIS 2.585–86). (The ostentatious and redundant use of jargon is, by the way, entirely characteristic of the pre-*Judith* Serov, whose insecurities about his own lack of training peep through everywhere.) All this smacks of effrontery, and one begins to understand the uncharacteristic and apparently calculated pedantry with which Balakirev, in turn, reviewed the first act of *Judith*—a gratuitous insult that infuriated Serov and made final the split between him and the "older generation" of kuchkists. That Serov never lumped together the whole kuchka (as we understand the term today) is evident from the cordiality with which he treated Rimsky-Korsakov to the end of his life. The *Serbian Fantasy* review is in SerIS 2.617. Serov lived to review one more Rimsky-Korsakov composition, the "symphonic picture" *Sadko*—once in Russian in his own *Muzïka i teatr* (no. 14, 1867) and once in French for the *Journal de St.-Petersbourg* (no. 279, 1869). In this second, very late review, animosity toward the senior kuchkists at last shows through: "Mr. Rimsky-Korsakov, alone among his whole party, is gifted with an enormous talent—settled, remarkable, profoundly appealing. Amid his ill-starred entourage he shines as a diamond among cobblestones. . . . Now here is a musical picture that really deserves its name, not merely arrogates it, like the pitiful potpourri of Mr. Balakirev [i.e., 'One Thousand Years'], with all its doomed pretension" (SerIS 2.627–28). Just how much *Sadko* impressed Serov was revealed by Vasiliy Vasilyevich Bessel, the music publisher, at a testimonial dinner tendered Rimsky-Korsakov on 17 December 1900, the thirty-fifth anniversary of his debut. When it came his turn to toast the jubilee, Bessel "informed us that when A. N. Serov came into his store after a rehearsal at which *Sadko* was played, he replied to Bessel's question how he liked that composition, after a moment's reflection: 'This is how much—after the very first page of that fantasia I was ready to go down on my knees, it impressed me so much.' And that was the proud and puffed-up Serov!" (YasVR-K 2.262). Given the nature of the occasion, we can assume that Bessel exaggerated a bit; but at the very least, all these pronouncements about Rimsky-Korsakov show that Serov was careful to distinguish between kuchkist generations. We ought to do the same in treating his relations with them.

(*Rayok*, 1870) he derided Serov without mercy. But one must bear in mind the circumstances. The letters dealing with Serov were mostly addressed to Musorgsky's seniors within the kuchka—Balakirev, Cui, and Stasov—who by the early sixties were united in their envious hostility to the critic, and, after *Judith*, to the composer as well. "The Peepshow," moreover, was dedicated to Stasov, and Serov was lampooned alongside other enemies of Stasov's, both real and imaginary: Alexander Famintsïn (who had successfully sued Stasov for libel), Rostislav (whose real name was Feofil Tolstoy, Serov's most enthusiastic exponent in the press), Nikolai Zaremba (acting director of Rubinstein's Conservatory) and the Grand Duchess Yelena Pavlovna (Rubinstein's German-born patroness). It was Stasov who inspired, nay, virtually *commissioned* this "musical pamphlet," as a retort to what he perceived as a concatenation of "hostile elements" that were threatening the kuchka and also, especially, as an insult to Serov, whom Stasov by now regarded with a fanatical, well-nigh paranoiacal hatred.

But Stasov can speak for himself. Here is how he described the circumstances surrounding "The Peepshow" in his 1881 biography-necrology of Musorgsky:

> The man who stood at the head of the hostile càmp, Serov, had long since ceased being the progressive human being, musician, and critic he had been in his youth. He was now writing bad operas, aimed at pleasing the coarse crowd. Long since frozen in the enthusiasms of his youth, he was maintaining that after Beethoven further symphonies were unthinkable and therefore with blind fanaticism attacked Franz Schubert and Schumann (whom he deemed a mere "demi-musician"), Berlioz, and Liszt. The summit of operatic music, he thought, was Wagner and his half-baked *Tannhäuser* and *Lohengrin*, and then he began dragging *Ruslan and Ludmila* through the mud, asserting (in 1868) that within five years that opera would lose the stage. On the occasion of Wagner's concerts in St. Petersburg, in 1863, he had written on his behalf the most monstrous puffs, claiming that Wagner had "brought whole worlds into being." In his musical critiques he was ever puffed up with himself, groundlessly captious, petty, and feebly impertinent, always going after personalities. In 1866, giving the public a press report on the performances of *Ruslan* in Prague under M. A. Balakirev's direction, I said that Balakirev and his talented fellow innovators made up a *"moguchaya kuchka,"* a mighty little bunch. Serov seized upon this expression and started persecuting the Balakirev party with it as a derisive epithet. Serov's cohorts in hatred of the new

musical trend, Messrs. Laroche, Zvantsov, etc., rejoiced in the nick-name and began using it like an expletive. They found in it, apparently, great wit and profundity. When in 1867 Berlioz was in Russia (for the second time), constantly surrounding himself with talented representa-tives of the New Russian School, Serov (who, by the way, had con-stantly attacked Berlioz in his journal *Muzïka i teatr*) was beside himself with annoyance. Such a personality and such writing about music (Ser-ov's former personality and writing were as far from the latter as heaven from earth, so much had he changed!) could not but be antipathetic and even somewhat contemptible to the talented group. Among the "mighty little bunch," in reaction, Serov and his comrades were a con-stant topic of conversation. César Cui wrote very often about them in his gifted and brilliant polemical articles, in which he, over a period of many years, gave voice not only to his personal opinions but to those of the whole group and in particular its chief, Balakirev. Combat seethed ever more bitterly, until one day in 1870 I advised Musorgsky to enter the fray once more with the same scourge of musical satire he had already tested with so much talent in "The Classicist" [*Klassik*, 1867].[7]

Stasov continues with a few halfhearted sallies at the other exhibits in Musorgsky's sideshow, but by now he is out of steam and soon goes on to other things. It is clear that the motive force behind the piece was Stasov's neurotic vendetta against Serov. And it is equally clear that Musorgsky's aim in composing the piece was to indulge his beloved confidant and mentor, to vent Stasov's spleen rather than his own. As he reported in a letter to Vladimir Nikolsky, he had given the manuscript to Stasov with a dedicatory letter containing a line of scripture: "Of thine own we have given thee" (1 Chronicles 29.14).[8]

Stasov's passionate invective—and the very fact that he went after Serov (already a decade deceased) at such length and with such gusto in a piece ostensibly dedicated to the memory of Musorgsky (as he later would do in the piece cited above, ostensibly devoted to Cui) betrays the uncontrollability and unassuageability of his ha-tred—amounts to a fairly comprehensive bill of kuchkist indictment against Serov. It is mostly absurd, its absurdest point being Stasov's ludicrous exaggeration of his rival's power and prestige. Serov led no camp in the 1860s, and it is especially risible to find him cast as men-

[7] StasIS 2.202–3. *Klassik*, according to a note on the autograph, was "an answer to Famintsïn's remarks on the heresies of the Russian School" (MusLN 2.182).
[8] MusLN 1.114.

tor to Laroche, one of the foremost public detractors of Serov's operas. Stasov also had his facts quite wrong on the origin and progress of his unfortunate coinage, *moguchaya kuchka*.[9] He had made it up not in connection with Balakirev's Prague activities but in connection with "Mr. Balakirev's Slavonic Concert," a festive affair performed before an audience of delegates to a Pan-Slavist congress in 1867. The program included works by Glinka, Dargomïzhsky, Alexey Lvov, Rimsky-Korsakov, Balakirev himself, and two non-Russians: Stanislaus Moniuszko and Liszt, the latter not even a Slav. Serov, whose music was conspicuously snubbed, had ample provocation to deride the newly christened party that would have no part of him, and loudly to dissociate himself from it. This he did in an article in *Muzïka i teatr* called "A Diplomatic Regret, but in Vain."

César Cui, reviewing Balakirev's concert in the guise of "Mr. Asterism" ("∗∗∗"), the anonymous music critic of the *Sanktpeterburgskiye vedomosti*, had gleefully called attention to the fact of Serov's exclusion from the Slavonic concert by affecting commiseration: "It is a pity that the Slavs did not have a chance to become acquainted with a single excerpt from Mr. Serov's operas."[10] Serov's infuriated reaction to this extra insult played no small part in putting the mighty kuchka on the map of Russian musical politics:

To this I respond as follows:

My musical arena is the *operatic stage*, so that I was indeed very sorry that for reasons beyond its control the Directorate of the Imperial Theaters was unable to stage *Rogneda* during the Slavonic guests' stay in St. Petersburg. [The reason was the refusal of Gennadiy Kondratyev, who played the Pilgrim Elder, to give uncontracted postseason performances.] If that was "fate," so be it. It was not the Theater's fault.

I trouble myself little over concert performances, . . . since I don't consider some "Maiden's Dance" or "Dance of the Buffoons" any sort of recommendation for an opera composer, nor have I the slightest inclination to join the ranks of "symphonists." . . .

On the other hand, the fact that our famous "Slavonic maestro" found room in his concert for the completely un-Slavic overture to [Lvov's] *Undina* and for a fantasy by the *Hungarian* Liszt on *Magyar* themes, but did not think to include a single scrap from a contemporary Russian opera that is not unknown even abroad (at least by name), an opera (whatever you make of it) that was written by a "Russian" on an

[9] On the term and its meaning, see the prefatory note in this book, pp. xxxiii–xxxiv.
[10] "Muzïkal'nïye zametki," *Sanktpeterburgskiye vedomosti*, no. 151 (3 June 1867); reprint, CuiIS, 93.

"old-Russian" subject—this is Mr. Balakirev's sole responsibility. There were no obstacles whatsoever.

M. A. Balakirev evidently thought, "the theater will take care of him." . . . The Slavonic maestro, evidently, also reasoned that my things don't belong among the works of the "mighty kuchka of young Russian musicians" (Mr. Stasov's term) just as my name doesn't belong in the programs of the "Russian" Musical Society (in St. Petersburg). In both cases the bearing on matters Russian is the same.

What is the same is the *ostracism* to which I am persistently subjected in the camp of the German pianist-concertgivers and in the "kuchka" of musical Slavophiles alike. To me it is a telling manifestation. And what it tells me is that I had best deal directly with the public, not with cliques or "kuchkas" [*ne s kruzhkami i "kuchkami"*].[11]

As for the other, more serious snub—when Serov was not invited to the testimonial dinner tendered Berlioz on his last birthday (11 December 1868) by the Russian Musical Society—this was Stasov's own doing, engineered through Balakirev, who was then enjoying his brief tenure as conductor of the Society's concerts, and also through the sick, enfeebled Dargomïzhsky (in his last month of life), its vice-president, who signed a letter Stasov drew up in answer to Serov's protest.[12] But neither the insult itself nor Musorgsky's taunting allusion to it in the text of "The Peepshow" could gratify Stasov sufficiently to quell his anti-Serovian mania. Not even Serov's sudden death in 1871 could do the trick. To the end of his life, Stasov's blood would boil and his pen run out of control at the thought of him. For no one, it would seem, had ever made Stasov feel quite so inferior as this former friend whose heinous crimes had been, first, to best Stasov in the *Ruslan* debate and, second, to achieve resounding success as composer in his own right.

But all this was Stasov's idée fixe, not Musorgsky's. Feuding with Serov was a favorite pastime of the kuchka's "older generation." The newer members—Musorgsky, Rimsky-Korsakov, Borodin—had little to do with it, understood it poorly, found it distasteful and burdensome.[13]

---

[11] *Muzïka i teatr*, no. 6 (1867); reprint, A. N. Serov, *Kriticheskiye stat'i*, vol. 4 (St. Petersburg: Tipografiya Departamenta udelov, 1895), pp. 1755–56.

[12] For Stasov's side of the story, see his "Liszt, Schumann, and Berlioz in Russia," in StasSEM, 167–68.

[13] As Rimsky-Korsakov put it in his memoirs: "Serov's relations with Balakirev, Cui, and Stasov in former days (prior to my appearance on the musical horizon) are a puzzle to me to this day. Serov had been intimate with them, but why the break occurred is unknown to me. This was passed over in silence in Balakirev's circle. Snatches of

Though it is hard to imagine that Musorgsky never met Serov, nothing ever passed between them that anyone, whether participant or onlooker, saw fit to record. That Musorgsky's personal feelings had little to do with either the text or the music of "The Peepshow" can be seen from the case of Zaremba, whom he mocked in 1870 and in whose house he lived (with Rimsky-Korsakov) in 1871. As for Serov, what "The Peepshow" chiefly reveals is how thoroughly Musorgsky had learned Serov's *Rogneda* (just as Musorgsky's forced derisive letter to Balakirev on Serov's *Judith* seven years earlier had shown how attentively he had listened to that opera).

The one epistolary reference to Serov that passed between Musorgsky and another member of the younger generation of kuchkists is contained in a letter to Rimsky-Korsakov (15 July 1867), in which Musorgsky advised him to remove a passage from *Sadko* reminiscent of the Witch in *Rogneda*. At the end of the letter Serov crops up again:

> My friends in St. Petersburg have written me about the sixth issue of Serov's paper. In this number he went after Mily [Balakirev] and impugned his education. Well, Serov is no one to talk; some fine educated musician, he, who thought up a High Priest for Perun in a Russian epic and who plants pilgrims in the Kievan bush. And as for the music, from the historical point of view it's lower even than Verstovsky [i.e., in *Askold's Grave*]; at Vladimir's feast he throws in a current tavern song and dancing girls—just as though Vladimir were Holofernes. But Serov really had a field day with Cui: on account of Cui's remark (an entirely tactless remark) that in the Slavonic Concert nothing of Serov's was played, this author of two five-act operas writes: *a diplomatic regret, but in vain* . . . How do you like that "diplomatic"? Too bad César was so tactless. They tell me we all caught it in this issue—and so it must be; on account of this Serov must hate us with a holy vengeance.[14]

reminiscences about Serov, chiefly ironical, reached me in passing. A scandalous story, of unprintable nature, was circulated about him, and so forth. When I came into Balakirev's circle, the relations between Serov and that circle were most hostile. I suspect that Serov would have been glad to make up with the circle, but Balakirev was incapable of conceding it" (R-KMusL, 70). Say, rather, Stasov was incapable.

[14] Musorgsky's reference is to the piece that followed "A Diplomatic Regret" in Serov's magazine, in the regular Cui-bashing department called *Zametki protiv zametok* ("Notes against Notes": the column by "****" in the *Sanktpeterburgskiye vedomosti* was called *Muzïkal'nïye zametki*, "Notes on Music"). It was subtitled "The Elephant and the Fly" (*Slon i mukha*) and took the form of a tiresomely extended colloquy on the enormities of "****" in which three fictitious characters took part: a "subscriber from Kolomna" (i.e., from a much-despised St. Petersburg suburb), a lawyer, and a justice of

So there we have Musorgsky's attitude. When all is said and done, after the pro forma defense of Balakirev and the predictable sniping at *Rogneda* (stale news, dutifully parroted from long-since-published articles by Cui and Stasov[15]), Musorgsky sounds a note of regret— genuine (unlike Cui's), not feigned. Where Balakirev and Cui glee- fully abetted Stasov's vendetta, Musorgsky and Rimsky could only watch disconsolately from the sidelines, cluck their tongues at one another and prepare to "catch it." And Musorgsky caught it not only from the "other camp." It was probably because he expressed his honest reaction to an unreasonable Stasov at the *Judith* première that Stasov shrieked to Balakirev that Musorgsky seemed "a perfect idiot."[16]

Serov and his work interested Musorgsky as deeply as they did Rimsky.[17] To paraphrase Satie's famous sally about Ravel and the Legion of Honor, Musorgsky rejected Serov but all his works

---

the peace. All express their amazement that the St. Petersburg critic can compare a pip-squeak like Balakirev to a titan like Wagner. Finally the justice of the peace ex- plains (Serov, *Kriticheskiye stat'i*, vol. 4, 1764):

> I am of the opinion that in criticism, in judgments on works of art, there is a very important law that is unfortunately all too seldom recalled, which is why critics fall into more or less amusing or pitiful error. This law, for which there is as yet no name, I will elucidate for you by means of a pertinent example. Note that from your window you can see the Church of the Blessed Shroud. Hold your hand up to your eyes—see, you have covered (for yourself) the whole building. But does it follow from this, Mr. Lawyer, that we, too, have also stopped seeing the church, or that your hand is larger than this church?
> SUBSCRIBER FROM KOLOMNA: Bravo! I don't think there can be any objection to this, and I see just where you're heading.
> JUSTICE OF THE PEACE (continuing): So, on a like basis, as a result of optic laws, the laws of perspective, a *fly*, which is crawling on the glass here right in front of your nose, might, for example, cover up a whole *elephant* that is standing half a verst away from us. If you were to announce for all to hear that *the fly is as big as the elephant*,—well, they'd think you were out of your mind. One can readily see that Balakirev is incomparably nearer to Mr. Asterism than Wagner. So he has equated them, forgetting that others will not experience the same optical illusion and that he will only bring laughter on himself for making an elephant out of a fly.
> LAWYER (annoyed): Comparison is no proof!

Despite what Musorgsky wrote to Rimsky-Korsakov, it is evident that Serov had not gone after "them all," only after those who had given him cause.

[15] Cf. Cui's review of *Rogneda* (*Sanktpeterburgskiye vedomosti*, no. 292 [1865]), and two articles of Stasov: "Arkheologicheskaya zametka o postanovke 'Rognedï' " (StasSM 2.65–69) and "Verit'li?" (StasIS 1.149–51; StasSM 2.69–81). The latter is given practi- cally in full (in English translation) in TarODR, 128–31.

[16] Letter of 17 May 1863. BalStasP, 203.

[17] For evidence of Rimsky's sympathetic interest and its effect on his work, see TarODR, 113–18.

EXAMPLE 1. *Rogneda*, introduction to act 1 (Moscow: A. Gutheil, n.d. [ca. 1885]), p. 2

accepted him. And his contemporaries were quick to notice. Laroche, whose reviews of *Boris Godunov* were as trenchant as they were ambivalent, made the most of it. "Mr. Musorgsky is more a follower of Dargomïzhsky than the other members of his circle," he observed, "but by a strange combination of circumstances that was stronger than the composer, in places of massive and colossal character he often falls into *Serovshchina*."[18] Laroche's catalog of Serovianisms in *Boris* is long. Some of them can be accounted for merely by the fact that Serov had set the sole Russian precedent for grand historical opera by the time of the composition of *Boris* (though by the time of the première, Rimsky's *Pskovityanka* had also reached the stage). But by no means can all of them be so written off. And some are quite astonishingly specific, testifying not only to the accuracy of Laroche's observations, but to the acuity of his ear.

In the introduction to the Coronation scene (the pealing bells) Laroche discerned an echo from the introduction to the first act of *Rogneda* (Example 1). And the characteristic, now-famous chord progression of Musorgsky's bells (oscillating between dominant sevenths

[18] *Golos*, no. 29 (1874).

EXAMPLE 2. *Rogneda*, from the Royal Hunt, act 3, p. 138

with roots a tritone apart, preserving a common tritone) was anticipated in the Royal Hunt from the same opera (Example 2).[19]

The dance songs in the Terem scene (the Nanny's song of the gnat,
the Clapping Game) reminded Laroche of the Jester's songs in the
second and third acts of *Rogneda* as well as of Yeryomka's songs in
The Power of the Fiend (the Shrovetide song in act 2 and the song to
the balalaika ["Pomogu-mogu-mogu-mogu-mogu"] in act 3). This
was a particularly injurious charge, since among the "models" cited
was the "current tavern song" that had called forth so much kuchkist
vitriol, including Musorgsky's letter to Rimsky-Korsakov. And it had
been parodied in "The Peepshow" to boot! The reference to Yeryomka, however, carries conviction. Not only must this dark character have appealed strongly to Musorgsky ("this Russian Bertram" he
called him in a letter to Stasov),[20] but the timing was right. *The Power
of the Fiend* was premièred posthumously in April 1871. Musorgsky
revised his Terem scene and added the dance songs in August of the
same year. The kind of folk-derived ostinato patter song he came up
with in the Clapping Game had Russian operatic antecedents only in
Serov (Example 3, p. 108).

The scene at the fountain was also composed in 1871, and a rather
improbable echo of *The Power of the Fiend* may lurk there as well. At

[19] This harmonic relationship, derived from Liszt (cf. the opening of *Orpheus*), pervades much Russian music and can be traced before *Rogneda* (e.g., Balakirev's Overture to *King Lear* [1859], as Rey Longyear points out in *Nineteenth-Century Romanticism
in Music*, 2d ed. [Englewood Cliffs: Prentice-Hall, 1973], p. 222). But Laroche was certainly right in tracing the oscillation effect to Serov.

[20] MusLN 1.121.

EXAMPLE 3a. *The Power of the Fiend*, Yeryomka's song to the balalaika, act 3 (Moscow: Muzïka, 1968), p. 243

Yeryomka:

uzh i ya li tvo-mu go-ryu po-mo-gu, po-mo - gu, mo-gu, mo-

gu, mo-gu, mo - gu, po-mo-gu, mo-gu, mo - gu, mo-gu, mo-gu!

For I can help you in your woe, yes I can, I can, I can, I can, I can!

EXAMPLE 3b. *Boris Godunov*, the Clapping Game, act 2 (MusPSS 1 [MusCW 2]), p. 173

Fyodor:

Ska-zoch-ka pro to i pro syo: kak ku - roch - ka bïch -

ka ro - di - la. Po - ro - syo-no-chek ya - ich - ko snyos.

A little tale about this and that: how the hen had a little bull . . .

least Rimsky-Korsakov thought so. On 29 September 1897, not long after he finished work on his first redaction of Musorgsky's opera, he told his disciple Yastrebtsev that a certain phrase in the Pretender's monologue (Example 4a) seemed to have been unconsciously borrowed from the notorious Drunkard's song in the fourth act of Serov's opera—itself a reworking of the folk song *Kapitanskaya doch' ne khodi gulyat' v polnoch'* (Lvov-Pratsch, no. 61), from which so much of the music in *The Power of the Fiend* derived (Example 4b).[21] But while the Serov snatch Rimsky cited certainly did turn up in his own *Snegurochka* (as, with characteristic candor, he acknowledged in the same conversation with Yastrebtsev), Musorgsky's phrase seems more plausibly a derivation from the Pretender's leitmotif, a more nearly literal citation of which immediately precedes it in the Fountain monologue (Example 4c).

Boris's monologue at the center of the Coronation scene Laroche

[21] YasVR-K 1.472–73.

EXAMPLE 4a. *Boris Godunov*, p. 262

Voz - ve - du ye - yo s so-bo - yu na tsar - skiy pre stol,

I will take her up with me onto the royal throne,

EXAMPLE 4b. *The Power of the Fiend*, p. 280

Med - nï de-nezh-ki zve - nyat, v ka - ba - chok id - ti ve - lyat.

Copper coins jingle, order us into the tavern.

EXAMPLE 4c. *Boris Godunov*, p. 262

Voz-ne - su ye - yo, go - lub - ku, pred vse - yu rus - skoy zem-ley

I will raise her up, my precious, before the whole Russian land.

compares with the Wanderer's recitative in *Rogneda*, act 3 (Example 5, p. 110). And the offstage chorus of monks in the Cell scene, Laroche avers, was inspired by the mourning chorus for Ruald in the same act of Serov's opera (Example 6, pp. 112–13). The critic sums up: "The general decorativeness and crudity of Mr. Musorgsky's style, his passion for the brass and percussion instruments, may be considered to have been borrowed from Serov." And then, no friend to either party, he twists the knife: "But never did the crudest works of the model reach the naive coarseness we note in his imitator."[22]

Long as Laroche's list is, it could be considerably extended. And his conclusion, purged of its malice, could be considerably strengthened. For the affinities between Musorgsky and Serov as creative personalities were fundamental, and their common creative leanings numerous. Our next witness will be Musorgsky himself. His well-known letter to Balakirev on *Judith* has been much analyzed.

[22] *Golos*, no. 44 (1874). The list of borrowings is drawn from this article and the one cited in n. 18.

EXAMPLE 5. *Rogneda*, the pilgrim elders' recitative, act 3, pp. 119–20

EXAMPLE 5, *continued*

Gerald Abraham has described it as a "weak attempt at exculp-
ation" after Stasov blew up at his younger colleague's "idiocy"
at the première.[23] With the single exception of the act 1 finale,
which Balakirev himself had mildly praised when shown the score
by Serov in 1861 in a last act of good will, Musorgsky dared not actually praise the opera or any of its parts. But even the passages chosen for blame show at least what interested him in *Judith*, and they
make a revealing list. Holofernes's act 4 delirium, for example, is singled out for special scorn: "Holofernes, dead drunk, starts having
hallucinations. . . . What a broad field for a musician, this feasting
sensualist-despot, how interestingly might his hallucinations have
been portrayed in the orchestra. But there is nothing of the sort—
just banal French melodrama with Wagnerian howls from the vio-
lins."[24]

So it would seem that Boris Godunov's hallucination—one of the
very few episodes in the first version of Musorgsky's opera that did
not come from Pushkin's play, and which is chiefly "portrayed in the
orchestra"—was prompted by the wish, as it were, to set Serov
straight. And so one might boldly extend Professor Abraham's just

[23] "The Operas of Serov," in Jack Westrup, ed., *Essays Presented to Egon Wellesz* (Oxford: Oxford University Press, 1966), p. 174. Abraham continues, "his true reaction to
Judith was to begin his own *Salammbô* five months later."
[24] MusLN 1.68.

EXAMPLE 6. *Rogneda*, the pilgrims' funeral chant, act 3, pp. 182–83

Example 6, *continued*

A. 2479 G.

EXAMPLE 7. *Judith*, opening of act 1 (Moscow: A. Gutheil, n.d. [ca. 1885]), p. 8

but cautious observation that Serov's scene suggested Musorgsky's "dramatically, not musically."[25] The musical suggestion was there, too, precisely in what Musorgsky found lacking in Serov's achievement.

There is another conspicuous example of Serov having planted an idea in Musorgsky's mind as it were by omission. The younger composer, writing to Balakirev, pointed with approval to a melody that accompanied the pacing of the elders at the raising of the curtain in act 1, typically Serovian in its tortuousness and angularity (Example 7). But Musorgsky called attention to what he regarded as a "serious dereliction": "This phrase, which portrays the predicament of the people lying exhausted upon the stage, is dropped with the beginning of the elders' recitative. I would have continued it, added some juice, and upon its development, upon the progress of this phrase, I would have constructed the elders' declamation."[26] And so he did, exactly, for Pimen's monologue in the Cell scene.

The one real plagiarism from *Judith* in Musorgsky's works is found neither in *Boris* nor in *Salammbô* but in the concert chorus after Byron, *Porazheniye Sennakheriba* [The destruction of Sennacherib, 1867], which treats of the same subject matter as Serov's opera: the war between the Assyrians and the Hebrews. Undoubtedly because of this congruence, Musorgsky copied Holofernes's war song from act 4 of *Judith* in the first theme of the chorus. It is something one cannot imagine Musorgsky doing consciously, yet the parallel is so obvious that one has to wonder how it escaped not only Musorgsky's notice but that of his fellow kuchkists as well. Had they noticed, they would scarcely have "permitted" it (Example 8).

[25] *Essays Presented to Egon Wellesz*, p. 177.
[26] MusLN 1.65.

EXAMPLE 8a. Holofernes's War song (A. N. Serov, *Judith*), pp. 264–65.

We cross the torrid steppe! The air breathes fire!

EXAMPLE 8b. *The Destruction of Sennacherib* (MusPSS 4 [MusCW 21]), pp. 56–57

Like a pack of famished wolves, the enemy has attacked us.

EXAMPLE 9. *Judith*, introduction to act 1, pp. 4–5. Reduced to block formation from harp arpeggios over pedal.

Yet interesting as all these specific points and parallels may be—and the list could be extended further still, to include enharmonic third relations, particularly the progressive reidentification of a given pitch as root, third, fifth, and seventh, such as we find in the fanfares in Musorgsky's Coronation scene, which reflect such typically Serovian passages as the harp arpeggios in the introduction to act 1 of *Judith* (Example 9)—they are neither as interesting nor as important as the more general aesthetic and dramaturgical parallels. Here we really see how indispensable a precursor Serov was for Musorgsky. Asafyev put it rather loftily and abstractly when he observed that "their paths were not at all far from one another . . . in the predominance of all that was *characteristic* over the generalizing and the harmonious."[27] What he meant was that Serov provided a spiritual source for some of the most basic tenets of Musorgsky's aesthetic credo—traits, as a matter of fact, that rather set him apart from his kuchkist elders Balakirev and Cui: his contempt for "beauty," his harmonic empiricism, his preoccupation with pathological psychology and its unvarnished, unflinching representation. One is almost tempted to say that what Musorgsky "got" from Serov was realism itself.

So much of what one is apt today to regard as characteristic of Musorgsky and of Musorgsky alone can be found in embryo in Serov's work, and the opera to look to first—Asafyev recognized this—is neither of the ones referred to by Laroche (and by a host of such lesser critics as Mikhnevich, Rappaport, and Solovyov),[28] but *Judith*. There one finds more than the Orientalism of *Salammbô*, which Musorgsky dismissed with a shrug when asked why he

[27] AsIT 3:40.
[28] Cf. GozROTIII, 94.

had never finished that first operatic attempt.[29] One also finds such patently "Musorgskian" devices as the fragmentation of the chorus, extreme harmonic "ugliness" in the interest of expression (and vocal ugliness, too, to the point where even Cui was offended),[30] and above all, an austerity amounting almost to asceticism in the dramaturgical plan (the Assyrian acts excepted, as one must except the Polish act of *Boris*). Some of this was developed further in Serov's later operas (the jeering of the Pecheneg prisoners in *Rogneda* as noted by Abraham,[31] the "murder chords" in *The Power of the Fiend*), but Musorgsky's reaction to *Judith* was fresh and as yet relatively unprejudiced. He acknowledged it to be "the first seriously treated opera on the Russian stage since [Dargomïzhsky's] *Rusalka*,"[32] and he could only have been kindly disposed at this point toward the work of the critic who had welcomed his own debut three years earlier.

When Musorgsky next heard from Serov as composer for the stage, it was not with *Rogneda* itself but with the preface to the libretto, published in September 1865, over a month before the première. This ringing, bellicose manifesto on behalf of "dramatic truth in tone" and against all " 'conventional' beauty"[33] is so close to Musorgsky's own creative aspirations (as he began to state them only later in his letters) that one easily imagines him, in different circumstances, hugging its author to his breast and bestowing upon Serov the epithet he accorded to Dargomïzhsky: "great teacher of musical truth." But St. Petersburg musical politics decreed otherwise, and Musorgsky joined the kuchkist chorus of gleeful abuse. It was all too easy to point up the gap between Serov's lofty preachments and his at times risibly inadequate practice. But Musorgsky's ears re-

[29] "We've had enough of the Orient in *Judith*. Art isn't a pastime, time is precious." Nikolai Kompaneysky, "K novïm beregam," *Russkaya muzïkal'naya gazeta* (1906), quoted in MR, 67.

[30] "In the entire fourth act what we hear from Mr. Sariotti [in the role of Holofernes] is not singing at all, but raucous bellowing. If Mr. Serov were really aspiring to this, then he probably would not have written a vocal part, but merely indicated, 'Holofernes declaims hoarsely.' " But as Cui himself realized, "Mr. Sariotti is . . . singing and acting on Mr. Serov's instructions." For more on the vocal style of *Judith*, including more of Cui's review, see R. Taruskin, "Opera and Drama in Russia: The Case of Serov's *Judith*," JAMS 32 (1979): 114–17.

[31] *Essays Presented to Egon Wellesz*, p. 180.

[32] MusLN 1.64.

[33] The preface is given practically in full in TarODR, 88–90.

EXAMPLE 10a. *Sorochintsï Fair*, opening of Fair scene, act 1 (Moscow: Mu-zïka, 1970), p. 7

EXAMPLE 10a, *continued*

mained open to the harmonic barbarities of the sacrifice to Perun, the naturalism of the choruses and, occasionally, of the declamation.[34] Serov's Christian Elder (see Example 4), though compared by Laroche with Boris Godunov, was sooner the natural prototype for Pimen. It seems Cui agreed, for how else is one to account for his odd hostility toward the Cell scene in *Boris*? He must have sensed the kinship between Musorgsky's "choppy, unmusical recitatives" and Serov's.[35]

As for *The Power of the Fiend*, no opera set a more powerful precedent for *Sorochintsï Fair*. Musorgsky's Fair scene, originally composed for *Mlada* in 1872, with its vendor's cries set contrapuntally against a continuously developing orchestral backdrop, inescapably evokes Serov's Shrovetide fair, first performed in 1871 (Example 10). But beyond that, and beyond Yeryomka, there is the matter of folk song

[34] See ibid., pp. 119–20 for some specific instances of Musorgskian borrowing from *Rogneda*.

[35] See his famous review of the *Boris* première, still unreprinted and untranslated in full (*Sanktpeterburgskiye vedomosti*, no. 37 [1874]).

EXAMPLE 10b. *The Power of the Fiend*, Shrovetide scene, act 4, p. 264

recitative. The whole concept so flies in the face of Musorgsky's practice (not to mention his theorizing) from *Marriage* to *Khovanshchina*, yet figures so prominently in *The Fair*, as to send one off in search of explanations. A comparison at random with Serov's recitatives in the earlier acts of his Ostrovsky opera suggests a compelling one (Example 11, p. 122).

This was an aspect of Musorgsky's work that his contemporaries could not judge, for *The Fair* remained an unknown quantity apart from a few excerpts until the second decade of this century. By then, of course, the realist ferment in Russian music had long since died down, and so had Serov's once mighty reputation. So no one seems to have drawn the perfectly obvious connections between Musorgsky's posthumous opera and Serov's.

EXAMPLE 10b, *continued*

But by now they should elicit no surprise. Musorgsky and Serov were kindred spirits who by rights should have been allies. Only the vagaries of musical politics, in which Musorgsky's role was a passive one, kept them apart in life and in conventional historiography. La-roche was already of the opinion that Serov "would have consider-ably softened his wrath at the '*moguchaya kuchka*' had he lived to see the production of *Boris Godunov*, [for] in the person of Mr. Musorgsky he would have found a composer who not only fulfilled but even exceeded" his own Gluck-derived operatic ideals.[36] "Amazingly, no one up to now has said so yet among us," wrote Stasov in 1883, "but Perov and Musorgsky represent in the world of Russian art an aston-

[36] G. A. Laroche, *Sobraniye muzïkal'no-kriticheskikh statey* (Moscow: J. N. Kushnerov, 1922), p. 116.

EXAMPLE 11a. *Sorochintsï Fair*, act 1, scene 1, pp. 24–25

—*Do you think you can approach my daughter just like that? Just like that?—Bah, it's Solopiy himself! Hello old pal! Hello, Pan Cherevik!*

EXAMPLE 11b. *The Power of the Fiend*, act 2, pp. 137–38

Now you leave off grieving, at least for today!—What a spell you've cast on me!

ishing parallel. It seems to me that anyone who will take the trouble to look into these two personalities will come to the same conclusion."[37] A century later, it is time to recognize that if we change the first letter of the painter's name to an *S*, Stasov's provocative assertion holds good.

[37] This is the opening of "Perov i Musorgskiy," one of Stasov's finest essays, which prompted the title of the present chapter. It was first published in *Russkaya starina* (May 1883), pp. 433–58, and is reprinted in StasIS 2.132–52. Vasiliy Grigoryevich Perov (1834–82) was one of the *peredvizhnik* painters [the so-called wanderers], whose highly individualized Daumieresque "types" have often been compared with Musorgsky's realistic songs of the sixties.

THE PRESENT IN
THE PAST

Russian Opera and Russian
Historiography, circa 1870

"Now *there* is a page of history," Nikolai Kostomarov is supposed to have exclaimed at the conclusion of *Boris Godunov*. For Stasov, who overheard (or perhaps elicited) the famous historian's remark, there could be no higher praise, and he advertised it repeatedly in his writings on Musorgsky.[1] Both the comment and the importance accorded it were symptomatic of the time. The seriousness with which historical drama and even historical opera were treated by educated Russians was one of the hallmarks of the Alexander II period, when the positivist outlook reached the high-water mark and art was seen as bearing an obligation, in Chernïshevsky's words, to embody a content "worthy of the attention of a thinking man."[2] The "thinking realist" was as much the literary archetype of the moment as the "superfluous man" had been a generation back, and the epithet was applied (not without some irony) to the composer of *Boris* by Herman Laroche in a surprisingly favorable review.[3]

---

[1] It appears in the biography-necrology of 1881 (StasIS 2.199), and, worded a bit differently, in *Pamyati Musorgskogo*, an essay marking the fifth anniversary of the composer's death (StasIS 3.34). Though Stasov implies in these articles that the remark was made after a performance in the theater, it seems rather likelier that the occasion for it was an evening at Stasov's own home (30 October 1874), at which Musorgsky played excerpts from his opera to a gathering that included, besides Kostomarov, the writer Daniyil Mordovtsev (who had contributed to the text of the Kromy scene), the painter Nikolai Ge (a specialist in historical subjects), and Golenishchev-Kutuzov. See OrTD, 404, where the date of the gathering is established on the basis of letters.

[2] Nikolai Chernïshevsky, *Selected Philosophical Essays* (Moscow: Foreign Languages Publishing House, 1953), p. 379.

[3] "Mïslyashchiy realist v russkoy opere," *Golos*, 13 February 1874.

The attitude of high seriousness with which people went to the theater in those days was a very self-conscious, somewhat affected thing. So was historicism. The two met in the pages of the *Vestnik Yevropï* [The European courier], a "thick journal" of historiography and liberal opinion. The very first issue contained a learned exchange between Kostomarov and Stasov on the historical verisimilitude of the production of Serov's opera *Rogneda*.[4] The editor, Mikhail Stasyulevich, saw fit to introduce it with this half-apologetic yet optimistic note:

> Perhaps a few of our readers will be surprised that in our "Historical Chronicle" section we speak of the theater and of scenic productions, even though the journal is devoted specifically to historical scholarship. But such doubts will not visit those who, like us, think of the theater not as an idle amusement but accord it a high significance among the organs that motivate and develop the intellectual life of man, and, consequently, have an influence on the history of societies.[5]

This positivistic, melioristic aesthetic was echoed a year later by Kostomarov himself, in the pages of the same journal, when he affirmed that "the theater has the means to disseminate throughout society information on past life, just as it can acquaint [society] with the trends and notions of the present; just as, in general, it can serve as an important weapon in broadening the intellectual horizon of society."[6] The view of art as a didactic tool, the very attitude a younger generation would brand a "slap in the face of Apollo,"[7] was among the factors contributing most to the efflorescence of historical drama at this particular juncture in Russian literary history. Relaxation of censorship was another, though the censor continued to exert a stronger grip on the theater than on printed literature (and stronger yet on opera, in curious ways we shall examine).

The stunning achievement of Nikolai Karamzin (1766–1826), the litterateur turned "official historiographer," had also played a part. His monumental *History of the Russian State*, which appeared in twelve volumes beginning in 1818 (the last one published posthumously), had an electrifying effect on Russian intellectual life. In-

---

[4] Part of Stasov's side of it is given in TarODR, 126.

[5] *Vestnik Yevropï* 1, no. 1 (1866): 84.

[6] "Po povodu noveyshey russkoy istoricheskoy stsenï, ibid., vol. 2, no. 2 (1867): 94.

[7] Alexandre Benois, "Vrubel'," *Mir iskusstva*, no. 3 (1910), quoted in John Bowlt, *The Silver Age: Russian Art of the Early Twentieth Century and the "World of Art" Group* (Newtonville, Mass.: Oriental Research Partners, 1979), p. 74.

tensely monarchist and nationalist, it made as important a contribution to the development of Russian national consciousness as it did to the development of historical thinking in the land. Its impact on imaginative literature was immediate: it began, in fact, before the *History* was even complete. Volumes 10 and 11, covering the reigns of Tsars Fyodor Ioannovich, Boris Godunov, and the False Dmitry, appeared in 1824; Pushkin wrote his famous tragedy in 1825 (though it was not published until 1831). *Boris Godunov* was the progenitor of the whole line of Russian romantic historical dramas in verse.

Such had been Pushkin's intention: with his "Shakespearean" tragedy he had hoped to break the stranglehold of French neoclassical drama on the Russian court theater. Karamzin's vivid portrayal of Boris in his *History* had provided Pushkin with the pretext he had been looking for to attempt the "reform of our stage."[8] If we discount for the moment the minor contributions made to the historical drama in the 1840s by romantic novelists like Mikhail Zagoskin and Ivan Lazhechnikov, the reform initiated by Pushkin was next taken up by the lyric poet Lev Alexandrovich Mey (1822–62), whose *Tsar's Bride* (1849) and especially *Pskovityanka* [The maid of Pskov] (1859) marked something of an epoch in the development of the genre, in terms of period atmosphere and seriousness of treatment.[9] Unlike Pushkin's play, moreover, Mey's were "well made" and effective and they inspired imitations. What in the forties and fifties had been a trickle turned, after *Pskovityanka*, into a flood, which reached its peak in the late sixties and early seventies—that is, just when the operas we shall consider were conceived. Dramatists great and small were caught up willy-nilly in this rising tide. Alexander Ostrovsky was temporarily diverted from his true métier, that of realistic domestic dramas in prose, to compose a series of "chronicles" in verse that culminated in a kind of trilogy: *Dmitry the Pretender and Vasily Shuisky* (1867),[10] *Tushino* (also 1867), and *Vasilisa Melentyeva* (1868). An actual historical

[8] Cf. the manuscript draft of a preface to the first edition (1831) in D. S. Mirsky, *Pushkin* (New York: E. P. Dutton, 1963), p. 154. Pushkin, of course, was only one of many "Shakespearean" reformers of nineteenth-century drama. Hugo was another, as was Verdi. See Piero Weiss, "Verdi and the Fusion of Genres," *JAMS* 35 (1982): 138–56.

[9] Both these plays were turned into operas by Rimsky-Korsakov, as was Mey's remaining play, *Servilia* (1853), on an ancient Roman subject. Another Russian historical play, on Vasilisa Melentyeva, remained unfinished at Mey's death and the manuscript has perished.

[10] It was first performed at the Malïy Theater in Moscow with an overture and mazurka specially composed by Chaikovsky.

trilogy was the magnum opus of Count Alexey Tolstoy: *The Death of Ivan the Terrible* (1866), *Tsar Fydor Ioannovich* (1868), and *Tsar Boris* (1870). And then there was the work of numerous stringers and hacks like Nikolai Chayev (*Dmitry the Pretender*, 1866; *Dread Tsar Ivan Vasilyevich*, 1868; etc.) and Serov's *Rogneda* librettist Dmitri Averkiyev (*Sloboda Nevolya*, 1866). The whole spate is often dismissed by modern critics for its excessive plot complications and superfluous characters (owing to a naive understanding of Pushkin's technique and its Shakespearean model), for its falsification of the conditions of old Russian life through the inevitable introduction of the theme of romantic love (here Pushkin alone had been blameless), and, finally, for its clumsy and stilted rhetoric—"the conventional language of contemporary poetry larded with idioms from old documents and from folklore."[11]

But, superficial though they may have been, these plays clearly answered a need. A clue to the nature of that need may be gleaned from the subject matter their authors all favored. Without exception the titles given above deal with the late reign of Ivan the Terrible and the "Time of Troubles" (*smutnoye vremya*) that followed it, that is, the period circa 1565–1613.[12] This may be partly explained by the conditions of the censorship, which forbade the appearance of any member of the Romanov dynasty as a character on the stage. The Time of Troubles, then, was the very latest phase of Russian history that could be used by a dramatist, at least if he adhered to Karamzin's "Caesaristic" mode of historiography, which viewed the history of Russia in terms of the personalities of the tsars. (And in those days, who didn't?)[13] As to the specific attractions of Ivan the Terrible and Boris Godunov, we again have Karamzin to thank, for his masterly and controversial character portraits of these two titanically flawed personages had turned them into veritable myths. The historical the-

[11] D. S. Mirsky, *A History of Russian Literature* (New York: Vintage Books, 1958), p. 254.

[12] Tushino was the encampment of the second False Dmitry, who led a campaign on Moscow in 1607; Vasilisa Melentyeva was Ivan the Terrible's sixth wife, whom he wedded without benefit of clergy; Sloboda Nevolya was the popular name of Ivan's domestic retreat at Alexandrovo.

[13] Even later it remained a feature of popular historiography: witness Kostomarov's bestseller, *Russian History through the Lives of Its Main Figures* (*Russkaya istoriya v zhizneopisaniyakh eyo glavneyshikh deyateley*, 7 vols. [St. Petersburg: Tipografiya M. M. Stasyulevicha, 1873–88], and reprinted continually thereafter up to the Revolution), which clashes curiously with the main thrust of Kostomarov's work, directed, as we shall see, very much against the Caesaristic approach.

ater of the 1860s was taking an increasingly psychological turn (it was the period, after all, that spawned *Crime and Punishment*), and Ivan and Boris provided an endless source of psychopathological speculation on the part of dramatists whose aims ranged from the loftiest (Tolstoy) to the most trivial (Averkiyev: "I wanted to show Ivan the Terrible not as the Tsar Ioann, but . . . [as] Vanya, Vanyusha, sweetheart").[14]

Finally, we may recall the social and civic themes invoked at the beginning of this chapter. Belinsky had observed in 1846 that "the study of Russian history has never had so serious a character as it has taken on recently," and went on to one of his most famous dicta: "We question, nay, we interrogate the past for an explanation of our present and a hint of our future."[15] All this was even more true in the 1860s. It was for Russia a new time of troubles, a period of social unrest unprecedented within living memory, brought about by the disastrous Crimean War, by the Emancipation, and by nationalist uprisings on the peripheries of the Empire. Art sought "relevant" themes, and in all media one can observe the swing away from the Kievan period as favored historical epoch to that of the Time of Troubles, matching the general swing from romanticism to realism as the reigning aesthetic.

That opera lagged a bit behind the spoken drama until the end of the sixties can be seen from the standpoint of *Rogneda*, which had a Kievan setting though it was produced as late as 1865, and which celebrated an "Official Nationality" hardly less egregious than that of Glinka's *Life for the Tsar*. For many, that was merely in the nature of the operatic beast. Kostomarov, though his admiration was sincere, greeted Serov's work in a way that can only seem patronizing:

> Such a remote period as the time of Vladimir [the tenth-century Kievan prince who Christianized Russia], virtually impossible for drama [owing to the absence of a sufficient fund of information for realistic treatment], suits opera better, as it generally seems that where the dramatic kernel is shrouded in an epic atmosphere, opera must replace drama, and will thus serve as a musical interpretation of such historical facts as would be, by virtue of the remoteness of their epoch, hardly accessible even to the strongest dramatic talent. And in that case it is necessary that any

---

[14] S. S. Danilov, *Ocherki po istorii russkogo dramaticheskogo teatra* (Moscow: Goslitizdat, 1948), p. 386.

[15] Vissarion Belinsky, "Vzglyad na russkuyu literaturu 1846 goda," *Polnoye sobraniye sochineniy*, vol. 10 (Moscow: Goslitizdat, 1956), p. 18.

opera with a historical subject, both in content and in its musical idea, leave us with the impression precisely of a historico-epic image, through which the subject may be conveyed to us out of the depths of the past, and in which it may be grasped and reproduced by artistic creation.[16]

But this is only the standard idealist view of music as an art with the "capacity to reach back into prehistory," as Vischer, for one, had put it.[17] Nor is it so far from what Wagner had to say on the matter. In *Opera and Drama* he had declared historical verisimilitude and "realization" of feeling irreconcilable, and had deplored the historical drama (which to a musician, of course, meant the French grand opera) as "romance turned to politics."[18] Serov, his Russian admirer and the author of *Rogneda*, followed Wagner in this view, going so far in one critical essay as to rule out Pushkin's *Boris Godunov* as a viable operatic subject, since the title character was one in whom "rational thought predominates," and this was "an element unmusical in essence."[19] Elsewhere Serov rejected Ostrovsky's *Dmitry the Pretender* for a similar reason: "it is a brilliant subject to be sure, but in essence not very musical. Politics plays the chief role in it and music, by virtue of its open, candid nature, is but a poor elucidator of political and diplomatic intrigue. Give us rather something *simpler*, more heartfelt."[20] We seem to be dealing here with what Dahlhaus has characterized as the "neoromantic" plight of music in the latter nineteenth century: "romantic in an unromantic age dominated by positivism and realism."[21] And yet, as anyone who knows the standard operatic repertory is aware, there were composers in Russia only too eager to embrace positivism and realism and to try their hands at the new historical drama without compromise. Their unprecedented success can be preliminarily measured in the startling paragraph with which Prince Mirsky concluded his not-too-admiring survey of the Russian costume play:

[16] *Vestnik Yevropï* 1, no. 1 (1866): 92.
[17] See Carl Dahlhaus, *Richard Wagner's Music Dramas*, trans. Mary Whittall (Cambridge: Cambridge University Press, 1979), p. 80.
[18] See *Richard Wagner's Prose Works*, vol. 2, trans. William Ashton Ellis (London: Kegan Paul, Trench, Trubner, 1895), pp. 168–79, 197–201.
[19] SerIS 1.259.
[20] Letter to O. Novikova (August 1866), quoted in GozROTII, 248.
[21] Carl Dahlhaus, *Between Romanticism and Modernism: Four Studies in the Music of the Later Nineteenth Century*, trans. Mary Whittall (Berkeley and Los Angeles: University of California Press, 1980), p. 5.

The principal interest of all this drama is its connection with the far more vigorous growth of the Russian opera; Rimsky-Korsakov's librettist, Belsky, was one of its best writers, and above all it can claim kinship with the greatest Russian tragic poet of the period, Modest Musorgsky. Musorgsky himself wrote the libretto of *Khovanshchina* and adapted with great skill Pushkin's *Boris Godunov* to make his popular opera. That he had dramatic as well as musical genius cannot be denied, but the literary historian unfortunately has no right to appropriate him or to sever the dramatic from the musical texture of his dramas.[22]

The mention of Belsky is both inappropriate and anachronistic, no doubt motivated by personal regard.[23] But Rimsky's first opera, *Pskovityanka*, after Mey's play, was one of the most remarkable achievements of the early kuchkist period (it is dedicated, in fact, to "my dear musical circle"). It stands with *Boris*, its exact contemporary, as the kuchkist opera par excellence: seeking as little compromise as possible with operatic convention, it attempts to harness music's power to realize not only transcendent feeling, but that "content worthy of the attention of a thinking man" that sets realist art apart from romantic. Like *Boris* and *Khovanshchina* it is not only "historical drama" but drama about history, in which the past is treated and confronted in the light of advanced historiographical thought, and in which an attempt is made to contribute to historical understanding.

We shall focus on *Pskovityanka* and *Boris* primarily from this standpoint, and, rushing in where Mirsky feared to tread, we shall (particularly in the case of Musorgsky's so much better known work) to a considerable extent sever the "historiographical" from both the dramatic and the musical textures of the operas. Our method will be comparative. But instead of comparing Rimsky's opera with Musorgsky's directly (except briefly, when passing from the one to the other), we shall compare *Pskovityanka* with another exactly contemporaneous work, Chaikovsky's *The Oprichnik*, which, like *Pskovityanka*, was concerned with Ivan the Terrible; and we shall compare *Boris* not with any other opera but with its own earlier version. The goal in both cases will be to place the operas in a precise historical as well as historiographical context and to show how the composers,

---

[22] Mirsky, *A History of Russian Literature*, p. 255.

[23] Belsky's collaboration with Rimsky-Korsakov only began in 1899, and in all cases involved not historical but fantastic subjects (*Tsar Saltan*, 1900; *Kitezh*, 1905; *The Golden Cockerel*, 1907).

unlike their "neoromantic" contemporaries, saw themselves as aspiring participants in their country's intellectual life.

I

In the *Vestnik Yevropï* article quoted at the outset of this chapter, Kostomarov went on to say:

> One has to allow the dramatist who deals with historical personages to invent whatever he likes, but only on the condition that the historian would say, "although history says nothing about this, the progress of events, the nature of the characters, the spirit of the era and the customs of the time are all presented by the poet just as they must have been." That, in our view, is what one must demand of a historical drama.[24]

It seems a pious Aristotelian platitude (all the more so since the object in view was *Rogneda*). Yet it contains the seeds of controversy without end, since historians inevitably differ, and never more than they did in the Russia of Alexander II's time. If from the civic point of view the most important of these controversies concerned an area that was off-limits to the drama—the reforms of Peter the Great and the church schism—the one that most closely concerned artists and dramatists was the one that revolved around the character of Ivan the Terrible and his place in history. It began in 1821 with the publication of the ninth volume of Karamzin's *History*. Up until then Karamzin had behaved like a servile aristocratic historian, foreshadowing Nikolaian ideology and (in words attributed to Pushkin) "proving the necessity of autocracy and the delights of the knout."[25] But although Karamzin did indeed view the autocracy as necessary, emphasizing again and again that "whenever the power of the sovereign was emasculated, Russia fell apart and her subjects turned into slaves,"[26] he had his doubts about the knout, especially when wielded by a sovereign with no respect for law. Having himself suffered under the despotic rule of Paul I, Karamzin passed a harsh judgment on the "unenlightened" sixteenth-century despot, sum-

[24] *Vestnik Yevropï* 2, no. 2 (1867): 98.

[25] A. S. Pushkin, *Sochineniya* (Moscow, 1964), vol. 1, p. 100. The anonymous little quatrain circulated widely in "samizdat," and has been assigned by Pushkinists conjecturally to the year 1818, when vols. 1–8 of Karamzin were issued.

[26] Richard Pipes, "Karamzin's Conception of the Monarchy," in J. L. Black, ed., *Essays on Karamzin* (The Hague: Mouton, 1975), p. 118.

ming it all up in a ringing passage that completely captivated the imagination of his contemporaries:

> Amid other sore trials of Fate, beyond the misfortune of the feudal system, beyond the Mongolian yoke, Russia had also to endure the terror of an Autocrat-Torturer. She withstood it with love for the autocracy, for she believed that God sends plagues, earthquakes, and tyrants alike; she did not break the iron scepter in Ivan's hands but bore with her tormentor for twenty-four years, armed only with prayer and patience, in order to have, in better times, Peter the Great and Catherine the Second (History does not like to name the living [i.e., Alexander I, Karamzin's patron]). In magnanimous tranquility martyrs died on Red Square like the Greeks at Thermopylae, for their fatherland, for Faith and Loyalty, without even a thought of rebellion. In vain did some foreign historians seek to excuse Ivan's cruelty by writing of the conspiracies he crushed by means of it: these conspiracies existed only in the tsar's troubled mind, as all our chronicles and state papers attest. The clergy, the boyars, the distinguished citizenry would not have summoned the beast from his lair at Alexandrovo had they been planning treason, of which they were accused just as absurdly as they were of sorcery. No, the tiger reveled in the blood of the lambs—and the victims, perishing in innocence, in their last look at the impoverished land, demanded justice and a loving memory from their contemporaries and posterity!
>
> Despite all hypotheses and speculations, the character of Ivan, beneficent Hero in his youth and ferocious bloodsucker in his manhood and old age, remains an enigma, and we would doubt the veracity of the most trustworthy accounts of him if the chronicles of other nations did not present us with examples just as astonishing: if Caligula, a *model sovereign* and a *monster*, if Nero, disciple of the wise Seneca, the *object of love* and the *object of disgust*, had not reigned in Rome. They were pagans; but Louis XI was a Christian and yielded to Ivan neither in ferocity nor in outward piety, by which both of them sought to expiate their iniquities. Both were pious out of fear, both were bloodthirsty and lecherous, like the Asiatic and Roman torturers. Miscreants beyond the law, beyond rule and all rational possibility, these horrible meteors, these will-o'-the-wisps of unrestrained passion illumine for us through the ages the chasm of potential human depravity—to see it is to shudder! The life of a tyrant is a calamity for mankind, but his History is always useful to sovereigns and peoples: to nurture aversion to evil is to nurture love of virtue—and glory to that time, when a historian armed with truth can, in an autocratic government, expose to shame such a ruler, may his like never again be seen! The grave is insensible: but the living

dread the eternal damnation of History, which, while not reforming villains, can sometimes prevent misdeeds, always possible since wild passions rage even in times of civic enlightenment, commanding the mind to keep still or else in a servile voice to justify its crimes.[27]

This totally unexpected diatribe burst like a bombshell on the Russian intellectual community. "What an Ivan! What a Karamzin!" exclaimed Rïleyev, the future Decembrist,[28] while at the other end of the political spectrum there were outraged condemnations: "A well-described virtue attracts people to goodness but it serves no purpose to expose and magnify forms of evil."[29] At least one purpose was served, however: a figure of epic proportions was bequeathed to Russian artists in all media, and to dramatists above all.

An excellent example of Karamzin's Ivan on the Russian stage can be found in Ivan Lazhechnikov's tragedy, *The Oprichnik* (1834), on which, some four decades later, Chaikovsky was to base his opera. Lazhechnikov (1792–1869) was primarily a novelist who favored exotic and patriotic themes after the fashion of his time. His *Basurman* [The infidel] (1838), which Serov briefly considered turning into an opera in his extreme youth, had contained a vivid, if trivially "realistic" portrait of Ivan III ("the Great," grandfather of "the Terrible"), drawn strictly from imagination, which sympathetic critics liked to contrast with the stilted magnificence of Pushkin's *Boris Godunov* on the one hand, and, on the other, with the hazy romanticism of Lermontov's *Song of the Tsar Ivan Vasilyevich* [i.e., "the Terrible"], *the Young Oprichnik, and the Brave Merchant Kalashnikov* (turned into an opera by Anton Rubinstein in the late seventies).[30] Meanwhile, the sensibilities of the defenders of Official Nationality were affronted. A review by the ultraconservative editor Faddey Bulgarin suggests that the portrait of Ivan III in *Basurman* was a kind of dry run at that of Ivan IV in *The Oprichnik*, and was probably already heavily influenced by the description of the latter in Karamzin's *History*:

---

[27] Nikolai Karamzin, *Istoriya gosudarstva rossiyskogo* [History of the Russian state; henceforth HRS] (St. Petersburg: Izdatel'stvo Yevgeniya Yevdokimova, 1892; reprint, The Hague: Mouton, 1969), vol. 9, pp. 273–74.

[28] Quoted in Alexandra Orlova and Maria Shneerson, "After Pushkin and Karamzin: Researching the Sources for the Libretto of *Boris Godunov*," in MusIM, 251.

[29] Metropolitan Filaret, quoted in J. L. Black, *Nicholas Karamzin and Russian Society in the Nineteenth Century* (Toronto and Buffalo: University of Toronto Press, 1975), p. 148.

[30] S. A. Vengerov, "Ivan Ivanovich Lazhechnikov: Kritiko-biograficheskiy ocherk," in Lazhechnikov, *Polnoye sobraniye sochineniy*, vol. 1 (St. Petersburg, 1899), p. ciii.

Ioann III is depicted in frantic terms, as one who flies into a fury at every word, seizes his nobles by the throat, curses them in the most extreme language, orders them beaten, rounded up, thrown into dungeons, picks fights but is really a coward who fears war, works solely by treachery, through his base courtiers. Shame and disgrace! This is our great Ioann! . . . It's unnatural and revolting. Ivan wasn't like that! . . . *[He] never bragged and never chattered about nonsense, but did his deeds heroically.*[31]

Undeterred, Lazhechnikov immediately embarked upon *The Oprichnik*, attracted particularly by the figure of Ivan the Terrible: "No one can dispute the fact," he boasted at the time of the belated première of the play, "that I was the first to think of putting the gigantic figure of Ivan on the stage."[32] His portrayal this time was so extreme as to provoke the censor, and the play remained unpublished until 1859 and unperformed for eight years more. Though trouble with the censor lends an inevitable glamour, all agree that Lazhechnikov's *Oprichnik* was no masterpiece. It concerns one of the murkiest and least understood phases of Ivan IV's reign, but its virtues are those of the well-made play; it broadened no one's intellectual horizon.

The *oprichnina*, or *oprichina* (from *oprich*, a thing apart), was Ivan's personal domain within Russia, created by decree in 1565 as an administrative entity distinct from the *zemshchina*, or territories belonging, as before, to hereditary landowners. Within the oprichnina, land was held by a special class of "serving people" known as the *oprichniki* (singular, *oprichnik*), sworn to stringent vows of personal loyalty to the tsar (for which reason they are often erroneously described as the tsar's bodyguards), who were assigned special tasks of surveillance over the rest of the population and of "tracking down traitors."[33] The quasi-monastic life of the oprichniki, their dread hound's-head-and-broom insignia, their documented excesses of zeal (or of simple plunder) in carrying out the tsar's program, contain all the makings of lurid melodrama, and Karamzin certainly did not miss his opportunity:

It quickly became apparent that Ivan had sacrificed all Russia to his oprichniki. They were always right in court, on them there could be

---

[31] *Severnaya pchela*, no. 47 (1839), quoted in Vengerov, pp. cv–cvi.

[32] Preface to *The Oprichnik* (St. Petersburg, 1867), quoted in Vengerov, p. cxvi.

[33] Leo Yaresh, "Ivan the Terrible and the *Oprichnina*," in C. E. Black, ed., *Rewriting Russian History* (New York: Frederick Praeger, 1956), p. 226.

CHAPTER 4

neither judgment nor restraint. An oprichnik, or hellhound [*kromesh-nik*]—for so they came to be called, as if they were monsters of hellish darkness—could oppress and plunder his neighbor with impunity. . . . In a word, the people of the *zemshchina*, from courtier to townsman, were disenfranchised, helpless before the oprichnik. The former were prey, the latter predators, and all so that Ivan might count on the zeal of his highwaymen-bodyguards in any new, murderous plan he might think up.[34]

This indignant view of the oprichnina as the instrument not of re-form, whether administrative, political, or social, but of terror in-flicted by a paranoiac sovereign on an innocent populace, was taken over not merely uncritically but enthusiastically by Lazhechnikov as the background to his tragedy. He gave the piece a veneer of histor-ical authenticity by drawing the names of his characters from Ka-ramzin (e.g., the ranking oprichniki Vyazemsky, Basmanov, and Skuratov), by having the oprichniki referred to as "*kromeshniki*," and by citing footnote references to the *History of the Russian State* to jus-tify or document such matters as the abduction of boyar maidens and wives to the tsar's *sloboda*, or retreat,[35] the ubiquity of spies and in-formers, the nature of the oprichnik oath, even the sport of bear wrestling. But despite this apparent diligence, Lazhechnikov really took from Karamzin little more than a hackneyed backdrop. The main plot line is adapted from a familiar stock situation.

It runs as follows: the young boyar Andrey Morozov joins the oprichniki with the object of settling accounts with Prince Zhem-chuzhnïy, who has cheated Andrey and his mother out of their in-heritance, and with whose daughter Natasha he is in love (she, of course, is plighted to another). But when she finds out that he has joined the hated band, Natasha rejects him. In despair, Andrey pe-titions the tsar for release from his vows. Ivan hypocritically assents, with the proviso that Andrey remain an oprichnik until after his wed-ding feast. In the midst of the celebration, the tsar sends word that he wishes Natasha brought to his chambers alone. Andrey forgets his oprichnik discipline and insists upon accompanying his bride against the tsar's orders, which gives Ivan the pretext to have him murdered. Natasha, throwing herself at the fatally wounded Andrey, herself falls accidentally upon a sword and is killed. As for Andrey's mother,

[34] HRS 9.54–55.
[35] This in fact had provided the main plot line for Lermontov's *Merchant Kalashnikov* and Averkiyev's *Sloboda Nevolya*.

she drops dead on the spot upon discovering that her son has joined the oprichniki.

It is obvious that this is no historical drama at all, but a drama of fate after the German romantic model.[36] Historical personages and conditions are merely the tools of the stars in their conspiracy against the pure love of a Russian Romeo and Juliet. The bloody denouement has the same character and significance as in, say, Heine's *William Ratcliff* (operaticized by César Cui)—the inexorable working-out of implacable forces beyond the protagonists' control. The Karamzinian persona of Ivan-as-evil-genius was a convenient Fury and little more. Shown as he is only in domestic surroundings and concerned with trivial affairs, the tsar emerges as a petty sadist, while the oprichniki are reduced to a band of rowdies and roisterers, a medieval motorcycle gang.

All this rendered Lazhechnikov's *Oprichnik* excellently suitable to Chaikovsky's creative strengths and needs. The composer attended the play's first Moscow production, three weeks after the belated première in St. Petersburg in September 1867. He remembered it as a play sufficiently close in setting to Ostrovsky's *The Voyevoda* to accommodate the transfer of music from his unsuccessful first opera. The fact that the historical data in *The Oprichnik* were merely circumstantial and of little specific relevance to the central, "universal" love-fate intrigue was for Chaikovsky not a minus but a plus. In the opera the purely historical element shrank to even less significance than in the play, for reasons both outside the composer's control and very much within it, as he wrote his own libretto.

To begin with, the figure of Ivan himself had to be removed for legal reasons. So his functions were taken over by the oprichnik Vyazemsky (renamed Vyazminsky in the opera, perhaps also in deference to the censor). The latter, not Ivan, administers the oath to Andrey, and this necessitated a further change in the plot. In Lazhechnikov's play Ivan exercises his arbitrary power and grants Andrey the exceptional favor of exemption from the requirement that he renounce all ties with his mother.[37] Vyazminsky could not do this in the opera, and so Andrey must renounce her, which motivates the

---

[36] Chaikovsky well understood this. In his last act Natasha sings of nameless forebodings as prelude to her final duet with Andrey immediately before the tsar's grisly "test," and the composer built the climax of the duet on a theme from his early tone poem *Fatum* (1868).

[37] Act 3, scene 8. Lazhechnikov, *Polnoye sobraniye sochineniy*, vol. 11, p. 352.

maternal curse that replaces Natasha's rejection and forms the climax of the third act. Also absent in the opera were the scenes that showed the oprichniki in action, whether plundering the *zemshchina* (act 2, scenes 1–4) or leading their peculiar monkish life at the tsar's retreat (act 3, scenes 4–5). The latter aspect was summed up operatically in the quasi-religious chorus that prefaces the oath-taking scene (act 2, scene 2), while the former was reduced to a few shouts of "Hoyda, hoyda" in the first and third acts.

Far more interesting were the changes Chaikovsky made out of artistic principle. As is usual in operatic adaptations, the cast of characters was radically scaled down (from thirty-two to eight) and the action was correspondingly streamlined. Chaikovsky succeeded in reducing the plot of his opera to a set of pliant stock elements that could be freely and effectively rebuilt and reordered so as to conform to a very specific, exigent, and, in its day, highly regarded set of dramaturgical conventions epitomized in Eugène Scribe's grand opera libretti. From this point of view, and despite the ridicule *The Oprichnik* continues to elicit even from those most kindly disposed toward the composer, Chaikovsky's adaptation of Lazhechnikov was quite impressively skillful, demonstrating not only his intimate acquaintance with Scribe's structural methods (as embodied at their most mature in *Le Prophète* and *Les Huguenots*), but a decided dramaturgical flair of his own. Everyone quotes Gerald Abraham's bon mot that *The Oprichnik* was "Meyerbeer translated into Russian."[38] But the translation really took place at the precompositional stage, and it is therefore much more interesting than the notorious comment would suggest. Moreover, as the first deliberate and principled attempt to "translate" the most complex and imposing international operatic method of its day into Russian, *The Oprichnik* deserves a far closer, more respectful look than it has yet received.

II

There is not space for a look that is both close and comprehensive, so let us focus entirely on the act that most closely reveals Chaikovsky's operatic methods, the third. It is a classic Scribian act. If the baroque opera is "exit opera," then the French grand opera is just the opposite: "entrance opera." After an opening decorative chorus, a

[38] Gerald Abraham, ed., *The Music of Tchaikovsky* (New York: W. W. Norton, 1946), p. 136.

soliloquy, or both, an act is typically given a steadily mounting tension through a progressive accumulation of characters, each of whose entrances marks an abrupt shift in plot. The crux is musically fixed by a huge ensemble with chorus, the latter now taking on a more active role, often, moreover, divided into various (and oft-times opposing) groups.

In order to achieve this dramaturgical rhythm in his third act, Chaikovsky made quite free with Lazhechnikov's plot. Events from numerous scenes in the original play were telescoped. Some of them bore only a slight resemblance to Lazhechnikov's scenario. Others were contrived for the occasion.

Following a brief, agitated entr'acte (which contains some striking common-tone progressions of the kind made famous by the Coronation scene in *Boris Godunov*), the curtain goes up on a typically Scribian scenic tableau:[39] a quite lengthy choral lament, in which the people of Moscow bewail Russia's "orphanhood" (i.e., the tsar's retreat from Moscow to his abode at Alexandrovo). The opening and closing quatrains of Chaikovsky's text are worth quoting for their ironic contrast with the libretto of *Pskovityanka*, to which we shall presently turn:

Vremena nastali zlïye:	Evil times have come:
Nas pokinul tsar' otets.	Our father tsar has left us
I volkov golodnïkh staya	And a pack of famished wolves
razoryayet nas v konets.	Is bringing us to ruin.
Nas pokinul pastïr' dobrïy	Our good shepherd has left us,
Stado zhalkoye svoyo,	His poor, forsaken flock,
Bed velikikh preispolnil	Horrendous woes have overwhelmed
Nashe gor'koye zhit'yo.	Our bitter existence.

The idea for this chorus came apparently from the speeches of the boyars Fyodorov and Viskovatov in Lazhechnikov's act 3, scene 3.[40] Morozova (Andrey's mother) now enters and soliloquizes an arioso about her loneliness. This material is drawn from Lazhechnikov's act 2, scene 6 (Morozova alone). She is taunted by a little chorus of street

---

[39] For the terminology employed in this description I have depended in part on Karin Pendle, *Eugène Scribe and French Opera of the Nineteenth Century* (Ann Arbor: UMI Research Press, 1979), especially the chapter entitled "The Technique of Grand Opera and the Transformation of Literary Models" (pp. 465–94).

[40] E.g., Viskovatov: "How bitter, how bitter it is for Holy Russia, how like a deserted widow she appears; it seems our Sovereign has forsaken us altogether!" (Lazhechnikov, vol. 11, 333).

urchins (the Boris-like progressions return here, and the resemblance of this scene to that of the taunting of the Holy Fool in *Boris* has often been remarked[41]). The text for this chorus (plus one line for "five basses [who] come out on stage and chase the urchins away") is taken from Lazhechnikov's act 3, scene 1.

The next entrance, and the plot situation it introduces, is Chaikovsky's invention. Natasha, having run away from home, comes rushing onstage and seeks protection from Morozova. This episode may have been tenuously suggested by Andrey's abduction of Natasha in Lazhechnikov, act 4, scene 1. And if so, then we have elements derived so far from three different acts of the original play forged into a new relationship by the requirements of the Scribian ideal.

That ideal further demands that each of the situations engendered by the successive entrances reach its own musical climax before the next ensues. And so Natasha and Morozova have a very extended duet *scena*, which may be broken down into a chain of interrelated but nevertheless discretely rounded and cadenced numbers, forming a definite musical progression as follows:

A. Arioso (Natasha): 172/202[42]

B. Arioso (Morozova), in which the accompaniment continues a fragment of melodic material from A: 174/205 (Recitative phrase: Natasha refuses to return home)

C. Arioso (Morozova): 176/208

D. Arioso (Natasha), derived from the main orchestral theme of B: 178/209

E. Duet, developing and recapitulating D and C: 179/211

The climax, replete with cadenza and ritornello (based on D), is succeeded by an abrupt tremolando on a dominant $\frac{4}{2}$ chord, over which Natasha expresses, in a line of recitative, her fear of her father's pursuit. He arrives on schedule, precipitating a three-way confrontation that has no counterpart at all in Lazhechnikov's drama. In order to give this scene a power greater than that of the duet, Chaikovsky (again according to the recipe of the grand opera) enlists the chorus, who come running out of the surrounding shops and tav-

[41] E.g., David Brown, *Tchaikovsky: The Early Years* (New York: W. W. Norton, 1978), p. 244. Not that there is any question of influence, for the two operas were composed simultaneously and premièred three months apart in 1874.

[42] The first page reference is to the vocal score published by Bessel in 1874; the second is to the standard Soviet edition (P. I. Chaikovsky, *Polnoye sobraniye sochineniy*, vol. 34).

erns, crying, "It's Prince Zhemchuzhnïy!" A dramatic tableau ensues, beginning with an arioso by Natasha in two parts, the first pitting recitativelike phrases in the voice against a continuous melody in the orchestra, and the second transferring the main melody to the voice part for climactic effect (189/219). Natasha's plea is taken up by Morozova, who sings a recitative and arioso of her own, the second part of which is a literal repetition to new words of Natasha's $\frac{12}{8}$ melody, transposed down a third to accommodate Morozova's range.

Zhemchuzhnïy's answering recitative takes place over a patch of "symphonic" modulation in the orchestra, which leads into the leitmotif of the oprichniki, heralding their entrance, and with it the fourth and final increment of dramatic tension. Chaikovsky now presses two choruses into service: the male chorus of oprichniki and the mixed chorus of "the people." They exchange repliques—the oprichniki limiting themselves to a menacing "Hoyda! Hoyda!" while the people, along with the boyar Zhemchuzhnïy, mutter curses— over a little orchestral fantasy combining the oprichnik theme with brass fanfares.

With Morozova's recognition of her son among the oprichniki, this hubbub comes brusquely to an end. The ensuing confrontation is drawn from act 5, scene 2, of Lazhechnikov's drama, where it had resulted, as already mentioned, in Morozova's instant demise. Since Chaikovsky needs Morozova's death for his final curtain, she survives her meeting with Andrey in the opera, pronouncing instead the mother's curse alluded to above. This seems a decided improvement on Lazhechnikov's improbable original, for all that it came about through the exigencies of the censorship, on the one hand, and those of the Scribian finale on the other.

The finale thus initiated represents the grand opera style at its grandest, its most typical and, one is even tempted to say, its best. It demonstrates the kind of close interdependence of stage situation and musical form that the critic Laroche had in mind when he spoke of "understanding the stage in musical terms," and was undeniably one of the chief attractions of the French style to Chaikovsky, Russia's first professionally trained composer and proud of it. The action, having come to a stunning halt with Morozova's recognition of Andrey, now slowly gets under way again, beginning at the lowest level of musical structure: a secco recitative in which Morozova gives vent to her amazement. Thus the composer seeks, as it were, a running start on the elaborate process of musical growth the finale must embody.

Andrey answers his mother with a reassurance of his filial love, set to yet another reprise of the $\frac{12}{8}$ melody first heard (but not by him) in the Natasha-Morozova duet. The oprichniki interrupt him with a stern, fugal reminder of his vows, but Andrey presses on to tell her the whole truth. This leads into an effective number in which Andrey retells his story accompanied by two choruses: the oprichniki continue their warnings while the people cluck their sympathy for Morozova. But she will not be moved. She reiterates her curse in a frenzied *accompagnato*, in which practically the whole gamut of romantic high-passion clichés is pressed into service: chromaticized and "dissonated" variants of the oprichnik leitmotif, enharmonic modulations by rising semitones, and finally the melodramatic harmonic progression that accompanies the utterance of the curse in its fullest form, full of augmented and Neapolitan sixths, unresolved six-fours, and final evasion of the cadence by means of a diminished-seventh chord, as Morozova sinks spent into a dead faint.

At this point the action freezes once again. Morozova's vehement curse, the more fearful for its having been so unexpected, hits all the assembled characters, oprichnik and boyar alike, like a thunderbolt. The simile comes readily to mind, since Chaikovsky's characters react precisely as Glinka's had reacted to the actual thunderbolt that accompanied the heroine's abduction in the first act of *Ruslan and Lyudmila*: they sing a canon. But the similarities go much further than the device itself, so much further as almost to amount to plagiarism: the same slow triple meter, the same dotted rhythms, the same prevalence of short repeated notes in the voice part, even the same insistent pedal on the second beat that represents the characters' transfixed, immobilized state.[43] Again, as in *Ruslan*, the chorus is brought into play at the end of the quartet. But where in Glinka's opera the choral entrance provided nothing more than a coda, in Chaikovsky's it forms a bridge to a new level of musical intensity: the monster *morceau d'ensemble avec choeurs*, a gigantic tableau, huge both in volume and in emotional weight, the crowning moment for which the whole preceding action had been a strategic preparation, an enormous dramaturgical upbeat (250/275). Like all Scribe-engineered musical

---

[43] Compare *The Oprichnik* 258/243 with *Ruslan and Lyudmila* (vocal score, Moscow: Muzïka, 1968), p. 81. Glinka's model, it seems pretty clear, was Rossini's act 1 sextet, "Fredda ed immobile," from *The Barber of Seville*.

climaxes, it takes place in a complete dramatic stasis. Further development of action waits while the mood of agony is fixed and monumentalized at length by the impressive music.

When the mood has run its course, the action is resumed with a recitative by Basmanov over the oprichnik leitmotif. He suggests the only possible way out for Andrey: to plead with the tsar for release. The idea is received enthusiastically by all, producing an instant change in affect and sending the *morceau d'ensemble* on to new heights of volume. All are now in agreement and join voices in one monolithic chordal mass: "To the tsar! To the tsar! He is God's chosen one! He is our lord and master!" (262/286). Chaikovsky works this into a lengthy musical coda, which ends with the exit of all the principals, the chorus meanwhile continuing its celebration in a second coda, tempo vivace, as the curtain falls.

The third act of *The Oprichnik* is a kind of monument to convention. In it, Chaikovsky can be seen as a genuine musical counterpart to Lazhechnikov: a sure-handed, highly professional dramatist who knows how to harness to their maximum effect the theatrical methods of his day. The operatic aesthetic within which he operated regarded the radical transformation of material appropriated from the spoken drama as a foregone conclusion (Meyerbeer: "One does not redo what has already been done perfectly").[44] The musical stage had its own requirements, which differed considerably from those of the spoken stage. And the aesthetic within which Lazhechnikov had operated regarded the radical transformation of historical fact for the sake of theatrical effect as equally to be taken for granted. But by the late 1860s all of these assumptions were being fundamentally questioned by radical artists, along with the view of history Lazhechnikov had accepted as his starting point.

III

Karamzin ended his assessment of Ivan the Terrible with a passage that was to prove extremely suggestive to historians of a later generation:

> But let us give even the tyrant his due: even in the very extremes of evil
> Ivan looms as the specter of a great monarch, zealous, tireless, often

[44] Letter to Dr. Schucht (1852), quoted in William L. Crosten, *French Grand Opera, An Art and a Business* (New York: King's Crown Press, 1948), p. 90.

shrewd in his political activity. Though (despite the fact that he always loved to compare himself with Alexander the Great) he hadn't even the shadow of courage in his soul, he remained a conqueror. In his foreign policy he steadfastly followed the grand designs of his grandfather. He loved the truth in courts of law, not infrequently tried cases himself, heard grievances, read documents and made decisions without intermediaries. He punished oppressors of the people, unscrupulous dignitaries and usurers, both corporally and by shaming them. . . . Ivan showed respect for the Arts and Sciences, showing favor to educated foreigners. He founded no Academy, but promoted the education of the masses through the propagation of church schools, where even laymen learned to read and write, learned Law and even History. . . . Finally, Ivan is celebrated in history as a lawgiver and as a founder of the state.[45]

This last distinction was for historians of a certain stripe sufficient to redeem all the rest, even (or especially) the oprichnina. In the 1850s the influence of German idealism and German historicism began to make itself felt in Russian historiography. The school of historical writing known as "statist" appeared, which took over from Hegel and Schelling the idea that all of history points in the direction of the nation-states of the post-Napoleonic period, and that historical judgments should be made not on the basis of contemporary morality but on the "objective" basis of this teleology. The state was a concept that transcended the personalities and the actions of rulers; any atrocity, any excess could be justified by the historian if it made a positive contribution to overriding historical processes.

Russian historians like Konstantin Kavelin (1818–85) and especially Sergey Solovyov (1820–79) believed in Hegel's concept of the world-historical individual, whose actions, whatever their ostensive immediate motivation, accorded with the demands of progress, that is, the progressive realization of freedom as vouchsafed in the nation-state. "The great man," in the words of Solovyov, "always and everywhere . . . satisfies the needs of the nation in a certain time. . . . The activity of the great man is always the result of all the previous history of the nation."[46] Accordingly, Solovyov "made an attempt to discover some political meaning in the series of events [i.e., those of the years 1565–72], which his fellow-historian [Karamzin] had taken to be nothing but a succession of horrors and acts of insanity."[47]

[45] HRS 9.275–76.
[46] Cited in Black, *Karamzin and Russian Society*, p. 179.
[47] K. Waliszewski, "The *Opritchnina* at the Bar of History," in *Ivan the Terrible*, trans. Lady Mary Loyd (Hamden, Conn.: Archon Books, 1966), p. 263.

This was the first serious challenge to Karamzin's hitherto unassailable historiographical preeminence, and it centered around the figure of Ivan the Terrible. The locus classicus of the "statist" interpretation of Ivan's reign was the sixth volume (1856) of Solovyov's supremely ambitious twenty-nine-volume *History of Russia from the Earliest Times*. This most comprehensive history of Russia ever attempted by a single author was a deliberate attempt to supersede Karamzin. It began coming out in 1851 and continued at the rate of a volume each year up to the author's death, by which time he had reached the year 1774. "Ivan the Terrible has long been an enigmatic figure in our history," wrote Solovyov. "For a long time his character and deeds have been an object of controversy." The reason for the controversy lay in "the immaturity of historical science, the disinclination to give attention to the connection, the causality of phenomena."[48] The founder of the oprichnina emerges as a far-seeing reformer: "The age posed important problems, and at the helm of state stood a man whose character equipped him to move resolutely toward their solution."[49] However great and real the cruelties with which Ivan realized his policies, the struggle with the boyar class was historically determined, inevitable, and hence "progressive."

And what were these policies? Statist historians located them first and foremost in Ivan's lengthy epistles to the renegade boyar Prince Andrey Mikhailovich Kurbsky, who had defamed and reviled him from his Lithuanian sanctuary, and whose treacherous defection is generally considered by modern historians to have been the efficient cause of the drastic administrative measures that led to the institution of the oprichnina. Kurbsky had challenged Ivan's right to rule autocratically. Ivan answered at furious length, defending not only his divine right, but his holy duty to wield his power without division or limit, as had his forebears, who "from the beginning . . . have ruled all their dominions, not the boyars, not the magnates." He bolstered his point with references to Greek and Roman history, showing in a passage that obviously impressed Karamzin that unless they were "under one authority," nations and empires inevitably fell from greatness. And, of course, Ivan cited copiously from the Bible: "Bethink yourself: did God, having led Israel out of captivity, appoint a

---

[48] Sergey Solovyov, *Istoriya Rossii s drevneyshikh vremyon*, vol. 3 (containing the original vols. 5 and 6 [Moscow: K. Soldatenkov]) (Moscow: Izdatel'stvo Moskovskogo Universiteta, 1963), p. 704.
[49] Ibid., p. 707.

priest to command over men, or numerous governors? No, he made Moses alone lord over them, like a Tsar."[50]

Defense of his autocratic power, his assertion of it against the claims of the once-powerful boyars, and his consolidation of it throughout the length and breadth of his domain (which increased greatly in territory during his reign) constituted Ivan's primary domestic policy, and in this he was a profoundly "historical" figure in the eyes of Solovyov. One of his greatest exploits in pursuit of this policy was the ruthless destruction in 1570 of the ancient city of Novgorod, on suspicion of conspiracy with Poland. For this, of course, Ivan was reviled by Karamzin, who bewailed the fate of one of Russia's great political entities, with her remarkable republican traditions (already smashed by Ivan's grandfather Ivan III, "the Great") and her ties to the West through the Hanseatic League. But there can be no question that Ivan's bloody act strengthened the Muscovite state, and so for Solovyov it counted as one of Ivan's typically resolute solutions to the problems of his age.

The new image of Ivan as the forerunner of Peter the Great, as visionary statesman and progressive historical force, quickly found expression in the arts. One thinks, for example, of Antokolsky's famous marble statue (1870), which depicts the tsar seated deep in thought, a commanding figure of strength and determination, but of great intelligence and obvious wisdom as well. The first play to embody the new Ivan was Mey's *Pskovityanka*, composed only three years after Solovyov's third volume had appeared. With Rimsky-Korsakov's adoption of Mey's play for operatic treatment early in 1868 at the suggestion of Balakirev and Musorgsky[51] (and while the play was still under the censor's ban), musicians now entered what was an arena of vital and vigorous intellectual debate.

Pskovityanka was the first attempt in the realm of fiction to "explain" the actions of the Groznïy [terrible, or threatening] Tsar along lines suggested by the new teleological historiography. Mey's Ivan seems to have read both Solovyov and Karamzin. He ponders and juxtaposes his various historiographical images. In one speech the tsar deftly summarizes the popular view of his character and reign

[50] Citations in this paragraph from J.L.I. Fennell, ed. and trans., *The Correspondence between Prince A. M. Kurbsky and Tsar Ivan IV of Russia, 1564–79* (Cambridge: Cambridge University Press, 1955), pp. 26–27, 61, 46–47. Recent scholarly doubts about the authenticity of these letters have no bearing on their significance for nineteenth-century statist historians and dramatists.

[51] R-KMusL, 80.

in terms patently Karamzinian: "A bloodthirsty blackguard, perse-cutor of the boyars and his zealous servants, a torturer, a killer, a monster!"

Gotov ya vsyu ikh pesen'ku propet':
"On, mol, kakoy: chem tol'ko kto praveye,
Tem na sude ego i vinovatey;
Kto zhitiyem, voistinu molchal'nïm
I monastïrskim, gospodu ugoden,
Tot u nego—khanzha i litsemer;
Kto lestyu gnushayetsya—zavistnik,
A kto stoit za pravdu, po prisyage
I tselovan'yu krestnomu—otmyotnik,
Zlokoznennïy izmennik i predatel'! . . .
I vot, mol, on muzhey, toliko doblikh,
Preslavnïkh tsartsva russkogo singklitov,
Vserodno istreblyayet, aki zver',
O nyom zhe nam glasit Apokalipsis . . .
Ni vozrasta, ni pola ne zhaleyet:
Grudnïkh mladentsev, startsev bespomoshchnïkh,
Nevinnïkh dev terzayet lyutoy mukoy
I teshitsya ikh krov'yu, so svoyeyu
Kromeshnoy t'moy, chto satana s besami . . ."[52]

[Word for word I'll sing you their whole song:
"This is how he is: the more you're in the right,
The more guilty in his court will you be judged;
If in your ways you are truly monklike
And humble, worthy of the Lord,
Then as far as he is concerned—you're a fraud and a hypocrite;
If flattery you shun—you're envious;
If you stand by the truth, swear oaths
And kiss the cross—you're a turncoat,
An insidious recreant and traitor! . . .
And look how he treats the mighty men,
Glorious defenders of the Russian realm—
He exterminates them one and all, like a very beast;
It is he of whom the Apocalypse forewarns . . .
He pities neither age nor gender;
Babes in arms, the helpless aged,
Innocent maids he racks with fearsome torture,

[52] *Pskovityanka*, act 5, scene 10, in L. A. Mey, *Dramï* (Moscow: Sovetskiy pisatel', 1961), pp. 194–95.

Amusing himself with their blood, in his
Hellish abyss, like Satan with his troop of devils . . ."]

But in a famous address to his son (modeled obviously on Boris's farewell in Pushkin), which Rimsky-Korsakov was to turn into a monologue, Mey's Ivan gives his reasons:

To tol'ko tsarstvo krepko i veliko,
Gde vedayet narod, chto u nego
Odin vladïka, kak v yedinom stade
Yedinnïy pastïr'. . . Yesli zhe podpaskam
Pastukh dast volyu—pogibai vsyo stado! . . .
Ne to chto volki, sami budut rezat'
Da svalivat' vinu svoyu na psov . . .
Net! tak bï mne upravit'sya khotelos',
Rus' skovat' zakonom, chto broneyu,
Da dast li Bog mne razuma i silï? . . . [53]

[Only that kingdom is strong and great,
Where the people know they have
A single ruler, as in a single flock
There is a single shepherd. . . . Let the shepherd
Grant the herd boys their will—and the whole flock perishes!
Never mind the wolves; they themselves will do the killing
And lay the blame to the dogs . . .
No! I would like to rule so that
Rus' will be bound by law, like armor,
But will God grant me the insight and the strength? . . .]

This direct embodiment of ongoing historiographical controversy made *Pskovityanka* a "thinking man's" play, even if Mey's handling of the tsar struck more than a few as faintly ridiculous. Apollon Grigoryev, for one, could only laugh: "How comical is this Ivan Vasilyevich, discoursing on his theories of government just like Mr. Solovyov, . . . almost a sweet and tenderhearted Ivan Vasilyevich, this."[54] But most found impressive the skill with which the author effected the "organic" integration and interpenetration of historical background and romantic intrigue. Neither the one nor the other can be viewed as superfluous in *Pskovityanka*, and the play therefore seemed to represent a breakthrough to a new level of responsibility and seriousness.

[53] Act 5, scene 1; in ibid., p. 181.
[54] *Sochineniya Ap. Grigor'yeva*, vol. 1 (St. Petersburg, 1876), p. 515.

Mey's plot is cleverly contrived so as to provide an answer to some real historical questions. The drama is set in the year 1570, at the time of the Novgorod campaign. The question was: why, having destroyed Novgorod, did the tsar come with all his retinue of oprichniki to Pskov, the other ancient Russian Hanseatic port, and yet spare it its sister's fate?

In a historical afterword to his drama, which bears the title "Annotations" (*Primechaniya*) in deliberate emulation of the famous documentary appendices Karamzin had provided for each volume of his *History*, Mey himself indicates that this problem was what had initially attracted his attention to this episode as the basis for a play:[55]

> At first glance this unexpected mercy will seem decidedly enigmatic, and Karamzin was unable to explain it in substance, giving himself up rather to farfetched psychological speculations and even mysticism.
>
> According to him, Ivan Vasilyevich visited the hermit monk Nikola Sadlos in the Pechersky Monastery and took fright at the latter's forthright speech.
>
> It was during Lent. Nikola handed the tsar a piece of bloody meat. "I do not eat meat during the fast," objected Ioann. "You do worse than that, Tsar!" answered the hermit, according to Karamzin, "You drink Christian blood!!!"
>
> And the ruler became not angry and he spared the city of Pskov . . .
>
> He pitched camp not far from Pskov on the river, and was awakened that first night by the peal of Pskovan church bells.
>
> "His heart was softened miraculously," once more according to Karamzin, "and . . ."
>
> . . . And Pskov endured longer than Novgorod . . .
>
> But is this so? Is this the reason?
>
> Hardly.[56]

Mey rejects any ascription of superstition to this Machiavellian tsar. Nor does he imagine that Ivan could have been taken in by protestations of fealty or hypocritical displays of bread and salt. "Tsar Ivan IV was above all else a politician," he avers, again echoing Solovyov. And so Mey prefers to believe that Ivan was motivated by concern lest both Russian Hanseatic cities be destroyed, thus cutting the country off from trade with the West (Ivan as proto-Peter, again).

---

[55] Here, too, Mey gives a liberal sampling of extracts from the Kurbsky correspondence to "document" the speeches quoted above.

[56] Mey, *Dramï*, p. 201. Cf. Karamzin, HRS 9.97–98. Solovyov passes over the Pskov episode rather cursorily (*Istoriya*, vol. 3, p. 561).

And that Pskov should have been the one spared Mey ascribes to the fact that Ivan had personal ties there. Pskov had been conquered and ruled by his father, the Great Prince Vasily Ioannovich, son of Ivan III, and Ivan the Terrible had been there in his youth.[57] Acknowledging that not everyone might find this explanation convincing—sentimentality in a sixteenth-century despot seems a mite harder to swallow even than superstition—the author proceeds to fabricate a plot that will motivate his reading of the events of 1570 even as it provides a central romantic intrigue.

The Pskovityanka—maid of Pskov—of the title, the central character of the drama, is an invented, deliberate symbol of the "blood ties" that bind Pskov and Moscow and stay Ivan's hand from carnage. Noting that Ivan had briefly visited Pskov, according to chronicle accounts, in 1555, Mey supposes an affair between the young tsar and the beautiful Pskovan boyarinya Vera Sheloga. Mey christens their fictitious love child Olga—an inevitable, symbolic choice, after the "Cross-receiving Olga" (*Krestopriyimnaya Ol'ga*), the half-legendary wife of the tenth-century Kievan Prince Igor, who, born at Pskov, embraced Christianity long before the general conversion of Russia and became her native city's patron saint.[58] Mey's Olga is brought up by her mother's sister Nadezhda and her husband Prince Yury Tokmakov, who happens to be the tsar's vice-regent in Pskov. The circumstances of her conception and birth are revealed in act 1 of Mey's drama, which takes place in the year 1555.[59]

[57] There is substantial documentation on this point from Pskovan chronicles in Mey's *Primechaniya*, though Karamzin and Solovyov are both silent on the matter.

[58] For more on Olga, see George Vernadsky, *Kievan Russia* (New Haven: Yale University Press, 1948), pp. 32, 38–42. Karamzin ends his account of the sparing of Pskov with these words: "[Nikola Sadlos] so frightened Ivan that he immediately left the city; he spent a few days in his camp nearby; he allowed his soldiers to pillage the estates of the wealthy, but commanded them not to touch the hermits or priests; he took only the monastery treasuries and a few icons, vessels, books, and having as it were involuntarily spared Olga's homeland, he hurried to Moscow, where he might slake his unquenchable thirst for torture with new blood" (HRS 9.98). It seems possible that this passing reference to the sainted Olga gave Mey the first glimmer of the idea whence *Pskovityanka* grew.

[59] In adapting Mey's play, Rimsky-Korsakov opted for the "unities" and dispensed with this act, preferring to reveal its contents as needed in strategically placed narratives. In the first of the two revisions of the opera (1877–78, never performed or published), the act was restored, only to be dropped again from the second revision (1891–92) and refashioned into an independent one-act "musico-dramatic prologue to L. Mey's *Pskovityanka*" in 1898. Another change made in the first revision stands out for its absurdity. Rimsky let Stasov (who was obviously thinking of the St. Basil scene in *Boris*) talk him into reinstating the confrontation between Ivan the Terrible and Nikola Sadlos—the very episode against which the whole of Mey's drama polemicizes!

The rest of the play (and the whole of the opera) concerns the events of 1570. A parallel with Lazhechnikov's *Oprichnik* is immediately suggested by the facile love triangle that motivates the surface action—a stock coherence-insuring device that few constructors of drama out of history could avoid (not even Musorgsky in *Khovanshchina*): Olga has been betrothed to the Pskovan boyar Nikita Matuta, who is old enough to be her father (he *is* the father of her best friend, Styosha). But she loves Mikhailo Tucha, the son of a landlord's overseer. When news of the tsar's imminent arrival with his troops gets out, citizens of Pskov convene a *veche* [republican council],[60] at which an emissary from Novgorod horrifies all with his account of the bloodbath there. In order to escape a similar fate, the council resolves that Ivan shall be met with a show of submission and with petitions for mercy.[61] But Tucha rejects this idea and calls for armed resistance. A band of hotheads joins him and they march off into the woods. Ivan arrives in triumph and is entertained by Tokmakov. He demands refreshment and Tokmakov calls for Olga to give him drink. Seeing her, Ivan recognizes Vera's features and knows that he is looking at his own daughter. It is then that he utters the climactic words "Let the killing cease! There has been too much blood. Make your swords blunt upon a stone: the Lord preserveth Pskov!"[62]

Olga tries to find Tucha to tell him of the tsar's change of heart, but she is waylaid by Matuta and brought before the tsar (it is at this point that he discourses on his historiographical image). While Olga is with Ivan, Tucha and his band mount an attack. The tsar orders that Tucha's life be spared for Olga's sake, but his soldiers fire indis-

---

For detailed information on the various versions of Rimsky-Korsakov's opera (only the first of which will henceforth concern us), see Gerald Abraham, "*Pskovityanka*: The Original Version of Rimsky-Korsakov's First Opera," *Musical Quarterly* 54 (1968): 58–73.

[60] This was an anachronistic touch. Vasily Ioannovich, Ivan the Terrible's father, had put an end to Pskovan republicanism, and the last *veche* had taken place in 1507. It was also a forbidden touch, and was one of the factors that caused the censor's ban on Mey's play. In Rimsky's opera, although he makes striking musical use of the famous Pskovan *veche* bell (another anachronism: it had been carried off by Vasily's father, Ivan the Terrible's grandfather, Ivan III), he never uses the word *veche*, replacing it at the censor's behest by the neutral *skhodka*, or "meeting."

[61] This much is faithful to Karamzin: "Coming into the city [Ivan] with astonishment saw that on all the streets, before each house, tables had been set out with viands (following the advice of Prince Yury Tokmakov). The citizens, their wives and children, all holding bread and salt, bent their knees to the tsar, blessed him, greeted him, and said, "Great Sovereign Prince! We, your faithful subjects, with zeal and with love do offer you our bread and salt; do with us and with our lives as you will, for all that we have, and we ourselves, are yours, great monarch!" (HRS 9.97).

[62] Mey, *Dramï*, p. 179.

criminately at the rebels and kill them all. When Olga learns that her beloved is dead, she picks up Ivan's own knife and stabs herself. The tsar sends for his physician (the Dutchman Bomelius), but he can do nothing for her, and utters the drama's curtain line: "Sovereign! Only the Lord can raise the dead!"[63] Olga dies in her father-tsar's arms.[64]

The symbolism is pretty thick, but it is effective. Olga's tragic situation—torn between the tsar, her father, toward whom she feels a strange and inexplicable attraction, and her lover, Tucha, the leader of the abortive insurrection—is the predicament of Pskov itself, torn between its independent republican traditions and the historical necessity of submission to Moscow. Olga's death, while melodramatic, epitomizes the historical moment. Not merely a historical drama, *Pskovityanka* is a drama about history—history conceptualized in the light of Solovyov's Hegelian historiography.

IV

It was already a measure of kuchkist idealism that the youngest member of Balakirev's circle should have chosen to turn into an opera a play that was under the censor's ban. The problem was compounded by an imperial decree of 1837, which stipulated that while Russian rulers antedating the house of Romanov could appear on the dramatic stage, they could not appear in opera. When Rimsky inquired at the Censorship Bureau as to the reason for this, he was told, "And suppose the tsar should suddenly sing a ditty? Well, it would be unseemly."[65]

But of course there was no danger of that in a kuchkist opera, as Rimsky and Musorgsky hastened to assure the censor in charge of the case, a certain Fridberg, who in any case was mainly intent upon toning down the republican trappings of the *veche* scene.[66] Rimsky

[63] Ibid., p. 198.
[64] In the opera the ending is somewhat modified. Instead of killing herself onstage, Olga rushes out to Tucha and is caught in the gunfire. She is then carried onstage dead.
[65] R-KMusL, 125.
[66] Ironically enough, a "ditty" for the tsar was added much later at Chaliapin's request, for performances of the third (i.e., standard) version of *Pskovityanka* by Mamontov's Private Opera. See the singer's autobiography, *Maska i dusha* (Fyodor Ivanovich Chaliapin, *Literaturnoye nasledstvo*, vol. 1 [Moscow: Iskusstvo, 1957], p. 300). It was never performed, even by Chaliapin, but it can be found in an appendix to the Muzgiz (the Soviet state music publishers) vocal score of the third version (Moscow, 1967).

secured permission for staging his opera by appealing to the tsar's brother, the Grand Duke Konstantin, for special dispensation.[67] But Fridberg himself had been impressed by the seriousness of Rimsky's opera and in his report (7 January 1872) urged that "high-level permission" be secured to circumvent the Nikolaian decree. "This would serve," he wrote in his pompous bureaucratic way, "to encourage young, talented creators (among whom Mr. Rimsky-Korsakov should be counted), to whose lot it falls to vouchsafe the existence of Russian opera, which has just begun to take on an independent character, thanks to the exemplary and typical works of Glinka, Dargomïzhsky, Serov, and others."[68]

Rimsky-Korsakov's *Pskovityanka* is as fully committed to a new conception of operatic dramaturgy as Chaikovsky's *Oprichnik* is to an old one. Whereas the Moscow professional viewed opera as an art form with its own peculiar and immutable laws, the St. Petersburg naval cadet was at the time completely under the sway of a realist canon that sought in the name of "truth" to compromise the canons of the spoken theater as little as possible. The outstanding artifact of that tendency was Dargomïzhsky's *Stone Guest*, which was in progress when Rimsky embarked on *Pskovityanka* in 1868, and which he himself was shortly to orchestrate upon Dargomïzhsky's death early the next year.

Accordingly, although Rimsky started out with a conventional libretto after Mey's play by the novelist Vsevolod Krestovsky (1840–95) in hand,[69] he quickly forsook it and worked directly from Mey's text, subjecting it for the most part only to a radical condensation both in length and in the number of characters (from forty-one to eleven), plus interpolating a few genre numbers for the chorus.[70] The

[67] R-KMusL, 126.

[68] A. A. Orlova and V. N. Rimsky-Korsakov, *Stranitsï zhizni N. A. Rimskogo-Korsakova*, vol. 2 (Leningrad: Muzïka, 1971), pp. 68–69. The censor cites three specific precedents for the lifting of the ban, and a curious assortment they are: Serov's *Rogneda*, which includes the Kievan prince Vladimir the Great among its dramatis personae; Rubinstein's *The Battle at Kulikovo* (*Dmitry Donskoy*); and (of all things) Glinka's *Ruslan*, with its purely fictitious Kievan prince, Svetozar.

[69] It had originally been prepared for Anton Rubinstein, and Chaikovsky seems to have had something to do with procuring it for Rimsky. See GozROTIII, 48n, and Abraham, "*Pskovityanka*," p. 58. Rimsky probably got the idea of transferring the action of act 1 to a later narrative from Krestovsky, who had had Vera Sheloga appear in act 4 as a nun who tells her whole story in a lengthy monologue.

[70] These were the songs sung by the maidens to entertain the tsar in the third act, for which the texts were composed (after models in Krestovsky) by none other than

role of Ivan the Terrible was the most "realistically" conceived one in the opera.[71] The scenes in which he appears are the ones in which the words are most closely based on the original text of Mey's drama, and Rimsky's opera comes closest to the ideal of the Dargomïzhskian "play set to music." The role is cast throughout in what Cui liked in his reviews to call "melodic recitative" (no ditties for the tsar!), usually played off against the leitmotif that follows Ivan wherever he goes, and which in fact had been adumbrating him for two whole acts before his first appearance on stage. This theme, which resembles the opening tune of the familiar Russian Easter Overture (and which is thought by some therefore to be, like it, a derivation from authentic Russian ecclesiastical—i.e., *znamennïy*—chant[72]), is actually sung—once only—by Ivan upon his first entrance, but thereafter is predominantly an orchestral theme, against which Ivan usually sings a counterpoint of naturalistic declamation.[73] At climactic moments, Ivan is apt to join his voice to the notes of his leitmotif, but to seemingly random ones that emphasize odd intervals and preclude any

---

Musorgsky, who hailed from the Pskov region (see MusLN 2.211–21, where documentation, texts, and settings are all given), and the tableaulike concluding chorus, for which both idea and text came from Vladimir Nikolsky, the Lyceum professor and adviser to the kuchka on the matter of historical opera. Nikolsky also wrote the text of the first scene of Rimsky's act 4, which portrays Olga's abduction by Matuta and the attempted capture of Tucha, events only narrated (by Matuta) in Mey's act 5.

[71] Except, that is, for the minor role of Matuta, who in the scene mentioned in n. 70 (one of the earliest to be composed) has music that for studied ugliness can be compared only with Musorgsky's *Marriage*, composed at exactly the same time. An evident embarrassment to the mature Rimsky-Korsakov, the whole scene was eliminated from later versions of the opera.

[72] E.g., Alexey Kandinsky, *Problema narodnosti v opernom tvorchestve N. A. Rimskogo-Korsakova 60–70-kh godov* (Moscow: Moskovskaya ordena Lenina Gosudarstvennaya Konservatoriya im. P. I. Chaikovskogo, 1956), p. 4.

[73] Even the one time it *is* sung, the peculiarities of the prosody show that the theme was not conceived in connection with the words, but is functioning as what in another context ("Tone, Style, and Form in Prokofiev's Soviet Operas: Some Preliminary Observations") I have called a "melodic mold." By this technique an abstractly conceived melodic idea is made to accommodate an infinite variety of naturalistically declaimed texts, and could therefore lend a higher level of musical organization and coherence to a "play set to music." The device is very thoroughly exploited in *Pskovityanka*, in which many scenes set in naturalistic declamation are tied together with a melodic thread—often of folklike character and in at least one instance a genuine folk song—that runs throughout in the orchestra. The scene that cites the actual folk song is the very first one in the opera, where the exchange between the two nannies is accompanied by the folk song *Ne son moyu golovushko klonit* [It is not sleepiness that makes me hang my head], which Rimsky-Korsakov had collected himself, and would publish in his anthology of 1876.

THE PRESENT IN THE PAST

hint of lyricism. The classic example is the third-act curtain, corresponding to the end of Mey's fourth act (Example 1, p. 154).[74]

Now the whole purpose of "realistic" declamation was that it enabled the composer to follow faithfully the smallest nuances of feeling. It was a kind of Camerata-like aesthetic, its object being the exploration and elucidation of character. And that is what made Mey's Solovyovesque Ivan an inviting personage for a kuchkist musicalization. He had many dimensions, and his portrayal by the dramatist had been eminently "psychological." Ivan's act 5 disquisitions on statecraft and on historiography were taken very seriously by Rimsky-Korsakov, and however stringently he otherwise condensed and streamlined the action of the play, these passages he preserved and prominently displayed. The opening of the last scene in the opera shows Ivan sitting alone, pondering the events that had befallen him in Pskov. The text, after a short expository preface presumably of the composer's devising, is a condensation of Mey's scene (act 1, scene 1) in which Ivan discusses kingship and statehood with his two closest and dearest, Boris Godunov and the Tsarevich Ioann, Mey further specifying the presence of the scribe Elizar Vïlïzgin (who reads to the tsar from scripture) and a guard of oprichniki crisscrossing the gate at the rear of the set. All these characters are eliminated in the opera, the tsar himself taking whatever lines Rimsky chose to retain from their parts (including the passages from scripture). The passage on statecraft quoted above is set in typical "melodic mold" technique (Example 2, p. 156). The mood evoked is as un-Karamzinian as can be imagined: contemplative, rational, moderate, and full of quiet lyricism suggesting a heart at peace. Though Rimsky's Ivan has often been compared with Musorgsky's Boris, the character that comes first to mind here is Pimen.

Even more Musorgskian is the tsar's "historiographical" monologue as set by Rimsky later in the same scene, when Ivan is trying to put Olga at her ease. "I can sing you their whole song," the passage begins, and Rimsky set it as an ironic little *pesenka*, or ditty whose passages *all'unisono* and whose noncadences on tritones over strangely voiced French sixths will bring to mind many of Musorg-

---

[74] Feality to Dargomïzhsky is proclaimed especially loudly at this moment in the opera: the curtain line is followed by an orchestral postlude based on a whole-tone transformation of Ivan's leitmotif, which practically plagiarizes the music of the Statue's entrance in the last scene of *The Stone Guest*.

EXAMPLE 1. *Pskovityanka*, act 3, scene 4, conclusion (Nicolai Rimsky-Korsakov, *Polnoye sobraniye sochineniy*, vol. 29a [Moscow: Muzïka, 1965]), pp. 212–13

EXAMPLE 1, *continued*

Let the killing stop! There has been too much bloodshed . . . Let us make our swords blunt
against the stones, for the Lord preserveth Pskov!

sky's realistic songs of the sixties, perhaps *Kozyol* [The billy goat,
1867] above all. When Ivan sings *Vot on, mol, kakoy!* [That's what he's
like!], one's inner ear resonates with Musorgsky's *Sushchiy chort!*
[The very devil!]—and so, one is tempted to think, had Rimsky's
(Example 3, p. 158).

Rimsky bent so far over backward to cast Ivan in a new, rounded,
humane, and unbloodthirsty light that even in the opinion of his
kuchkist confrères the role was somewhat vitiated. Borodin, for example, found it "cold."[75] For Cui, the best characterization was that
of Matuta, the very one that so embarrassed Rimsky later that he
removed it bodily from the opera. As for Ivan, though Cui praised
the role's "sharp, strong, somber" features, he sternly criticized the
handling of the voice in dramatic scenes.[76]

Sure enough, when Rimsky revised the opera, the role he changed
the most was Ivan's: the range was broadened, the tessitura significantly raised, the durations increased, the whole effect inflated. It
was not dissimilar to the change the title character's monologue underwent when Musorgsky rewrote the Terem scene in *Boris Godunov*
and it had a similar motivation, to cast the character into greater relief. But while the changes certainly do show a far more practiced
hand and a far surer gauging of effect, it is only hindsight that judges
the original to have been mere "throwaway recitative."[77] What was
really thrown away was the Karamzinian stereotype. Rimsky's original Ivan was a more faithful counterpart to Mey's than the more the-
atrically effective character familiar to this day on the Russian oper-

[75] BorP 1.310. Borodin claims to be concurring with Stasov's opinion.
[76] CuiIS, 215.
[77] Abraham, "*Pskovityanka*," p. 69.

EXAMPLE 2. *Pskovityanka*, act 4, scene 5, pp. 248–49

EXAMPLE 2, *continued*

mu - drïm, chto bro - ne - yu.   Da dast li bog mne ra - zu - ma i si - li?

Only that kingdom is solid and strong, where the people know they have one ruler, as in a single flock there is a single shepherd. I would like to have it so that Rus is bound in wise laws as in a coat of armor. But will God give me the insight and the strength?

atic stage. Ivan was not meant to dominate the opera, as (particularly thanks to the example of Chaliapin) he now does.[78]

V

Who, if not Ivan, did dominate the original version? It was the chorus, and this was the most radical (and characteristic) stroke of all. Without exception reviewers in 1873 singled out the act 2 *veche* as the most successful and significant scene in the opera. Critics of the original play had also singled this scene out, and the censor had obliquely concurred by making it the chief obstacle to the play's production. It was just the kind of scene to capture the imagination of Slavophiles and *pochvenniki*. As Grigoryev put it in 1861,

> The Pskovan *veche* looms heavily over the whole of *Pskovityanka*, and, in the breadth of its conception, its profound attainment of Russian national spirit, its artistic serenity combined with true dramatic content, it crushes before it everything in our contemporary drama except, of course, the plays of Ostrovsky.[79]

The censor, on the other hand, considered that the scene's inflammatory potential outweighed its artistic merits:

[78] When *Pskovityanka* was presented to Paris by Diaghilev in 1909 as a Chaliapin vehicle, the title was actually changed to *Ivan le Terrible* to strengthen the parallel with the wildly successful production of *Boris Godunov* the previous year.

[79] Quoted in GozROTIII, 46.

EXAMPLE 3a. *Pskovityanka*, act 4, scene 7, p. 266

Go - tov ot slo-va i do slo-va ya

vsyu ikh pe - sen - ku pro - pet'! Vot on, mol, ka-koy!

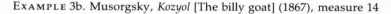

I can sing their whole song through, word for word! This is what he's like!

EXAMPLE 3b. Musorgsky, *Kozyol* [The billy goat] (1867), measure 14

su - shchiy chort!____

The *veche* constitutes the focal point of the struggle between Pskovan autonomy, in particular the Pskovan *vol'nitsa* [rebels], and Muscovite sovereignty, the lawful power. . . . The youthful faction at the meeting instigates an actual secession from the lawful power of the Muscovite state, leaving in scorn those who remain submissive, loyal to the tsar. . . . All this can hardly make a seemly impression on the mass of spectators.[80]

That the censor's fears were not groundless is indirectly confirmed by Rimsky-Korsakov's recollection of his opera's reception, which strikingly parallels Stasov's report of the reception of Musorgsky's Kromy scene. The *vol'nitsa*, according to Rimsky, "struck the fancy of the young students, who could be heard bawling the mutineers' song to their hearts' content up and down the corridors of the [Medical] Academy."[81]

Indeed, thanks in part to the music, the *veche* is even more the focal point of the opera than it was of the play. It was a heaven-sent opportunity for the broad choral dramaturgy so highly valued in kuchkist theory, the one ingredient missing from the Dargomïzhskian operatic recipe. Rimsky's *veche* was the most specifically kuchkist music yet written for public consumption, and, after Serov's Shrovetide carnival in *The Power of the Fiend*, it was the most ambitious choral scene in Russian opera (excepting the static epilogue to *A Life for the Tsar*). But where Serov's choral scene had concerned itself chiefly with setting a genre background to the action, Rimsky's *was* the action at the point at which it occurred. The *veche* embodied the crux of the opera's dramatic conflict and projected it on a heroic scale. It attempted an unprecedented and specifically kuchkist solution to the problem of actively integrating the chorus into the unfolding drama, along lines called for in numerous articles by Cui and, perhaps even more to the point, one by Rimsky-Korsakov himself.

Early in 1869, Cui called on Rimsky to pinch-hit for him twice as music reviewer for the *Sanktpeterburgskiye vedomosti*. Once was for the première of his own *William Ratcliff*. The other occasion was the première of the opera *Nizhegorodtsï* [Men of Nizhny Novgorod], a historical opera on a subject dealing with the end of the Time of Troubles, that is, the Muscovite uprising against the Poles under Minin and Pozharsky. The composer was Eduard Nápravník, who had just been engaged as chief conductor at the Mariyinsky Theater, and who was slated shortly to direct the première of Cui's opera. The young, ide-

---

[80] Ibid., p. 47.

[81] R-KMusL, 113. Compare Stasov: "More than once a crowd of young people would break into song at night on the street, approaching the Liteynïy Bridge on the way to the Vïborg side, taking up the chorus of 'glorification of the boyar by the people' and other choruses" (StasIS 2.202).

alistic Rimsky's review of *Nizhegorodtsï* had for him the consequence that Cui had sought to avoid: it soured relations between Rimsky and the conductor for life.

The review appeared on 3 January 1869 over the initial "N." and treated Nápravník's work as an object lesson in how historical operas were not to be composed. Special attention was accorded the treatment of the chorus. The libretto by Pyotr Kalashnikov, an operatic translator employed by the theater (he would later compose the fourth act of *The Power of the Fiend* for Serov), provided magnificent opportunities in its "scenes of popular agitation" in the third and fourth acts. The effect of these scenes, in which the composer had sought to give the chorus an enormous active role, was vitiated first, in the reviewer's opinion, by the "monolithic" treatment of the choral mass, and second, by the excessive respect Nápravník had shown "the routine forms of old." "How often," exclaims Rimsky-Korsakov, "do all these procedures work not only against sense but even against effect!" He gives one rather extreme example:

> Minin, exhorting the people, proposes that they sell their property to raise funds:
>
> "We must mortgage our wives, our children,
> But we will ransom our beloved country!
> Will you do it?"
>
> he asks; but the people wait in silence for the orchestral coda. The orchestra sounds the final E♭, and only then does the chorus shout, "We will!"[82]

In fairness to Nápravník it should be pointed out that the young critic exaggerated the point, both as to text and as to music. (He even had the key wrong.) Example 4 (p. 162) gives the spot in question as it appears in the vocal score. Similarly exaggerated, but very revealing, is Rimsky-Korsakov's more general critique of the unhealthy influence of conventional libretto construction upon musical dramaturgy. Here the target is not just the poor scapegoat at hand but a whole dramaturgical procedure and strategy so notably embodied, as we have seen, in the third act of the as-yet-unwritten *Oprichnik*:

> Formal duets, trios, quartets, choruses, all with thoroughly defined endings, often thoroughly contrary to common sense, linked by the in-

[82] This and all preceding quotations from Rimsky's review in Nikolai Rimsky-Korsakov, *Polnoye sobraniye sochineniy*, vol. 2 (Moscow: Muzgiz, 1963), p. 15.

sertion of recitatives—that is the format in which most of the operas that exist in the world are written. The text of each number is itself written in such a way as to allow the music to achieve the most uncomplicated "symphonic" form. From this proceed those numberless and senseless repetitions of lines and individual words. From this proceeds the librettist's striving to write such a text that several characters might sing it at the same time, with only the pronouns changed. "How I love you!" sings she. "How you love me!" exclaims he at the same time. "How she loves him!" accompanies the chorus. All operas, unfortunately, are full of such absurdities. Sometimes, because of the dictates of the action, the librettist cannot invent a text with the needed repetitions of lines, but the composer does not despair and forces the text into a routine symphonic frame anyway. From this proceeds the common situation where two completely different texts are sung to the same music. Many similar incongruities were decreed by entrenched routine, but the public listened and enjoyed itself because it had no wish to see in opera anything but a concert in costume. But in the course of time even tastes change. By now it has become impossible to write operas in such forms. We now demand a fully rational text and the total solidarity of text and music. If one gives every number in an opera a discrete, rounded, and uncomplicated symphonic form, with symmetrical layout of sections and repetitions, this goal cannot be achieved.[83]

So here is the crux of the complaint against Nápravník's choral scenes: they are too orderly. In Example 4, both Minin's exhortations and the choral responses are cast in eight- and sixteen-bar periods, and they are almost invariably separated by full cadences. Protagonist and chorus practically never overlap or sing simultaneously, except in large, formal, perorative ensembles. Not only that, but choral responses are often parallel-period repetitions of the soloist's phrases. The one exception, which Rimsky-Korsakov calls the "single dramatic moment in all of Mr. Nápravník's music," comes where the composer invokes old *loi des contrastes* and pits two choruses against each other. The "people" stand on the town ramparts and listen to the offstage choir that accompanies the wedding ceremony of two of the opera's protagonists. The quick *parlando* commentary of the onstage chorus in juxtaposition with the measured *falsobordone* of the offstage group is effectively handled (Example 5, p. 164). Even this is ultimately an orderly affair, though, and Rimsky finds further

[83] Ibid., pp. 14–15.

EXAMPLE 4. Eduard Nápravník, *Nizhegorodtsï* (1868), act 3, scene with chorus, no. 19 (Moscow: Jurgenson, 1884), pp. 188–89

EXAMPLE 4, *continued*

EXAMPLE 5. *Nizhegorodtsï*, act 3, prayer, pp. 236–37

Example 5, *continued*

cause for complaint in the style of the church choir's anachronistically Bortnyanskian music. He praises the orchestration, calling special attention to the "exquisite effect of the woodwinds playing in imitation of the organ, while the gong is struck pianissimo." But he is quick to turn praise to blame even here, noting that such an effect has "little to do with Russian church singing," which is never accompanied.[84]

How ironic, then, that Rimsky began his *veche* scene with a comparable anachronism—the famous *veche* bell, which had been carried off from Pskov by Ivan III some sixty years before the time of *Pskovityanka*'s action. But this was an anachronism of the right tendency according to the tacit kuchkist double standard, that is, backward rather than forward in time. It imparted a greater aura of antiquity and of national character—of "authenticity," in short—than scrupulous historical accuracy might have achieved.

From the very beginning of the scene, Rimsky's efforts are bent at destroying orderliness and symmetry. The chorus enters gradually in response to the tolling bell. A spirit of confusion is created by dividing the singers into five groups who converse among themselves with mounting intensity until all five are singing (shouting) at once to different words:

BASS I: Who has summoned the *veche*?

TENOR I: A messenger from Novgorod.

BASS I: Well, this can bode us no good!

SOPRANO AND ALTO: A *veche* has been called, but no word as yet why.

TENOR I: Well, let the messenger tell us: let him have his word with Pskov.

SOPRANO AND ALTO: And here come the boyars with the generals and judges.

TENOR I: Let him speak! What are we waiting for?

BASS I: No, my lords! Let's observe the forms and protocols: let the good people all gather first.

BASS II: By the old peaceful ways!

SOPRANO AND ALTO: And the deacons, and the scribes, and the prince–vice-regent himself has deigned to come.

TENOR I: A *veche* has been called, but no word as yet why. Let him speak!

TENOR II: Really, fellows! Let him speak! What are we waiting for?

[84] Ibid., p. 16.

BASS I: The prince–vice-regent must come.

BASS II: No, that's no way! My lords of Pskov, judge: Shall there be a *veche*, or is there no need for one?[85]

In answer to this last question from the second basses, the whole chorus comes together for the first time: "Yes! Yes! Let there be a *veche*, according to the will of all Pskov!" This cry is set to the first of five homorhythmic choral themes that recur for most of the full-chorus utterances. They bind the scene musically, doing multiple textual duty. What never changes is their affective content. This first motive (theme A), for example, is used consistently for assertions of popular will (Example 6, p. 168). In its other appearances, it takes words like "Ring for the *veche*!" and "Let Tucha have a word!"

The other recurrent choral motives are shown in Example 7 (pp. 169–70). They are handled freely, reappearing in many keys and with many modifications in texture, tempo, and harmony. Extended choral passages are often constructed mosaic-fashion out of these elements. The longest one (vocal score [Rimsky-Korsakov, *Polnoye sobraniye sochineniy*, vol. 29A (Moscow: Muzïka, 1966)], pp. 118–25), for example, is built on the succession C–B–D–A. Even in these full-chorus passages, the choral mass is often divided against itself, bristling with dissension and dramatic conflict, as far as possible from the conventional "monolithic" chorus upon which the kuchka so loved to heap scorn. Thus, in the passage just mentioned, the first tenors and first basses, who later will form the core of Tucha's *vol'nitsa*, cut through the texture of the rest of the chorus with cries to give Tucha the floor (Example 8, pp. 172–75). In an even more striking passage, the basses actually attempt to shout the rest of the chorus down (Example 9, pp. 176–77).

But extended passages for the full chorus are only a part of the chorus's role in the *veche*. Just as characteristic is the realistic breakup of the chorus into its component sections, who react and interact freely among themselves and with the soloists. One example of this is the muttered exclamations of groups of choristers at the fearful tale of Yushko, the Novgorod messenger (Example 10, pp. 178–79). Another is the dialogue between Tucha and the crowd, where the choral repliques are written in a recitative style indistinguishable from Tucha's own (Example 11, pp. 180–81). Cadences rarely separate the

---

[85] In this extract the words changed by the censor are reinstated, following the latest vocal score (Moscow: Muzgiz, 1965).

EXAMPLE 6. *Pskovityanka*, act 2 (the *veche*), choral theme A, pp. 97–99 (vocal parts only)

Let there be a veche! It is the will of all Pskov!

EXAMPLE 7a. The *veche*, Theme B, p. 105 (vocal parts only)

What? Have the walls come down? Have the locks become rusty?

EXAMPLE 7b. The *veche*, Theme C, p. 106 (soprano, alto, tenor)

For our native Pskov, for our veche, for the sake of old times!

EXAMPLE 7c. The *veche*, Theme D, p. 107 (vocal parts only)

If it comes to that we will don our shields, lads. Stand by great Pskov!

EXAMPLE 7d. The *veche*, Theme E, p. 112 (sopranos only)

Lord Prince, by thy well-being our Pskov endures.

utterances of the full chorus and the soloists. The composer dovetails their passages so that they are continually breaking in on one another, maintaining at once a high dramatic tension and a seamless, asymmetrical continuity (Example 12, pp. 182–85).

The end of the scene—the secession of Tucha and the *vol'nitsa*—is the most strikingly novel of all. Having announced his intention to resist Ivan the Terrible, and having gathered to his side the first tenors and first basses, Tucha breaks into a mocking "farewell song," for which purpose Rimsky-Korsakov appropriated a folk song from Balakirev's recently published anthology (no. 30, *Kak pod lesom, pod lesochkom*). Tucha takes the part of *zapevala* [precentor] and the *vol'nitsa* enters on the refrain, maintaining not only the tune but also the harmony as notated by Balakirev in the field. Against this the composer pits the anguished protests of Tokmakov in recitative style, along with similar ejaculations from the rest of the chorus, while the orchestra sounds the *veche* bell and reminiscences of the melody to which Tucha had previously sung his call to arms. The resulting combination of almost unretouched folk song, choral recitative, and mimetic orchestral effect makes for a texture that is the very epitome of kuchkist ideals, and the group's tribunes heralded it with encomium upon encomium. The normally tight-lipped Cui, for example, proclaimed:

> You forget that before you is a stage, and on it choristers performing a more or less skillfully constructed crowd scene. Before you is reality, the living people, and all of it accompanied by matchless, meaty music from beginning to end. A crowd scene like this has never appeared in any existing opera. Even if everything else in *Pskovityanka* had been completely worthless, this *veche* scene alone would have been enough to give the opera significance in the history of art and a prominent place among the most remarkable of operas, and its author a place among the best operatic composers.[86]

What prompted this remarkable musico-dramatic concatenation, it is worth reemphasizing, was Mey's original text, unmediated by any librettist and handled with a literalness that was unheralded in historical opera. Like Ostrovsky,[87] Mey himself had realized the theatrical potency of folk songs and had thought up the idea of having the

[86] CuiIS, 221.
[87] See TarODR, 144–47.

EXAMPLE 8. The *veche*, pp. 119–20

mutineers march off to the strains of one. He had even directed that Tucha produce a balalaika to accompany it.

After the mutineers have marched off, Rimsky appends a little epilogue for the portion of the chorus remaining on stage. It has no analogue in the original drama: "Thy end is coming, great Pskov! Heavy is the hand of the Groznïy Tsar!" This little passage would hardly merit special notice except that it prefigures the larger choral epilogue that brings the whole opera to an end. That epilogue-conclusion, which has been pointed to with a certain wry admiration as "the most 'ineffective' end of any opera in existence,"[88] sits oddly

[88] Abraham, "*Pskovityanka*," p. 70.

EXAMPLE 8, *continued*

with the rest of the work. It was suggested, and its text composed, by Vladimir Nikolsky (who suggested something very similar to Musorgsky: the *yuródivïy*, or Holy Fool at the end of the Kromy scene), and though it is modest in length, it has an effect similar to that of the choral epilogue to *A Life for the Tsar*.[89] After all the action of the opera has been completed, and Ivan the Terrible is grieving over Olga's corpse, Rimsky-Korsakov brings the chorus onstage (rather improbably, that is, into Ivan's inner sanctum), to sing a lament (in an authentic folk meter) that spells out the equation of Olga's fate and Pskov's, the symbolic underpinning of the whole foregoing drama:

[89] It was, inevitably, grossly inflated in the third (standard) version of the opera.

EXAMPLE 8, *continued*

Lyudi pskovskiye pravoslavnïye,
Sovershilas' volya bozhiya.
Za svoy rodnïy Pskov, za liubov' svoyu
Otdala tï zhizn', krasu, molodost'.
Lyudi russkiye, lyudi pskovskiye!
Pozabudemte raspryu staruyu
A pomolimtes' o dushe yeyo.
Da prostit ey gospod' grekhi yeyo,
Bozh'ey milosti net kontsa vo vek.

[Orthodox people of Pskov,
God's will is done.
For thy cherished Pskov and for thy love

EXAMPLE 8, *continued*

*Chorus (Theme C): Come milords, let us meet him in peace! We have made no seditious
    alliances! Why should Ivan Vasilievich turn in anger against Pskov?*
Bass I: But we would have it differently!
Tenor I: Hey there, Mikhailo Andreich, thou overseer's son!

> Hast thou laid down thy life, thy beauty, thy youth.
> People of Russia, people of Pskov!
> Let us forget our ancient strife
> And pray for her soul.
> May the Lord forgive her her sins,
> For God's mercy is everlasting.]

Like the *yuródivïy*'s lament on the battlefield, this curiously impersonal little choral sermon on the theme of reconciliation is the mu-

EXAMPLE 9. The *veche*, p. 132

sico-dramatic equivalent of the historian's *primechaniye*. It is a perfect encapsulation of the "statist" view of the events of 1570 in Novgorod and Pskov. The triumph of the tsar's absolute power, though purchased at a painful price, was inevitable and just. It was the working-out of historical necessity. It was God's will.

VI

Among the most fervent admirers of Rimsky's achievement in the *veche* scene was a close friend and fellow kuchkist, who for a short but significant time was also his roommate and hence knew the scene earlier and better than anyone else. On 18 June 1870, Musorgsky

EXAMPLE 9, *continued*

*Soprano, alto, tenor (Theme C): For our great Pskov, for our native Pskov, for the sake of
old times!*
Basses: Not so fast! Quiet! Wait! Quiet! Quiet! Wait, I say!

wrote to the Purgold sisters: "Before [Rimsky-Korsakov's] departure
from Petrograd I went to see him and experienced something extraordinary. This something is none other than a milestone in Korsinka's
talent. He has realized the dramatic essence of musical drama. He,
that is, Korsinka, has concocted some magnificent history with the
choruses in the *veche*—just as it should be: I actually burst out laughing with delight."[90]

Indeed, it took another composer facing the same problems to re-

[90] MusLN 1.110.

EXAMPLE 10. The *veche*, pp. 103–4

alize the full import of the scene. At the time Rimsky wrote his *veche*, Musorgsky was between versions of *Boris*. It had been submitted to the Imperial Theaters directorate, whose opera committee, as everyone knows, rejected it in February 1871, on the grounds that there was no prima donna role. But of course the changes Musorgsky made went so much further than anything required or envisioned by the committee that one can only conclude that the impetus that

EXAMPLE 10, *continued*

mla-den-tsev vya-zhut k ma-te-ryam ver-yo-vko

Bass: Lzhosh', Yush-ko!

i tekh tu-da zhe, v vo-du.

Lzhosh' ti!

Al' de-ti tozh po-vin-no?

Yushko (the Novgorod messenger): Soon it will be a month since the victims were thrown from the bridge into the seething whirlpool. Babies were tied to their mothers and both were thrown in the water.
Altos: My God!
Tenors: Could it be true?
Sopranos: Could the tsar punish so harshly?
Basses: You're lying!
Tenors: As if children were also guilty . . .

EXAMPLE 11. The *veche*, p. 127

caused him to rethink his opera lay elsewhere. According to Stasov, the scene at Kromy, in which the people are shown in the act of re- bellion, and which had nothing to do either with the committee's wishes or with the Pushkin tragedy on which the first version of the opera had been so closely modeled, was conceived "during the win- ter of 1870–71." In the fall of 1871 Musorgsky and Rimsky moved in together, sharing a furnished room in an apartment belonging to the Conservatory professor Nikolai Zaremba. According to Rimsky's ac-

EXAMPLE 11, *continued*

Tucha: As if we did not fend off those awful Lithuanians! As if we spared the Germans
our battle-axes! Why should we now hang our heads?
Tenors: We haven't done anything! Lithuania, indeed!
Basses: Like hell we spared them!

count, during the time they lived together, *Pskovityanka* was orchestrated and the Polish act and Kromy scene were added to *Boris*.[91] The
Kromy scene in completed full score bears the date 23 June 1872.

All this circumstantial evidence merely confirms what comparison
of the two scores already suggests: that the Kromy scene was inspired by Rimsky's *veche*, and emulates it. The parallels are far-reach-
ing and astonishing: the portrayal of the crowd in revolt; the device
(later, by Musorgsky, regretted) of mocking glorification; perhaps
above all the use of folk song as an integral part of the action. The
song of the *vol'nitsa* at the end of the *veche* found echo in two Kromy
numbers, the very ones Stasov claimed he heard the students singing:[92] the choral song about the falcon (the mocking of the boyar
Khrushchov) and the "Revolutionary" chorus, *Raskhodilas', razgulyalas'*. Like the *vol'nitsa* chorus, both of them incorporate tunes collected by Balakirev[93] and work them up into large-scale numbers that
(unlike the *Slava!* in the Coronation scene) carry action. This was a
new kind of choral dramaturgy for Musorgsky: in the first version of

[91] R-KMusL 1.123.
[92] See n. 81.
[93] For identifications, see Chapter 5, p. 272.

EXAMPLE 12a. The *veche*, p. 101 (chorus interrupts solo)

EXAMPLE 12a, *continued*

Yushko: . . . keep its memory alive.
Chorus: Oh my God! Great Novgorod, dear Novgorod, can it be thy end has come?

Boris the crowd had been treated for the most part like a single Dargomïzhskian character, in recitative declamation.

If the plain fact of correspondence between Rimsky's *veche* and Musorgsky's "tramps"—let alone the importance of the former as background, subtext, and perhaps even efficient cause of the latter—has remained as unremarked as it has, this reflects a number of bad habits that have affected Musorgsky research. First, he is often treated as a complete naif without a historical context. Second, when antecedents are sought they are usually sought in the realm of ideology, not in prior music or opera. Third, when Rimsky-Korsakov is thought of in conjunction with Musorgsky it is all but invariably in connection with their "posthumous" relationship, in which they are often viewed as adversaries. Thus, the Kromy scene is usually treated by Soviet writers (and not only by them) as a more or less direct reflection of "populist" thought: as an unmediated response to the peasant uprisings of Musorgsky's own time, or else as a kind of musicalization of the writings of Shchapov, or worse, of Khu-

EXAMPLE 12b. The *veche*, pp. 109–10 (soloist interrupts chorus)

dyakov.[94] And attempts are often made to show why the Kromy scene is a kind of complement to the scene at St. Basil the Blessed in the first version, rather than—as the sheer physical evidence of the manuscripts already proves—its replacement. The impulse to write Kromy, it should be emphasized, was not only an ideological one or

[94] Such interpretations are rife even in the most recent Soviet literature. Gozenpud, for example, flatly asserts without documentation that "the conception of the scene at

EXAMPLE 12b, *continued*

Chorus: Hey, a veche, a veche!
Boyar Matuta: Quiet, milords of Pskov! Our vice-regent has the floor!

a historiographical one. It was also a musical one: the wish to replace one form of choral dramaturgy with another.

But even if we acknowledge this much, a historiographical problem remains. Having determined to write a scene of popular rebellion on the order of Rimsky's *veche*, Musorgsky was faced with a task Rimsky had not encountered. The *veche* scene was provided ready-made within the play from which Rimsky adapted his libretto. The scene Musorgsky wanted to write had no counterpart in Pushkin's *Boris Godunov*. To motivate and justify it, Musorgsky was forced to do something unprecedented in Russian opera: he went directly to

---

Kromy was influenced not so much by Karamzin's account as by the peasant uprisings of the sixties, which gripped a significant part of Russia," and "the chorus demanding bread in the scene at St. Basil the Blessed was conditioned not only by the events of the late sixteenth century but also by the famine that had seized many provinces of Russia at the beginning of 1868" (GozROTIII, 72–73). Mikhail Pekelis, in his introductory essay to the second volume of MusLN, in which the libretto of Boris is published with annotations, builds a blatantly factitious case for the influence of the fugitive revolutionary populist Ivan Khudyakov's inflammatory (and anonymously published) historical tract, *Ancient Russia (Drevnyaya Rus'*, 1867) on the second version of *Boris*, basing his argument on the fact that a different publication of Khudyakov's, his *Anthology of Great Russian Historical Folk Songs (Sbornik velikorusskikh narodnïkh pesen)*, had furnished Musorgsky (through Stasov) with the model for Varlaam's song about the taking of Kazan in the *first* version of the opera ("Musorgsky—pisatel'-dramaturg [writer-dramatist]," MusLN 2.18–20, 26–30). Unfortunately this hypothesis was accepted uncritically by Hoops in "Musorgsky and the Populist Age" (see MusIM, 288–89). For a similarly factitious case regarding the supposed influence of the *narodnik* historian and political exile Afanasy Prokofyevich Shchapov on Musorgsky, see Marina Rakhmanova, "Musorgsky i ego vremya," SovM 9 (1980): 101–10. Hardly better, of course, is the doggedly revisionist position that would completely deny the influence of even liberal, let alone populist thought on Musorgsky. Orlova and Shneerson's discussion of the *Boris* libretto ("After Pushkin and Karamzin") is a case in point (MusIM, 249–70).

historical sources (as he and Stasov would later do for the whole of *Khovanshchina*) and made an original selection and interpretation. In the end, his scene thus attained an authenticity his immediate model (that is, Rimsky's *veche*) had neither possessed nor needed. The obvious question: what were those sources?

Before attempting to answer it will be necessary to identify and characterize the historiographical tradition within which Pushkin had worked, so as to show the distance between the Kromy scene and Pushkin's drama, and hence the distance between Kromy and Musorgsky's own first conception of the opera. Once again we shall be dealing with Karamzin, for he was Pushkin's sole source.

It is well known by now that twentieth-century historians have rejected the premise on which Pushkin based his play: that Boris Godunov had engineered the murder of the Tsarevich Dmitry, Ivan the Terrible's youngest son, so as to pave his own way to the throne. George Vernadsky, summarizing this new view of the events of May 1591 (largely from the work of V. I. Kleyn and Sergey Zavadsky), has called attention to the fact that the documents implicating Boris all come from the early Romanov years and must be treated as Romanov propaganda, while there is no serious reason to doubt the veracity of the one important document contemporaneous with the events, the *Sledstvennoye Delo*, an investigative report prepared by a commission headed by Prince Vasily Shuisky, which attributed the tsarevich's death to a self-inflicted stab wound.[95] But Karamzin thought otherwise. He rejected the *Delo* as a Boris-instigated falsification and believed the testimony of the post-1613 chronicles. On the basis of his assumption of Boris's guilt, he created another vivid historiographical figment to rival the bloodthirsty Ivan—this time a wise, just ruler tragically doomed by his one misdeed. Karamzin ends his first chapter on the reign of Boris Godunov with this singing peroration:

> But the time was approaching when this wise sovereign, rightly acclaimed throughout Europe for his high-minded policies, his love of enlightenment, his zeal to be a true father of his country, finally for the fine conduct of his social and familial life, would have to taste the bitter fruit of lawlessness and become one of the most astounding victims of heavenly judgment. Its harbingers were the inner anxiety of Boris's heart and the various calamities against which he as yet still intensely struggled with all the steadfastness of his spirit, only to find himself all

[95] See Vernadsky, "The Death of the Tsarevich Dmitry: A Reconsideration of the Case," *Oxford Slavonic Papers*, vol. 5 (Oxford: Oxford University Press, 1954), pp. 1–19.

at once feeble and as it were helpless against the ultimate manifestation of his awesome fate.[96]

Here we have, as the Russians would say, the whole *zamïsel'*, the whole conception–in–embryo of Pushkin's drama and its tragic protagonist. Even Karamzin's rhetoric found its way into some of Pushkin's most famous lines. The very next paragraph in the *History*, the one that begins the second chapter on Boris, starts with a phrase that will bring both Pushkin and Musorgsky forcefully to mind:

> Having attained his ends, having risen from petty servility to the heights of power by dint of tireless effort and inexhaustible resources of guile, perfidy, intrigue, and villainy, could Boris enjoy to the full the grandeur his soul had so craved—a grandeur purchased at so high a price? And could he enjoy the pure satisfaction of the soul, a soul so beneficent toward his subjects and therefore so deserving of his country's love? At best, not for long.[97]

Dostignuv tseli [Having attained his ends], . . . *Dostig ya vïsshey vlasti* [I have attained the highest power], . . . this was the model for the great central monologue (Pushkin's scene 8, combined in Musorgsky's first version with Pushkin's scene 11) in which the "Tsar-Herod" bares to the audience the soul so dramatically described by Karamzin. Pushkin was chided by Belinsky for his "slavish adherence" to the official historiographer, but of course his motives in writing *Boris* were hardly those of a historian. Few plays were so purely literary in conception and execution, and even Musorgsky assumed that "Pushkin wrote *Boris* in dramatic form, [but] not for the stage."[98] One may hesitate to hold with the modern formalist that Pushkin's tragedy, "a premeditated and experimental work," was "written not so much for the subject as for the literary form,"[99] and still conclude that for the poet the subject consisted not in the facts of history but in the tragic character of the protagonist and in the theme of nemesis, all wholly set forth by Karamzin in prose that, in the words of Musorgsky's friend and adviser, the Pushkinist V. V. Nikolsky, already "reads like poetry."[100]

Now if this be a drama of nemesis, who, to use Mirsky's word,

[96] HRS 11.55.

[97] Ibid., p. 56.

[98] Musorgsky to Golenishchev-Kutuzov, 15 August 1877. MusLN 1.232.

[99] Mirsky, *Pushkin*, p. 153.

[100] Lecture notes, quoted in Orlova and Shneerson, "After Pushkin and Karamzin," MusIM, 252.

was the "Eumenid"? Quite obviously, the False Dmitry, and not, as is so often supposed, "the people." The widespread conception, based on knowledge of the second version of Musorgsky's opera, that Pushkin's drama already embodied the theme of kingship and legitimacy, of the relationship between ruler and ruled (*vlast' i narod*—"power and people"—as the Soviet cliché would have it), is quite erroneous. And the idea that the source of this conception lay in Karamzin is still more so. Karamzin's conception of legitimacy derived from anything but "the consent of the governed" (cf. his treatment of Ivan IV), and "the people" play no active or essential role at any point in his narrative. Neither do they play any such role in Musorgsky's first conception of his opera. Soviet critiques of Pushkin's play, as may be expected, always fabricate a "social" or "civic" subtext. But ostensibly un-Soviet, revisionist interpretations often commit the same error. Orlova and Shneerson, for example, assert that "the dramatic conflict of Musorgsky's opera, as well as of Pushkin's tragedy, is based on the confrontation of the people with the 'criminal Tsar Boris,' "[101] and go on to emphasize the famous stage direction with which the drama ends: *Narod bezmolvstvuyet* [The people keep silent]. Following the traditions of Soviet criticism, they call this a "sinister stillness pregnant with menace," and claim that "behind this brief phrase, we feel the invisible presence of the poet-seer who foresees the misfortunes and upheavals to come."[102] But the poet-seer had inserted the famous closing direction at the behest of the censor. Pushkin's intended ending was to have been the crowd acclaiming the False Dmitry on command, as it had earlier acclaimed Boris. The people, then, for Pushkin as for Karamzin, remained passive to the end.

Nowhere is the passivity and impotence of the people more apparent than in the scene at St. Basil the Blessed, often touted as the scene that shows the tsar and the people in sharpest confrontation,

---

[101] "After Pushkin and Karamzin," p. 255. This seems a paraphrase of a passage on the first version of the opera from Gozenpud: "Everything is concentrated on the collision of *two* forces—the people and the tsar. The theme of enemy intervention is not visually present. Grishka Otrepyev, having jumped from the window of the inn, disappears forever from the stage. The appearance of the Pretender is only alluded to in Shuisky's report, in the scene at St. Basil the Blessed, and at the tsar's council. The first version of the opera excluded everything that was not directly connected with the central conflict. Boris Godunov perishes because the tsar-criminal is rejected by the people" (GozROTIII, 71). Ultimately, the source of this misinterpretation is Asafyev. His three articles on the dramaturgy of *Boris* are reprinted in AsIT, vol. 3.

[102] "After Pushkin and Karamzin," MusIM, 266.

and which therefore is often viewed as the heart of the dramatic conception of the play and opera alike. Its kernel in Karamzin was an incident wholly unrelated to the matter of the Tsarevich Dmitry: Boris's encounter with a *yuródivïy* following the death of his own first-born son in 1588, ten years before he became tsar.

> Godunov, . . . having at the time only one infant son, took him reck-lessly with him, though the boy was sick, to the church of St. Basil the Blessed, paying his doctors no heed. The infant died. At the time there was in Moscow a fool in God [*yuródivïy*], esteemed for his real or imaginary holiness. Walking naked through the streets in bitter cold, his hair hanging long and wild, he foretold calamities and solemnly calumniated Boris. But Boris held his peace and dared not do him the smallest harm, whether out of fear of the populace or because he believed in the man's holiness. Such *yuródivïye*, or blessed simpletons, appeared frequently in the capital wearing chains of penance called *verigi*. They were privileged to reproach anyone, no matter how important, right in the eye, if their conduct was bad. And they could take whatever they wanted from shops without paying. The merchants would thank them for it as if for a great favor.[103]

Pushkin (and following him, Musorgsky) tied this story to the events of 1604 in the following way: seizing upon another choice item from Karamzin—that Boris, in response to the growing threat from the False Dmitry, ordered memorial services for the slain tsarevich and anathema services for Grishka Otrepyev[104]—the poet had Boris emerge from St. Basil's after such a service to be greeted by a howl from the starving populace: "Bread, give bread to the hungry, batuyshka, for Christ's sake!" There follows the searing exchange between the tsar and the *yuródivïy*, who is usually portrayed as the voice or personification of the people.[105] Boris is confronted with his crime: the *yuródivïy* asks him to have the little boys killed who had stolen his kopeck, just as he had had the little tsarevich killed. As in the incident cited above, Boris does not react to this unspeakable offense; instead he asks the *yuródivïy* to pray for him. But, the *yuródivïy* says in refusal, "Our Lady forbids us to pray for the Tsar-Herod."

Now even in this scene the crowd is passive. Boris is still their *batyushka*, their "little father." The people do not threaten him, rather

---

[103] HRS 10.169.

[104] Cf. HRS 11.95.

[105] E.g., Gozenpud: "The *yuródivïy* pronounces judgment on the tsar in the name of the people" (GozROTIII, 78).

they go down on their knees to him in supplication. And when the *yuródiviy* refuses to pray for the tsar, the crowd, according to *Musorgsky's* stage direction, "disperses in horror."[106] The *yuródiviy* is at best an ambiguous figure; to see him here as the people's spokesman is an unwarranted extrapolation. One detail, in fact, positively separates him from the crowd. In the beginning of the scene the chorus indicates its belief in the False Dmitry's legitimacy; that is, they believe that he is the real Dmitry, alive and well. The *yuródiviy*, on the other hand, knows that the tsarevich is dead by Boris's hand. How, in the face of this, can one go on seeing his words as the voice of the people? Clearly, the *yuródiviy* is no such thing, but rather the embodied voice of Boris's remorse.

Quite the best evidence that this interpretation is correct is the very fact that having written the scene at Kromy, Musorgsky deleted the one at St. Basil's—physically ripped it out of his score, in fact—and, moreover, made conflation impossible by recycling the episode of the *yuródiviy* and the boys, along with the *yuródiviy's* concluding lament.[107] Indeed, the two scenes, meant originally to occupy the same (penultimate) position in the opera's sequence of scenes, are ideologically incompatible, and one has to wonder at the ingenuousness of those who claim that "what caused Musorgsky to delete one of the best scenes remains unknown."[108] For it was with Kromy, and only with Kromy, that Musorgsky finally introduced the theme of *vlast' i narod*—actual conflict between the tsar and the people—into his opera as motive force in the drama. In Kromy (and only in Kromy) one can speak accurately of the people as the real tragic hero of the opera (their tragic flaw being their credulity).

So, clearly, the Kromy scene had little to do with Pushkin. It is true

[106] MusLN 2.122.

[107] That Musorgsky's wishes are regularly flouted in this matter, particularly in performances that pretend to authenticity, in no way changes the fact. Attempts to justify the inclusion of both scenes on ground that the Kromy scene realizes what is already implicit in Pushkin/Karamzin, or else on the assumption that the versions "do not replace but complement one another" (Pekelis, MusLN 2.9) are untenable. Altogether preposterous is the claim first made by Asafyev and repeated as recently as Orlova and Shneerson's "After Pushkin and Karamzin," that the scene at St. Basil's was deleted for reasons having to do with the censorship. In that case, why was the far more radical Kromy scene permitted? Such arguments, moreover, fail to consider that when Pushkin's play was finally produced in 1870, the scene at St. Basil's was passed. (For more on the censorship question, see OldBGC.) One senses that what lies behind the rage to conflate is simply the desire not to lose any of Musorgsky's music. And who can fail to sympathize? But let the rationalizations cease.

[108] "After Pushkin and Karamzin," MusIM, 263.

that the penultimate scene in the original drama ends with the crowd, having been incited to riot by the speech of the poet's namesake, the boyar Pushkin, rushing off toward the palace now occupied by Boris's helpless son, shouting, "Bind him, drown him! Hail Dmitry! Crush the race of Godunov!"—an episode that comes straight out of Karamzin, and, mutatis mutandis, went straight into Musorgsky. But the relationship of these events to those in the Kromy scene is at best oblique. The violence is being committed not spontaneously but at the behest of Dmitry's minion; the angry mob is one of Muscovites at home, not tramps in the woods; finally, the target is Fyodor Borisovich, not the boyar Khrushchov.[109] Something perhaps a bit closer to Musorgsky's scene is suggested in the scene immediately preceding in Pushkin, when the boyar Pushkin, conferring with the boyar Basmanov (another defector to the Pretender's cause), confidently predicts victory, and on these grounds:

> . . . Basmanov, dost thou know
> Wherein our true strength lies? Not in the army,
> Nor yet in Polish aid, but in opinion—
> Yes, popular opinion. Dost remember
> The triumph of Dimitry, dost remember
> His peaceful conquests, when, without a blow
> The docile towns surrendered, and the mob
> Bound the recalcitrant leaders?[110]

But that is all one finds in Pushkin—a suggestion, not a conception, hardly a *zamïsel'*. The first actual spark of the eventual scene at Kromy may have been touched off, interestingly enough, by a couple of lines on the Pretender's progress, which Musorgsky himself inserted into the text of the scene at St. Basil the Blessed: "He's already got as far as Kromy, they say. —He's coming with his troops to Moscow. —He's blasting Boris's troops to smithereens."[111] Even this, however, is a long way from the eventual "Revolution scene." It refers to the siege and pitched battle described in detail by Karamzin, at which Dmitry's Polish troops were joined by several hundred Don Cossacks. It was they who had bound and taken prisoner the boyar

[109] Khrushchov makes only the briefest of appearances in Pushkin, in a passage from scene 12 that was cut by censors when the play was first published in 1831. In it, Khrushchov, an early defector to the False Dmitry, appears before the Pretender with news of Boris's condition.

[110] Trans. Alfred Hayes, in Avrahm Yarmolinsky, ed., *The Poems, Prose, and Plays of Pushkin* (New York: Random House, 1936), pp. 406–7.

[111] MusLN 2.120.

Khrushchov, whom Boris had sent to lead them against the Pretender. They presented Khrushchov to Dmitry as a trophy at Kromy. This was, at least according to Karamzin, the turning point in the Pretender's campaign.[112]

Was it in Karamzin, then, that Musorgsky found the makings of his Kromy scenario? Most historians agree it was, taking their cue from Stasov's account of the planning of the scene, in which he claimed to have been a direct participant:

> Karamzin's story of the popular rebellion and of the Jesuits Czernikowski and Lawicki was decided upon by us as the basis for the magnificent scene of the people jeering at the boyar Khrushchov, the commander at Kromy, and for the scene of the people's settling of accounts with the Jesuits at the moment the victorious Pretender approaches with his troops.[113]

But there is no such story in Karamzin. What there is is the vivid description of the siege at Kromy to which reference has been made (and which was fairly irrelevant to Musorgsky's concerns), the mere names of the Jesuits (given at the end of n. 240 to vol. 11), some documents from which Musorgsky derived the rhetoric of Dmitry's proclamation at the end of the scene,[114] and some scattered references to the famine of 1604 and the widespread unrest it caused among the people. One of these references is interesting for its mention of "tramps" (*brodyagi*), the word Musorgsky habitually used in his correspondence to refer to the Kromy scene:[115]

> Whereas in good times the nobility willingly augmented their retinues, in times of famine they began to disperse them. Their temper turned toward executions and cruel punishments! Even people of good conscience expelled their servants from their homes, or at best forced them to take a leave. . . . The unfortunate perished, or else turned to robbery together with many exiles of the nobility, Romanovs and others, who were condemned to lead the lives of tramps (for no one dared take in the servants of the disgraced)—together with Ukrainian fugitives, wan-

[112] The whole story may be read in HRS 11.86–87, 104–6.

[113] StasIS 2.197.

[114] HRS 11.83n. 217, etc.

[115] As he wrote to Stasov, "I acquainted myself in *Boris* with the origins of the Time of Troubles through the tramps" (6 September 1873, MusLN 1.169), meaning through the study of the phenomenon of vagrancy mentioned by Karamzin. The translator of Orlova and Shneerson's article on the sources of *Boris*'s libretto committed a serious error here, rendering the words *v brodiagakh* as "while tramping [through the woods]" ("After Pushkin and Karamzin," p. 267).

dering far from their nests into the heart of Russia in quest of plunder. Gangs appeared on the highways, . . . people were robbed and murdered at the very outskirts of Moscow.[116]

But as this phenomenon is described by Karamzin, it had little to do with the progress of the False Dmitry. The one concrete borrowing attributable uniquely to Karamzin that may be verified in the scene at Kromy is the reappearance in that scene of the monks Varlaam and Missail, both of whom are named by Karamzin among the Pretender's supporters.[117] And that is all, despite the fact that the earliest printed libretto of the Kromy scene carried a number of footnote references to the official historiographer. These have been exposed as "fictitious" (presumably for the benefit of the censor) by Orlova and Shneerson, who, though they attempt to prove the derivation of Kromy from Karamzin, admit that "revolt is not even mentioned in [his] history."[118] Indeed, missing altogether from Karamzin is the crucial factor: any sense that "the people" played any active "revolutionary" role that may have contributed to the fall of Godunov and the triumph of the False Dmitry. The closest Karamzin ever comes to such an idea is the following rather caustic remark:

> In the cities, the villages, and along the highways, proclamations of Dmitry to the inhabitants of Russia were circulated, containing news that he was alive and would soon be among them. The people were astonished, not knowing whether to believe it. But the tramps, the good-for-nothings, the robbers long since inhabiting the northern regions, rejoiced: their time was coming. Some came running to the Pretender in Galicia; others ran to Kiev, where . . . a banner had been set out to rally a militia [vol'nitsa].[119]

But this passage already suggests Karamzin's harsh judgment of the "tramps." They were an anarchic element at best, not a "historical force," and explicitly distinguished from "the people." Here is a fuller description:

> It was not a host that assembled against Boris, but a scum. An entirely insignificant portion of the [Polish] nobility, in deference to their king, . . . or else flattering themselves with the thought of deeds of derring-do with the exiled tsarevich, showed up in Sambor and Lvov. Also there

[116] HRS 12.71.
[117] HRS 11.84 (Varlaam), 85 (Missail); also n. 224, in which the presence of two orthodox monks among the Pretender's retinue is documented.
[118] "After Pushkin and Karamzin," MusIM, 253.
[119] HRS 11.85.

hurried thither all manner of tramps, hungry and half-naked, demanding arms not for victorious battle but for plunder and favors, which
Mniszek granted generously in hopes for the future.[120]

This is the riffraff from which Musorgsky is supposed to have
drawn inspiration. Not that the point is one of moral attitude, for
Musorgsky, too (as Orlova and Shneerson quite rightly point out),
judged his "tramps" harshly.[121] The point is that Karamzin altogether
minimized the importance of "the people"—tramps or otherwise—
as a historical force, and never drew an unambiguous connection between the famine-inspired lawlessness in the Russian countryside
and the progress of the False Dmitry. In order to find an authentic
historiographical sanction for a choral scene to match Rimsky's *veche*,
or on a more philosophical plane, to find an account that viewed the
people, as he did, as a "great individual, inspired by a single idea,"[122]
Musorgsky would need a historian who viewed the people as an essential, motivating force for the events of the Time of Troubles, not a
mere reactor to those events, as in the accounts both of aristocratic
historians like Karamzin and of "statists" like Solovyov.

There was such a man, and his name was Kostomarov—the very
one whose admiring comments about Musorgsky's opera furnished
us with our point of departure. He and Musorgsky were well acquainted. Kostomarov was among those named by Musorgsky, in
the autobiographical sketch he wrote for Riemann during the last
year of his life, as having contributed the most to "the arousal of the
young composer's mental activity and to giving it its serious, strictly
scientific inclination."[123] Musorgsky further stated, in the same
sketch, that Kostomarov participated directly, along with Stasov and
Nikolsky, in planning *Khovanshchina* and *Sorochintsï Fair*.[124] That
would imply that his period of close relationship to the historian be-

[120] Ibid., p. 84.
[121] "After Pushkin and Karamzin," MusIM, 265: "The scene at Kromy, despite the
accepted opinion among Soviet musicologists, does not represent the apotheosis of
popular uprising but demonstrates that revolt is a profoundly tragic phenomenon."
According to Golenishchev-Kutuzov's memoirs of the composer, Musorgsky, in his
late, "idealistic," period, is supposed to have had second thoughts about his brutal,
unidealized portrayal of his "tramps." For a detailed discussion, see the Introduction
to this book, pp. 31–33.
[122] Manuscript dedication on title page of the published vocal score, 21 January 1874
(MusLN 1.326).
[123] MusLN 1.268.
[124] Ibid., p. 269.

gan right before those works were planned, or precisely as he was revising *Boris*. But it further implies that Kostomarov's influence on the earlier opera was probably exercised not in person but through his published works. And so we shall find.

Of all Russian historians, Kostomarov showed the greatest interest in theater and the arts as bearers of historical lessons. Besides the articles in the *Vestnik Yevropï* quoted at the beginning of this chapter, in the late sixties Kostomarov wrote many reviews of historical dramas for the newspaper *Golos*. So widely noticed were these columns that in the 1870s Kostomarov was retained (along with Stasov) as consultant on matters of historical verisimilitude by the Imperial Theaters directorate under the intendant Stepan Gedeonov.[125] Of the radical historians of his day, Kostomarov was by far the most influential, thanks to a vivid writing and speaking style that made his books and lectures very popular among students and the liberal-minded intelligentsia. He was the major proponent of the view that the prime historical mover was not tsar but populace. His idealization of the peasantry made it inevitable that Kostomarov should specialize in the chronicling of popular uprisings. His first big success was *Stenka Razin's Revolt* (*Bunt Stenki Razina*, 1859), one of the first fruits of the liberalized censorship under Alexander II. Its popularity was phenomenal and made its author a hero. In the early sixties his lectures were so appealing to the St. Petersburg University students who crowded his auditorium that more than once Kostomarov was carried out on their shoulders.[126]

Kostomarov's magnum opus was *The Time of Troubles of the Russian State in the Beginning of the Seventeenth Century* (*Smutnoye vremya moskovskogo gosudarstva v nachale XVII stoletiya*), first published serially in the *Vestnik Yevropï* in 1866. It was the most recent authoritative word on the subject when Musorgsky composed *Boris*. It began at the year 1604, the year of the False Dmitry's victory over the forces of Boris Godunov. In the scene-setting introduction to the main narrative, Kostomarov wrote an extended paragraph that directly related the unrest caused by famine to the progress of the Pretender, thereby setting out the whole *zamïsel'* of Musorgsky's Kromy scene:

[125] GozROTIII, 20.

[126] For interesting oblique references to this, see Stasov's hysterical letter of 17 May 1863 to Balakirev on Serov's *Judith*: "Immediately, from the very first note Serov became the idol of St. Petersburg, just such an idol as Kostomarov was recently" (BalStasP 1.199).

If old-timers couldn't remember such a horrible famine in Russia, neither would they remember such vagrancy [brodyazhnichestvo] as then was rife. Lords had turned out their servants when it became excessively dear to feed them, and later, when the price of bread had fallen, wanted to get them back. But their former serfs, if they had managed to survive the famine, were living with other masters or else had developed a taste for wandering—and did not wish to turn themselves in. Lawsuits and prosecutions multiplied. Hunted fugitives gathered in gangs. To these tramps were added a multitude of serfs who had belonged to fallen boyars. Boris had forbidden taking them as serfs, and this had been just as hard on them as the prohibition on transfers had been on the peasants. Having been indentured to one master, it was a rare serf who wanted to leave the status of serf altogether; practically all ran away to find another place. These "fallen" serfs gathered at that time by the thousands. Deprived of the right to roam from court to court, they attached themselves to the robber gangs, which sprang up everywhere in varying numbers. Most serfs had no other way of feeding themselves. The only exceptions were those who knew some trade. There were a multitude of fugitives from noble courts, from monasteries, from outlying settlements. They ran wild during the famine, and later, when they were sought by their former masters, they couldn't buy themselves off, especially since so many died in the famine. On the survivors a huge tax was declared before they could be free of their obligations. And so they ran, cursing the extortion, the injustice of the bailiffs and elders, the violent measures of their henchmen. Some ran off to Siberia, others to the Don, still others to the Dnepr. Many settled on the Ukrainian plains and there evaded their state-imposed obligations. The fact that the northern Ukraine had happily been spared the worst of the famine was the reason for an extreme concentration of people in that region. The government began to take measures for the return of the fugitives, and they for their part were prepared to resist. This whole fugitive population was naturally unhappy with the Moscow authorities. They were prepared to throw themselves with joy at whomever would lead them against Boris, at whomever would promise them an advantage. This was not a matter of aspiring to this or that political or social order; the huge crowd of sufferers easily attached itself to a new face in the hope that under a new regime things would be better than under the old.[127]

Kostomarov presents not a scum, then, but a mass of insulted-and-injured with whom one can (and he does) sympathize. As for the

[127] *Sochineniya N. I. Kostomarova*, vol. 3 (St. Petersburg: Tipografiya M. M. Stasyulevicha, 1903), pp. 42–43.

people as an active force that, when aroused, can threaten tsars, consider Kostomarov's description of the gang of Khlopka Kosolapïy (and substitute the name Khrushchov for Basmanov):

> Khlopka did not limit himself to attacking travelers on the highway; with an enormous gang he went straight to Moscow, threatening to annihilate the throne, the boyars, and all that was sanctioned by authority, powerful, rich, and oppressive in Russia. In October 1603, Boris sent troops to destroy this gang, under the leadership of the *okol'nichiy* Ivan Fyodorovich Basmanov. They had not gotten far from Moscow when suddenly "thieves" fell upon Basmanov. They attacked the tsar's troops on a path that cut through the underbrush. Basmanov was killed.[128]

As for Khrushchov himself, the story of his capture by the Don Cossacks and his acceptance of the False Dmitry (which last is part of the action of Musorgsky's Kromy scene) is related by Kostomarov in much greater detail than in the work of any previous historian:

> Here [on the left bank of the Dnepr near Kiev], there came again to Dmitry emissaries from the Don Cossacks with representations of the willingness of the whole independent population of the Don basin to serve the miraculously spared tsarevich. As an earnest of their fidelity they lay at their feet the nobleman Pyotr Khrushchov, who had been sent by Boris to incite them against Dmitry. The prisoner, brought before him in shackles, no sooner caught sight of the Pretender than he fell at his feet and said, "Now I see that you are the natural-born, true tsarevich. Your face resembles that of your father, the sovereign Tsar Ivan Vasilyevich. Forgive us, Lord, and show us mercy. In our ignorance we served Boris, but when they see you, all will recognize you."[129]

Finally, Kostomarov narrates several incidents that furnished Musorgsky with the model for his chorus of mockery. They relate, actually, to the period immediately following Boris's death, when his son and family were routed from the palace. Here are two:

> Meanwhile, on the other side of the river there were still those who, having sworn loyalty to Boris's widow and son, wished to remain true to their vows and persuaded others in the name of church and duty not to turn traitor. They reviled Dmitry, proclaiming, "Long live the children of Boris Fyodorovich!" Then Korela shouted: "Beat them, beat them, not with swords, not with sticks, but with poles; beat them and say, 'There you are, there you are! Don't you be picking fights with

128 Ibid., p. 43.
129 Ibid., p. 83.

us!' " This appealed to the assembled troops, especially the ones from Ryazan. The Godunovites were turned loose, and the Dmitryites chased them with laughter and beat them, some with whips, some with sticks and some with fists.[130]

[The supporters of Boris] were robbed and plundered without any mercy, from those marked by the people's hatred even the clothing was ripped, and many were seen that day—so eyewitnesses report—covering their nakedness as Adam did, with leaves. The mob, who had suffered long and much, who had been so long humiliated, rejoiced in this day, amused themselves at the expense of the noble and wealthy, paid them back for their former humiliation. Even those who had not sided with the Godunovs suffered on that day; it was enough to have been rich. And the general plunder and drunkenness continued until nightfall, when all slept like the dead.[131]

So when Kostomarov said of *Boris* that it was a "page of history," one understands what he meant—it was a page of *his* history. That he was referring to Kromy, the scene that concludes the opera, goes without saying. The difference between Kromy and the rest of *Boris* was precisely the difference between Karamzin and Kostomarov. As one of Musorgsky's intimates, Alexandra Molas (*née* Purgold), put it much later to the young Boris Asafyev, "the Kromy Forest scene arose in connection with the fact that Musorgsky [wished to] recast the denouement of his tragedy in keeping with the burgeoning populist [*narodnichestvennïye*] tendencies" of the time.[132] This much is true; but it will not do to assert with Asafyev that "precisely that which Nikolai I's regime did not permit Pushkin to do was done here by Musorgsky."[133] For Musorgsky's conception derived from a historiographical viewpoint that did not so much exist in Pushkin's time, nor indeed until the 1860s. It was as much a denial of Solovyov's "statism" as the latter had been of Karamzin's absolutism, the source of Pushkin's view of the Time of Troubles and, at first, of Musorgsky's, too.

All of the foregoing notwithstanding, to claim that the Kromy scene is an example of ideologically committed *art engagé* would be facile. The evidence, as we have seen, suggests a rather more tortu-

---

[130] Ibid., p. 117.
[131] Ibid., pp. 127–28.
[132] Boris Asafyev, "Boris Godunov' Musorgskogo, kak muzïkal'nïy spektakl' iz Pushkina," AsIT 3.132.
[133] Ibid., p. 137.

ous conception, in which Musorgsky's initial stimulus may have been musical, not political, not an a priori commitment to populism but admiration for Rimsky-Korsakov's choral dramaturgy in that quintessentially "statist" opera *Pskovityanka*, where the theme of popular rebellion had, from the purely historiographical standpoint, sounded a curiously discordant note. If we call Musorgsky a committed populist in *Boris*, we shall have to explain his apparent retreat from that ideology in *Khovanshchina*.[134] This self-created problem has led researchers into endless difficulties: some have seen fit to censure, others to devise elaborate rationalizations. Neither the one nor the other is justified by the evidence. It is enough to view Musorgsky's "populism" as an exterior manifestation of his overriding commitment to realism on the one hand, and to his alertness to the intellectual currents of his time on the other. It is already sufficient praise to note that for him it was not enough merely to contrive an emulation of Rimsky's *veche* by hook or crook, which he might easily have done by revamping his own scene at St. Basil's. No, he was impelled to seek an authentic historical basis for his crowd music, and he found it in the "tramps" so vividly described by his friend and mentor, Kostomarov.

VII

"History in a certain sense is the Holy Book of nations," wrote Karamzin at the very outset of his gigantic labors. "It is the chief thing, the indispensable thing. It is the mirror of their existence and their deeds, a tablet of revelations and laws, the testament of the forebears to posterity, the amplification and explication of the present and an example to the future."[135] The new birth of historical studies in the nineteenth century, its significance and its fundamentals of aim and method are among the brightest testimonies and finest fruits of the heightened national consciousness the new century was witnessing everywhere in Europe. In Russia, where that consciousness was newer and stronger, perhaps, than anywhere else, interest in the past became obsessive. Its effect on opera is but a small facet of that

[134] The curious mixture of romanticism and historicist pedantry that characterizes the libretto of *Khovanshchina* is well reflected in Musorgsky's comments to Golenishchev-Kutuzov on historical drama and on the work of Vladislav Kenevich. See especially the letter of 2 March 1874 (MusLN 1.177–78).

[135] "Predisloviye," HRS 1.xvii.

general obsession. But the fact that the three most important Russian operatic composers of the latter nineteenth century should have been so directly involved with the works and issues raised by the three most eminent Russian historians of their time lends a new credence to the oft-heard claim that in Russia the arts mattered as nowhere else. Musorgsky, it goes without saying, but also Rimsky-Korsakov and even Chaikovsky viewed themselves in the period around 1870, the most quintessentially "civic" moment in Russian intellectual history, not as "mere" musicians but as participants and contributors to their country's seething intellectual life. If history was the mirror of the nation, what better role for opera than to mirror history if, as Chaikovsky put it, the composer wished to become "the property not merely of separate little circles but—with luck—of the whole nation"?[136] Though their angles of reflection differed considerably, the three operas we have examined were all honorable constituents of the great mirror that was nineteenth-century Russian art.

[136] Chaikovsky to Nadezhda von Meck, 27 September 1885. Quoted in *The Music of Tchaikovsky*, p. 126.

5

MUSORGSKY VERSUS MUSORGSKY

The Versions of *Boris Godunov*

When an artist revises, it means he is dissatisfied.
Musorgsky to Rimsky-Korsakov, 15 August 1868.[1]

PRACTITIONERS of literary hermeneutics draw a fundamental distinction between meaning and significance. The former term refers to the intrinsic sense of a text, the latter to its contextual relevance. A complete act of understanding involves both interpretation and critique,[2] that is, it attempts to take account of both meaning and significance—what Husserl described as the "inner and outer horizons" of any cognition.[3] When contexts are chosen for their historical bearing on an object or text, the establishment of significance amounts to a historical explanation of the object, as conversely it contributes to the comprehension of the context. As any whole is comprehended, its parts are explained.

This roundabout and perhaps gratuitous little disquisition is offered by way of justification for a fresh approach to what may seem

---

[1] MusLN 1.107.

[2] Cf. August Boeckh's division of the science of hermeneutics. *Kritik* he defines as "that philological function through which a text is understood not simply in its own terms and for its own sake, but in order to establish a relationship with something else, in such a way that the goal is a knowledge of this relationship itself" (*Encyclopädie und Methodologie der philologischen Wissenschaften*, 2d ed. [Leipzig: B. G. Teubner, 1886], p. 170, as quoted in E. D. Hirsch, Jr., "Objective Interpretation," *PMLA* 75 [1960]: 463). To Hirsch's article, and to his later expansion of its theoretical premises in *The Aims of Interpretation* (Chicago: University of Chicago Press, 1976), I owe the way I have framed my point of departure here.

[3] See Helmut Kuhn, "The Phenomenological Concept of 'Horizon,' " in *Philosophical Essays in Memory of Edmund Husserl*, ed. Marvin Farber (Cambridge: Harvard University Press, 1940).

a tired and refractory subject. *Boris Godunov*, among major operas, shares the dubious distinction with *Don Carlos* of having the most complex creative history and the most bafflingly abundant "wealth" (as Budden put it of Verdi's opera) "of alternative and superseded material, so little of which can be dismissed out of hand."[4] Its purely textual problems have been admirably addressed by three generations of scholars, beginning with Pavel Lamm's epoch-making edition of 1928 and extending through Robert Oldani's meticulous dissertation, completed exactly half a century later.[5] But clarification of the chronological, philological, and bibliographical record has not put an end to debate as to what the opera's optimum form should be, or what its composer's true intentions were (whether or not these two questions are regarded as identical—a debate in itself). In fact the clarification has only exacerbated the debate. As long as the focus has been mainly on establishing the texts of the two authentic (i.e., authorial) versions of the opera and on describing their structures more or less independently—that is, on "meaning," as defined above—no convincing rationale has ever been offered for the revision in all its aspects, nor has any serious rationale for choosing between them ever been proposed.

As a result, conflation has become the rule. The more music (from both versions) a production includes, the greater its claim to authenticity. Since absolute inclusiveness is impossible, for reasons that will emerge in the discussion that follows, no two productions seem ever to be textually identical, and hardly any production—whether the text is Musorgsky's "original" or one of the many subsequent redactions—precisely conforms to either of the versions Musorgsky made himself.

[4] Julian Budden, *The Operas of Verdi*, vol. 3 (London: Oxford University Press, 1981), p. 38.

[5] The Lamm edition of the vocal score of *Boris Godunov*, containing a full critical report, was the first volume of MusPSS. (In MusCW, the *Boris* vocal score is the second volume, not the first.) Also of primary importance is Lamm's article describing his source work: "Vosstanovleniye podlinnogo teksta 'Borisa Godunova,' " in *Musorgskiy: "Boris Godunov," Stat'i i issledovaniya* (Moscow: Muzgiz, 1930), pp. 13–18. The most authoritative edition of the full score of the opera is that of David Lloyd-Jones (London: Oxford University Press, 1975), also with a full critical report. Valuable for its clarification of the tangled mess of editions and redactions in which Musorgsky's music has appeared over the years is RMusMus. The section on *Boris* originally appeared as a "Scorography" in the *Musical Newsletter* 4 (Fall 1974): 10–17, 23. Finally, Oldani's dissertation, *New Perspectives on Mussorgsky's "Boris Godunov"* (University of Michigan, 1978), contains a chapter on "Stemmata," which has been published as "Editions of *Boris Godunov*" in MusIM, 179–214.

In part this situation has arisen from the composer's reputation as an idiot savant, to be second-guessed with confidence in one's own better judgment. This is a view that even the composer's staunchest supporters still seem at least tacitly to share, and one becomes used to reading self-righteous carping at Rimsky-Korsakov's editorial excesses offered as preface to justify editorial intrusions just as radical. But in truth, the situation *is* difficult and in some ways unique.

In the case of a composer like Verdi, who was a dominant presence on the operatic stage of his day, tracing the versions—say, of *Macbeth, Simon Boccanegra*, or *Don Carlos*—means tracing the history of their productions. The changes made can be accounted for at least partly in terms of the practical exigencies of the stage. Not only do these considerations provide explanations, they also provide a great diversity of supporting documentation—performance material, letters, theatrical archives, and so on. *Boris Godunov*, as is well known, was completely revised before there were any productions. Indeed, revision was a precondition for production. Thus, not only is there very little documentary evidence to explain the revision but in addition the few practical factors bearing on it—the demands of the Imperial Theaters directorate, the looming Russian censorship—have been traditionally emphasized far out of proportion to their true role in accounting for it. The question of censorship has been effectively disposed of by Oldani.[6] But even he accords the rejection by the Imperial Theaters directorate the status of prime (or sole) motivating force for the revision.[7] Less cautious writers have seen fit to attribute everything about the revision, even its harmonic idiom, to the demands of the Theater directorate.[8]

It is here that considerations of "significance" can be of assistance. If Musorgsky's versions are not only described but compared, and not only compared but "inserted"[9] into such vaster structures as the

[6] See chapter 5 of his dissertation, also published as OldBGC. His conclusion: "The censors may have provided Musorgsky with a rationalization that the loss of the Cell scene [from the premiere production in 1874] was perhaps for the best, but their direct effect, it now seems clear, was minimal."

[7] *New Perspectives*, p. 143.

[8] E.g., Maureen Carr, "The Sound of Mussorgsky," *Opera News* 39, no. 12 (25 January 1975): 25: "The playing down of modality in the revision probably indicates an attempt to make the opera more pleasing to the Imperial Theater committee."

[9] Cf. Lucien Goldmann: "The illumination of a meaningful structure constitutes a process of comprehending it; while insertion of it into a vaster structure is to explain it" ("Genetic Structuralist Method in the History of Literature," in *Marxism and Art*, ed. B. Lang and F. Williams [New York: McKay, 1972], p. 249).

history of Russian opera, that of Russian historiography as embodied in Russian art and literature, and Musorgsky's own aesthetic attitudes and their vicissitudes, we may come closer to an understanding, even an explanation of the way he revised his masterpiece. We may even arrive at an account of the revision coherent enough to suggest motivation at last for all its aspects: the scenes added as well as the scenes removed and the scenes revised, the deletions in the remaining scenes as well as the interpolations. To achieve this we shall have to consider the two *Borises* afresh from many angles: their ideological and historiographical conceptions, their relationship to the literary source in Pushkin, their dramaturgical structures, their musical styles (involving questions of form, declamation, and the use of leitmotif), influences and models (including some quite unexpected), and the elusive yet all-important matter of "tone."

The thesis that will emerge from this fundamental reexamination will be one that views the second version as no mere retouching, supplement, or bowdlerization of the first, but a new opera, in many ways opposed, both ideologically and musico-dramatically, to the old. The Imperial Theaters directorate and its opera committee, it will be argued, played an altogether negligible role in determining the nature of the new *Boris* (though its rejection of the opera may have been the spur that set the revision in motion). A clear understanding of the divergent tendencies represented by the two *Borises* will perhaps inhibit the rage to conflate. Such inhibition should arise, in any case, not out of any a priori ethical compunction but out of a better knowledge of Musorgsky, his time and place, his work, its "meaning" and its "significance."

The primary purpose here is not prescription. As Budden put it, referring to *Don Carlos*, "when performed with sufficient musical and dramatic understanding any combination of versions can be made to sound convincing."[10] And in the case of Musorgsky's work, one is even prepared to add "anybody's version." We need hold no moral grudge against Rimsky-Korsakov, Diaghilev, Shostakovich, Rathaus, or any of the other arrangers and impresarios whose so easily derided labors have ensured the opera's survival into our own enlightened time; in fact we ought to thank them. But what sounds convincing under the impression of a great performance is not always convincing upon reflection, and there is a dimension of understand-

[10] *The Operas of Verdi*, vol. 3, p. 156n.

ing that transcends individual performances. Each of Musorgsky's versions possesses a good deal more integrity than either, but particularly the second, is usually given credit for. A clearer pinpointing of their unique qualities will render them more distinct as musico-dramatic entities. These distinctions, perhaps, will make a difference in their appreciation.

I

The first public inkling that there was more than one completed version of *Boris Godunov* was given by V. V. Stasov in his lengthy biography-necrology, published in two installments by the journal *Vestnik Yevropï* within months of Musorgsky's death in 1881. "Originally," wrote Stasov,

> the opera *Boris Godunov* was to have consisted of only four acts and was almost wholly devoid of the feminine element. All those closest to Musorgsky (myself included), ecstatically though we admired the miracles of dramaturgy and of fidelity to the folk with which these four acts were filled, nevertheless remonstrated to him whenever we had the chance that his opera was incomplete, that much that was needed was lacking, and that however great the beauties that already existed in the opera, it could seem occasionally unsatisfactory.[11]

Though (by Stasov's account) Musorgsky resisted these importunings as long as he could, the opera's rejection by the Imperial Theaters directorate in February 1871 (Stasov incorrectly has "fall 1870") forced him around. It may surprise those who have been conditioned by conventional accounts to despise the much-maligned directorate, to read how thoroughly Stasov approved of their decision. "The rejection," he declared, "was extremely beneficial to the opera; Musorgsky decided to expand it," as a result of which "*Boris Godunov* achieved its completed form [as] one of the greatest works not only of Russian but of all European art."

Stasov went on to list the additions Musorgsky made to his opera in 1871–72. First and foremost he placed the scene at the Fountain, which, he claimed, had been part of the conception all along, and had been almost fully composed, but then dropped—"God knows why"—and restored at the urging of Stasov and of Victor Hartmann

[11] This and the following quotations from Stasov's article are taken from StasIS 2.197–98.

(the artist of the *Pictures at an Exhibition*). For some reason Stasov failed to mention the rest of the Polish act, that is, the scene in Marina's boudoir or the confrontation between the Pretender and Rangoni, although from Musorgsky's letters to Stasov himself we now know that it was "the Jesuit" (Rangoni) that chiefly inspired him in composing the Polish scenes.[12] Next, Stasov listed the genre interpolations for the minor women's roles (animal ditties all): the Hostess's song about the drake in the scene on the Lithuanian Border (hereinafter the Inn scene), and the three that went into the scene in the tsar's quarters in the Kremlin (hereinafter the Terem scene)—the Nanny's song about the gnat, the tsarevich's Clapping Game, and his song about his pet parrot. Third, Stasov listed the episode with the chiming clock at the end of the Terem scene. Fourth, the Kromy Forest scene, whose position at the end of the opera was suggested by Musorgsky's friend, the history professor V. V. Nikolsky, who in 1868 had given him the idea of an opera on Pushkin's *Boris Godunov* to begin with. ("I confess," wrote Stasov, who enjoyed taking credit for things, "that I was in despair and deeply envied Nikolsky that it was he and not I who imparted to Musorgsky so brilliant, so magnificent an idea.") And finally, Stasov listed the offstage chorus of monks at the end of the Cell scene, forgetting to mention the other one earlier in the scene at the end of Pimen's monologue and the awakening of Grigory, the future Pretender. "None of these wonderful creations of Musorgsky's would have existed," he observed in conclusion, "if his opera had been accepted immediately by the directorate and mounted on the stage."

But Stasov did not tell the whole story. His account of the revision of *Boris* was one-sided and self-serving, emphasizing his own contributions in the form of research—texts and situations from Karamzin's *History of the Russian State*, P. V. Sheyn's *Russian Folk Songs*, and other sources, many of them incorrectly identified.[13] His version stood, however, until the year of the Revolution, when an extremely important article on *Boris Godunov* appeared in the short-lived and now virtually forgotten journal *Muzïkal'nïy sovremennik*, the work of

[12] 18 April 1871. MusLN 1.122.

[13] For correctives see Mikhail Pekelis, "Musorgskiy—pisatel'-dramaturg," introductory essay to MusLN 2.18–19; Alexandra Orlova and Maria Schneerson, "After Pushkin and Karamzin: Researching the Sources for the Libretto of *Boris Godunov*," MusIM, 253, 267; as well as Chapter 4 of this book, where Stasov's assertions vis-à-vis Karamzin are scrutinized. For more on P. V. Sheyn's folklore anthology and Stasov's use of it on Musorgsky's behalf, see the Appendix to this chapter.

the journal's editor Andrey Rimsky-Korsakov, son of the opera's most notorious arranger.[14] Rimsky-Korsakov had followed in Stasov's footsteps as caretaker of musical manuscripts at the Imperial Public Library in St. Petersburg (from 1918 to his death in 1940 he would be head of the music division). As a result both of his family background and of his professional activities, he was intimately acquainted with the manuscript sources of Musorgsky's chef d'oeuvre, some of which still belonged to his mother, and in his article he gave a detailed description of them. From this it emerged that the revision process had been no simple matter of expansion and completion, but that much had also been deleted; and that what remained had been extensively recast.

For the first time it now became public knowledge that a whole scene in the first version had been done away with: the scene at St. Basil's, in which the Holy Fool (yuródivïy) had originally made his appearance and had confronted the tsar directly, as he no longer did in the revised version of the opera.[15] And for the first time it was revealed that the alterations in the Terem scene went so much further than the handful of additions listed by Stasov as to amount to a wholly new musico-dramatic conception, far less directly indebted to Pushkin than the original version of the scene had been. Rimsky-Korsakov reported further that the opening scene of the prologue, in the courtyard of the Novodevichy Monastery (Rimsky-Korsakov mistakenly called it the Chudov Monastery, confusing it with the one in which the Cell scene takes place) had originally ended not with the chorus of pilgrims but with another crowd scene, and that the Cell scene had included a lengthy narration by Pimen describing the murder of Tsarevich Dmitry, with a text drawn (like the rest of the scene) verbatim from Pushkin. The only alterations Rimsky-Korsakov failed to tabulate were fairly minor ones involving the end of the Inn scene[16] and the Death scene. In the case of Shchelkalov's monologue in the latter scene, the relevant manuscript was unavailable to him;[17]

[14] Andrey Rimsky-Korsakov, " 'Boris Godunov' M. P. Musorgskogo," Muzïkal'nïy sovremennik, nos. 5–6 (January–February 1917): 108–67.

[15] Actually a very brief and inaccurate reference to this scene had been included in Nikolai Rimsky-Korsakov's discussion of Boris in R-KMusL, 110, originally published eight years earlier, in 1909.

[16] Unknown to even Lamm, this was first made known by Lloyd-Jones in the critical notes to his edition (vol. 2, p. 23). He also printed a facsimile of the original ending of the scene (plate 4, following p. 71 of the second volume of the edition). The facsimile has since reappeared in the New Grove Dictionary 12.871.

[17] Lamm discovered it among Stasov's papers in the Public Library, Leningrad. See

the rest of the changes in the death scene (all deletions) were small and escaped his notice. As we shall see, however, some were far from insignificant.

Having given his description, Andrey, his father's loyal son, proceeded to ratify Stasov's judgment as to the relative merits of the versions, and in terms even stronger than Stasov's.[18] His account at least suggested, though, that there had been differences in conception, not merely in quality of execution, between them, and that the earlier of the two was recoverable from the extant sources. This was big news, but poorly timed. For the next half-dozen years there was little leisure in Russia for musicological pursuits. But in the mid-to-late twenties Rimsky-Korsakov's hints began to bear fruit in the form of more detailed research and publication.

As it happened, the next stage in the progressive revelation of the first *Boris* was contributed by a non-Russian scholar, though one with strong ties to Russian musicological circles. Oskar von Riesemann (1880–1934), who had been born in Reval (Talinn), Estonia, and had lived and worked chiefly in Moscow, published a biography of Musorgsky as the second (and, as it turned out, last) of a projected series of *Monographen zur russischen Musik*.[19] His discussion of the versions of *Boris* is a garbled hash derived (at times verbatim) from Rimsky-Korsakov's article. But he included, as an appendix, a vocal score of the entire scene at St. Basil's, which constituted the first publication anywhere of material belonging exclusively to the earlier version of the opera.[20] Riesemann's publication was immediately superseded, of course, by Lamm's edition, which made both authorial versions of the opera available for study and comparison at last. Owing to some curious ambiguities in its presentation, however, the Lamm edition did not make the relationship between the two versions optimally

the critical notes to his vocal score, pp. xxiv–xv (Russian), xxxvi (German); also Lamm, "Vostanovleniye podlinnogo teksta 'Borisa Godunova,' " p. 21.

[18] "At this stage of life, Musorgsky—by nature not at all disposed (unlike, for example, his friend Rimsky-Korsakov) to merciless self-criticism—had not yet had time to nurture in himself that pathological amour propre which manifested itself later, after the première of *Boris*; he was still young, his talent had matured too much in his own eyes; the shortcomings of the original version of *Boris*, partly connected with its text . . . partly attributable to Musorgsky's inexperience as an operatic composer, called attention to themselves far too loudly for him long to remain deaf and insensible to them" (" '*Boris Godunov*' M. P. Musorgskogo," p. 117).

[19] *Modest Petrowitsch Musorgski* (Munich: Drei Masken Verlag, 1926).

[20] The English-language edition, which appeared after the publication of Lamm's vocal score (*Moussorgsky*, trans. Paul Englund [New York: Alfred A. Knopf, 1929; reprint, 1971]) did not include this appendix.

clear. Because the first and second versions of the opera had so much music in common, Lamm deemed it expedient to present the two of them running as if concurrently. The St. Basil's scene and the Kromy scene, for example, are part of the same apparent continuity (with the death of Boris between them). The two versions of the Terem scene are found side by side—with the misleading labels "preliminary redaction" and "principal redaction." In addition, all passages that had been deleted from the first version in the process of revision are as it were reinstated, so that the Cell scene, for another telling example, which had been subjected to both addition (the offstage choruses) and deletion (Pimen's narrative), is presented in a form containing both the added and deleted items, that is to say, in a conflated form that represents neither of Musorgsky's own "redactions" but rather what amounts to a "supersaturated" redaction of Lamm's. Also presented in this fashion is the deleted excerpt that Lamm was the first to discover: Shchelkalov's monologue (the "reading of the ukase") at the beginning of the Death scene. Unknown to all previous writers, it brought to four the number of major deletions from the first version of the opera. All were duly "restored" by Lamm in his edition of 1928.

LAMM'S presentation gave rise to a persistent misapprehension that the additions first described by Stasov and the deletions first described by Rimsky-Korsakov represented two different layers of work on the opera, and that there were in fact *three* versions. These were the original (1868–69); an "1872" version (dated after the latest autograph full score, that of the Kromy scene), which contained the 1869 version plus the additions; and an "1874" version (dated after the vocal score published by Bessel), which contained the 1872 version minus the deletions. The deletions could then be variously explained away as the result of the censorship, or of meddlesomeness on the part of the Imperial Theater directorate or on the part of Eduard Nápravník, the conductor of the première. This hypothesis seems to have been explicitly articulated for the first time by Gerald Abraham in his supplementary contribution to Calvocoressi's posthumously published biography of Musorgsky in the Dent "Master Musicians" series (1946), where he asserted that the end of the Novodevichy scene and Pimen's narrative in the Cell scene were deleted only for the vocal score of 1874 and represented cuts made for the first production "on the advice of Nápravník and others."[21] But this thesis, unsupported as it is by any evidence, has been rejected by all recent Musorgsky scholars. It does not and cannot account for the alternative versions of the Terem scene, or for the episode with the *yuródiviy* and the boys that the St. Basil's scene and the Kromy scene have in common. It rests, moreover, on the mistaken assumption that the vocal score of 1874 represents the version of the text performed at the première. Not only Pimen's narrative but the whole Cell scene was cut for the first production, as was the song of the parrot in the Terem scene, yet the two latter items were included in the vocal score. Indeed, the score bore a legend on its title page proclaiming that it was a "complete arrangement for piano and voice, including the scenes not offered for production on the stage."[22]

This erroneous interpretation of *Boris Godunov*'s creative history was nowhere stated or implied by Lamm. While his chronological table on p. xvii of the vocal score does list three versions of the opera, his "second version" (representing the manuscript orchestral score of 1872) incorporates both the additions and the deletions, along with the "principal redaction" of the Terem scene. The "third version" (representing the published vocal score), elsewhere referred to by Lamm as the "principal version," differs from the second only in relatively minor textual matters (both emendations and shortcuts). The most recent commentators—Lloyd-Jones, Reilly, Oldani—prefer not to regard these differences as sufficient to constitute a full-fledged "version" (and Lloyd-Jones has mildly rebuked Lamm for according the printed vocal score precedence over the autograph full score[23]). But all agree that the differences between the orchestral and vocal scores represent a last layer of editorial work on Musorgsky's part. (What is not agreed upon, and what is not particularly relevant to our present concerns, is which layer—printed or autograph—was the later one.) So to assert that Lamm was so naive as to think that "Musorgsky, while revising the opera, continually expanded it but made no cuts . . . until after the revision had been composed and scored"[24] is both incorrect and disrespectful toward the work of a great scholar.

[21] *Mussorgsky* (New York: Collier Books, 1962), p. 166.

[22] A photograph of this title page may be seen in OrTD, facing page 288.

[23] See his discussion of "Editorial Method" in the second volume of his edition, pp. 19–21.

[24] Oldani, "Editions of *Boris Godunov*," p. 198.

Nevertheless, while it is possible to disengage the two authorial versions from each other in Lamm's vocal score (though not in the "supersaturated" orchestral score prepared with the assistance of Boris Asafyev), one needs to read the footnotes and the critical report to do so, and few, it seems, have bothered. Shostakovich, for instance, orchestrating the opera from Lamm's score, simply took the opera as he found it there, so that his orchestration represents Lamm's supersaturated redaction, with all deletions (including St. Basil's) back "in place."

Lloyd-Jones's newer critical edition, while an improvement in clarity over Lamm's (since St. Basil's is relegated to an appendix along with the earlier version of the Terem scene) is still, like Lamm's, a conflation. Thus the "world première recording of the original version," which reinstates St. Basil's before the Death scene (according to what is by now a tradition fostered by the Bolshoy Theater, Moscow, which commissioned an orchestration of the scene from Mikhail Ippolitov-Ivanov to insert into the Rimsky-Korsakov redaction), but which otherwise follows the Lloyd-Jones text, also presents a supersaturated version of the opera.[25] Ironically enough, to find a recorded version of the opera that accords with Musorgsky's own final version, one must now turn to one of the several based on Rimsky-Korsakov's second orchestration, which followed the vocal score of 1874 more closely than either Lamm or Lloyd-Jones.[26]

THE first major commentator to make use of the new material published by Lamm was his collaborator in the preparation of the full score, Boris Asafyev, writing under his pen name Igor Glebov, in the year of the new score's publication, 1928. Predictably enough, his was a revisionist account, partly intended as a promotion for the 1928 Leningrad production of the 1869 version, aimed squarely at the received Stasovian–Rimsky-Korsakovian idea that the second version was the true (or "complete") realization of Musorgsky's conception of the drama. Against all expectation, wrote Asafyev, the "preliminary version" turned out to be "more integrated, more profound, more complete, and more penetrating than any of the revisions, in-

---

[25] Angel SDLX-3844, Jerzy Semkow conducting. The same is true of more recent "authentic" recordings conducted by Vladimir Fedoseyev and Mstislav Rostropovich.

[26] E.g., Angel 3633, André Cluytens conducting, or the classic HMV recording, conducted by Issay Dobrowen, with Boris Christoff in three roles.

cluding those of the author himself."[27] He went on to claim that the earlier version had a better-focused dramatic theme (conflict between tsar and people, "a social and political tragedy, not the tragedy of Boris's conscience"[28]), and a more concentrated dramatic structure, while the second version ran off in all directions, both external (the Dmitry-Marina subplot) and internal (Boris's melodramatically portrayed psychological torment), with the result that the opera was reduced to "the personal drama of Tsar Boris against a romantic background of popular revolt."[29]

It is easy to see this thesis as typical of its early-Soviet time and place, and Asafyev to a considerable extent recanted it later.[30] It proved influential, however, and even became something of a received idea in its own right. It came westward in a rather crudely articulated form with Victor Belyayev's popularizing essay on the versions of *Boris*, which, as it happened, was published in English by Oxford University Press (the British agents for the Lamm edition) two years before it appeared in Russian.[31] This account was heavily reliant on Asafyev, as Belyayev indirectly acknowledged in his foreword.[32] The latter was even rasher than Asafyev in his claims for the first version, to the point of flatly contradicting the Stasovian position: "The composer did not revise the opera because he himself found, after its first production, that it was in some respects unsatisfactory, but because its staging depended upon a number of alterations required by irrelevant persons and external circumstances"[33]— an assertion as unsubstantiated as it was crass. Thus was the legend of the malign directorate born. "In view of this," continued Belyayev,

[27] Igor Glebov [Boris Asafyev], "Muzïkal'no-dramaturgicheskaya kontseptsiya operï 'Boris Godunov' Musorgskogo," AsIT 3.79.

[28] Ibid., p. 90.

[29] Ibid., p. 91.

[30] See his lengthy postwar study, " 'Boris Godunov' Musorgskogo kak muzïkal'nïy spektakl' iz Pushkina," which, however, remained unpublished until the posthumous (1954) Academy of Sciences collection of Asafyev's works (AsIT 3.100–59).

[31] Victor Belaiev [sic], *Musorgsky's Boris Godunov and Its New Version*, trans. S. W. Pring (London: Oxford University Press, 1928); the Russian version, "Dve redaktsii 'Borisa Godunova,' " was incorporated in the anthology "*Boris Godunov," Stat'i i issledovaniya*, referred to in n. 5.

[32] The acknowledgment is to Sergey Popov, who, Belyayev writes, "made me acqainted with a series of unpublished papers relating to the subject in which I was interested" (*Musorgsky's Boris Godunov*, p. v). This could only have been the collection *K vosstanovleniyu "Borisa Godunova" Musorgskogo*, in which two articles by Asafyev, including the one cited above, first appeared. Popov was the editor of this volume, which was published in Russia the same year Belyayev's piece appeared in England.

[33] Belyayev, p. 7. This sentence is italicized in the original text.

"the 'final' version of *Boris* (the composer's vocal score, published by Bessel in 1874 and now reissued) cannot possibly be considered *authentic* in the full meaning of the term."[34]

The aura of exclusive authenticity that now attached to the 1869 version of the opera lent it a prestige that few who wrote about it could resist. A certain aesthetic snob appeal engendered by its arrant unstaginess no doubt played a part as well. Thus Calvocoressi:

> What strikes us when we consider the original version of *Boris* are its starkness and terseness. It does not, like the later version, afford its hearers any opportunity for relief. It pursues its grim course without an instant of intermission, except when the tension is relieved awhile by touches of character-comedy in the dialogue. . . . And even at these points, there is nothing (except Varlaam's song . . .) that comes as an intermezzo inducing a halt, however brief, in the action. Every one of these touches is part and parcel of the whole.[35]

Or Gerald Abraham, writing of the relationship between Musorgsky's opera and Pushkin's play, in terms whose very casualness makes clear the unquestioned ascendancy of Asafyev's position:

> Some of Musorgsky's changes are easily understandable and quite justifiable; others—particularly the minor verbal alterations—seem pointless. Some of the major changes—such as the introduction of Rangoni, the melodramatic treatment of Boris's hallucinations in the Terem Scene (particularly its second version) and in the council of boyars, the banalization of the scene between Marina and Dmitry by the fountain—are altogether regrettable. But one point does emerge very markedly; the seven scenes which constitute the 1869 version are *not only the best musically and make a more satisfactory dramatic whole* than either the 1872 version or the cut version of the latter which Musorgsky published in 1874 (the original Bessel score); they are also much more faithful to Pushkin.[36]

[34] Ibid., pp. 7–8. All these italics may well have been added by Oxford University Press, since the Bessel reissue of *Boris* had been published in 1926 by Oxford's rivals J. and W. Chester.

[35] *Mussorgsky*, p. 143. On matters of detail Calvocoressi uncritically accepts Asafyev's ("Glebov's") judgments, quoting him verbatim and at length. He stops short of declaring an absolute preference for the first version, however, opening the door to conflation: "The complete [i.e., "supersaturated"] version is longer than the primitive version, but makes up for its length by affording opportunities for relaxation and points of repose which, far from breaking or unduly delaying the course of action, co-operates in it" (p. 156). On the other hand, the Polish act is "merely a long intermezzo, charming or impressive in parts, but at times, I think, tedious" (p. 155).

[36] "Mussorgsky's 'Boris' and Pushkin's," originally published in *Music and Letters* 26 (1945), quoted from Gerald Abraham, *Slavonic and Romantic Music* (New York: St. Mar-

Some moderation of this view has lately become the norm, as the pendulum has continued to swing on the matter of Stasov's testimony, and as the novelty of the discovery of the 1869 version has worn off.[37] The last serious claim on behalf of the 1869 version of the opera was made implicitly in 1970 by the ultraorthodox Soviet musicologist Yuriy Tyulin, who argued for the suppression of the Kromy scene on the basis of its alleged "slander" of the Russian people. But Tyulin's article was printed together with no less than four invited refutations by other Soviet musicologists.[38] Abram Gozenpud, the outstanding contemporary Soviet authority on nineteenth-century Russian opera, considers it "impossible to agree with the generally accepted point of view" that "the newer version was the result of concession and adaptation to the demands of the Theatrical directorate," for in that case, "Musorgsky, knowingly mutilating his own work so as to secure its production, would be not a great and principled artist but a man of compromise. The testimony of Stasov and Rimsky-Korsakov [i.e., the much later *Chronicle of My Musical Life*] refutes the notion of forced revision."[39] Though he puts it tautologically, Gozenpud is undoubtedly correct about this, and quite rightly, too, he adduces the evidence of Musorgsky's letters during the period of revision, which show that "in actuality he applied himself to the making of the new version with great enthusiasm."[40]

But if one stops short, as Gozenpud does, of assenting to Stasov's (and Rimsky-Korsakov's) preference for the second version—"the two versions of *Boris* differ not in the degree of the sharpness of social conflict [*pace* Asafyev] or that of artistic merit [*pace* Stasov], but rather represent two distinct conceptions"[41]—then one is left with the problem of accounting for Musorgsky's enthusiasm, not to mention the problem of motivating the new conception. N. Isakhanova has argued that Musorgsky's primary impulse to revise came from his increasing musical mastery. This she tries to demonstrate by

tin's Press, 1968), p. 187. Italics are mine. On the erroneous matter of the "1872" and "1874" versions, see above.

[37] Still, Joseph Kerman was following the Belyayev line as recently as 1975: "The plain fact is that all versions of *Boris Godunov* except the first are pastiches, and that even the composer's own pastiche—the second version—lacks final authority" ("The Puzzle of Boris," *Opera News* 39, no. 12 [25 January 1975]: 12).

[38] See the Introduction to this book. The 1869 version enjoyed a new vogue in the 1980s: see the Epilogue.

[39] GozROTIII, 70.

[40] Ibid.

[41] Ibid., p. 71.

means of a detailed comparison of the two versions of the Boris-Shuisky confrontation in the Terem scene, the superiority of whose *first* version, ironically enough, had been one of Asafyev's main contentions. She concludes, in the unmistakable jargon of Soviet musicography:

> Acknowledging the great intonational merits of the musical language of the first version, which acutely underscores the content of the text, one must nonetheless give preference to the second version, as being dramatically more fully realized, more effective, and for that reason more responsive to the specific demands of the operatic stage. It is important to emphasize that such an opinion was maintained . . . by Musorgsky's very close friends and admirers, Stasov and Borodin [cf. the latter's letter to his wife of 12 November 1871, in BorP 1.322]. To continue to prefer the first version is futile: it inevitably leads to affirming that which Musorgsky himself denied in his later work. The composer created the new version of his opera with authentic inspiration led by his own artistic taste and by the exceptionally augmented mastery of an authentic dramatist. His second version of *Boris Godunov* is a magnificent artistic achievement.[42]

Quite so! And the point about "that which Musorgsky himself denied in his later work" is a perceptive one that will reward pursuit. Still, Isakhanova has far from "explained" the new *Boris*. For if increased mastery can be thought to account for the *revisions*, strictly construed, it can account for neither the additions nor the deletions. To explain the additions, one must still invoke the Theatrical directorate, and no one has yet explained the deletions satisfactorily.

The latest major contribution to the debate, that of Edward Reilly, illustrates the dilemma well. Like Gozenpud, Reilly refrains from stating a preference for either version. He calls the 1869 *Boris* "one of the most striking attempts at operatic reform in the entire nineteenth century . . . a highly compressed closed drama, a single dramatic arch with a well-defined beginning, middle, and end,"[43] and claims that Musorgsky tampered with this excellent structure in order to "meet some of the criticisms he had received." But Reilly's list of criticisms (some of them extrapolated rather than documented, which tends to bend the argument into a circle)—the lack of a love story, the lack of a major feminine role, and the cutting short of the part of the False Dmitry, "the potential tenor hero"—in no way corresponds

---

[42] N. Isakhanova, "Put' k sovershenstvu," SovM 30, no. 7 (1966): 60.
[43] RMusMus, 5, 6.

with the list of revisions he gives one paragraph later: the Hostess's song, the songs of the tsarevich and the nanny in the Terem scene, the "chiming clock," the rewritten dialogue of Boris and Shuisky, the introduction of Rangoni, the excision of the St. Basil's scene, and the addition of the one at Kromy. Only those aspects of the Polish act directly involving Marina and the Pretender answer to the needs Reilly indicated. The resulting version of the opera "is more overtly complex, somewhat less tightly organized, and more varied in musical style" than its predecessor.[44] It merits performance on a par with the first version because of its greater accessibility: it is "much broader in scale, longer, more varied and at certain points more overtly theatrical and 'operatic' in the conventional sense. Musically it is somewhat less even in quality, but the new passages include some of the most lyrical and immediately appealing portions of the work."[45] While Reilly's personal preference is clearly for the first version, he grants that "both versions . . . have distinct merits of their own, closely bound up with the composer's carefully thought-out conceptions, and each deserves independent productions."[46]

But Reilly does not really show that the conceptions were carefully thought out. He merely asserts that they were.[47] And as always, the deletions are a stumbling block: St. Basil's is passed over in silence, while with regard to what Reilly (following Abraham) calls the "major cuts in the 1874 vocal score," that is, the end of the first scene of the prologue and Pimen's narrative, he remarks that they "will (and should) always remain a subject for debate. Both episodes are so rich dramatically and musically that it is painful to see them removed. Yet I think Musorgsky was quite properly concerned by the length of his greatly expanded new version, and felt that some of the strong inner relationships of the first version should be de-emphasized in his new scheme of things."[48]

The last remark seems a non sequitur, and the whole passage may be questioned on grounds of chronology, since it still assumes that

[44] Ibid., p. 8.
[45] Ibid., p. 11.
[46] Ibid.
[47] One should mention, however, Reilly's perceptive rationalization of the Polish act as having been conceived "not as a vehicle for the display of Romantic passion, but to show the *deceptiveness* of such passion and how it can be used and diverted to other ends" (p. 9).
[48] RMusMus, 10.

Musorgsky first expanded, then cut.[49] But neither of these points is the chief problem. Whether to include this or that item within a freely conflated *Boris* will (and should) be endlessly debated, as Reilly says, for these will always be matters of taste. But unless an account of the revision of *Boris* can show why precisely those numbers that were cut had to go, then it is really no account at all, if by "account" a coherent explanation, rather than a mere inventory, is meant. I believe that by bringing a number of hitherto neglected factors, both internal and external, to bear upon the problem, such an explanation can be attempted. The rest of this essay is that attempt.

II

The version of *Boris Godunov* that Musorgsky began in the fall of 1868 and completed on 15 December 1869 was exactly the sort of opera that those who knew him would have expected from him at that particular point in his career. The original *Boris* was an *opéra dialogué*, a "numberless" recitative opera based not only in subject but in actual text on a preexistent play. Its immediate model was Dargomïzhsky's *The Stone Guest*, to the text of Pushkin's "Little Tragedy" of 1830, begun in earnest in 1867 (though conceived as early as 1863) and still in progress alongside *Boris* up to its creator's death at the beginning of 1869. Its immediate predecessor was Musorgsky's own unfinished *Marriage*, to the text of a comedy by Gogol, on which he had worked during the summer of 1868.

The motivating premise behind all these works was an extremist-realist contempt for operatic librettos with their provision for "musical forms," and the belief that the highest realization of opera's potential would come about when composers would "perform" great plays like inspired actors. Music would be used to fix and control the rendition of the lines, thus imparting to them an emotional impact they would otherwise lack, just as the words would lend the music in return an otherwise unattainable specificity of intention. The need for specificity reveals the positivist basis of the aesthetic that ruled these works—a bias much more pronounced in Musorgsky than in Dargomïzhsky, who sometimes complained that his younger colleague went too far in his musical empiricism. The same bias is re-

[49] For a more elaborate refutation of this view than the one offered earlier in this chapter, see Oldani, "Editions of *Boris Godunov*," pp. 197–99, or his dissertation, pp. 76–82.

vealed in the emphasis on accurate declamation as key to an authentic musical expression based on the "natural" model of speech.[50]

In *The Stone Guest*, Dargomïzhsky had completely rejected melismatic prosody (and with it, the possibility of vocal display) and had adopted a fairly regular and moderate tempo akin to that of declaimed poetry. In *Marriage*, based on a prose text, Musorgsky, while adopting an aesthetic stance no less ascetic, went in a somewhat different direction. His declamation was far more naturalistic than Dargomïzhsky's, full of "antilyrical" augmented and diminished intervals, wide leaps reflecting the comically exaggerated contours of agitated speech, and exceedingly finicky rhythms set to a faster, more "conversational" tempo. By the time he had set one act, however, Musorgsky found his "experiment in dramatic music in prose" confining—"a cage," as he put it in more than one letter—owing both to the paltriness of the subject matter and to the tendentious rigor of his method. He was eager to turn his attention to something more significant and creative, the more so since his friend Rimsky-Korsakov had just embarked on the grandiose project of turning Lev Alexandrovich Mey's historical drama *Pskovityanka* [The maid of Pskov] into a modified *opéra dialogué*. So he fairly leapt at Vladimir Nikolsky's suggestion that he do the same with Pushkin's *Boris Godunov*.

This play had everything, starting with an important historical theme, something that was especially relevant in the late 1860s, when historical drama, chiefly involving the period of Ivan the Terrible and the Time of Troubles that followed, was becoming the dominant theatrical genre in Russia.[51] Pushkin provided a "Shakespearean" mixture of poetry and prose, tragedy and comedy, which would vouchsafe the opportunity to combine the approaches of *The Stone Guest* and *Marriage* and evade the monotony of style that had plagued both works; a wide range of character types from boyar to beggar, to be portrayed naturalistically through declamation in the manner of the songs Musorgsky had been writing since 1866; and a large role for the crowd, making good the one lack César Cui, speaking for the kuchka, had noted in evaluating *The Stone Guest* as an operatic "canvas." And, perhaps not least, owing to the "predominance of politics" in it and the absence of romance, *Boris Godunov* had

---

[50] For a thorough treatment of this aesthetic and its musical embodiments in Dargomïzhsky and the young Musorgsky, see TarODR, chapter 5.

[51] See Chapter 4.

been pronounced unfit for operatic treatment by Alexander Serov, the chief musical pundit of the day, to whom the Balakirev circle had grown increasingly hostile, especially since his unexpectedly success-ful 1863 debut as an opera composer in his own right.[52] Selecting Pushkin's play as a subject was thus an act of typically realist aes-thetic bravado. Political bravado, too (or was it just kuchkist quixoti-cism?), since until 1866 Pushkin's *Boris*—like Mey's *Pskovityanka*, for that matter—was under the censor's ban. (It was finally staged, heavily bowdlerized, in 1870.) Censorship, as all composers knew, was even stricter for operas than for spoken drama.

The only drawback *Boris Godunov* presented was its length. As a full-scale play, unlike the extremely compressed *Stone Guest*, it would have to be adapted for operatic use, not set in toto as it stood. Com-parison of the 1868–69 libretto with Pushkin's play will show how determined Musorgsky was that the adaptation be kept to a mini-mum; at this point in his career he was very much the aesthetic doc-trinaire. Examination of his specific selections and omissions will also show how he viewed the drama, and might cast doubt on some com-monly held points of view, notably those that tout the first *Boris* as a "single dramatic arch" (Reilly) or as a "social and political tragedy" (Asafyev).

THERE is no need to proceed in detail, scene by scene, as that has long since been definitively accomplished by Gerald Abraham.[53] But since Abraham's main purpose was to compare the various *Borises* rather than to compare the first version with its literary source, there

---

[52] "Drama and opera are by no means identical, and a subject that is excellent in itself and excellently developed in a play can be completely unsuitable for opera. The best examples: Goethe's *Faust* (the first part), Shakespeare's *Hamlet*, Pushkin's *Boris Godunov*. These very profound dramas are founded on characters in whom rational thought predominates, and thought is an element by its very nature unmusical." SerIS 1.259.

[53] "Musorgsky's 'Boris' and Pushkin's" (see n. 36). One small corrective to Abra-ham's admirably thorough survey may be offered. In Musorgsky's first scene (the courtyard of the Novodevichy Monastery), Pushkin's scenes 2 (Red Square) and 3 (No-vodevichy) are not quite so freely conflated and adapted as Abraham reports. Much of Shchelkalov's speech is found in the opening exchange between two members of the crowd in scene 2, an exchange whose very first word is the striking participle, "*Neu-molim!*" [implacable], with which Shchelkalov begins his appeal in the libretto. Some of the contents of Musorgsky's chorus of pilgrims is found in the lines Pushkin gave Shchelkalov in the play—e.g., the reference to processions with the holy images of the Vladimir and Don madonnas. The words of the *pristav* [policeman] and of Mityukha— roles for choral coryphées in Musorgsky's text—are in large part prefigured in the lines Pushkin gave the crowd.

was no need for him to make the kind of general observations our present purposes require. These may be easily extracted from his data, however. Musorgsky's fidelity to Pushkin in 1869 was nearly total. With the sole exception of the hallucination in the Terem scene there is nothing in the action of Musorgsky's drama that was not present at least by implication in Pushkin's. As to the actual words of the libretto, while it is something of an exaggeration to claim, as Musorgsky did on the title page of his 1874 vocal score, that "[the] subject [was] borrowed from A. S. Pushkin's dramatic chronicle of the same name, preserving the majority of his verses,"[54] it is certainly true that the majority of the 1869 libretto's verses are in Pushkin— the very great majority.

Two scenes in the opera—the Cell scene and the Inn scene—were full-fledged, verbatim *opéra dialogué* settings of complete scenes in Pushkin, only slightly abridged. The former took as its text a scene cast, like all of *The Stone Guest*, in blank iambic pentameters. The latter was set to an extended comic scene in prose, like all of *Marriage*. The melodic and declamational styles of these two scenes closely resemble those of their respective prototypes. A comparison of a typical passage from Pimen's part with one from that of Don Juan in *The Stone Guest* (disguised, as it happens, as a monk) will demonstrate the similarity of Musorgsky's and Dargomïzhsky's approaches to setting Pushkin's poetry (Example 1).

These two passages, perfect specimens of what César Cui called "melodic recitative," have been chosen to illustrate two declamatory features in particular. The first is the manner of starting phrases with anacruses of a full beat's duration, even though this does not naturalistically reflect Russian speech patterns. It produces, rather, what one Soviet writer has called "rounded intonational periods,"[55] and its "natural model," if such it be, is not conversational speech but the emotionally exalted tone Russians invariably assume when, even to-

---

[54] Of course, the claim was even more of an exaggeration in 1874 than in 1869, but by 1874 it was merely a slogan identifying the opera's "tendency," a paraphrase of the formula first used by Dargomïzhsky on the title page of his *Rusalka* (1856)—"Libretto by the author after the drama of A. S. Pushkin, preserving many of his verses"—and echoed by César Cui on the title page of *William Ratcliff* (1869), the first kuchkist opera to achieve publication: "Text borrowed from the dramatic ballad of Heinrich Heine, in the translation of A. N. Pleshcheyev." The publisher of *Ratcliff* (Bessel), not catching the kuchkist nuance in Cui's use of the word "text," faced it with an inaccurate German translation: "Das Sujet ist der Heinischen Tragödie *William Ratcliff* entlehnt."

[55] Mikhail Druskin, *Voprosï muzïkal'noy dramatugii operï* (Leningrad: Muzgiz, 1952), p. 83.

EXAMPLE 1a. *Boris Godunov* (MusPSS 1 [MusCW 2]), p. 53

[Some laborious monk will] kindle, as I, his lamp, and from the parchment shaking the dust of ages, will transcribe my chronicles, that thus posterity, the bygone fortunes of the orthodox of their own land may learn . . . (trans. Alfred Hayes, The Poems, Prose, and Plays of Pushkin, p. 343)

EXAMPLE 1b. *The Stone Guest* (Moscow: Muzgiz, 1932), pp. 104–5

How long I've been in love I do not know, but only that since that hour I've known the value of this brief life, yes, only since that hour I've understood what happiness could mean. (trans. A.F.B. Clark, Poems, Prose, and Plays of Pushkin, p. 453)

day and even in casual surroundings, they recite poetry. The passage from Dargomïzhsky exhibits the trait in a more consistent fashion, for his style of melodic recitative is more unremittingly lyrical than Musorgsky's. The younger composer reserves the device for the climactic couplet, *"Da vedayut . . . ,"* where he draws out the concluding notes (e.g., *"pravoslavnïkh"*) as well, thus "rounding" the "intonational period."

The other characteristic declamational device has been termed the "mute ending" (*glukhoye okonchaniye*): the naturalistic rendering of words that end on unaccented syllables, producing, typically, a pair of eighth notes (or a triplet) on a beat, with the beginning of the next beat void. In the *Boris* excerpt this happens on *"perepíshet"*; in the one from Dargomïzhsky, compare *"nedávno"* and *"ne znáyu"* in the first line. In settings of poetry, this trait is special effect, honored as often in the breach as in the observance. In the examples cited, Musorgsky uses it as a foil against which the lyrical climax (including the drawn-out *"pravoslávnïkh"*) is set off. Dargomïzhsky uses it as an expressive device, to impart a sense of breathless (and, to be sure, affected) urgency to Don Juan's seduction of Donna Anna.

In Musorgsky's settings of prose, however, the mute ending is very much the rule, for here naturalism in declamation is the main concern. Virtually any passage from *Marriage* or from the Inn scene in *Boris* could serve as illustration. Example 2 shows one from each.

The plethora of rests effectively precludes any hint of "lyricism" here. And note how thoroughly mixed are the note values, and how freely duple divisions of the beat alternate with triple. These traits are "drawn from life." In normal, conversational Russian speech, the tonic accent is very strong and tends to fall into a pattern of fairly isochronous "beats," with the unaccented syllables arranging themselves evenly between them like gruppetti. Triplets are superabundant in the "conversational" Inn scene; they are almost absent in the "declaimed" Cell scene. The two scenes sum up between them the state of the declamatory art in extremist-realist Russian music, vintage 1860s. That, in fact, was to a large extent their raison d'être.

These fully incorporated scenes account for only two out of Musorgsky's seven (in 1869), and—more to the point—only two out of Pushkin's twenty-five. How were Pushkin's remaining twenty-three boiled down to Musorgsky's remaining five? The solution was of the Gordian Knot variety. Musorgsky simply threw out all the scenes in

EXAMPLE 2a. *Boris Godunov*, pp. 110–11

Here's why: Alyokha! Have you got the ukase? Give it here! Look: A certain heretic, Grishka Otrepyev, has escaped from Moscow. Did you know that?

EXAMPLE 2b. *Marriage* (Moscow, 1933), pp. 14–15

It's a troublesome thing, marriage, devil take it! This, that, and the other thing . . . everything has to be just so. No! What the devil, it's not as easy as it seems.

which the title character failed to appear, leaving a total not of twenty-three but only six from which to adapt his text.

For Boris himself loomed not nearly as large in Pushkin's scheme of things as in Musorgsky's. Indeed, calling his play *Boris Godunov* was merely the poet's tendentious nod in the direction of Shakespeare's Henry IV and his heavy crown. The tradition to which his play belonged was that of the "Demetrius play," a genre that had its heyday in the Spanish and English theaters of the early seventeenth century (Lope de Vega, Fletcher), and continued to produce specimens well into the nineteenth. Immediate predecessors of Pushkin's Demetrius drama included plays by Kotzebue (1782), Schiller (1805), and, in Russia, Sumarokov (1771). In all of these plays the Pretender was the title character, the tsar merely his target (the same would be true of Hebbel's *Demetrius,* completed in 1864, and Ostrovsky's *Dmitry the Pretender and Vasily Shuisky* of 1867).[56]

Now, while the balance between the two main characters is more even in Pushkin than in the work of his predecessors, the fact remains that Dmitry is on stage more of the time than Boris (eight scenes), and is portrayed just as imaginatively and "roundly" as the title character. Neither tsar nor Pretender can be said to dominate Pushkin's drama. It is a true "chronicle," for which reason "Russia," or, more sentimentally, "the Russian people" is often cited as its protagonist. Dmitry could just as easily have been the central character of the opera but for the inevitable attractions exerted by the tortured figure of the tsar on the imagination of a composer reared in the Dostoyevskian sixties and the opportunities the role afforded a practitioner of *opéra dialogué* by its wealth of beautiful (and famous) soliloquies. Perhaps, too, the relative brevity of Boris's role was itself seen as an asset, since the scenes containing it, when isolated and reshuffled a bit, produced a highly concentrated (if not altogether coherent) drama.

Here is a summary of how Musorgsky distributed and dovetailed the material of Pushkin's six Boris scenes to make the rest of his 1869 libretto:

SCENE 4 (The Kremlin Palace): Boris's speeches to the assembled boyars and patriarch (his first appearance in the play) were excerpted and adapted to produce the central monologue in the Coronation scene. The decorative choral tableaux on either side of the monologue were Musorgsky's idea. The added text, though, amounts to no more than that of the famous *Slava!* and two lines for Shuisky.

SCENE 11 (The Tsar's Palace): This scene provided, in course of action and in words, the framework of the Terem scene. A fairly lengthy exchange between the tsar and the boyar Semyon Godunov was replaced by a heavily abridged paraphrase. The hallucination at the end was original with Musorgsky (probably prompted by Holofernes's hallucination scene in Serov's *Judith*). Twice this scene is interrupted by interpolations from—

---

[56] For a history of the genre—more comprehensive, in fact, than its title implies— see Ervin C. Brody, *The Demetrius Legend and Its Literary Treatment in the Age of the Baroque* (Rutherford, N.J.: Fairleigh Dickinson University Press, 1972).

SCENE 8 (The Tsar's Palace): After a brief exchange for two courtiers who exit immediately upon Boris's entrance, this scene consists wholly of the tsar's great Shakespearean soliloquy about kingship and conscience. The first thirty-seven lines, boiled down to twenty-nine, became the central monologue, "I Have Attained the Highest Power" (*Dostig ya vïsshey vlasti*), while seven of the last nine lines became the closing monologue immediately preceding the hallucination.

SCENE 19 (Square in Front of the Cathedral in Moscow): This scene closely corresponds with the St. Basil's scene in the opera. Musorgsky added the chorus of the people begging bread and the concluding reprise of the *yuródivïy*'s song.

SCENE 17 (The Tsar's Council) and Scene 22 (The Tsar's Palace): Episodes from these two scenes were conflated to produce the Death scene. Scene 22 furnished the farewell to the tsarevich and the "beginning of the ceremony of the tonsure," as Pushkin put it in the concluding stage direction, that is, the ritual of monastic vows with which the Russian tsars prepared for death. This gave Musorgsky the idea for the chorus of monks at the conclusion of the scene. The actual death agony was Musorgsky's; Pushkin let the curtain fall on the tonsure ceremony. Shuisky's report to the boyars of the tsar's hallucination was obviously Musorgsky's, as the hallucination itself had been.

From scene 17, curiously enough, Musorgsky cut out Boris's own lines. One of his speeches, however, became the basis for the decree read by Shchelkalov at the beginning of the Death scene.[57] The main appropriation from scene 17 was the tale of the miracle worked by the sainted infant Dmitry, told in the play not by Pimen—who, of course, logically has nothing to do with the tsar—but by the patriarch.

To this Musorgsky attached a prefatory scene (Novodevichy) derived from two crowd scenes (scenes 2 and 3) near the beginning of Pushkin's play, and his libretto was complete.[58]

It was in every way an *opéra dialogué* libretto, and in setting it Musorgsky maintained with fair consistency the two declamational styles illustrated above with respect to the Cell and Inn scenes,

[57] A few words from one of the patriarch's speeches, "You do not wish destruction to the sinner" (*Tï greshniku pogibeli ne khochesh'*), were transformed and transferred to the conclusion of Musorgsky's hallucination episode at the end of the Terem scene, where Boris sings, "You do not wish the sinner's death" (*Tï ne khochesh' smerti greshnika*). The irony is that in the opera Boris addresses the lines to God with reference to himself, while in the play the patriarch addresses them to Boris with reference to the Pretender.

[58] For more details on this conflation, see Abraham, "Musorgsky's 'Boris' and Pushkin's," and n. 53.

depending upon whether the text at a given moment was verse or prose. The St. Basil's scene was the only other scene besides the Inn scene written entirely in prose; elsewhere, wherever Musorgsky set Pushkin directly, the text is verse. The only (partial) exception is the Terem scene, which in the Pushkin original mixes prose and verse. Musorgsky furthered the mixture by frequently paraphrasing the text, especially in the concluding monologue and in the episode with Shuisky, substituting his own prose for Pushkin's verse. And in these passages, accordingly, the second declamational manner takes over from the first. This applies as well to the crowd music in the opening scene at Novodevichy, especially the closing section, after the chorus of pilgrims has ended. Here, in one of the boldest declamatory strokes in the entire opera, Musorgsky wrote a scene for the chorus in naturalistic prose recitative, over an orchestral continuity derived from fragments of themes from the orchestral introduction and the pilgrims' chorus.

THIS device of orchestral continuity was one that Musorgsky had just recently hit upon, and which he now cultivated very deliberately. In composing *Marriage* he was confronted with a severe problem of musical coherence (one that, in the opinion of many—including his fellow kuchkists—he did not adequately solve), caused by his deliberately asymmetrical and athematic prose recitative. This hurdle was so troublesome that it forced Musorgsky to rewrite completely the single act of Gogol's play he managed to finish, which therefore exists in two distinct versions contained in two autograph fair copies: the standard version, inscribed to Stasov (at the Public Library in St. Petersburg), which served as the basis for both publications of the work,[59] and what we may in this case justly designate a "preliminary version," now at the Glinka Museum in Moscow.[60] The revisions affected the vocal parts hardly at all—a pitch or note value here, a rest there. But the accompaniment was altogether transformed. From a virtual secco it became a fairly elaborate affair, commenting on the dramatic goings-on at times wittily (e.g., the "curlicues" that so amused Dargomïzhsky that he could never proceed at private run-

[59] Ed. Rimsky-Korsakov (St. Petersburg: Bessel, 1908); ed. Lamm (Moscow: Muzgiz, 1933).
[60] See Yelena Antipova, "Dva varianta 'Zhenit'bï,' " SovM 28, no. 3 (March 1964): 77–85.

EXAMPLE 3a. *Marriage*, first version (after facsimile in SovM 3 [1964]: 83)

Well, then, you agree!—I? Well, no, I don't yet entirely agree.

throughs in St. Petersburg without stopping to laugh[61]), at times in a naive "Mickey Mouse" fashion. Occasionally, the revisions in the accompaniment aspired to a higher, structurally unifying purpose. One such instance, especially striking as it bears direct witness to the composer's intentions, comes near the end. Over the phrase given in Example 3a, in which the bachelor antihero Podkolyosin expresses his perennial inertia and cold feet, Musorgsky penciled in a note to himself, "on the opening phrases of the first scene" (*na khodakh l-i stseni*). In the revised version (Example 3b), the accompaniment is made to incorporate a reference to the melodic phrase that opens the opera (Example 3c), producing a sort of primitive leitmotif.

Nor is this the only instance of recurring motives in the second version of *Marriage*. Even the first version had a few, but they were as skimpy and haphazard in their development as in *The Stone Guest*, where the only characters to sport identifying themes[62] were Donna

[61] See Nadezhda Purgold's (Rimskaya-Korsakova's) memoir in MR, 124.
[62] For this term, cf. Joseph Kerman, "Verdi's Use of Recurring Themes," *Studies in Music History for Oliver Strunk*, ed. Harold Powers (Princeton: Princeton University

EXAMPLE 3b. *Marriage*, second version (Moscow: Muzgiz, 1933), p. 60

Well, then, you agree!—I? Well, no, I don't yet entirely agree.

EXAMPLE 3c. *Marriage*, p. 1

Anna, the Statue, and, most improbably, one of the smallest roles of all, the Monk (or rather "monks in general," since the theme is also associated with the disguised Don Juan). These themes of Dargomïzhsky's were mere tags, used mainly to accompany entrances and exits; rarely were they called upon to sustain the kind of continuity

---

Press, 1968), pp. 495–510. "Identifying themes," or what are usually loosely designated leitmotifs, are usefully distinguished there from "recalling themes," Kerman's rendering of *Erinnerungmotive*.

(one hesitates to use the word development) found on so many pages of *Boris*. In the revised *Marriage*, on the other hand, identifying themes are applied and deployed far more systematically, and it is evident that by using them Musorgsky sought to compensate for the "formlessness" of his setting, in which the vocal lines are so much less structured than Dargomïzhsky's. Every character in the revised *Marriage* (except for the manservant Stepan) has at least two identifying themes, which recur so often that the accompaniment seems at times a veritable patchwork. However abundant, though, these themes remain static components of what remains, by and large, a "punctuating" orchestra, and they do grow tiresome as the act wears on. But there is one outstanding exception to this generalization: the matchmaker's Fyokla's lengthy enumeration of a dowry (the longest speech in the play). Musorgsky set the whole thing as continuous elaboration, *moto perpetuo* style, of the signature tune that announced her first entrance (Example 4).

These methods of deploying identifying themes were a permanent acquisition for Musorgsky. Nor should we forget his *Salammbô* of 1863–66, where recurring motives had also played a conspicuous role, not only structural but also dramaturgical. Mato's prison monologue in act 4, evidently modeled on Ivan Susanin's act 4 monologue in *A Life for the Tsar*, makes striking use of recalling themes as Mato reflects upon the past action of the drama.[63]

The leitmotif treatment in *Boris* represents a kind of synthesis of the identifying-theme technique one finds in *Marriage* and the recalling-tune device one encounters in *Salammbô*, just as *Boris* itself represents a kind of synthesis of the operatic genres represented by Musorgsky's two earlier attempts. The use of identifying themes is pervasive. In his analysis of the opera, Andrey Rimsky-Korsakov identified and discussed motives for the six most important characters in the first version of the opera: Boris (actually a whole complex of themes about which there will be more to say later), the Pretender, Prince Shuisky, Pimen, Varlaam, even Fyodor (the tsarevich).[64] He could have gone a good deal farther, as he noted himself in calling an arbitrary halt to his survey: "The dimensions of an article do not permit us in the present connection to dwell in detail on the minor characters";[65] but it is precisely here, among the small fry, that one

[63] See MusPSS 4/1 (MusCW 19), pp. 172–87.
[64] " 'Boris Godunov' M. P. Musorgskogo," pp. 141–49.
[65] Ibid., pp. 148–49.

EXAMPLE 4. *Marriage*, p. 17

can best appreciate the rigor of Musorgsky's procedure. Literally every character who appears in more than one scene has an identifying theme, whether Shchelkalov at the two ends of the opera,[66] or the police officer (at Novodevichy, the inn on the Lithuanian border, and—by implication—St. Basil's: quite a beat!).[67] Even Mityukha, the representative of the crowd, has a fleeting phrase that identifies him in both the Novodevichy and St. Basil's scenes (Example 5). And although Xenia appears in only one scene, Boris sings to her or about her in two, and in both he does so to the same orchestral music.[68]

As for Boris himself, we have already noted that no one theme is used to characterize him in all his manifestations. This befits the complexity of the role. But what is striking is the extent to which the accompaniments to his utterances—particularly the two big soliloquies in the Terem scene—are woven out of a practically seamless fabric of leitmotifs. "I Have Attained the Highest Power" is based

[66] Cf. the Lamm vocal score, pp. 20, 329.

[67] Cf. ibid., pp. 3, 12, 29 (Novodevichy); pp. 106–7, etc. (the Inn); p. 306 (St. Basil's). No police officer sings in the St. Basil's scene, but according to the stage direction they are "often to be seen among the crowd." Even though the list of dramatis personae includes only one officer ("Nikitich," as he is addressed by the women in the opening scene), and even though a single bass-baritone sings the role both at Novodevichy and at the Inn, one wonders whether Musorgsky meant literally (as Gozenpud, for one, assumes he did) that the same officer turns up in both scenes, or whether his leitmotif characterizes the police in general, as Dargomïzhsky had characterized monks in general in *The Stone Guest*.

[68] Cf. the Lamm vocal score, pp. 128, 136 (Terem scene), 359 (Death scene).

EXAMPLE 5a. *Boris Godunov*, p. 10

EXAMPLE 5b. *Boris Godunov*, p. 307

rigorously on two themes—both salvaged from *Salammbô*—which seem to have been meant to present the tsar's two contrasting sides. The first, an arching, aspiring melody that had permeated the big Temple scene in the earlier opera,[69] seems to be associated with Boris's noble qualities and frustrated good intentions. It is first heard where he complains (in Lloyd-Jones's translation), "In vain the wise astrologers foretell long life, and years of glory, free from turmoil,"[70] and later it accompanies his promise of mercy to Shuisky (Example 6). The other motive, filled with dissonant chromatic intervals, seems to be associated with the tsar's agony of remorse, and with punishment. In *Salammbô* it had been the melody to which the Pentarchs pronounced the death sentence on Mato.[71] In *Boris*, it is first heard where the title character laments, "God in his wrath sent famine to our land," and in the scene with Shuisky it contrasts directly with the first motive, when Boris follows his promise with threats (Example 7). At the end of the Terem scene, a lengthy sequence built out of this second motive gives form to the soliloquy before the hallucination.[72]

[69] MusPSS 4/1 (MusCW 19), pp. 111, 115–17, 121, 125, 136–37.
[70] Lamm, pp. 132–33.
[71] MusPSS 4/1 (MusCW 19), p. 193.
[72] Lamm vocal score, p. 154, figs. 63–65. Circumspection, of course, is always in order

EXAMPLE 6. *Boris Godunov*, Lloyd-Jones edition
(London: Oxford University Press, 1975),
vol. 2, p. 978

EXAMPLE 7. *Boris Godunov*, Lloyd-Jones edition,
vol. 2, p. 984

There are more. Boris's first appearance in the opera in the Coronation scene, his speeches in the St. Basil's scene, and his central monologue in the Terem scene are all introduced by the same motive, which thus takes on the attributes of an identifying theme for the title character on a par with those associated with all the other personages in the opera.[73] And finally, two subsidiary recalling themes may be noted: the hallucination, as first witnessed and later described by Shuisky,[74] and the melody to which, in the Terem scene, Boris hints obliquely to the tsarevich of his own death ("Some day, and soon perhaps, this whole kingdom will be yours"). It returns, as if on schedule, in the Death scene, and is used to introduce the farewell monologue.[75]

But if the role of Boris is the one most thoroughly permeated with leitmotifs and reminiscences, it nevertheless does not contain the most conspicuous and significant theme in the opera that bears his

when interpreting the meaning of a leitmotif when it seems to transcend the function of a mere identifying theme. Oldani, for example, calls Ex. 6 (as it appears in "I Have Attained the Highest Power") the theme of "Boris's Majesty and Authority" (*New Perspectives*, p. 248); this leads him to interpret the final recurrence of this motive, as the curtain descends on the Death scene, as "irony" (p. 287), surely a jarring construction of its pathos.

[73] Cf. Lamm pp. 44, 131–32, 323. On the other hand, one does tend to associate the motive with the famous opening line in the title role—"My soul is sad" (*Skorbit dusha*)—which lends it some of the resonance of a recalling theme. Perhaps that is why Oldani calls it "Boris's Anxiety" (*New Perspectives*, p. 247).

[74] Lamm, pp. 155–56 (Terem scene), 343–45 (Death scene).

[75] Ibid., pp. 131, 346, 356.

EXAMPLE 8a. *Boris Godunov*, Lamm edition, p. 73

The murdered tsarevich lay in a pool of blood:

EXAMPLE 8b. *Boris Godunov*, p. 76

A miracle! . . . All at once the corpse began to shake . . .

name. That one, which Oldani has aptly termed "the opera's idée fixe,"[76] belongs to Dmitry. The progress of the Dmitry theme through the course of the drama, the way it stalks the tsar and, in particular, the vagaries of its signification, have always been among the special fascinations of *Boris Godunov*.

In the initial version of 1869, the theme, when we first hear it, re-fers unambiguously to the "real" Dmitry, the one who died at Ug-lich. This happens during Pimen's narrative, at the words "the mur-dered tsarevich lay in a pool of blood" (Example 8a), and then again at the words "all at once the corpse began to shake" (Example 8b). When, at the end of the narrative, Pimen tells Grigory that had he

[76] *New Perspectives*, p. 252.

EXAMPLE 8c. *Boris Godunov*, p. 77

He would be your age and would be reigning! . . . But God decreed otherwise.

lived, the tsarevich would have been "your age, and would be reigning" (Example 8c), the motive comes back, this time adjusted to the major mode, in which form it is often associated with the Pretender.

Before the appearance of this transformation of the tsarevich motive, Grigory (not yet the Pretender) had actually been given a different identifying theme in the 1869 version of the Cell scene, to accompany his two accounts of his prophetic dream (Example 9). This motive disappeared from the opera in 1871 when the passage in which it first appeared was rewritten to provide the offstage chorus. But since the chorus does not sing during the passage that replaced the second appearance of the motive, we may deduce that Musorgsky had other reasons for removing the theme when revising the opera, reasons to which we shall return.

The tsarevich-Pretender theme thus having been given its "double exposition," it continues to refer ambiguously either to the "real" or to the "false" Dmitry, depending upon the context. Throughout the

EXAMPLE 9. *Boris Godunov*, p. 56n

EXAMPLE 10a. *Boris Godunov*, p. 137

They allege that I willed the death of Dmitry, the tsarevich . . .

Inn scene, of course, it refers to Grigory, the character on stage. But in the next scene (the Terem) it reverts to its original meaning as Boris, at the very end of his central monologue, recalls his crime (Example 10a). When Shuisky brings news of the Pretender, and informs the tsar that he has taken the name Dimitry, the motive comes back in precisely the key, the harmony, and the orchestration (woodwind octaves over tremolo strings) that had marked its first associa-

EXAMPLE 10b. *Boris Godunov*, p. 144

. . . the resurrected name of Dmitry. Dmitry! Tsarevich, go away!

tion with Grigory in the Cell scene (Example 10b; cf. Example 8c). And from here on the motive begins to take on its sinister ambiguity within the tsar's terrified mind.

In the remarkable passage given in Example 11, Boris's mounting fear is conveyed in a passage constructed wholly out of intensifying iterations of the Dmitry motive. It is impossible to decide whether the reference here is to the real or the false Dmitry. And that is precisely the point of it: in Boris's mind they have meshed.

Three more times the Dmitry motive is sounded during the Boris-Shuisky exchange, in contexts where the text makes it clear that the real Dmitry is its referent.[77] But the third time (at the beginning of Shuisky's arioso), the motive sounds forth ironically in the Pretender's major mode—we are hearing it through Boris's ears (Example 12, p. 240).

In the St. Basil's scene, there is no ambiguity. The considerable

[77] Cf. Lamm, p. 147, fig. ⨳50⨳; p. 148, fig. ⨳52⨳; p. 151, fig. ⨳56⨳.

spate of music built on the Dmitry motive (figs. ⌷13⌷ to ⌷15⌷) accompanies
a passage in which the crowd discusses the Pretender's advances.
(When the "real" Dmitry is mentioned, between figs. ⌷10⌷ and ⌷11⌷, the
motive is withheld, as the text makes reference to a requiem service
for the slain tsarevich, and the crowd believes him alive in the person
of the Pretender.) At the beginning of the Death scene, the boyars
refer (fig. ⌷15⌷) to just such gullible popular support for the Pretender
as the St. Basil's scene had shown, and once again the Dmitry theme
is heard in unambiguous reference to the Pretender—the "risen Dmitry" as the people believe him to be. Once Boris is on stage, however,
ambiguity returns. To which Dmitry does the motive refer in conjunction with Boris's hallucination (fig. ⌷27⌷)—the "live" one or the
"dead" one? And when Pimen recounts his insidious tale of the an-
gel-Dmitry, one again hears the major-mode leitmotif (fig. ⌷44⌷) as if
through Boris's ears. It is through these touches above all that we are
made to "see" musically into Boris's soul, and are made so painfully
aware of the tsar's predicament—in Reilly's words, "Boris himself finally cannot distinguish what is real, and is literally frightened to
death at the specter that has risen in his mind to taunt him"[78]—that
we seem to experience it along with him. This magnificent ambiguity, and the empathy to which it gives rise, are clearly the work of a
musical psychologist of genius.

BUT however impressed we may be with the cumulative impact of
the Dmitry theme, it will not do to claim for the 1869 *Boris*, as so
many have done, a structural unity it does not possess. Those who
assert the original version to be a "single dramatic arch" or a concentrated "collision of *two* hostile forces—tsar and people"[79]—are simply
forgetting the pair of scenes amounting to the entire "second part"
of the initial version, and to the entire first act of the revised version,
devoted to the early stages of the Pretender's career. This pair of
scenes—whole scenes from Pushkin, recall, not conflations—gives a
much closer view of Grigory-Dmitry than the preceding pair had
given of Boris, even though Grigory is given no long monologues
(since Pushkin had given him none). And then, at the end of the Inn
scene, he jumps out of the window—and out of the opera! It is hardly
reasonable to suppose that Musorgsky would have followed the career of the future Pretender so closely up to this point if it had been

[78] RMusMus, p. 8.
[79] Ibid., p. 6; GozROTIII, 71.

EXAMPLE 11. *Boris Godunov*, pp. 145–46

EXAMPLE 11, *continued*

Have you ever heard of dead children rising from their graves to question tsars? . . .
lawful tsars, named, elected of the people and consecrated by the great Patriarch . . .
Ha ha ha ha ha ha ha . . .

his prior intention to drop him so abruptly from the cast of characters. It is for this reason that we can readily credit Stasov's contention that the scene at the Fountain, at least, had been part of the original plan, even though not a shred of documentary evidence survives in support. One can even surmise when Musorgsky sketched it for the original version of the opera.

The seven scenes comprising the initial version of *Boris Godunov* were composed in order, as may be verified by the dates on the autograph vocal scores.[80] Five out of the seven scenes are dated, and the missing dates can be easily extrapolated. For the undated Inn scene, we have Stasov's testimony that Dargomïzhsky heard it,[81] which means that it was at least sketched out before 5 January 1869,

[80] See the table in Lamm's vocal score, pp. xvii (Russian), xviii (German).

[81] StasIS 2.200: "In the last months of his life Dargomïzhsky also heard excerpts from the opera, including some of the choicest: the first scene and the Inn scene, and . . . with magnanimous enthusiasm repeated before all and sundry that 'Musorgsky is going even farther than I.' "

EXAMPLE 12. *Boris Godunov*, p. 151

[Tranquillo] Not rushing, relaxed

Shuisky: Whispers secretively

For three days in Uglich cathedral I stood by the boy's body.

when Dargomïzhsky died[82]—a date that falls comfortably between those of the scenes immediately preceding (the Cell scene, completed 5 December 1868) and following (the Terem scene, completed 21 April 1869).[83] The other undated scene is the Death scene, whose period of composition may be extrapolated by comparing the date of the St. Basil's scene (22 May 1869) with that of Stasov's letter to his brother Dmitry, in which he follows the information that "Musorgsky has finally finished *Boris Godunov*" with a description of Pimen's Death scene monologue (18 July 1869).[84]

These dates allow us not only to ascertain the order in which the scenes were composed but also to judge the speed at which Musorg-

[82] There is another bit of circumstantial evidence for dating the composition of the Inn scene. As Orlova has persuasively argued, the concert at which Stasov gave Musorgsky the text for Varlaam's first song took place on 9 December 1868 (OrTD, 168).

[83] The last page of the newly discovered autograph vocal score of the Inn scene (see n. 16), which differs interestingly from the standard version in its use of the Dmitry theme, carries the date *1869 god* [the year 1869]. This probably signifies the very beginning of 1869, which corroborates the date arrived at by extrapolation.

[84] StasPR 1/2.46.

sky worked. If we take "October 1868," the date inscribed by Musorgsky in his volume of Pushkin interleaved with blank pages for
writing the libretto,[85] as the starting point, then the Novodevichy
scene (4 November 1868) was composed in something like a month;
the Coronation scene (14 November) in a mere ten days; the Cell
scene (5 December) in three weeks; the Inn scene ("1869") in something like a month. The next date of completion is that of the Terem
scene: 21 April 1869, or close to four months later. Even if we allow
for the greater length of the Terem scene and assign it, say, a two-
month gestation, and even if we assume that Stasov's letter to his
brother was written very close to the actual date of the completion of
the Death scene, which would allow that relatively short scene a gen-
erous two months in the writing, there definitely seems to be some
lost time between the Inn and the Terem scenes. One may hazard a
guess, then, that this is when Musorgsky sketched an initial version
of the Fountain scene.

One can guess, too, that this version would have borne scant resemblance to the one we know. It would have been, like the rest of
the 1869 libretto, a severe *opéra dialogué* adaptation of Pushkin's text.
So there would have been no Rangoni, though there might have
been Pushkin's very different Pater Czernikowski; there could
scarcely have been a polonaise (though Pushkin had one), given the
inordinate kuchkist-realist scruples about *divertissement* that Musorgsky would have had to overcome in order to write one; and of course
there would have been no culminating love duet. Marina's exit lines
in Pushkin are cold and haughty as ever: "Until you've overthrown
Godunov, I'll hear no talk of love." Pushkin's Fountain scene, despite
its romantic setting, was just one more scene of political intrigue.
(Pushkin thought of this as a tour de force: "A tragedy without love
appealed to my imagination," he wrote in 1829 to Nikolai Rayev-
sky.[86]) No wonder, then, that Serov and even Cui thought it impossible for music. Musorgsky, having tried to set the Fountain scene,
probably came at first to the same conclusion.

But if this is why the Grigory-Dmitry plot line came to its sudden
end, one has to ask why the pair of scenes devoted to the Pretender
were left in place. For it is absurd to argue that with the loss of the

[85] "Conceived in autumn 1868; work began in October 1868. For this very work this
little book was furnished by yudmila Shestakova" (OrTD, 166–67).

[86] *Letters of Alexander Pushkin,* ed. and trans. J. Thomas Shaw (Madison: University
of Wisconsin Press, 1969), p. 365.

Pretender the opera suffered no loss in dramatic unity. Explaining this lacuna away became a major stumbling block for those committed to establishing the superiority of the 1869 *Boris*. The usual solution was to claim it as a virtue by sheer critical fiat. Thus Calvocoressi:

> A very remarkable feature of the original version (one, indeed, that makes it something unique in the history of lyric drama) is that Grigory never reappears after he has effected his escape into Lithuania and begun his activities as the Pretender. He remains in the background, evoked time after time by references made by Shuisky, by Boris, by the people and by the councillors [i.e., the boyars].[87]

Or as Reilly puts it, "the impostor Grigory is given just enough concrete reality to become an ever more menacing psychological reality as Dmitry in the remainder of the work."[88] Just enough for whom, though? Not for those he menaces, for they never see him at all. The "psychological reality" is Boris's perception; the "concrete reality" is (presumably) the audience's. The one does not contribute to the other; Reilly's point is self-contradictory. If the Pretender is powerful because he is unseen, then omitting the "second part" of the 1869 version would be a gain in dramatic intensity, not a loss. No information is conveyed to the audience by the Cell or Inn scenes that would be indispensable to follow the course of a drama shorn of them. The audience could as well be told of the Pretender's rise along with Boris, when Shuisky brings his terrible news in the Terem scene. In short, the Cell and Inn scenes are superfluous to the "single dramatic arch" that the initial version is so often purported to be, and which indeed it *would* be without them.

If, after dropping the Polish scene, Musorgsky had gone back and removed the "second part" as well, he would have been left with a drama derived single-mindedly from the Boris-dominated scenes in Pushkin's sprawling chronicle. This would have been a drama focused entirely on Boris's rise and fall. It would have been an unprecedentedly terse, yet sweeping and wholly logical progression—a *pièce* decidedly more *bien faite* than Pushkin's. By turning the poet's unruly play into a wholly personal and psychological drama of conscience and nemesis, Musorgsky would have indeed achieved his "single dramatic arch," and achieved a unity of impression that

[87] *Moussorgsky*, pp. 143–44.
[88] RMusMus, pp. 6–8.

would virtually have turned Pushkin's historical scenes into another "Little Tragedy" like *The Stone Guest*.

But this he did not do, for how could he have dispensed with his "second part"? The reason he needed it lay partly in Pimen's narrative, which, it could be argued, makes a substantive contribution even to a conception of the drama wholly centered on Boris, for it contains the only account in the play of the details of Boris's crime. And the Cell scene also introduces the all-important Dmitry leitmotif in a dramatic and "organic" fashion that would have been difficult or impossible to achieve elsewhere. But there cannot be any such "strict" justification for the Inn scene. Its raison d'être has to be sought not in the contribution it makes to the dramatic structure of the opera, but in its specific qualities as a scene. As the most extensive prose scene in Pushkin's play, and one that fulfilled the "Shakespearean" requirement of comic relief, it was doubly a must for Musorgsky, fresh from the composition of *Marriage* and still so deeply committed to the most uncompromising brand of post-Dargomïzhskian realism. Setting the Inn scene was another "experiment in dramatic music in prose"; it recommended itself not on the basis of its dramatic function, of which it possessed little in Musorgsky's radically scaled-down version of Pushkin's drama, but as an inviting, nay compelling, musical opportunity. And once the Inn scene was retained, the Cell scene did become a dramaturgically necessary preface.

What we have then in the 1869 version of *Boris* is a set of scenes very roughly hewn from Pushkin's unwieldy block of poetic marble, selected according to diverse and unrelated criteria. On the one hand we have the "dramatic arch" achieved by the radical expedient of extracting and conflating all the scenes from Pushkin in which the title character appears; on the other, a couple more scenes that recommended themselves for musical and stylistic reasons. Far from showing how carefully Musorgsky structured his dramatic conception, the first *Boris* boldly displays a quintessentially realist disdain for a well-made play.

IT REMAINS to examine the ideological and historiographical content of the initial version of *Boris*. This can perhaps best be done by omitting the "second part" altogether from consideration, for reasons related to the foregoing discussion, and inquiring into the way the fate of the title character is understood and treated. In particular it will mean testing Asafyev's idea, which has been faithfully echoed since (especially in the Soviet Union, but not only there), that the central theme of the initial version of the opera is that of "popular unrest," "the loss of popular faith in the powers that be and their downfall, which takes place in parallel with the rise of popular discontent." "All the rest," Asafyev stoutly maintained, "are outcroppings on the surface: the palace intrigues, the personal tragedy, the adventure stories—all this is merely the coloring, the 'anecdotal' content, and also the consequences of the main premise—consequences that could have been otherwise."[89]

In testing this hypothesis, we must remember that it is really Pushkin's ideology we are investigating. The nature of the relationship of opera to play in the first version was such that the composer was more or less bound willy-nilly to adopt the poet's vision of events, however selective that adoption may have been. Once this is admitted, Asafyev's contentions become not only untenable but downright paradoxical.

As all students of Russian literature know, Pushkin found the subject of his drama, and even in large part its treatment, ready-made in Karamzin's *History*, a very paradigm of Caesaristic historiography and a prime prop of the Official Nationality of the Nikolai I era. To recapitulate what was learned in Chapter 4, Karamzin's idea of legitimacy depended on anything but the consent of the governed—witness his famous treatment of Ivan the Terrible, whom he despised and condemned, but whose right to rule he never questioned. He even praised Russia for having endured Ivan's monstrous tyranny "with love for the Autocracy, for she believed that God sends plagues, earthquakes, and tyrants alike."[90] Boris Godunov was presented as a just ruler tragically doomed by a crime—exactly as Pushkin presented him, and, following Pushkin, Musorgsky.

The 1869 *Boris*, derived from Karamzin via Pushkin, is a drama of nemesis and of the defiled conscience of a just man—the very stuff of personal tragedy since Aeschylean times. The Pretender, not the people, was the Fury. What topples the tsar is not popular unrest but "heavenly judgment." That unrest is characterized, with anything but approval, as the "bitter fruit of lawlessness," a scourge on crown

[89] AsIT 3.91; see also his argument on p. 82.
[90] Nikolai Karamzin, *Istoriya gosudarstva rossiyskogo* (St. Petersburg: Typografiya N. N. Moreva, 1892), vol. 9, p. 273.

and populace alike. What Karamzin, with a scholar's reserve, merely called the "inner anxiety of Boris's heart,"[91] became for Pushkin his defining trait. And Musorgsky, going much further than Pushkin, translated this anxiety into a palpable specter—palpable not only in the famous, if melodramatic, hallucination but throughout the opera in the form of the Dmitry leitmotif.

Musorgsky strengthened the theme of conscience over anything in Pushkin in other ways, too—not all of them of the subtlest. The end of the Terem scene proceeds from the closing speech of Pushkin's scene 11, in which Boris, reeling from Shuisky's revelations, momentarily falters before (how unlike Musorgsky's portrayal!) regaining his composure:

> I choke! . . . Let me draw breath!
> I felt it; all my blood surged to my face
> And heavily receded.[92]

to the concluding lines of Pushkin's "Highest Power" soliloquy in scene 8, with which Musorgsky prepared Boris's hallucination:

> But if she [i.e., conscience] be found
> To have a single stain, then misery!
> With what a deadly sore the soul doth smart;
> The heart, with venom filled, beats like a hammer
> And dins reproach into the buzzing ears;
> The head is spinning, nausea tortures one,
> And bloody boys revolve before the eye.[93]

[91] Ibid., vol. 11, p. 55.

[92] Translated by Alfred Hayes (*The Poems, Prose, and Plays of Alexander Pushkin*, ed. Avrahm Yarmolinsky [New York: Random House, 1936], p. 370 ["Ukh, tyazhelo! . . ."]). Pushkin's Boris continues:

> For thirteen years together I have dreamed
> Ever about the murdered child. Yes, yes—
> 'Tis that!—now I perceive. But who is he,
> My terrible antagonist? Who is it
> Opposeth me? An empty name, a shadow.
> Can but a ghost tear from my back the purple,
> A hollow sound makes beggars of my children?
> This is pure madness! What is then to fear?
> Blow on this phantom.—and it is no more.
> So, I am fast resolved. I'll show no sign
> Of fear, but let no trifle be ignored.
> Ah! Heavy art thou, crown of Monomakh!

[93] *The Poems, Prose, and Plays of Alexander Pushkin*, p. 353 ("No yesli v ney yedinoye pyatno . . .").

EXAMPLE 13a. *Boris Godunov*, 1869 version, p. 153

EXAMPLE 13b. *Boris Godunov*, 1872 version, p. 223

O cruel conscience, how horribly you punish me!

At the joint, Musorgsky interpolated a line of his own—"O cruel conscience, how horribly you punish me!" (*O sovest' lyutaya, kak strashno tï karayesh'!*)—and, lest anyone miss the point, gave it climactic setting, which contains not only the highest but also the longest notes in the whole title role as of 1869 (Example 13a). In view of what we shall have to say later about the ideological differences between the first *Boris* and the second, it seems apropos to note here, in advance, that the setting this line received in the second Terem scene is wholly devoid of this climactic quality (Example 13b).

Even more telling is the way Musorgsky handled the tale of the miracle-working tsarevich. In Pushkin's play the tale is narrated by the patriarch Job in the course of a meeting of the tsar's council at which methods are being sought to deal with the spread of popular support for the Pretender. The tale of the miracle is offered as proof that the tsarevich is indeed dead and the Pretender an impostor. The patriarch follows the tale with this advice:

> To Uglich then I sent, where it was learned
> That many sufferers had likewise found
> Deliverance at the grave of the Tsarevich.
> This is my counsel: to the Kremlin send
> The sacred relics, place them in the Minster
> Of the Archangel; clearly will the people
> See then the godless villain's fraud; the fiend's
> Dread might will vanish as a cloud of dust.[94]

[94] Ibid., p. 391.

In Musorgsky's version the tale—rather improbably given to Pimen, an unlikely visitor to the tsar's council, but well known to the audience as Boris's implacable foe, and associated furthermore with the Pretender's beginnings—becomes the final instrument of nemesis and brings on the fatal seizure.

The argument that the central conflict in the 1869 version of *Boris* was between ruler and ruled usually centers on the Terem monologues and especially on the St. Basil's scene, their one and only direct confrontation. Of the first version of "I Have Attained the Highest Power," Asafyev has written that "from the point of view of the dramatic impulse—popular discontent—Boris's aspect and the character of his thoughts . . . are more clearly motivated [than in the revision]."[95] But while popular discontent is mentioned in both versions of the monologue, only in the second version is it connected with the crime and usurpation. Given below is Pushkin's original passage (scene 8, lines 19–31)—Musorgsky set all of it in 1869 except the lines "The living power . . . / Only the dead they love"—followed by the composer's own text for the revised Terem scene:

PUSHKIN:

> I thought
> *to give my people glory and contentment,*
> *To gain their loyal love and by generous gifts,*
> *But I have put away empty hope;*
> The living power is hateful to the mob—
> Only the dead they love. *We are but fools*
> *When our heart shakes because the people clap*
> *Or cry out fiercely. When our land was stricken*
> *By God with famine, perishing in torments*
> *The people uttered moan. I opened to them*
> *The granaries, I scattered gold among them,*
> *Found labor for them; yet for all my pains*
> *They cursed me! Next, a fire consumed their homes;*
> *I built for them new dwellings; then forsooth*
> *They blamed me for the fire! Such is the mob,*
> *Such is its judgment!*[96]

[95] AsIT 3.90.
[96] *The Poems, Prose, and Plays of Alexander Pushkin*, p. 352.

MUSORGSKY:

> Famine, and plague, and fear and devastation . . .
> Like wild beasts the people roam, stricken with disease:
> And Russia groans in hunger and in poverty . . .
> In this affliction dire, sent down by God
> For all my grievous sins a punishment,
> They name me cause of all these evil things.
> And curse the name of Boris everywhere![97]

Only in the 1871 revision, in other words, and only to the extent that Musorgsky departed from Pushkin's text, are the people cast in the role of nemesis, a role solely reserved in the original version for Boris's conscience and its "objective correlative," the Pretender.

In the St. Basil's scene it is the *yuródivïy* who is usually cited as personification or representation of the people's wrath. But he is neither. He stands apart from the crowd in every way. The people think the tsarevich is alive; the *yuródivïy* knows he is dead at Boris's hand. The people remain submissive to Boris. They do not threaten him. In their chorus of supplication (Musorgsky's idea, not Pushkin's) they address him as their "little father" (*batyushka*); the *yuródivïy* challenges and insults Boris, calling him the "Tsar-Herod." At this the crowd, according to a stage direction by Musorgsky, not Pushkin, "disperses in horror." The *yuródivïy*, then, far from representing the people, is one more embodiment of dread nemesis, one more personification of Boris's conscience.

But the people do not lack a representative. For what else is Mityukha? He epitomizes everything that characterizes the crowd in play and in opera alike—passivity, gullibility, dull-wittedness, ignorance, apathy. For Pushkin, the crowd was no more than a comic foil on a par with the drunken monks in the Inn scene. It has been amply demonstrated how the poet farcically (and "realistically") caricatured the monolithic crowd behavior chronicled by Karamzin.[98] As for the *yuródivïy*, Pushkin, with characteristic heartlessness, described him as "a very funny young fellow" in an offhand letter to a friend.[99]

There is no "tsar versus people" theme in Pushkin, nor is there any such theme in the original musical drama that Musorgsky so sedulously modeled on Pushkin. That came later. And Asafyev knew it.

[97] Translated by J. P. Smith and N. Anderson (Angel SDLX–3844).
[98] Brody, *The Demetrius Legend*, pp. 241–42.
[99] To Pyotr Andreyevich Vyazemsky, 7 November 1825 (*Letters of Alexander Pushkin*, p. 261).

Obliquely recognizing that the people play no active role in the events depicted by the opera, he was reduced to asserting that they hate Boris not for his crime but with a mere "instinctive hate"[100]—only in this way could he draw them at all into the essential dramatic framework. An unprejudiced view of the drama has to leave them outside, as passive sufferers, and as part of the background to the events portrayed.

Thus the initial version of *Boris Godunov* was precisely that "personal drama of Tsar Boris on a romantic background of popular unrest" that Asafyev affected to discern in the revised version.[101] But of course this was the very task for which *Marriage*, and the general example of Dargomïzhsky's realism, had prepared Musorgsky—the revelation of character and emotion through musical speech, or, as he put it to Stasov, "the living man in living music."[102] Where Musorgsky had gone even further than his predecessor was in the application of Dargomïzhskian techniques to the chorus,[103] and in his incredibly detailed remarks and stage directions to the principals, not only on the delivery of lines but, even more tellingly, on reactions to them.[104] The first version of *Boris Godunov* is the apogee of that tendency in Russian opera that viewed the role of composer as a kind of exalted dramatic executant or *régisseur*.

III

Musorgsky finished the full score of the first version of *Boris Godunov* on 15 December 1869, and by early spring of the next year he was busy with all the details involved with its submission to the Imperial Theaters—copying the score for the opera committee, copying the libretto for the censor. All these matters were fully attended to by 13

[100] AsIT 3.80.

[101] Ibid., p. 91.

[102] MusLN 1.143.

[103] To judge by the autograph libretto (as given in MusLN 2.57–123), Musorgsky originally thought of virtually abolishing the chorus in such places and assigning its repliques to coryphées. In the end he settled on the compromise of assigning lines to small groups from within the chorus. Stasov (StasIS 2.199n) claimed that this idea was forced upon him by Nápravník. Whether or not this was so, there was a prototype for such choral fragmentation in Serov's 1865 *Rogneda* (see TarODR, 110, 120), an opera whose influence on Musorgsky's work Stasov would scarcely have wished to acknowledge.

[104] See, for example, the directions for Boris during Pimen's narrative in the Death scene (MusLN 2.103–4). These were prompted by Pushkin's single remark in scene 17, "During this speech Boris wipes his face several times with a handkerchief."

July 1870, when Stepan Gedeonov, director of the Imperial Theaters, told Musorgsky he would have to wait until the next season for the decision. This came on 10 February 1871, and as all the world knows, it was negative.

The bearer of bad tidings was Shestakova, *Boris's* "godmother," who, as Glinka's sister, knew all the parties concerned with the decision and was informed of it in advance. (Musorgsky did not receive official notification of his opera's rejection until the eighteenth.) Shestakova was quite surprised by Musorgsky's reaction to the news:

> I knew that this news would be unpleasant for Musorgsky and did not want to tell him right away, so then and there I wrote to him and to Stasov, asking them to come and see me around nine in the evening. Returning home, I found them waiting. I told them what I had heard, and Stasov with heated enthusiasm began talking over with him the new parts to be inserted into the opera; Musorgsky began playing over some themes, and the evening passed in a very lively fashion.[105]

Her surprise was even more explicitly corroborated by Rimsky-Korsakov:

> [Musorgsky] knows everything concerning *Boris's* fate and reacted completely differently from how one might have expected, and therefore, completely differently from how we all had predicted.[106]

Musorgsky was eager, not reluctant, to revise his opera.

When this fact is set alongside the lack of congruence between the requirements of the theatrical directorate and the actual revisions, the rejection must lose its status as motivation for the revision; nor can the changes in the opera be regarded any longer as forced. They were motivated deeply and from within, and therefore deserve both understanding and respect. Open-minded examination of the scanty but nonetheless persuasive external evidence, on the one hand, and of the actual revised score, on the other, leads to the conclusion that the revisions were primarily motivated by considerations of historiographical ideology, dramatic tone, and consistency in the deployment of leitmotifs. Taken together, they amounted to a complete rethinking of the basis of Musorgsky's operatic aesthetic and his operatic style.

Although these considerations (perhaps needless to say) over-

---

[105] Ludmila Shestakova, "Moi vechera," quoted in OrTD, 213.
[106] To Alexandra Purgold, 14 February 1871. OrTD, 214.

lapped and intertwined, thoroughly "overdetermining" the revision process, we shall take them up one by one for clarity's sake. But first, like Musorgsky himself, let us briefly dispose of the demands of the directorate and consider the extent to which they were reflected in the revision.

THE seven-member committee that rejected *Boris Godunov* in 1871 was not required to state its reasons. The double-bass player Ferrero, who reported to the directorate, simply informed the head of repertoire, P. S. Fyodorov, that the vote had been six to one against the opera (the one white ball, it turned out, had been cast by Nápravník), and that was that. The only document to give even indirect evidence of the committee's actual deliberations and reasoning is Shestakova's memoir:

> There was a luncheon at [Mariyinsky prima donna] Julia Platonova's on the occasion of her bénéfice. She came to invite me, and added that on that very day in the morning the fate of Musorgsky's opera would be decided, and that Nápravník and [chief *régisseur*] Kondratyev would be coming to her house afterwards. I went, and with great impatience awaited the arrival of these personages. Understandably, I greeted them with the words, "Is *Boris* accepted?" "No," they answered me, "it's impossible. How can there be an opera without the feminine element?! Musorgsky has great talent beyond doubt. Let him add one more scene. Then *Boris* will be produced!"[107]

Before proceeding further, we may note parenthetically that the directorate required one scene, while Stasov and Musorgsky, as noted in the other extract from the same memoir given above, immediately began discussing the "new parts to be added"—plural, not singular. These plans, evidently, had been made before the rejection. To this point we shall return.

There is simply no evidence that the committee ever asked for more than a prima donna role and a single scene to contain it. The three other reports of the rejection that have often been cited in the scholarly literature were fanciful kuchkist embroideries without any documentary authority. The best-known account is Rimsky-Korsakov's, from his *Chronicle of My Musical Life*, written in 1905–06 and first published in 1909:

[107] "Moi vechera," quoted in OrTD, 213.

The freshness and originality of the music nonplussed the honorable members of the committee, who reproved the composer, among other things, for the absence of a reasonably important female role. . . . Much of the fault-finding was simply ridiculous. Thus the double-basses *divisi* playing chromatic thirds in the accompaniment of Varlaam's song were entirely too much for Ferrero, the double-bass player, who could not forgive the composer this device. Musorgsky, hurt and offended, withdrew his score, but later thought the matter over and decided to make radical changes and additions.[108]

Comparison of the last sentence in this extract with Rimsky's own letter to his sister-in-law some thirty-odd years closer to the event, as given above, will show how far this account is to be trusted. Not only that but the double-bass passage, cited as exemplary of the "freshness and originality" that occasioned the rejection, survived the revision.

Stasov, who, as we have seen, approved the rejection for the pretext it afforded for revision, distorted the reasons for it in the account he gave in his biography-necrology of 1881, mentioning only the "plethora of choruses and ensembles and the too-conspicuous lack of scenes for individual characters."[109] But again, the "offense" (at least vis-à-vis the chorus; the rest of the passage is obscure) not only survived the revision, but was actually aggravated by it.

The remaining kuchkist witness was César Cui. On 9 March 1871 he published a small note appended to his regular column in the *Sanktpeterburgskiye vedomosti*, in which the French-Lithuanian composer-critic lamented the fate of Russian composers, and made much of the fact that out of seven members of the "vaudeville committee," as he called it, only one—the ballet conductor Alexey Papkov—was ethnically a Russian.[110] Further raillery against the "vaudeville committee" found place in Cui's review of the three scenes that were performed, despite their ruling, at Kondratyev's *bénéfice* in February

[108] R-KMusL, 110.

[109] StasIS 2.197.

[110] "Muzïkal'nïye zametki," *Sanktpeterburgskiye vedomosti*, no. 68 (1871). Cui also pointed to the fact that "the single true musician member of the committee, Mr. Nápravník, sensitive to the new musical tendency, sensitive to what is good and new, sensitive to dramatic truth, to faithful, strong declamation, stood fast behind *Boris*." But this was merely flattery addressed to the conductor who had presided over Cui's own *Ratcliff*, and did not represent Nápravník's true reasons for casting a favorable ballot, which as he recalled them much later, were of the "we could do worse" variety. See E. F. Nápravník, *Avtobiograficheskiye, tvorcheskiye materialï, dokumentï, pis'ma* (Leningrad: Muzgiz, 1959), pp. 11–12.

1873. "The committee boiled over with righteous indignation against the music of this opera," fumed Cui, the master propagandist, who then proceeded subtly and deliberately to confuse the committee with the critical press, and *Boris* with the "New Russian School" in general:

> The new tendency is rebuked for its alleged destructive aspirations. . . . What has Musorgsky destroyed, who created the grandest of all existing comic scenes, boiling with life and inimitable truth, in his "Inn"? The old exists as before, only something new has been added to it. . . . But how easy it would be to support Russian opera at a remarkably high level! . . . What will become of it in reality, however, is known only to Allah—and the Theaters directorate.[111]

Thus was born the durable legend of a *Boris* rebuked and rejected for its modernism when all that was asked, according to reliable testimony, was a prima donna role.

This was supplied in short order by the Polish act, on which Musorgsky embarked immediately after the rejection came down. By 5 April 1871 he was able to play the completed scene of Marina and Rangoni to an assemblage at Shestakova's.[112] A couple of days later, at the Purgolds', Musorgsky became inspired and composed Marina's aria then and there: "In the course of the evening he went to the piano several times, played over some fragments, and before his friends [including the Stasov brothers and Rimsky-Korsakov] there gradually arose the whole monologue [*sic*]. . . . Musorgsky had the knack of composing 'in company.'"[113] According to the date on the autograph vocal score, the scene in Marina's boudoir was completed on 10 April 1871. Now Musorgsky had done all that the Imperial Theater directorate had asked of him. But logic demanded that Marina be brought into contact with the Pretender, so Musorgsky revived the abandoned Fountain scene. A letter of 18 April to Stasov shows him at work on the confrontation between Dmitry and Rangoni in that scene.[114]

[111] CuiIS, 231–35.

[112] Letter of Stasov to his brother Dmitry, 6 April 1871. StasPR1/2.

[113] Oral recollection by Nadezhda Purgold (Rimskaya-Korsakova), in OrTD, 216.

[114] Its oft-quoted text reads, "I am finishing the scene—the Jesuit has given me no rest for two nights running. That's fine. I love this, that is, I love it when work goes like this" (MusLN 1.122). It is strange that previous commentators—Andrey Rimsky-Korsakov, Orlova, Pekelis—have assumed that the reference to the "Jesuit" is a reference to the scene with Marina, which, as we have seen, was finished two weeks earlier. The reason seems to be that the autograph vocal score of the Fountain scene is

Many have cited Marina's conventional aria and the rhetorically inflated love duet at the end of the Fountain scene, with their un-Pushkinian texts, as evidence of cynical capitulation to the committee, unworthy of the rest of the opera (or of further comment). But the Polish act cannot be written off so easily. Not only does the enthusiasm evident in Musorgsky's letter to Stasov contradict such a view; so does his subsequent behavior. Having supplied the requested Polish act, he did not resubmit the opera to the Directorate, confident (as per Shestakova's assurances) of its acceptance. Far from it. By August, he was happily de-Pushkinizing the text of the Terem scene, and "perpetrating an arioso" for the title character, to paraphrase another well-known letter to Stasov.[115] The Polish act was just the beginning. It set the tone for the whole revision and can serve as the yardstick by which to measure the stylistic distance separating the two *Boris*es.

The most fundamental difference between the Polish act and the 1869 *Boris* is the fact that it is no longer an *opéra dialogué*—and a more fundamental difference there could not be, since the *opéra dialogué* ideal had been the defining essence of the Dargomïzhskian reform in the late 1860s. In part the change arose out of practical necessity, since Pushkin had given Marina no extended, self-characterizing speeches, and, as we have seen, had deliberately avoided a love scene at the Fountain. If Musorgsky had insisted upon modeling his Polish act on Pushkin's text as closely as he had the rest of the opera, he could not have complied with the opera committee's one demand.

But in matters far beyond what directly concerned Marina, Musorgsky threw to the winds the ideals to which he had hitherto adhered so zealously. He wrote his own text for the Polish act, freely paraphrasing Pushkin even when it was possible to quote him directly (e.g., in the Pretender's opening monologue at the Fountain), and more often fabricating not only lines but entire situations and even characters out of whole cloth. Cui, who was Dargomïzhsky's press champion par excellence, was predictably disappointed. At the Kondratyev *bénéfice*, the three scenes selected for advance exposure

dated 14 December 1871, and in the April letter Musorgsky already wrote that he was "finishing the scene." Oldani (*New Perspectives*, p. 144) has speculated that Musorgsky "was not quite satisfied with the first Polish scene and returned to it." But the Russian word *stsena* is just as ambiguous as the English word "scene." When he wrote that he was "finishing the scene," Musorgsky probably meant only the episode between Rangoni and the Pretender, not the larger scene at the Fountain from which it comes.
[115] 10 August 1871. MusLN 1.122.

were, as it happened, the Inn scene and the Polish act, the very paradigms of Musorgsky's old and new approaches, and Cui in his review emphasized the stylistic gulf that separated them. His paean in praise of the Inn scene was a summation of the ideals and criteria of realist "dialogue opera," touching all the kuchkist bases—truth of declamation, national character, and the intensification by musical means of the forms and values of the spoken theater. When it came to the Polish scenes, Cui's first observation was the somewhat rueful one that here "Musorgsky departed from Pushkin. . . . Both these scenes are done completely differently." And though Cui was quick to offer excuses—"in Pushkin these scenes are too rational, poorly suited to music, and in the first of them there is a new character, Ruzia, who would have increased still further the opera's roster and the obstacles to its production"—they are halfhearted and none too logical (if Ruzia was *de trop*, what of Rangoni?). His disapproval shows through once he gets down to cases:

> In its conception this act is, compared with the Inn, weaker and cruder.
> . . . The music of this act possesses great merits, but it is not so impeccable throughout as in the Inn. Its character is different: we get a chorus, we get lyrical outbursts, in consequence of which melodies are rounder and undergo a certain amount of development. [The dramatic confrontations]—Marina with the Jesuit and the Pretender with the Jesuit and with Marina—are written a bit unevenly. They contain amazing, inspired episodes, but they also contain weak phrases of insufficiently well defined melodic character, and even some meaningless tones in two or three spots.[116]

Cui persists in measuring the dramatic scenes in the Polish act by the same kuchkist yardstick he had applied to the Inn scene: the success or failure of the individual *répliques*, or "musical thoughts." The relative "unevenness" he thus purports to uncover testifies not only to the circularity of his judgment but also to the dubious relevance of his measuring tool. For in these scenes Musorgsky veered sharply away from the pithy naturalistic manner of the Inn scene, seeking a more exalted level of expression through a greater "aesthetic distance." The accompaniment is more regular and generalized; the *répliques* are longer, attaining at times the quality of short monologues; the phrase structure is regularized, with frequent recourse to both literal and sequential repetition. It is senseless to attempt to separate,

[116] CuiIS, 228–29.

as Cui does, the component phrases of these long speeches for individual critical evaluation, since, unlike the *répliques* in the Inn scene, they are not contrasted and "characterized" at so local a level, but are used as blocks in the construction of relatively long musical periods of unified mood.

Cui's critical stance—perfect for the Inn scene, whose felicities he describes in masterly fashion—is far too close for the Polish act. By so plainly missing the forest for the trees in the review, Cui unwittingly dramatized the crucial issue for understanding the revision of *Boris* in all its multifaceted aspects: the problem of tone.

IV

It is of course a truism that tragedy requires a greater aesthetic distance—what Serov called "aerial perspective"—than comedy. Where comedy can be set forth in details and in sharp *aperçus*, tragedy traditionally demands the broad brush stroke, the heroic scale. It was a preeminent aim of realistic theater in the nineteenth century to break down this distinction: to portray, as Gerald Abraham put it so well of Musorgsky, "the prose of life as well as its poetry,"[117] and to do it seriously, with high moral purpose. Ostrovsky's signal contribution, for example, had been the construction of serious plays out of elements previously associated exclusively with comedy. It is noteworthy, however, that even Ostrovsky reserved the designation "tragedy" for historical verse plays, using the neutral word "drama" or "popular [*narodnaya*] drama" for works in prose with domestic (*bïtovoy*) settings. Ostrovsky's tendency had been intensified by Serov, who turned one of the playwright's "popular dramas," *Live Not the Way You'd Like* (*Ne tak zhivi, kak khochetsya*), into his last opera (*The Power of the Fiend*), and by changing the resolution of this drama of domestic strife from one of reconciliation to one of murder, sought to elevate it explicitly (and over the playwright's vociferous objections) to the rank of full-fledged tragedy. In this experiment in Ostrovskian musical verismo, special interest attaches to the figure of the evil blacksmith Yeryomka, whose role is cast in musical idioms whose roots lie obviously, if only in part, in the traditions of opera buffa (a tradition whose very origins lay in the deflation and mockery of tragic opera). The tension between traditional genres and the novel

---

[117] *Slavonic and Romantic Music*, p. 170.

use to which they were put imparted to the music of *The Power of the Fiend* a pervasive and insidiously fascinating irony.[118]

A necessary part of theatrical realism was the rejection of large-scale form—the rhetorical soliloquy, the genre set piece, what Cui called "Karamzinian stanzas." Hence operatic thinkers who considered themselves realists worked programmatically to divest the musical theater of its repertoire of conventional formal practices—concerted aria, "monolithic" chorus, *morceau d'ensemble*. The trick was not easy to turn in opera, however, outside of experiments of relatively narrow scope, such as the "recitative operas" composed by Dargomïzhsky and Musorgsky to preexisting plays (or such successors as Prokofiev's early stage pieces, not to mention *Pelléas, Salome,* or *Wozzeck*). Most operatic composers thought the prospect too far limiting, and their number even included one from within the bosom of the kuchka. In an often-quoted letter to the singer Lyubov Karmalina, Borodin wrote:

> In my view of matters operatic I have always parted company with many of my comrades. The pure recitative style has always gone against my grain and against my character. I am drawn to singing, to cantilena, not to recitative, even though, according to the reactions of those who know, I am not too bad at the latter. Besides, I am drawn to more finished, more rounded, more expansive forms. My whole manner of treating operatic material is different. In my opinion, in the opera itself, no less than in the sets, small forms, details, niceties should have no place. Everything should be painted in bold strokes, clearly, vividly, and as practicably as possible, from both the vocal and the orchestral standpoints.[119]

"Small forms, details, niceties": these had been the very essence of the Dargomïzhskian reform that was to have revolutionized musical drama. For Borodin, though, it meant the loss of the tragic style, which would have spelled the ruin of an opera on the epic scale of *Prince Igor*. But what of *Boris Godunov*?

Dargomïzhsky, *The Stone Guest* notwithstanding, was best remembered by his admirers as a comic talent. In his obituary notice, Serov called particular attention to the late composer's "inimitable comic gift."[120] And Musorgsky himself had paid Dargomïzhsky the tribute

---

[118] See TarODR, chapter 4 ("Drama Revealed through Song: An Opera after Ostrovsky") for a detailed treatment of *The Power of the Fiend*.

[119] 1 June 1876. BorP 2.109.

[120] *Journal de St.-Pétersbourg*, no. 9 (1869). SerIS 2.53.

of emulation with *Marriage*, an out-and-out farce. Even Dargo-mïzhsky's magnum opus was universally regarded as a "chamber" opera (Laroche: "[its] true domain is the salon; its true orchestra, the pianoforte").[121] But if Dargomïzhsky could forego the grand manner, could Musorgsky afford to do so in a historical opera like *Boris*?

There is evidence to suggest that he came to feel he could not. During 1870, the year in which the first *Boris* was in limbo between completion and rejection, Musorgsky played selections from the opera to interested parties on a number of occasions. One of these was a gathering at Stasov's dacha in Pargolovo toward the end of July. Stasov described the impression Musorgsky made in a letter to his brother Dmitry, full of his usual blustery, myopic optimism: "Musorgsky arrived for dinner and in the evening he sang *so*, that all the ladies and girls applauded him and he had a sort of triumph. I recalled the days of Glinka, when he himself would sit down at the piano. Since then I haven't seen anyone make such a *unanimous* impression on everyone without exception."[122] But that is certainly not the impression one gets from a rather bemused Musorgsky's description of the same event in a letter to Rimsky-Korsakov. In fact he was considerably disconcerted at the *lack* of unanimity. "As regards the peasants in *Boris*, some found them to be *bouffe* (!), while others saw tragedy."[123]

The annotators of the various editions of Musorgsky's letters have assumed that he could only have meant the peasants in the opening scene of the prologue (Novodevichy), since (to quote the most recent annotation), "the Kromy Forest scene did not yet exist at the time, and in the scene at St. Basil's there are no comic elements at all."[124] But, as we have seen, to say this is to misunderstand Pushkin, as Musorgsky himself had evidently misunderstood him. The fact that the St. Basil's scene, in late nineteenth-century realist eyes, seemed to contain no comedy, is precisely the reason why that scene must have been the one Musorgsky meant (along with Novodevichy, perhaps). Else why the parenthetical exclamation point? Both crowd scenes employed identical radical techniques of choral writing and choral dramaturgy, and as these techniques were derived from the prose recitative of the Inn scene, they themselves were what constituted the "comic element." Andrey Rimsky-Korsakov, in a percep-

---

[121] *Russkiy vestnik* 87 (1887): 385.
[122] StasPR 1/2.61.
[123] MusLN 1.117.
[124] A. Orlova and M. Pekelis, commentary to MusLN 1.304.

tive aside, noted that the comic elements implicit in Pushkin's handling of the drama "came out all the more vividly underscored with
Musorgsky."[125]

And the elder Rimsky-Korsakov, to whom Musorgsky had con-
fided his bewilderment, so far agreed that the peasants in *Boris* were
"*bouffe*," that he parodied them wickedly in his comic opera *May
Night* (1879) after a story by Gogol. At the very end of act 2, when
the pusillanimous town bailiffs cringingly beg the mayor not to force
them out into the night on a perilous errand of justice, they do so to
a musical phrase obviously modeled on Musorgsky's chorus of
forced supplication in the Novodevichy scene (Example 14).

The humor here was not entirely friendly to Musorgsky. *May Night*
was the first major work Rimsky composed after putting himself
through the rigorous and painful course of self-instruction he undertook upon being unexpectedly appointed to the faculty of Rubinstein's Conservatory. So this passage probably contains an ironic
backward glance at his own musical origins. But Musorgsky himself
no doubt began to view his peasants with a similar irony after his
experience at Pargolovo, when he perceived that in the eyes—or
rather, ears—of his audience the prose recitative of his choral scenes
ineluctably spelled "comedy," its traditional medium. From this experience, perhaps, dates his first impulse to revise his opera.

To meet the immediate need only some local surgery was required:
deletion of the concluding episode in the Novodevichy scene—
which, though one of the opera's boldest and most original strokes,
broke the poignant mood of the pilgrims' chorus—and the physical
removal of St. Basil's. This would be replaced later by the Kromy
Forest scene, in which the dramatic intentions could hardly be mistaken. For that scene to be achieved, however, the whole drama
would have to be reshaped and rethought along new and thoroughly
un-Pushkinian ideological lines.

In constructing a rationale for the revision of *Boris*, it turns out to
be exceptionally fruitful to make the assumption suggested here: that
Musorgsky's first impulse to revise came in the form of a reconsideration of his operatic technique with an eye toward clarifying the
"genre" of the opera—that is, toward making decisive the contrast
between what was "*bouffe*" and what was not, and generally toward
elevating the tone of the opera, as Prince Odoyevsky had said of *A*

[125] " 'Boris Godunov' M. P. Musorgskogo," p. 138.

EXAMPLE 14a. *May Night* (Moscow: Muzïka, 1970), p. 167

Have mercy, Mr. Mayor!

EXAMPLE 14b. *Boris Godunov*, p. 18

Our father! Our provider!

Life for the Tsar so many years before, "to the level of tragedy."[126] For in light of this assumption (and only in light of it) much that has appeared paradoxical or otherwise inexplicable in the revision—as regards the choral scenes, to be sure, but most particularly as regards the Terem—falls into place.

V

"Woe to them," Musorgsky wrote later, "who blithely take Pushkin . . . only as a text."[127] That is what he himself had done the first time around. By treating the utterances of the title character strictly according to kuchkist-realist principles of musical song-speech, Musorgsky had diminished him vis-à-vis the literary prototype. To restore Tsar Boris to full tragic dimension on the operatic stage he would have to "perpetrate an arioso," and to define and focus its tone more effectively, he would have to surround the arioso with a baffling profusion of trivial genre pieces, so abundant that (ironically enough) at least one of them is almost always cut in performance today.

In revising the Terem scene, Musorgsky resolved its excessively even tone into two precipitates, so to speak, one higher in tone than before, the other lower. In doing so he had a specific model to follow: César Cui's *William Ratcliff*, which enjoyed enormous prestige within the Balakirev circle as the first opera by one of its members to achieve production (and the only one as of the date of the revision of *Boris*). Though in view of their respective historical statures, and in view of Cui's notorious perfidy toward the finished *Boris*, it seems almost indecent to cite his work as a model for Musorgsky's, the parallels speak for themselves.

Like so many kuchkist productions, *Ratcliff* had had a long and checkered gestation. It was begun in 1861 and only finished in the summer of 1868, right before Musorgsky embarked upon *Boris*. When Cui began work on the opera, his operatic gods were Glinka, Auber, and Schumann (!); by the time he finished it, his operatic ideals had been completely transformed under the influence of Dargomïzhsky. The last stages of work were carried out under the watchful eyes of Dargomïzhsky himself and the whole kuchka, to the point

[126] V. F. Odoyevsky, *Muzïkal'no-literaturnoye naslediye* (Moscow: Muzgiz, 1956), p. 119. Cf. TarODR, 2–3.

[127] To Golenishchev-Kutuzov, 15 August 1877. MusLN 1.232.

where Musorgsky could exclaim to Cui, in a letter greeting the news of *Ratcliff's* completion, that the opera was "as much ours as yours."[128] These vicissitudes left an unmistakable mark on the extremely uneven and disparate style of the opera. As Herman Laroche very astutely sensed after the February 1869 première, "the differences in execution are not premeditated but involuntary. . . . All the inconsistencies can be explained by a difference in maturity and a radical change of taste."[129]

Laroche's comment, though valid for the opera as a whole, was made with specific reference to the second act. This begins with a tavern scene consisting of a drinking chorus, a sort of blindman's bluff game in which a drunken robber chases a girl around the room to the accompaniment of a laughing chorus, and a strophic song with choral refrains about the jolly robber's life. The merriment is peremptorily interrupted by the title character's entrance. He sends the robbers off to bed, and the rest of the scene is given over to his lengthy narrative monologue, in which he reveals to his lieutenant Lesley (but mainly to the audience) all the secrets of his heart.

The abrupt shift in tone is matched by a radical shift in style, and indeed the two halves of the scene were composed years apart. The opening choral *divertissement* was the earliest layer of all, and shows that as originally conceived, *Ratcliff* was to have been a kind of *Fra Diavolo, à la russe*. The text was the work of one Victor Krïlov, a school friend of Cui's who had furnished him with his previous libretti (*The Mandarin's Son, The Prisoner of the Caucasus*) and also wrote the words for Borodin's farcical pastiche *Bogatïri* (1867). Beginning with Ratcliff's narrative, however, the text is drawn direct, Dargomïzhsky-style, from Pleshcheyev's translation of Heine's original play, without benefit of librettist. The music, too, takes on an air of high seriousness, the vocal line aspiring to what Cui called "melodic recitative," while the orchestra aspired to symphonic continuity and eloquence by virtue of a texture heavy with pedal points, chromatic appoggiaturas, and leitmotifs.

Musorgsky copied the dramatic shape of this scene of Cui's in recasting the opening of his Terem scene. In both, a rather lengthy *divertissement* full of songs and games is suddenly interrupted by the entrance of the stern baritone protagonist, who, having dispersed the

---

[128] 15 August 1868. MusLN 1.104. For a detailed discussion of *Ratcliff* and its creative history, see TarODR, chapter 6, especially pp. 358–66.

[129] G. Larosh, *Muzïkal'no-kriticheskiye stat'i* (St. Petersburg: Bessel, 1894), p. 96.

revelers, proceeds to sing a crucial and self-revealing monologue. And the Boris who thus presents himself in the revised Terem is even more noble than his 1869 predecessor, even more the complex "Dostoyevskian" protagonist uniting aspects of hero and villain. This, too, seems indebted to the example of Cui's Ratcliff, who is portrayed with some subtlety, in Laroche's words, as "the victim of his hallucinations and his morbid sensitivity, musically realized by giving his music, whatever the bloodthirsty situation, a tender, lyrical cast."[130] The difference between the central monologues in the two Terem scenes is precisely a matter of heightened lyricism (for which purpose Musorgsky borrowed another theme from *Salammbô*, and gave it broad development not only in the orchestra but in the voice as well[131]), and the difference between the two concluding monologues is precisely a matter of heightened portrayal of a victimizing hallucination.

So what had been a kind of happenstance in *Ratcliff*, brought about by the juxtaposition of Cui's early and mature styles, became a calculated dramatic device in *Boris*. Musorgsky even aped the device of comic relief Cui had provided at the conclusion of the protagonist's monologue. In *Ratcliff* it had been a snoring chorus; in *Boris* it was the commotion caused by Popinka, the tsarevich's pet parrot.[132]

In light of his dictum about Pushkin-as-text, the most striking aspect of the revised Terem was the extent to which Musorgsky now found it desirable to rewrite the words even as he was straying musically from the Dargomïzhskian straight-and-narrow. Clearly the criteria of the musical and spoken dramas were no more synonymous to the creator of the revised Terem than they were to the author of the Polish act, which in so many ways it now resembled; in light of its "influence" on the Terem, the very heart of the opera, the Polish

[130] Ibid., p. 93.

[131] The heightening of the lyricism seems to have been influenced to some extent by some additional models from within the kuchka. In the big monologue for the title character in the scene at the Black Stone from *William Ratcliff* (act 3), Cui had constructed a large-scale *scena* around a recurrent, climactic melody that, unlike the other leitmotifs in *Ratcliff* (or in the 1869 *Boris*), is sung, not merely sounded by the orchestra. And the melody Musorgsky chose for this purpose from *Salammbô* is quite similar in contour and rhythmic design to the leading melody in Yaroslavna's arioso from act 1 of *Prince Igor*, one of the very few numbers from that opera to have been composed by the time Musorgsky undertook the revision of *Boris*.

[132] Musorgsky's debt to *Ratcliff* was "repaid" with interest several years later, when Cui invented a "revolutionary" subplot to Victor Hugo's *Angelo* when turning it into an opera, just so he could include a scene modeled in every way on Musorgsky's "Revolutionary" scene at Kromy.

EXAMPLE 15a. *Boris Godunov*, 1869 version, pp. 141–42

EXAMPLE 15b. *Boris Godunov*, 1871 version, pp. 209–10

In Lithuania a pretender has appeared! The king, the lords, and the pope are backing him!

act can hardly be looked upon as a mere "concession." Equally symptomatic of Musorgsky's changed aesthetic is the fact that the recitative declamation in the "new" scenes was far less naturalistic than in the old. This, too, can best be measured in the Terem scene, particularly in the episode where Boris and Shuisky face off. For here the composer retained a good deal of Pushkin's text but set it to new music. We can thus compare different settings of identical lines, for instance, the *réplique* of Shuisky shown in Example 15.

The 1869 setting betrays all the earmarks of kuchkist naturalism as described in connection with the Inn scene and *Marriage*. Particularly characteristic are the rest before the word *samozvánets* [pretender] and the triplet to which the beginning of the word is sung. There is no punctuation to justify the rest; it is the result of fastidiously moving the unaccented first syllable of *samozvánets* off the beat.[133] According to what is by now a familiar habit, the metrical pulses take nothing but accented syllables or rests. At the other place in this excerpt where three unaccented syllables follow in a row (*pápa za negó*), they are all crowded, along with the accented syllable, into a single beat.

Observe now how comparatively relaxed Musorgsky's standards of declamation had become by 1871. The rhythm of *samozvánets* is

[133] The device is immediately repeated in Boris's *réplique*—omitted here—"What? What pretender?" (*Chtozh? Chto za samozvanets?*).

smoothed out for musical reasons, allowing its first syllable to occupy a beat though unaccented. And the rhythm of *pápa za negó* has been spread out over two beats (evidently in the interest of singability), producing a similar case of an unaccented syllable (*za*) on the beat—and a preposition, at that. But most telling of all is the placement of the unaccented conjunction *i* [and] on a beat all by itself, so as to prepare the climax of the phrase more effectively. The shaping of the melodic line has been given precedence over correctness of declamation. In other words, abstractly "musical" considerations have taken precedence over the declamatory values that had been sacrosanct in the heyday of Dargomïzhskian realism only a few years before. There is no doubt that the 1871 setting of the line is a more effective and memorable "musical thought." But it has lost the special and instantly recognizable stamp of vintage kuchkism, now tainted with ineluctable associations of comedy.

From all these various perspectives, the revision of *Boris* can be viewed as harbinger of the general swing in Russian opera away from realism and kuchkism in the 1870s and 1880s. In this regard, *Boris* was fully as symptomatic, in its way, as Rimsky's revisions of *Pskovityanka* or Chaikovsky's transformation of *Vakula the Smith* into *Cherevichki*.[134] And, of course, Musorgsky continued in the "new-old" direction in the two unfinished operas that followed *Boris*, *Khovanshchina* and *Sorochintsï Fair*. The behests of the Imperial Theaters directorate played no part in Musorgsky's change of direction beyond furnishing him with an opportunity. But this is something we can see far better than Musorgsky's contemporaries. Outside his intimate circle the first version (to say nothing of *Marriage*) was not available for comparison. And withal, the revisions were only a harbinger of the swing, far from its culmination.

So it should not surprise us to find that, revisions notwithstanding, *Boris Godunov* struck its earliest audiences as a veritable ne plus ultra of musical realism. This is shown best, if ironically, by the fact that nothing Musorgsky was able to do in revising *Boris* could save it from making a "*bouffe*" impression on conservative critics. Thus V. S. Baskin intransigently refused to see any merit in the work beyond those

---

[134] See Gerald Abraham, "*Pskovityanka*: the Original Version of Rimsky-Korsakov's First Opera," *Musical Quarterly* 54 (1968): 58–73, and David Brown, *Tchaikovsky: The Early Years 1840–1874* (New York: W. W. Norton, 1978), pp. 308–35.

of the Inn scene, nor any merit in the composer beyond his lively comic sense:

> His humor and genuine wit, which up to now have found expression only in several comic songs (e.g., "The Billy Goat," "The Seminarist," etc.), have brought a large measure of authentic comedy to the opera, and have enlivened many scenes. Thus, Varlaam and Missail, the wandering vagrant monks, are not marionettes or caricatures, but are presented as two "types" drawn from life; the same may be said of the innkeeper, the policeman, the *yuródivïy*, and the two Jesuits [in the Kromy scene]. If Mr. Musorgsky, given his aptitudes, wished to write comic operas, of which we have none, he might have the place within Russian musical literature occupied by Auber [!] within the French.[135]

And if this is damning with faint praise, the notorious open letter to Musorgsky from the pseudonymous "D. Pozdnyakov" was an all-out attack:

> You, along with your whole circle, have too high an opinion of yourself. . . . You'll never go higher than your gifts allow. Your genre is petty comic operas of everyday life [*malen'kaya bïtovaya komicheskaya operï* (sic)]. And you, meanwhile, are rooting around in Russian history.[136]

The greatest antirealist indignation was aroused by the Polish act, of all things, for it represented to Pushkin lovers a typically "utilitarian," anti-aesthetic debasement of the poet's romantically metaphorical language. Particularly severe were the strictures of Nikolai Strakhov, one-time *pochvennik* par excellence,[137] who wrote a scathing critique in the form of three letters to the editor of the journal *Grazhdanin*, none other than Fyodor Dostoyevsky, his closest friend. "To this composer," he wrote:

words like—

> " . . . Beneath the roof of quiet night?
> How slowly passed the tedious day!
> How slowly the glow of evening died away!"[138]

---

[135] OrTD, 339.

[136] Ibid., p. 347.

[137] For a characterization of the romantic nationalist movement known as *pochvennichestvo* and its musical connections, see TarODR, chapter 3 ("*Pochvennichestvo* on the Russian Operatic Stage"), especially pp. 81–85.

[138] An excerpt from the Pretender's first speech to Marina. The translation is by Alfred Hayes (*Poems, Prose, and Plays of Pushkin*, p. 380).

—are out of place and unsuited to music. He is, after all, a musical Re-alist. He realized that he would have had to represent in sounds the quiet night, the close of day, the dimming of the twilight. Who needs all this? And so he throws it all out and sticks in his own words: "an-guished," "agonizing doubts," "torments of the heart," and even "the renunciation of my joy"! There you have an example of realism and, alas, the level of contemporary artistic feeling.[139]

Strakhov even professes to find a kind of Chernïshevskian nihilism at work in the Fountain scene, citing its author as one of those who "reason thus: why paint a picture if the same thing can be expressed in a modest journalistic article? And conversely: in a picture there must be only what can be set forth in a good piece of journalism. Everything else is nonsense."[140]

It is only too easy to dismiss these fulminations as a particularly obtuse period piece, especially as we have seen how closely Musorg-sky had cleaved to Pushkin's text *before* his realism had begun (*pace* Strakhov) to ebb. But Strakhov's testimony is a salutary reminder that the second *Boris* was not quite the neoromantic retreat it has seemed to the likes of Asafyev. It was right *after* revising *Boris*, after all, that Musorgsky wrote his celebrated "Toward new shores" letter, in which he delivered himself of his most famous realist slogan, his oft-quoted "credo" that "artificial representation of beauty alone, in the material sense of the word, is coarse childishness, the babyhood of art."[141] The adaptation of the Fountain scene is a case in point: Musorgsky rejected the "material" aspects of "external" beauty in Pushkin's text, replacing it with direct emotional reportage. As one sympathetic Soviet writer has put it, "in rewriting the poet's text, though much of the poetic enjoyment and beauty was lost, [Musorg-sky] undeniably achieved a rough and gaudy theatricality that had been lacking in Pushkin."[142]

"Rough and gaudy theatricality": Borodin could not have put it better. It was the opera composer's perennial stock-in-trade, not the

[139] Nikolai Strakhov, *Zametki o Pushkine i drugikh poètakh* (Kiev: Tipografiya I. I. Sho-kolova, 1897), pp. 83–84.

[140] Ibid. For a brief exposition of Nikolai Chernïshevsky's aesthetic and its implica-tions for music, see my "Realism as Preached and Practiced: The Russian Opéra Dia-logué," *Musical Quarterly* 56 (1970): 431–54.

[141] To Stasov, 18 October 1872. MusLN 1.141.

[142] GozROTIII, 74.

property of any aesthetic camp. The phrase aptly describes the quality Strakhov labeled "realist"; but just as aptly it defines what we have seen as evidence of a retrenchment from the hard-line realist doctrines of the 1860s. As a matter of fact, Strakhov gives us an unwitting hint as to the sources of Musorgsky's newfound "theatricality." He volleys off a particularly noisome blast at the opening of the Pretender's monologue at the very beginning of the Fountain scene: "Midnight . . . in the garden . . . by the fountain." These words, he indignantly observes, are to be found not in Pushkin's text but in his stage directions. "Astonishing is the only word for this musician, who prefers to write music to prose and not to verse, who does not even distinguish prose from verse, and who is so illiterate that he cannot even tell our poet's headings from his verses."[143] But though we balk at the critic's diagnosis, the symptom to which he calls attention is indeed an odd one. Why, indeed, set Pushkin's stage direction as if it were an actual line of text? Could it have been because it carried for Musorgsky an altogether different kind of resonance, one that had nothing to do with Pushkin? The third act of an opera whose triumphant Russian première had taken place on New Year's Day, 1869, had opened as in Example 16.

The kuchkists, whose contempt for Verdi had reached its climax with the much-touted première of *La Forza del destino*, his "Russian" opera, in 1862, had rather ambivalent feelings about *Don Carlos*, belonging as it did to a genre of which they approved, and to which a couple of them were already striving to contribute. At the time of the Russian première, Cui announced that *"Don Carlos* bears witness to the total collapse of the Italian school and to the great Maestro Verdi's complete lack of individuality,"[144] but by the time he came to write his testamentary essay on "Contemporary Operatic Forms" in 1889, Cui looked back upon *Don Carlos* as the first in a series of works (he also names *Aida* and *Otello*) that may "represent the progressive decline of Verdi's creative powers, but at the same time a progressive turn toward new forms, founded upon the criterion of dramatic truth."[145] One can deduce from this that *Don Carlos* had impressed the kuchkists in spite of themselves, much as *Lohengrin* had done a decade earlier, and so it does not strain credibility to suppose that

[143] Strakhov, p. 83.
[144] CuiIS, 148.
[145] *"Neskol'ko slov o sovremennïkh opernïkh formakh"* (1889) in Ibid., p. 415.

EXAMPLE 16. *Don Carlos* (1867), beginning of act 3

Musorgsky (perhaps not altogether consciously) turned to Verdi as a natural model for the kind of "rough and gaudy theatricality" to which he aspired in recasting *Boris*.[146]

VI

The remaining conspicuous addition to the revised *Boris* is the one that was most completely "overdetermined" by all the various im-

[146] This is not the first linking of Musorgsky's name with Verdi's in the recent literature. Oldani (*New Perspectives*, pp. 250–51) has given evidence suggesting Musorg-

pulses—stylistic, dramaturgical, ideological—that conditioned the revision. For that very reason, therefore, it demands close examination.

The so-called scene "near Kromy" (*pod Kromami*)—often referred to in the secondary literature as the Revolution scene, invariably referred to by Musorgsky as the scene of the "tramps" (*brodyagi*), and officially designated in the autograph libretto as "Sokolniki on the Dnepr"—has always posed an insurmountable problem to those who have tried to portray the revision of *Boris* as the undertaking of a composer at the mercy of sundry *forces majeures*. It had nothing to do with the theatrical directorate's strictures, and it was a much greater potential affront to the censor than St. Basil's, the scene it replaced. The initial impetus toward its composition was most likely the concern we have already noted over the "tone" of the opera, particularly as concerned the portrayal of the "peasants." But the specific realization was primarily conditioned by the influence of revisionist historiography, particularly rife in the 1860s and early 1870s, on the composer's view of the events of the Time of Troubles. These two factors were symbiotic: they can be disentangled only artificially, and that must be kept in mind during the discussion that follows.

We have associated Musorgsky's initial dissatisfaction with *Boris* with its private reception in July 1870, half a year before the committee that rejected the opera met to consider it. The first specific conception pertaining to the revision, moreover, seems to have been connected not with the Polish act but with Kromy. Stasov assigned Musorgsky's decision to end the opera with it to the winter of 1870–71.[147] And there is reason to believe it was written, or at least sketched, before the Polish act was completed. Some more chronology is called for at this point.

We have seen that the first scene of the Polish act (Marina's boudoir) was composed immediately after the rejection—it was completed 10 April 1871—and that Musorgsky then embarked directly on the Fountain scene. But the next recorded date of completion (10 September 1871) was not the Fountain but the revised Terem scene, on which Musorgsky was at work during August (as we know from a

---

sky's close acquaintance with a number of Verdi scores, and Roland John Wiley has persuasively argued (with specific reference to another Musorgsky-Verdi parallel) that the list of Musorgsky's musical "creditors" needs to be expanded beyond those whom a kuchkist would have been necessarily proud to acknowledge. See R. John Wiley, "The Tribulations of Nationalist Composers: A Speculation Concerning Borrowed Music in *Khovanshchina*," MusIM, 168–78.

[147] StasIS 2.198.

letter to Stasov). The next scene to which he turned was the Cell scene, a small task that took him only three days to complete: the revised full score, minus Pimen's narrative and with the offstage choruses, bears the date 13 September 1871. The next dated score is that of the Fountain scene at last, completed on 14 December 1871—a full three months later.

Once again there is lost time—and a lost manuscript, too—to account for. No autograph vocal score of the Kromy scene survives. But in the same letter that gave Stasov the news about the Cell scene revisions (11 September 1871), Musorgsky enthusiastically announces that he was "planning the *tramp scene*: novelty upon novelty / novelty of novelties—tremendously pleasing."[148] So that is where Kromy fit in: mid-September to, say, November 1871, if we allow two months for its completion in vocal score. That he waited until last to finish the Fountain scene may be taken as an additional confirmation that he was basing it on a prior draft, as Stasov maintained. Or perhaps it was simply the scene that interested him least.

ONE CAN be sure, though, that it was Kromy that interested him most. This scene took Musorgsky further from Pushkin than anything else in the revision. Its conceptual source can be found neither in Pushkin's play nor in Pushkin's factual source, Karamzin's *History*. It is to be found in the writings of Musorgsky's contemporary Nikolai Kostomarov, the very one (naturally enough) who, in a remark much publicized by Stasov, called the opera a "page of history."[149] Kostomarov was a neopopulist who "insisted that the simple people rather than tsars were the proper subject of the true historian."[150] The incorporation into *Boris Godunov* of this view of the people, as an active historical force rather than an obtusely passive bystander, altered the fundamental conception of the opera and went directly counter to the ideological and dramaturgical thrust of the scene it replaced.[151] The

[148] MusLN 1.125.

[149] See Chapter 4 for a full defense of this assertion.

[150] James Billington, *The Icon and the Axe* (New York: Vintage Books, 1966), pp. 409–10.

[151] Thus to include both Kromy and St. Basil's in a single performance of *Boris*, as has become the fashion of late, is to juxtapose scenes of flatly contradictory ideological contents. Far from intending such a thing, Musorgsky in fact thought he was making it impossible by transferring the episode of the *yuródivïy* and the boys, plus the *yuródivïy*'s concluding lament, from the one scene to the other. And his original plan, of course, was to insert the Kromy scene into the same position in the opera as had been formerly occupied by St. Basil.

crowd is now anything but *"bouffe,"* and so is the genre of the music it sings.

Instead of the realistic, Pushkin-derived prose of the recitative in St. Basil's, we now have a frankly "operatic" text put together by Musorgsky himself with help from Stasov and a few others. It consists of what amounts to seven large-scale, self-contained "numbers" linked occasionally by short snatches of the choral declamation that had formerly been the standard procedure. It may seem at first ironic or even paradoxical for Musorgsky to have sought to depict the crowd in active, quasi-anarchistic revolt by means of music so much more "orderly" than before. But this orderliness and roundness of form served the same "tragic" elevation of scale and tone as we have encountered in the revised Terem scene, and avoided the miniaturistic, detail-heavy effect of the recitative style, which had evoked for early hearers an unwanted impression of comedy.

The Kromy scenario consists of the following musically discrete sections.

1. Orchestral introduction, entrance of the chorus with the captive Khrushchov (through fig. ⑫). This is the one section that makes use of choral recitative in the older style.

2. The "glorification" of Khrushchov (figs. ⑫–⑳). Strophic choral song based on the folk song *Chto ne yastreb sovïkalsya s perepyolushkoyu* [Did the hawk not soar aloft with the quail?]. Interjections of prose recitative between the verses.

3. Episode of the *yuródivïy* with the boys (figs. ⑳–㉕), transferred from the St. Basil's scene.

4. Entrance of Varlaam and Missail (figs. ㉕–㉙). Strophic song, based on the bïlina *O Vol'ge i Mikule* [Of Vol'ga and Mikula], some interjections of choral recitative.

5. "Revolutionary" chorus, *Rakhodilas', razgulyalas' udal' molodetskaya* (figs. ㉙–㊾). Freely handled da capo form. Middle section based on the folk song *Zaigrai, moya volïnka* [Play, my bagpipes, play].

6. The False Dmitry's procession (figs. ㊾–㉘), including hymns of the Jesuits, Dmitry's proclamation, and the crowd's glorification of the False Dmitry. The procession music is adapted from the procession of the priests in the Temple scene of *Salammbô*.

7. The *yuródivïy*'s lament (fig. ㉘ to end), transferred from the ending of the St. Basil's scene.

Although the Kromy scene begins very much in the style of the *"bouffe"* choral writing of 1869, prose recitative is quickly abandoned as carrier of the dramatic thread. Starting with the second section, recitative does not even link the sections. This results in a certain episodic, static quality in the scene's progress, but also lends it a friezelike monumentality unlike anything in the opera save the much simpler Coronation choruses. Such a scene is hardly meant to play like spoken theater. It is closer to pageant, even oratorio.

Except for the opening section in which Khrushchov is strung up, and the episode of the *yuródivïy* and the boys—which actually belonged to the 1869 version, and hence derives from Pushkin—action in the Kromy scene is limited to entrances and exits. The characters, and in particular the chorus, do not so much act (unless the director cooks up some stage business for them) as report their feelings and thoughts in broad, simple musical constructions—"opera seria" answers *"bouffe"*!

The same desire to counteract the *bouffonnerie* of *opéra dialogué* may also underlie Musorgsky's decision to bring Varlaam and Missail back as leaders of the revolt against Boris—a strange decision, for surely they, if anyone, know that the Pretender is only Grishka Otrepyev in a plumed hat. On one level, their return can be seen as merely another manifestation of the composer's habit of "economizing" in the cast of characters, already noticeable in the early version of the opera (the policeman in the Inn scene, Pimen in the Death scene). But it has a deeper significance, too. Asafyev recalled being told by Stasov that Musorgsky meant Varlaam in Kromy to be a "horrifying and terrible" figure, the very opposite of what he had been in the Inn.[152] And Musorgsky himself averred to Golenishchev-Kutuzov that "Varlaam and Missail . . . evoked laughter until they appeared in the 'tramps' scene. Then everyone realized what dangerous beasts these seemingly funny people are."[153] So even the comedy of the Inn scene was to be, as it were, retroactively neutralized. Through Musorgsky's departures from Pushkin in Kromy, Kostomarov may be seen polemicizing with Karamzin. Characters who were initially spoofed are "recapitulated" in a spirit of grim and threatening earnestness.

Nor is this the only ironic recapitulation to be found in the Kromy scene. Two characters, Khrushchov and the Pretender, are hailed by

[152] AsIT 3.132.
[153] 10 November 1877, MusLN 1.235.

the crowd with shouts of "*slava!*" as Boris had been hailed in the prologue. The first of these glorifications is contemptuous and sarcastic; the irony is conventional. But when the Pretender is hailed with offstage trumpets mimicking the Coronation fanfares, the effect is chilling. Once again, for all its apparent newfound autonomy, the crowd has been manipulated. Here the ironic resonance goes beyond *Boris* to another opera that had ended on a note of popular rejoicing, Glinka's *A Life for the Tsar* with its concluding *Slavsya* chorus. As the crowd blindly follows the "risen" Dmitry offstage and their *slava*s die away, the ironic pathos becomes almost unbearable as the lonely *yuródiviy*, left behind amid fires and ruin, croons his prophecy of darkness and woe.

THE NEW monumentality of the Kromy scene, its reliance on the kind of thing Serov had called "musico-scenic frescoes," and in particular its heavy reliance on folk song motives—all this was really the resurgence of musico-dramatic means the Dargomïzhskian reform had rejected. It was Rimsky-Korsakov who had shown how they could continue to be employed within a realist context in *Pskovityanka*, particularly in the scene of the Pskov council, the so-called *veche*, which was composed while Musorgsky was between versions of *Boris* and at a time when the two composers were especially close—living together, in fact. Musorgsky was particularly impressed with the way Rimsky had succeeded in giving the chorus the quality of a collective character—an active participant in the drama—without debasing the tone of the opera. "Korsinka has concocted some magnificent history with the choruses in the *veche*—just as it should be," wrote Musorgsky to the Purgold sisters,[154] exactly one month before his own choruses were pronounced "*bouffe*" by Stasov's hand-picked audience. During the fall of 1871, the Kromy scene was composed by a Musorgsky who had daily contact with the sounds of *Pskovityanka*, then in the process of orchestration.[155] Recalling Borodin's comment on the mutual benefit Musorgsky and Rimsky derived from their brief cohabitation—"Modest has perfected Korsinka's recitative and declamational side, while the latter has eliminated . . . the incoherence of [Musorgsky's] formal construction, in a word, made Modest's

[154] 18 June 1870. Ibid., p. 110.
[155] R-KMusL, 123.

things incomparably more musical"[156]—the Kromy scene may be viewed as one of its most notable offspring.

Rimsky-Korsakov was always careful to maintain musical continuity—"coherence in formal construction," as Borodin put it—and this was saliently imparted to Musorgsky. In Kromy, once the initial episode with Krushchov is past, what choral recitative there is takes its place against a backdrop of leading melody elsewhere in the musical texture. In section 4 (see p. 272) this leading melody is furnished by Varlaam's and Missail's song. In section 6, when the chorus (led by Varlaam) threatens the Jesuits while they are singing for help to the Virgin Mary, the orchestra "organizes" the whole episode with an ostinato bass melody resembling, if not actually based on, a folk song (Example 17).

This technique of hanging recitative on a melodic thread, often symmetrical or else "developmental," and often of folklore character, was borrowed directly from *Pskovityanka*. It has little precedent in the first *Boris*, but pervades Rimsky's opera from the very opening scene, in which a game of catch for the chorus of maidens is accompanied by a quite elaborate orchestral fantasy on an eighth-note ostinato theme that is never sung on stage but is so fully realized in the orchestra as to be performable in its own right. Thereafter some form of the technique is used in many scenes, notably in the *veche*.[157]

Musorgsky had tried this trick once or twice in the earlier *Boris* (e.g., Grishka's interrogation of the Hostess in the Inn scene while Varlaam sings his second song, or Boris's death agonies against a chorus of monks), but had employed it strictly "empirically." That is, he used it when the specific stage situation called for it, never elevating it, as Rimsky had, into an abstract constructive device. More typical of Musorgsky's earlier procedure was the opening of the Cell scene. The tortuous viola figure running in sixteenth notes accompanies Pimen's writing but not his singing. It comes to an end the moment he opens his mouth, and thereafter (with the exception of the climax at the end of the opening monologue) is confined to filling

---

[156] BorP 1.313.

[157] Rimsky's music at the beginning of the *veche*, with its stately common-tone progressions, obviously owed a debt to the opening of Musorgsky's preexistent Coronation scene. But just as surely it influenced the beginning of Kromy, where the crowd rushes onstage and sings its recitatives against a frenzied orchestral ostinato. The resemblance of this opening orchestral idea to both the *Pskovityanka veche* and the Coronation scene is clear. It provides yet another ironic parallel with the early scenes of *Boris*, and at the same time most clearly shows Rimsky's influence.

EXAMPLE 17. *Boris Godunov*, pp. 408–9

the gaps between his phrases. When Pimen sings, the orchestra is reduced to a melodically neutral punctuation, as it is for most of the Inn and (unrevised) Terem scenes as well.

In the second *Boris*, the Rimskian device of organizing and unifying recitative scenes by means of a continuous and internally coherent orchestral fabric went beyond Kromy: it also motivated the famous chiming clock in the Terem scene. The clock's mechanical whirr

EXAMPLE 17, *continued*

and clang provided an ideal formalizing backdrop to set off Boris's free *parlando*, fixing and intensifying the emotion through an externalized musical structure—however minimal—that is discrete and differentiated from what had preceded it, and hence the more memorable in its generalized impression.[158] Indeed, a comparison of the

[158] Chaliapin's legendary success with this scene is telling in this regard. In his recorded performances of it (especially the one that captures a live 1928 performance at

1869 versions of both Terem monologues with their 1871 counterparts will illustrate this point perhaps better than anything else in the revision. What in the second version are two totally distinct, indeed contrasting impressions—the noble "arioso" based on a broad melody out of *Salammbô* versus the melodramatic hallucination with the clock, the two sharing no musical material whatever—were originally a pair of very similar recitatives, quite undifferentiated in musical means. The accompaniments to both had been woven out of a common fund of leitmotifs (up to the moment of the hallucination, at any rate) and were to that extent literally interchangeable; moreover, because of their leitmotivic base, the two monologues shared material with their surrounding passages as well, and thus tended to fade a bit into the musical woodwork.

To RETURN to Kromy: the scene shows its kinship with Rimsky's *veche* also in its new way of treating folk material. The two songs in the 1869 *Boris* had been handled with true kuchkist-realist circumspection—both the Coronation *Slava!* and Varlaam's second song represent actual singing in the course of the action.[159] They frame the action with elements of genre, of local color. The three folk songs in Kromy, on the other hand, *are* the action at the points where they occur.[160] And in the case of at least one of them, actual singing is not the object of "depiction" but the distilled essence of a mood.

First is the mocking glorification of Khrushchov. It is precisely the kind of thing Musorgsky would have set to a bold, *"bouffe"* recitative in the first *Boris*. If we are to believe Golenishchev-Kutuzov's memoirs (Soviet writers have understandably preferred not to), this very

---

Covent Garden) his departures from Musorgsky's notation are so radical as to turn the scene into virtual melodrama. Thanks to the regular, indeed rigid, orchestral accompaniment, however, the scene retains a musical backbone despite the musically unstructured rendition of the solo part. Any attempt to render the 1869 version of the hallucination in this fashion would surely have produced not a magnificent Chaliapinesque effect, but chaos.

[159] The *Slava!* is the subject of Chapter 6. Varlaam's song was adapted to an as-yet unpublished tune, imparted to Musorgsky by Rimsky-Korsakov, who had received it from his mother. See the Appendix at the end of this chapter.

[160] Of these songs, only one (*Zaigrai, moya volïnka*, which forms the middle of the "Revolutionary chorus") was available by 1872 in published form; Balakirev had included it in his anthology of 1866, described in Chapter 1. The Glorification song was given to Musorgsky privately by Balakirev, and the *bïlina* sung by Varlaam and Missail was taken down by Musorgsky himself from the performances of Trofim Ryabinin. Both of these were published in 1877 by Rimsky-Korsakov in his collection *One Hundred Russian Folk Songs* (nos. 18 and 2, respectively). For additional details see Chapter 6.

mannered, ritualized expression of so sophisticated an emotion as sarcasm later embarrassed the composer.[161]

Varlaam's and Missail's rabble-rousing song, which incites the crowd to the riot expressed musically in the "Revolutionary" chorus, parallels, in means and effect, the conclusion of Rimsky-Korsakov's *veche*, and was unquestionably modeled upon it. The relationship between Rimsky's scene and Musorgsky's is suggested not only by the former's chronological antecedence but also by the fact that the use of folk song was somewhat better motivated there. In Mey's *Pskovityanka*, a band of mutineers calls for a formal song of farewell to Pskov. The folk song that follows in Rimsky's setting, therefore, is one that would have been sung even were the play presented in its original, spoken form, and hence conforms wholly to kuchkist standards of "organic" relationship to the action. There is no comparable preparation of Varlaam's and Missail's song, though in its inexorable strophic unfolding (abetted by orchestration of steadily mounting sonority) it has precisely the same function as in *Pskovityanka*. It symbolizes the sweeping, spontaneous spread of an idea through the populace, in this case revenge upon Boris and the acceptance of the False Dmitry as rightful tsar. The deployment of forces in *Boris* is the reverse of that found in Rimsky's scene: in *Pskovityanka* the folk song is sung by a chorus of mutineers punctuated by recitative ejaculations by the principals, whereas in Kromy, the folk song is sung by the two soloists and the interjections of recitative come from the chorus. But so characteristic is the texture, and so unlike anything else in Musorgsky's work, that its conceptual derivation from Rimsky's *veche* is clear.

The most radical use of folk song in the Kromy scene, however, is the "Revolutionary" chorus, *Razkhodilas', razgulyalas'*.[162] This chorus represents the crowd not in the act of singing but in actual, spontaneous revolt. The use of so formal a set piece for such a purpose is as far from the dramaturgical principles that ruled the first *Boris* as can be imagined. Lingering kuchkist scruples can be perceived in the way Musorgsky fragments the chorus into sections so as to avoid the static "monolithic" effect so frequently derided in Cui's reviews of

---

[161] See the Introduction to this book.

[162] Only the middle section utilizes a folk melody, but the entire text is of popular origin, according to Stasov, who reports that it was supplied to Musorgsky by D. L. Mordovtsev (StasIS 2.198). If there was a published source it has not yet been identified.

operas by Chaikovsky and Serov.[163] But a conventionally conceived "chorus" it nonetheless remains. It carries no overt action, but functions dramaturgically as an "aria"—and a da capo aria at that. The use of folk song in this type of formal context also had antecedents in *Pskovityanka*, particularly the act 1 love duet. When Rimsky's opera was performed in 1873, as a matter of fact, the composer was rebuked by Cui for using a folk song to express "personal" emotions.[164] No such stricture could be applied to Musorgsky's chorus: its sentiment is entirely and properly collective. But the characterization of the crowd is monolithic—a single collective personage giving voice to a single, unanimous collective sentiment, rather than an unruly, internally divided collection of "types." While the crowd's unanimity is not unmotivated, this chorus (along with the revised Terem monologue) represents the clearest retreat from kuchkist realism in the interest of monumentality, of aesthetic distance—in a word, of "tragedy."

VII

If one of the traits of the extremist realism to which Musorgsky adhered in the 1860s was pettiness of scale and the resulting debasement of tone, another was casualness of overall form. This was a point of principle. "Formlessness," as preeminently exemplified by *The Stone Guest*, was one of the great kuchkist shibboleths. Stasov, who revered Dargomïzhsky for "destroying all conventional rules and forms" for the sake of truth to life,[165] could praise Wagner and even Serov to the extent that they shared the "general aspiration to formlessness" that characterized "all the latest and best music of our time."[166] Crudely construed, formlessness meant simply the avoidance of academic "forms." More subtly understood, it meant the whole realist value system that emphasized the piquancy of the individual moment over the coherence of the whole in artworks of all media.

To the committed realist, then, a whole was simply a sum of parts. And we have seen how well the 1869 *Boris* exemplified this view in

---

[163] Because the first pair of entries—basses and tenors—are pitched a fourth apart this chorus has been occasionally described as a fugue.

[164] CuiIS, 220.

[165] StasIS 3.725.

[166] BalStasP 1.163; StasSEM, 86.

its lopsided dramatic structure. In this, as in so many other ways, the revised opera contrasts so strikingly with its predecessor as to connote a fundamentally changed aesthetic. The composer now aimed at a unity in the narrative shape of the opera such as he had formerly despised. Perhaps precisely because Musorgsky was challenged by the task of ordering the many new elements in the opera, the revised version became a coherent, even shapely theatrical unity, which strives hard to impose a sense of artistic order on the sprawling plot it embodies, and to hold all the disparate elements in an artful and consistently sustained balance. This fact alone argues strongly against conflating the two *Borises*.

Many, beginning with César Cui, have complained that the libretto of the revised *Boris* is (in Gerald Abraham's words) "not an organic whole but a series of disconnected scenes."[167] But that is because they have not noticed the extraordinary symmetry that binds the scenes together. The three focal "characters" in the revised scenario—tsar, Pretender, crowd—are balanced in a fashion that can be demonstrated best in tabular form:

Prologue:	1. Novodevichy Courtyard	Crowd
	2. Coronation	Boris
Act 1:	3. Cell in Chudov Monastery	
	4. Inn on Lithuanian Border	Pretender
Act 2:	5. The Tsar's Terem	Boris
Act 3:	6. Marina's Boudoir	
	7. The Fountain	Pretender
Act 4:	8. Death of Boris	Boris
	9. Sokolniki on the Dnepr (Kromy)	Crowd

The sequence is palindromic, with the opera framed by two big choral scenes. The people, seen from two radically differing points of view, are the alpha and the omega (and is this not the reason why Musorgsky jumped with such alacrity at Nikolsky's idea that he end the opera not with Boris's death but with Kromy?). Their tragic history, viewed à la Kostomarov, is now the all-essential theme hovering over the drama. The middle of the sequence—the keystone of the arch—is the Terem scene, where we get our closest view of the title character. And while viewing the scene as a keystone, we ought to note that thanks to the genre interpolations at the beginning, the central monologue—where, in words no longer Pushkin's but Musorg-

---

[167] *Slavonic and Romantic Music*, p. 178.

sky's, the tsar laments the disaffection of the people in terms quite explicitly linked with his crime—now comes almost precisely at the midpoint. The other scenes in which Boris is dominant, the Coronation and Death scenes, are paired with the choral scenes, thus bringing tsar and people into radically contrasting juxtaposition at the beginning and the end of the drama. They trace opposite trajectories. The crowd begins in cowed and passive submission to authority—as they are portrayed throughout the 1869 version—but ends in rebellion. (The policeman in the first scene and the *voyevoda* Khrushchov in the last, both embodiments of state power, may be viewed as complementary figures symbolizing this progression: the first oppresses the people, the latter is their victim.) Boris, on his part, is shown first in the Coronation scene at the zenith of his power. From then on he is portrayed in a state of steady decline unto death.

The central Terem scene is flanked on either side by acts depicting the progress of the False Dmitry. (The opening scene of the Polish act, in which he does not appear, is nonetheless dominated by him, for he is its sole topic of reference.) It may be argued that an organic connection is still missing between the Pretender scenes and the Boris scenes: that if acts 1 and 3 were omitted, the coherence of the remaining scenes would be unaffected; or conversely, that if these acts were to be performed by themselves they would constitute in their own right a short but self-sufficient opera that could take its place alongside the many dramas entitled *Dmitry the Pretender*. But that opera, too, would have to end with the Kromy Forest scene, since that scene brings Dmitry's story to its culmination. The Kromy scene thus takes on the significance of a multiple resolution. It is the connecting link among all the simultaneously unfolding, symmetrically intercut stories that comprise the expanded plot of Musorgsky's opera.

A COMPARABLE concern for overall dramatic coherence seems to have ruled Musorgsky's radically altered deployment of leitmotifs in the revised *Boris*. On the face of it, their importance seems much diminished. In the newly composed scenes their role is minimal. Rangoni, for example, has only the most perfunctory identifying theme (a descending chromatic scale), and Marina has none at all. In revising the Terem scene, moreover, Musorgsky so attenuated the occurrences of leitmotifs associated with the title character that they tend to lose their significance as such altogether. One of the most important ones, the theme on which the concluding monologue had been based (see Example 7) was actually eliminated from the Terem scene, so that when it appears in the Death scene as a part of the farewell to the tsarevich ("Do not ask how I attained the throne" [*Ne sprashivai, kakim putyom ya tsarstvo priobryol*]), it is no longer a recurrence, hence no leitmotif.

This lessened reliance on leitmotifs has been noted before, and is usually cited as evidence of disaffection from Wagnerian methods. But that is an unwarranted extrapolation, since there is no reason to call the use of leitmotifs in the earlier *Boris* Wagnerian to begin with: models in *The Stone Guest* and particularly in Cui's *William Ratcliff* were far closer to hand.[168] What the suppression of the Boris motives actually suggests is that Musorgsky was sensitive to their "leveling" propensity, which made for a sameness among Boris's utterances that was especially undesirable in the Terem monologues.

A further incentive toward curtailing the Boris motives may perhaps be found in the greatly expanded role the Dmitry motive plays in the revised version, a role so spectacularly spotlit that a wish to suppress its competitors is plausible. To be sure, the motive's enhanced prominence was partly a mere by-product of the Pretender's much greater presence in the revised opera. (He now appeared in two more scenes than before, for a total of four to Boris's three.) But a careful comparison of the progress and deployment of the Dmitry motive in the two versions will show that the situation was not that simple, that the difference affected not only the portrayal of the Pretender but that of Boris as well, and that there may be some better explanations for some of the deletions from the 1869 score than have hitherto been offered in the literature.

Our discussion of the 1869 *Boris* emphasized the dual nature of the Dmitry theme: that it shifted in reference between the murdered tsarevich and the Pretender, and that the ambiguities in its treatment were an important contributor to the portrayal of Boris's psychological deterioration. All of this remains true of the revised version as well, with one telling and immensely clarifying refinement: in the new version the motive refers *only* to the Pretender—except in Boris's deranged mind. The consistency with which certain otherwise inex-

---

[168] For a discussion of the leitmotifs in *Ratcliff* and their significance for Russian opera, see TarODR, 367–79.

plicable, even paradoxical alterations realize this change leaves no doubt as to its purpose.

Cuts and revisions in the Cell scene, the Terem scene, and the Death scene, all contribute to the newly clarified significance of the leitmotif. With Pimen's narrative of the murder at Uglich gone, the first appearance of the motive now coincides with Grigory's first glimmer of ambition, at Pimen's line "He would have been your age, and would be reigning." The leitmotif comes in at the last word, while in Musorgsky's typically detailed stage direction, "Grigory majestically draws himself to his full height, then, with feigned humility, settles down again." Thus an unmistakable bond is forged between the leitmotif and the Pretender's progress; the slain tsarevich is no longer directly involved with it. The motive recurs only once in the revised Cell scene, shortly before the end, when Grigory hangs back at the door while Pimen goes off to matins, and utters his threat to Boris. Although mention is made in this speech of the dead tsarevich, its true significance is the formal launching, as it were, of the Pretender's career. The link forged here between the opera's main leitmotif and the progress of the False Dmitry is amply reinforced, of course, by the Inn scene that immediately follows.

Now the clarification of the Dmitry motive's significance (particularly, as we shall see, in light of the role it will play in the revised Terem) might already be deemed sufficient motivation for cutting Pimen's narrative, however regrettable or inexplicable the cut may now appear to us, who revere Musorgsky and all his works. And I believe it in fact to have been the main reason, especially in view of the fact that cutting the narrative was the very next step Musorgsky took after revising the Terem scene.[169] But another reason may be adduced as well: the failure of Cui's *William Ratcliff*, whose dramaturgical progress was fatally impeded by a plethora of narratives in place of directly portrayed action. Every critic fixed upon this flaw,[170] and, indeed, anyone who sat through the opera would have found it trying. Now while Musorgsky did refer to the removal of Pimen's narrative as an "abbreviation" in his report to Stasov,[171] abbreviation as such could hardly have been his aim, considering how much that was dramaturgically unessential was added (particularly to the Terem scene) in the course of revision. So what led him to Pimen's narrative must

---

[169] According to his letter to Stasov on 11 September 1871. MusLN 1.125.
[170] See TarODR, 364–66.
[171] MusLN 1.125.

have been the fact that it contained two references to the infant Dmitry through the motive he now wanted to refocus exclusively on the Pretender. Indeed, comparison of the use of the motive in the two versions of the Terem scene supports the hypothesis that the main objective in dropping the narrative was to get rid of the motive's associations with the slain tsarevich.

In the 1869 version of the Terem scene, the Dmitry motive figures very prominently. It is first heard at the very end of Boris's central monologue in unambiguous reference to the slain tsarevich. Thereafter, it sounds repeatedly and with shifting significance during the exchange with Shuisky, as described above. In the 1871 version its use is sharply curtailed. It is heard only twice, and is completely avoided in Boris's rewritten part. The first reference now corresponds to what had been the second occurrence of the motive in 1869: the climactic moment when Shuisky reveals that the Pretender is calling himself the risen Dmitry, and plants the thought for the first time in Boris's mind that it might be true. The only remaining use of the motive comes in Shuisky's narrative in the events at Uglich, where in place of the very prominent display the motive had received in 1869 (cf. Example 12), we get only a couple of quiet, veiled allusions, in which the motive appears in a kind of inchoate state, identifiable by its major-sixth *initium*, but minus its falling-fourth cadence (Example 18). The ambiguity of the reference, in which the motive is insinuated by Shuisky but never quite sung by him, suggests that a hint is being dropped: that it is left for Boris (and the audience) to draw the conclusion.

And draw it he does. The references to the Dmitry theme in the Death scene are fraught with an unbearable irony. When it is first heard, in the boyars' chorus, it refers unambiguously to the Pretender (Lamm score, fig. 15). But when Boris rushes onstage in the grip of his hallucination, it sounds forth as an embodiment of the specter haunting him (fig. 27). And finally, when Pimen sings of Dmitry as miracle-working angel (fig. 44) we know that we are hearing the leitmotif through Boris's ears. By now it is clear that the double significance of the Dmitry motive is consistent and ironic: it means the Pretender to everyone but Boris, for whom it means the risen tsarevich.

One of the least-remarked cuts in the revised *Boris*—mentioned neither by Andrey Rimsky-Korsakov nor by Asafyev, and mentioned by Lamm only in his critical notes—offers the ultimate proof that this

EXAMPLE 18. *Boris Godunov*, pp. 220–21

But the tsarevich's childish face was bright, pure, and clear; the wound gaped deep and fearful . . .

masterstroke of psychological penetration was carefully calculated. It is a twelve-measure passage from Boris's farewell to his son, in the course of which the Dmitry motive is associated with the Pretender (Example 19).

The reason why this apparently insignificant cut in the otherwise untouched farewell should have been deemed necessary is obvious by now. It is part of the general clarification we have traced, and takes its place alongside the removal of Pimen's narrative and the rewriting of the Terem scene. Musorgsky combed the opera for all instances in which the motive stood for the "true" Dmitry in the minds of any but Boris, and conversely for all instances in which it stood for the False Dmitry in Boris's utterances. As for the central monologue in the Terem, use of the motive had to be cut from it because it is only after the exchange with Shuisky, in which he first hears of the Pretender, that Boris can "hear" the Pretender's motive,

EXAMPLE 19. *Boris Godunov*, p. 357

Strong is the evil Pretender!

let alone cathect it as an embodiment of his superstitions and his nemesis.

When the versions of *Boris* are conflated so as to conserve a maximum of music, this fastidious and dramatically effective refinement in the opera's leitmotivic structure is lost. Another undesirable result is a gross harping on the Dmitry motive such as Musorgsky never intended. For surely another reason for curtailing it in the Cell, Inn,[172] Terem, and Death scenes must have been its extreme prominence in the new scenes devoted to the Pretender, particularly the Fountain and Kromy. The composer strove to avoid precisely the kind of overload one now encounters in most performances, with Pimen's narrative and the St. Basil's scene reinstated alongside the Polish act and Kromy.

The ingenious transformations *à la polacca* to which the Dmitry motive is subjected in the Fountain and Kromy scenes recall the Russian-Polish contrasts that lay at the heart of Glinka's *Life for the Tsar* and would continue to resonate in Russian opera at least as far as Prokofiev.[173] And here, of course, we have the ultimate reason why the leitmotif had to stop referring (except delusionally) to the infant Dmitry and refer only to the Pretender. For once the Dmitry motive had been turned into a polonaise it would have been ideologically unaccept-

[172] See the original conclusion, published in facsimile as cited in n. 17.

[173] See my "Tone, Style, and Form in Prokofiev's Soviet Operas: Some Preliminary Observations," in *Studies in the History of Music*, vol. 2 (New York: Broude, 1988), pp. 215–39.

able to let it go on representing genuine tsarist legitimacy. Unacceptable, that is, to Musorgsky himself, whose xenophobic and rabidly anti-Catholic interpretation of the events of the Time of Troubles is luridly embodied in Rangoni, which Mephistophelian character he invented without benefit of Kostomarov or any other responsible historian. By cutting the Pimen narrative and rewriting the Terem scene, Musorgsky protected his opera's ideological integrity. In light of the Polish act and Kromy, to have allowed the Dmitry motive to retain its former double meaning would practically have amounted to ultramontane propaganda.

FROM the double perspective of ideological updating and elevation of tone it has been possible to account for virtually all aspects of the revised *Boris*—in particular, the deletions from the 1869 score as well as the additions. The one cut one is willing to believe Musorgsky made primarily in the interests of dramatic pacing was Shchelkalov's monologue (the reading of the tsar's ukase to the assembled boyars) at the beginning of the Death scene. Its content merely recapitulates information already familiar to the audience, and it therefore delays the action to no good purpose save the weaving of a new concatenation of significant leitmotifs—Shchelkalov's own, Boris's, the Pretender's—after the fashion of the two discarded monologues from the Terem scene. It was a technique with which Musorgsky was evidently disenchanted.

Yet even here additional, aesthetically more substantial reasons could be adduced if desired. One is the nature of the vocal writing. Kuchkist recitative at its most ascetic, it amounts, for most of the monologue's duration, to no more than a "lection tone" that rises by chromatic degrees through an octave and more. It was the kind of thing even his fellow kuchkists had begun to tire of in Musorgsky from the time of *Marriage*. "One cannot acknowledge as a musical thought a multitude of repeated notes taken from the components of this or that chord," carped Cui about the Cell scene, far less an offender in this respect than Shchelkalov's monologue.[174] The latter is a prime example of what Borodin called Musorgsky's "clumsy originalizing" (*koryavoye original'nichaniye*)[175] at its most extreme, particularly in view of the bizarre harmonic sequence that underlies the chromatic ascent of this unmelodic recitative. It is easy to imagine a

---

[174] *Sanktpeterburgskiye vedomosti*, no. 37 (1874).
[175] BorP 1.313.

passage like this being received with condescension and reproof at kuchkist soirées, dismissed, like *Marriage*, as a "curiosity" and a *"chose manquée."*[176]

The state of the sources, moreover, suggests that the reading of the ukase had already been cut from the 1869 version of the opera by the time Musorgsky had the full score bound for submission to the theaters committee. The pagination of the full score is unaffected by this excision (unlike those of the end of the Novodevichy scene or of St. Basil's, which left gaps). Thus the particular deletion is not, properly speaking, part of the 1871 revision at all. It is also not insignificant that Lamm should have made his serendipitous discovery of the monologue among Stasov's papers at the Public Library in Leningrad. For Stasov, who could always be counted on to praise and cherish Musorgsky's wildest productions, had also been the recipient of the *Marriage* autograph after the rest of the kuchka had rejected that most aberrant of all Musorgsky's children.

VIII

We have come to the end of our lengthy and discursive investigation of the revision of *Boris Godunov*, but something is lacking. If we are to maintain that the version Musorgsky made in 1871, orchestrated in 1872, and published in 1874 represents his intentions and not his concessions; if we are to maintain that the revision was prompted by fundamental aesthetic and ideological reconsiderations and not by mere considerations of expedience; if, finally, we are to maintain that the revised *Boris* is the authentic masterpiece and the earlier version a document of a particular moment in the history of Russian opera and of its composer's creative development—then we are missing some corroboration from the composer, some explicit rather than merely circumstantial indication that he shared our view.

Such a document exists. In presenting Stasov with the autograph of *Marriage* as a forty-ninth birthday present on 2 January 1873, Musorgsky wrote a warmly moving dedicatory epistle that reads in part:

> How shall one please a dear one? The answer comes without the slightest hesitation, as it does to all hotheads: give him of yourself. And so I am doing. Take my youthful labor on Gogol's *Marriage*, look upon

[176] These are the epithets applied to *Marriage* by Balakirev and Cui (as reported by Rimsky-Korsakov) and by Borodin, respectively. See MR, 124–25.

these experiments in musical speech, compare them with *Boris*, set 1868 alongside 1871, and you will see that I am giving you myself irrevocably.[177]

Implicit in Musorgsky's comparison of 1868 and 1871 (and not 1869) is his judgment of the first *Boris*, a judgment quite in accordance with the Stasovian assessment with which we opened our investigation. As the composer now saw it, the first *Boris* represented the last stage of his apprenticeship. It was only as a result of revisions taken after, but not because of, its rejection, that the opera achieved what his friend called "its completed form, [as] one of the greatest works not only of Russian but of all European art." That completed form possesses an integrity of structure, style, and significance such as the earlier version had notably lacked. Attempts at second-guessing it run a serious risk of compromising this integrity. For it was the fruit of a thorough critical reassessment born of an artistic maturity that the popular image of Musorgsky as the Oblomov of music still unjustly denies him. The rage to conflate, on the other hand, rests on no such serious critique but on a mass of uncritical assumptions and reliance on positivistic scholarship over artistic judgment.

[177] MusLN 1.144.

APPENDIX

Folk Texts in *Boris Godunov*

———■———

PUSHKIN, like Ostrovsky after him, was fond of interpolating songs into his plays. Sometimes, as in the case of the *yuródiviy*'s lament in *Boris*, he wrote the words himself, evidently expecting a tune to be improvised in performance. At other times, as in act 2 of *The Stone Guest*, he would simply tell a character to sing without specifying what. On still other occasions he would call for a specific song by title or incipit.

There is a famous instance of this last device in *Boris Godunov*: Varlaam's song in the Inn scene. It is usually thought that Varlaam sings two songs. The first indication, after the wandering monks drink for the first time, reads, "Varlaam strikes up a song: 'As It Was in the Town of Kazan' " (*Kak vo gorode bïlo vo Kazani*). A page later, as Varlaam begins to get drunk, Pushkin indicates, "He drinks and sings: 'The Young Monk Was Tonsured' " (*Molodoy chernets postrigsya*). Actually, though, these are the first and second lines of a single song. Pushkin's indications seem to call for a typical piece of stage business: Varlaam strikes up a song, but is distracted by Grigory's refusal to join him in drinking. After a brief argument, he waves Grigory away in disgust, turns his attention to his drink, and takes up his song where he left off.

The text of the song Pushkin meant Varlaam to sing was first published in 1780 by Nikolai Novikov in his famous *Pesennik* [Songbook], and was first identified as Pushkin's source by V. I. Chernïshev in 1907. It runs as follows (the italicized line is a refrain that is to be sung after each line, adapted to the respective concluding words):

> Kak vo gorode bïlo vo Kazani,
> *Zduninai, nai, nai vo Kazani,*
> Molodoy chernets postrigsya,
> Zakhotelos' chernetsu pogulyati,
> Chto za te li za svyatïye za vorota,
> Za vorótami besedushka sidela,
> Kak vo toy li vo besede starï babï;

Uzh kak tut chernets ne vzglyanet,
Chernechishche klabuchishche prinakhlupil.

Kak vo gorode bïlo vo Kazani . . .
   [first five lines, plus refrains, repeat]
Kak vo toy li vo besede moloditsï;
Uzh kak tut chernets privzglyanet,
Chernechishche klabuchishche pripodnimayet.

Kak vo gorode . . .
Kak vo toy li vo besede krasnï devki,
Uzh kak tut chernets privzglyanet,
Chernechishche klabuchishche doloy sbrosit,
Tï sgori moya skuchnaya kel'ya,
Propadi tï moyo chernoye plat'ye,
Uzh kak polno mne dobro molodtsu spasat'sya
Ne pora l' mne dobru molodtsu zhenit'sya,
Chto za dushechke na krasnoy na devitse.[178]

[As once it was in Kazan town,
   Hey, hey, in Kazan town,
A young monk got himself shorn,
But then he wanted to live it up,
What were the holy gates to him?
For outside the gates there was an arbor,
And in this arbor were some old women.
Oh you can bet our monk didn't look in there,
But shut his monk's cowl tight!

As once it was in Kazan town . . .
And in this arbor were some young brides.
And you can bet our monk looked right in
And lifted his monk's cowl up just a bit!

As once it was in Kazan town . . .
And in this arbor were some pretty young maids,
And you can bet our monk looked right in
And threw his monk's cowl down on the ground.
"Oh burn up, drab cell of mine!
Oh get lost, black robe of mine!
Oh how tired I am of salvation, sweet youth that I am!

---

[178] V. Chernïshev, "Pesnya Varlaama," *Pushkin i yego sovremenniki* 2, no. 5 (1907): 127–28. Chernïshev asserts that the song is not included in the standard anthologies, naming those of Sheyn and Sobolevsky in particular, but it is indeed found in the latter collection, together with two variants. See Alexey Ivanovich Sobolevsky, *Velikorusskiye narodnïye pesni*, vol. 7 (St. Petersburg, 1902), pp. 302–4 (nos. 337–39).

FIGURE 1. Ivan [i.e., Johann Gottfried] Pratsch, *Sobraniye russkikh narodnykh pesen s ikh golosami* (2d expanded ed., St. Petersburg: K. Frelov, 1806), vol. 2, part 3 (Pesni khorovodnïye), no. 4, p. 58

Isn't it time I got married, sweet youth that I am,
To one of these fine sweet pretty young maids?"]

This is really a song Varlaam would sing. As Chernïshev remarks, "An exuberant song about a monk who likes carousing with pretty girls, of course, goes much better with Pushkin's Varlaam than a heroic song about the taking of Kazan. What does he care about Kazan?"[179] As a matter of fact, performers of Pushkin's play can even interpolate the song with its authentic tune, for this was published (as Pushkin undoubtedly knew) in the collection of Lvov and Pratsch, *Sobraniye narodnïkh russkikh pesen s ikh golosami* (1790) as no. 90, in the section devoted to round dances (Figure 1).

Now Stasov, who researched this song for Musorgsky and missed this source, certainly knew Lvov-Pratsch. He may have been misled, in checking its table of contents, by the garbled first word (*Chto* in place of *Kak*). But more likely he merely assumed that any song with Kazan in the title would belong to the large and noble family of his-

[179] Chernïshev, p. 129.

torical songs about Ivan the Terrible's conquest of the Tatar capital in 1552, despite the obvious fact that if Varlaam had been with Ivan on this campaign he would have to have been much older than the age of fifty, which is the age Grigory ascribes to him on faking Boris's edict later in the scene.

About half a dozen songs on the conquest of Kazan had been published by December 1868, when Stasov gave Musorgsky the text he had chosen for *Boris*.[180] In his biography-necrology of 1881 Stasov cited as his source the famous collection of Kirsha Danilov, *Drevniye rossiyskiye stikhotvoreniya*, first published in 1818, which does in fact contain a historical song about Kazan.[181] That was not the song he gave Musorgsky, however. Instead, he chose one that had been taken down by the *pochvennik* poet Apollon Grigoryev from the singing of a Gypsy singer in Moscow. Grigoryev then imparted this song to Pavel Yakushkin, who published it in 1860 in the journal *Otechestvennïye zapiski* (and later the same year in book form).[182]

But this still was not Stasov's source. From Musorgsky's scrupulous notation in the autograph libretto, we know that the book Stasov gave him was a small and relatively little known collection adapted for children by Ivan Khudyakov (1842–76) entitled *Sbornik velikorusskikh narodnïkh istoricheskikh pesen*, published in Moscow toward the end of 1860.[183] In Figure 2, Khudyakov's text (which he took from Yakushkin, as a footnote acknowledges) is set side by side with Musorgsky's song text for comparison. The first four lines of Khudyakov's text, a sort of exordium, [184] were omitted by Musorgsky. He replaced them with five of his own, which linked the body of the song

[180] On this date see OrTD, 168.

[181] StasIS 2.198. Stasov has "*russkiye*" in place of "*rossiyskiye*." The Kazan song in this collection is entitled *Seredi bïlo Kazanskogo tsarstva* and headed "Vzyatiye Kazanskogo Tsarstva" [The taking of the kingdom of Kazan].

[182] For this and all other published historical songs on Kazan, see B. N. Putilov and B. M. Dobrovolsky, *Istoricheskiye pesni XVIII–XVI vekov* (Moscow: Izdatel'stvo Akademïi nauk SSSR, 1960).

[183] Khudyakov was exiled to Siberia in 1866 for his connection with the perpetrators of an attempt on the life of Tsar Alexander II (the so-called Karakozov affair). He committed suicide ten years later. Soviet historians (and, unfortunately, a few Westerners, too) have predictably exploited Musorgsky's factitious connection with such a romantic revolutionary figure to the hilt. See Mikhail Pekelis, "Musorgskiy—pisatel'-dramaturg," the introductory essay in MusLN 2.18–20, 26–30; also Richard Hoops, "Musorgsky and the Populist Age," in MusIM, 288–89 (Hoops's discussion derives wholly and uncritically from Pekelis). See n. 94 in Chapter 4.

[184] They run as follows in translation: "O men of yore! / Listen, you valiant youths, / I will tell you yet of the Tsar's campaign, / Of the terrible Tsar Ivan Vasilyevich."

"The Taking of Kazan" (Ivan Khudyakov, *Sbornik velikorusskikh narodnïkh pesen* [Moscow, 1860], pp. 112–13)

Boris Godunov, Varlaam's song, act 1, scene 2

Vzyatiye Kazani

Uzh vï lyudi li, vï lyudi starodavnïye!
Molodïye molodtsï poslushaite,
Yeshcho ya vam rasskazhu pro tsaryovyïy pro
    pokhod,
Pro grozna tsarya Ivana Vasil'yevicha.

On podkhodom podkhodil pod Kazan' goro-
    dok,
A podkopï podkopal pod Kazanku pod reku.
Chto tatarï zhe po gorodu pokhazhivali,
Chto grozna tsarya Ivana Vasil'yevicha pod-
    draznivali.

Chto i tut-to nas grozen tsar' prikruchinilsya,
On povesil buynu golovu na pravnoye plecho,
Utupil on yasnï ochi vo sïru-mat' zemlyu,
On velel-li gosudar' tsar' pushkarey sзïvat',
Pushkarey sozïvat', zazhigal'shchikov,
On velel sudar' skoro kaznit', skoro veshati.

Ne uspel molodoy pushkar' slovo vïmolvit',
Vosku yarogo svecha zateplilasya,
Chto i s porokhom bochka zagorelasya,

Chto pobilo tatar' sorok tïsyachey i tri tïsyachi.

Kak vo gorode bïlo vo Kazani,
Groznïy tsar' piroval da veselilsya.
On tatarey bïl neshchadno,

Chto-b im bïlo da ne povadno
Vdol' po Rusi gulyat'.

Tsar' podkhodom podkhodil, da, pod Kazan'
    gorodok,
On podkopï podkopal, da, pod Kazanku reku.
Kak tatare, to, po gorodu pokhazhivayut,
Na tsarya Ivana, to, poglyadïvayut,

Zli tatarove!
Groznïy tsar', zakruchinilsya,
On povesil golovushko na pravoye plecho.

Uzh kak stal tsar' pushkarey sзïvat',
Pushkarey vse zazhigal'shchikov.

Zadïmilasya svechka vosku yarova,
Podkhodil molodoy pushkar', to k bochechke.
A i s porokhom to bochka zakruzhilasya.
Oy! k podkopam pokatilasya, da i khlopnula.
Zavopili, zagladili zli tatarove,
Blagim matom zalivalisya.
Poleglo tatarovey t'ma t'mushchya,
Poleglo ikh sorok tïsyachey i tri tïsyachi.

Tak, to, vo gorode bïlo, vo Kazani!

FIGURE 2.

to Pushkin's incipit, *Kak vo gorode bïlo vo Kazani*. Thereafter, many small changes were made in the wording and the scansion so as to adapt to Musorgsky's melody, but the only real departure was a three-line interpolation toward the end. (For a translation, see any libretto.)

Since Stasov did not know the source of Pushkin's incipits, neither he nor Musorgsky knew that the next time Varlaam sang he was merely continuing the same song as before. So in the opera Varlaam has a second song. The text, about a broken-down tramp, has so far eluded identification, and may have been either adopted directly from oral tradition or else even invented by the composer. The music was adapted from a wedding song Rimsky-Korsakov had taken down from the singing of his mother and would publish later as no. 71 in his *One Hundred Russian Folk Songs* of 1877: "The Bells Were Ringing in Novgorod" (*Zvonili zvonï v Novgorode*).

In his necrology, Stasov claimed that the three folk songs that were interpolated by Musorgsky into the second version of *Boris*—the Hostess's song of the drake, the Nanny's song of the gnat, and the tsarevich's Clapping Game—were all "taken by Musorgsky from the collection of Sheyn, which I had learned about not long before" the period of revision.[185] He meant Pavel Vasilyvich Sheyn's huge collection, *Russkiye narodnïye pesni*, published in eight installments between 1868 and 1870 in the quarterly *Chteniya v Imperatorskom Obshchestve Istorii i Drevnosti Rossiyskikh pri Moskovskom Universitete* [Papers read in the Imperial Society of Russian History and Antiquities at Moscow University], and reissued in book form in 1870, just before Musorgsky's revisions got under way. The collection is better known in its revised and still further expanded second edition, *Velikoruss v svoikh pesnyakh, obryadakh, obïchayakh* [The Great-Russian in his songs, rites, and customs (St. Petersburg: Tipografiya Akademii nauk, 1898)]. Since Stasov's citation of the source for Varlaam's song has proved incorrect, it is surprising that this other assertion of his has never been put to the test, but has been repeated endlessly and uncritically in all subsequent literature. As it turns out, some correction is again required.

Sheyn's 1870 collection contained 871 songs plus many variants, arranged by category. The first category, an unprecedented assemblage of 122 children's songs, was the one on which Musorgsky chiefly drew for the songs at the beginning of the Terem scene. But there is no one-to-one correspondence between any of the songs in Sheyn and the texts in the libretto. Rather, the composer freely conflated and embroidered, making reconstruction of his sources a difficult task. In Figure 3, the text of the tsarevich's Clapping Game is set alongside the songs from Sheyn on which it drew. No translation is offered, for the texts are largely nonsense and "mouth music," and the object of comparison is merely verbal correspondence. For an idea of what these nursery rhymes are about, any translation of the libretto will do (Lloyd-Jones's is perhaps the most faithful).

It will be seen that Musorgsky drew upon at least eight different

[185] StasIS 2.198.

Legend: 1. = Section 1, *Detskiye pesni* [Children's songs]
       3. = Section 3, *Plyasovïye* [Dance songs]
      The number following the period designates the song within a section; that following the slash, the lines within a song. Thus 1.7/35–36 means section 1 (*Detskiye pesni*), song no. 7, lines 35–36.

LIBRETTO	SHEYN	
Skazochka pro to i pro syo,		
Kak kurochka bïka rodila,		
Porosyonochek yaichko snyos.		
Skazka poyotsya,	Pryaniki pekutsya,	1.7/35–36
Durnyam ne dayotsya.	Kotu v lapki ne dayutsya.	
Turu, turu, petushok,	Turu, turu, petushok,	
Tï dalyoko l' otoshol?	Deleko li otoshol?	
Za more, za more,	Ot morya do morya,	
K Kievu-gorodu.	Do Kieva goroda,	1.44/1–7
	Tam moya rodina:	
Tam dub stoit	Na rodine dub stoit,	
Razvesistïy,		
Na dubu sïch sidit	Na dubu sova sidit.	
Uvesistïy.		
Sïch glazom morgnyot,		
Sïch pesni poyot:		
Dzin', dzin', peredzin',	Dzin', dzin',/Peredzin',	1.91/1–4
Postriguli, pomiguli,	Postriguli,/Pomiguli	
Ten', ten', poteten',	Ten', ten', poteten'	1.26/1–2
Zakolodu da ne pen',	Vïshe gorodu pleten'	
Shagom, magom,	Shagom, magom	1.64/3–4
Chetvertagom,	Chetvertagom,	
Kak odnazhdï popad'ya	Kak i nasha Popad'ya	
Zavodila vorob'ya	Zavodila vorob'ya,	
Sovsem vorobyoy,	Sovsem vorobyoy,	
Sovsem molodoy,	Sovsem molodoy,	3/40.27–34
Dlinnonosen'kiy,	Vostonosen'kiy,	
Vostronosen'kiy.	Klinonosen'kiy;	
Poletel vorobey	Poveli vorob'ya	
Pryamo v gosti k sïchu . . .	Na Boyarskiy dvor . . .	
Stal sheptat' na ushko		
Usatomu:		
Parni popovï	Popovï rebyata	
Gorokh molotili	Gorokh molotili	
Tsepï polomali,	Tsepï perlomali,	
V ovin pobrosali,	Za ovin pobrosali.	
Ovin zagorelsya,	Ovin zagorelsya,	
Polïmem pïshet,		1.44/17–30
Popu v okno		
Stalo vidno yego.		
Pop ispugalsya,	Pop ispugalsya,	
Zalez pod podushku,	Polez pod kadushku,	
Shchemil sebe ushko.	Prishchemil sebe ushko.	
D'yakon s pechi	D'yakon s pechi	
Oborval plechi.	Oborval plechi.	
Popova zhena	Nasha khozyaika dobra,	
Kalachey napekla.	Kalachey napekla:	
Nabezhali chernetsï,	Prileteli chernetsï	
Vse poyeli kalachi.	Podobrali kalachi	
Otets Luka	Nikolashka/Trebushka	1.92/11–17
S'yel korovu da bïka,	S'yel korovu/Da bïka,	
Sem'sot porosyat,	Sem'sot porosyat:	
Odin nozhki visyat.	Odni lapochki/Visyat.	
Khlyost! Khlyost!	Klest! Khrest!	1.93/5; 1.107/1

FIGURE 3. The Clapping Game and its sources in Sheyn, *Russkiye narodnïye pesni* (1870)

songs in Sheyn to supply the text of the Clapping Game. As children's song no. 44, *Turu, turu petushok*, is used the most, and as most of it is used, one might call it the basic source. And sure enough, that is the title by which Stasov referred to the Clapping Game in the necrology. The various Sheyn texts are linked by connective lines of Musorgsky's presumable invention, and substitutions and minor alterations in word form and word order are the rule rather than the exception. Still, it is fair to say that the text of the Clapping Game came from Sheyn.

One cannot say as much of the other two songs, however. Three lines from the Nanny's song of the gnat may be related to dance song no. 40 in Sheyn, which figures also in the Clapping Game (see Figure 3):

NANNY'S SONG

Line 1: Kak komar drova rubil
      2: Komar vodu nosil
     16: Rebra komaru slomalo

SHEYN, DANCE SONG NO. 40

Line 1: Tarakan drova rubil
      3: Komar vodu vozil
      8: Rebra polomala

And a couple of other lines are to be found scattered elsewhere in Sheyn, to wit:

NANNY'S SONG

Line 3: Klopik mesto mesil
     24: Zhivotochek nadorval

SHEYN

Klop banyushku topil (Children's Song no. 69, line 10)
Zhivot nadorvali (Children's Song no. 71, line 9)

But that seems to be all. The twenty-five-line text seems to be four-fifths original.

As for the Hostess's song of the drake, no trace of it whatever can be found in Sheyn. Though songs about drakes abound in Russian folklore anthologies, up to now the one Musorgsky set has not turned up. It, too, may be original.

The nonsense songs on which Musorgsky drew for the Clapping

Game sounded a new note in serious Russian music, even if the style of Musorgsky's setting had been anticipated in works by Glinka and Serov. The class of texts to which they belong is often designated *Pribaútki*—a term that brings Stravinsky to mind. These texts are in fact very similar to the ones Stravinsky selected from collections by Afanasyev and others during his Swiss years,[186] and the concluding section of *Renard* is set to a very close relative of the song that counts as the "basic source" for the Clapping Game. Stravinsky and Musorgsky were the only two Russian composers to have interested themselves in this class of text—a rare common trait for two composers who seem in most ways to be light-years apart.[187] What is most surprising is that Musorgsky, the realist-nationalist who approached folklore as a kind of natural artifact to lend his music verisimilitude, treated the texts he found in Sheyn very cavalierly, while Stravinsky, the modernist aesthete who approached folklore as a stylistic resource and who cared nothing (or so we think) for surface verisimilitude, handled his texts far more carefully, even reverently.

[186] Stravinsky found at least one text in Sheyn: "Tilimbom," the first of the *Trois Histoires pour enfants* (1917), comes from the expanded edition of 1898, where it is children's song no. 130.

[187] Robert Craft confirms that Stravinsky felt great rapport with Musorgsky's "birds and animals" (*Stravinsky in Pictures and Documents* [New York: Simon and Schuster, 1978], p. 28).

6

SLAVA!

ONE WAY or another, over a dozen Russian folk songs figure in the text and music of *Boris Godunov*. We will never know the exact number, since without documentation there is no way to tell for sure whether a folklike number is authentic or invented. The Hostess's song at the beginning of the Inn scene ("I've Caught Me a Grey-Blue Drake") certainly sounds like the real thing, and we have the word of no less an authority than Vladimir Stasov, Musorgsky's great friend and collaborator, that the song is genuine. In his long obituary for the composer, Stasov even tells us where Musorgsky found it: a then recent anthology by an ethnographer named Pavel Vasilyevich Sheyn.[1] Anyone who has scoured the book in search of the song, however, knows that Stasov was mistaken. And although songs about drakes abound in Russian folklore collections, up to now the one Musorgsky set has not turned up anywhere. Like the tsarevich's equally folklike "Song about the Parrot" in act 2, the Hostess's song may be presumed original until proven otherwise.

Four known folk songs are represented in *Boris* by their melodies only. Three of them come from the Kromy Forest scene, at or near the end of the revised version of the opera (depending on whether Musorgsky's order of scenes or Rimsky-Korsakov's is followed). When the crowd gathers round to mock the bound and gagged Boyar Khrushchov, they do it to the strains of a folk song ("Did the Hawk Not Soar Aloft with the Quail?") that Balakirev had taken down in 1863, and that Rimsky-Korsakov would publish in his anthology of 1877.[2] When Varlaam and Missail suddenly appear in the entourage

---

[1] P. V. Sheyn, *Russian Folk Songs* (*Russkiye narodnïye pesni*) (Moscow, 1870). The contents of this book had appeared in eight installments between 1868 and 1870 in the quarterly *Papers Read in the Imperial Society of Russian History and Antiquities at Moscow University* (*Chteniya v Imperatorskom Obshchestve Istorii i Drevnosti Rossiyskikh pri Moskovskom Universitete*).

[2] "Chto ne yastreb sovïkalsya s perepyoloshku," in Nikolai Andreyevich Rimsky

of the False Dmitry, they announce their presence with the tune of an ancient *bïlina*, or epic song ("Of Vol'ga and Mikula"), which Musorgsky himself had taken down from the singing of an aged bard named Trofim Ryabinin on 4 December 1871.[3] In the middle of the so-called Revolutionary chorus, the crowd celebrates its newfound power with a swaggering tune ("Play, my bagpipes, play!") that Balakirev had published in his anthology of 1866.[4] When Varlaam sings himself to sleep in the Inn scene, he strikes up an old wedding tune ("The Bells Were Ringing in Novgorod") that Rimsky-Korsakov had learned in childhood from his mother and passed along to Musorgsky, his roommate at the time of writing. (Rimsky would publish it in 1877.)

A larger number of folk songs are represented in *Boris* by their words alone. Musorgsky cobbled together the texts of the little game songs at the beginning of act 2 (the Nanny's song of the gnat and the tsarevich's Clapping Game) out of at least nine different children's songs from Sheyn's anthology, which contains only texts, no tunes.[5] The text of the Revolutionary chorus, according to Stasov, was adapted from a Volga robbers' song Musorgsky had learned from his friend Daniyil Mordovtsev, a writer. Stasov himself furnished the text of the famous "Song about Kazan" that Varlaam sings in the Inn scene, which was published in 1860 in a children's anthology of historical songs edited by Ivan Khudyakov, a romantic revolutionary figure convicted of participating in an attempt on the life of Tsar Alexander II.[6] It is worth pointing out that except for Varlaam's singing in the Inn scene, which was actually specified by Pushkin in the play from which Musorgsky derived the libretto,[7] all of the authentic folk

---

Korsakov, *One Hundred Russian Folk Songs* (*Sto russkikh narodnïkh pesen*) (St. Petersburg: Bessel, 1877), no. 18.

[3] "O Vol'ge i Mikule," first published in Musorgsky's transcription as a paste-in to *Epic Songs from the Onega Region, Transcribed by Alexander Fyodorovich Hilferding in the Summer of 1871* (*Onezhskiye bïlinï, zapisannïye Aleksandrom Fyodorovichem Gil'ferdingom letom 1871 g.*) (St. Petersburg, 1873), then by Rimsky-Korsakov (*One Hundred Russian Folk Songs*, no. 2).

[4] "Zaigrai, moya volïnka," in Miliy Alexeyevich Balakirev, *An Anthology of Russian Folk Songs* (*Sbornik russkikh narodnïkh pesen*) (St. Petersburg: Johansen, 1866).

[5] For details see the Appendix to Chapter 5.

[6] Ivan Khudyakov, *A Collection of Great-Russian Historical Folk Songs* (*Sbornik velikorusskikh narodnïkh istoricheskikh pesen*) (Moscow, 1860). Khudyakov's source was Pavel Yakushkin, who had learned it from the poet Apollon Grigor'yev and published it in the journal *Notes of the Fatherland* (*Otechestvennïye zapiski*). See B. N. Putilov and B. M. Dobrovolsky, *Istoricheskiye pesni XIII–XVI vekov* (Moscow, 1960).

[7] See the Appendix to Chapter 5.

material in *Boris Godunov* is found in the more conventional revised version of the opera completed in 1872, not the radically "realistic" version of 1869.

ALL, that is, but the most celebrated item, the only folk song in the opera that is represented by its text and tune together. The great *Slava!* [As to the red sun on high, glory!], the tintinnabulating chorus of exaltation that frames Boris's central monologue of foreboding in the Coronation scene, was based on what was by 1869 already the most famous Russian folk song of them all. Its text had been published almost a century before, in the very first printed anthology of Russian folk verse, Mikhaíl Chulkov's *Collection of Various Songs (Sobraniye razni̇kh pesen)*, a vast compendium containing upward of nine hundred items, issued in four installments between 1770 and 1774. The tune saw print a couple of decades later, in the first major anthology to include music, the legendary *Collection of Russian Folk Songs with Their Tunes (Sobraniye narodni̇kh russkikh pesen s ikh golosami*, 1790) by Nikolai Alexandrovich Lvov, a noble dilettante who assembled the texts, and Johann Gottfried Pratsch, a Bohemian-born music teacher who arranged the tunes.

The Lvov-Pratsch collection quickly became world-famous, and went through many editions. Throughout the nineteenth century it was "the wellspring into which everyone dipped in search of material on Russian folk song: composers, poets, amateurs, and compilers of other anthologies," in the words of its most recent editor.[8] The great majority of Russian folk tunes known to concertgoers stems ultimately (if often through intermediary anthologists and cribbers) from Lvov-Pratsch. Composers who helped themselves to its contents included virtually the whole nineteenth-century Russian school—as well as such later Russian composers as Glazunov, Grechaninov, Rachmaninoff, and even Stravinsky—not to mention a whole slew of Westerners in search of exotic material. The latter group included Rossini, Hummel, Weber, the guitarist-composer Fernando Sor, and of course Beethoven, who paid Count Andrey Kirillovich Razumovsky, the Russian ambassador in Vienna, the compliment of including a couple of *thèmes russes* from the famous anthology in the quartets the violin-playing count had commissioned

[8] Margarita Mazo, Introduction to *A Collection of Russian Folk Songs by Nikolai Lvov and Ivan Prach [sic]* (Ann Arbor: UMI Research Press, 1987), p. 76.

FIGURE 1. The *Slava!* as Beethoven knew it: Nikolai Lvov and Johann Gottfried Pratsch, *Sobraniye russkikh narodnïkh pesen* (1790), Yuletide song no. 1

in 1805 for himself and his friends to play at their amateur quartet readings.

Razumovsky very likely specified the tunes himself on presenting Beethoven with the book, and one of them was our *Slava!*[9] Upon seeing it in its Lvov-Pratsch incarnation (Figure 1), Beethoven spotted the tune for a natural fugue subject, and that is how it appears in the middle of the scherzo of op. 59, no. 2. Beethoven's imprimatur gave the song a pedigree in Western classical music, and unquestionably contributed to its later popularity among composers. It is probably the reason why Rimsky-Korsakov, for example, chose the *Slava!* as one of the three songs on which he composed his "Overture on Russian Themes" in 1866.

[9] The other was "Ah, Is Such to Be My Fate?" (*Akh! talan li moy, talan takoy*) a sorrowful song of the *protyazhnaya* type (see Chapter 1) in which a mother bitterly laments the fate of her conscript son. Beethoven changed Pratsch's tempo indication from Molto andante to Allegro and used the tune as the basis of the merry finale to op. 59, no. 1.

But just what kind of song was it? We tend to think of it in terms of Musorgsky's Coronation scene, and assume that it was in fact some sort of imperial acclamation or civic hymn. Its text in Lvov-Pratsch, obviously the model for the text of Musorgsky's chorus, only seems to confirm such a notion:

Uzh kak slava Tebe Bozhe na nebesi! slava!
Gosudaryu nashemu na sey zemle! slava!
Yego tsvetnoye plat'ye ne nositsya, slava!
Yego vernïye slugi ne stareyutsya, slava!
Yego dobrïye koni ne yezdyatsya, slava!
Mï pesnyu siyu Gosudaryu poyom, slava!
Gosudaryu poyom, Yemu chest' vozdayom! slava!

[Just as there is glory to thee O God on high! Glory!
There is glory to our Sovereign on this earth! Glory!
His colored gown will never wear out, Glory!
His faithful servants will never grow old, Glory!
His stalwart steeds will never ride themselves out, Glory!
We sing this song to our Sovereign, Glory!
We sing to our Sovereign, we render honor unto him! Glory!]

One would never guess from these words that they were meant to accompany no civic ceremony but only a girlish fortune-telling game. And yet anyone looking up the song in Lvov-Pratsch would have found it in the section labeled *Svyatochnïye*, and would have understood—as did Rimsky-Korsakov, when he incorporated the *Slava!* into his own folk song anthology of 1877 under the somewhat broader heading *Pesni igrovïye* [Game songs].

Songs grouped as *svyatochnïye* are those sung during the *svyatki*, which is how the Russians designate what in English are known as the "twelve days of Christmas," the Yuletide. Since it includes the New Year, it was in Russia a time not for "resolutions" but for wishes and for guessing fortunes. The chief fortune-telling ritual involved a big bowl or dish (*blyudo*) full of water, into which unmarried girls dropped trinkets. A magically allegorical divining song, known as a *podblyudnaya* because it was sung "in the presence of the dish," was performed by all the girls in chorus, and then the married woman administering the dish drew out someone's trinket. The fortune foretold in the song would be the owner's fate.[10] Figure 2, after a mid-nineteenth-century print, shows the ritual in progress.

[10] Stravinsky set three *podblyudnaya* songs as part of his collection *Four Russian Peas-*

Новый Годъ.

НАСТУПАЕТЪ НОВЫЙ ГОДЪ
СКОЛЬКО НОВЫХЪ СНИМЪ ЗАБОТЪ
ВЪ ПОЛНОЧЬ ДѢВИЦА ВСТАЕТЪ
РУКОЙ ТРЕПЕТНОЙ ВЕРТЕТЪ
СЪ СОБОЙ ЗЕРКАЛО ОНА
СЪ СВѢЧАМИ И ОДНА

ВЪ НЕМЪ ЖЕЛАЕТЪ УВИДАТЬ
КТО ЕЙ БУДЕТЪ ОБЛАДАТЬ
НЕ БОЯСЬ НЕ ЧУТЬ ГРѢХА
ВИДѢТЬ ХОЧЕТЪ ЖЕНИХА
И НЕ ДУМАЯ О ТОМЪ
ЧТО СВИДАНЬЕ СЪ ЖЕНИХОМЪ
ПРЕЖДЕ СРОКА И ЧАСА

ЗАПРЕЩАЮТЪ НЕБЕСА
ЖЕНИХА СЕБѢ ЖДАЛА
ЧТО ЖЕ ВЫШЛО? НЕ КЪ ВѢНЦУ
ЭТО ПРИЗРАКЪ КЪ МЕРТВЕЦУ
НО ОСТАВИМЪ МЫ ТАКИХЪ
И ПОСМОТРИМЪ НА ДРУГИХЪ.

FIGURE 2. New Year's wishes, circa 1850, showing (upper left) the
ceremony that the *Slava!* accompanied in its natural habitat

You can always spot a *podblyudnaya* because its lines all end in the
word *Slava!* [Glory!] or *Slavna!* [Glorious!], and because the words are
cryptically allegorical. The Lvov-Pratsch *Slava!* is an archetype of the
genre. (To the lucky maiden whose trinket was extracted at its conclusion it foretold inexhaustible wealth.) So how did this song, associated in its natural habitat with a girls' game, come to represent the
majesty of the Russian throne in an opera famed for its realism?

The missing link was a little singspiel in three acts, *The Old-Time
Yuletide* (*Starinnïye svyatki*), by Franz Xaver Blyma (1770–ca.1812), a
composer, violinist, and conductor of Bohemian birth, who made his
career as a theatrical musician in Russia. For two years beginning in

---

ant Songs for women's chorus (1914–17). In later life he forgot what a *podblyudnaya* was,
mistranslated the word from its literal roots (*pod* = under; *blyudo* = dish) as "saucer"
(for which the Russian word is *blyudtse*), mistitled the choruses "The Saucers" (which
has, alas, become standard in English), and invented a folk ritual to accord with his
mistranslation: "Choruses of this sort were sung by the peasants while fortune-tellers
read their fingerprints on the smoke-blackened bottoms of saucers" (Igor Stravinsky
and Robert Craft, *Expositions and Developments* [Garden City, N.Y.: Doubleday, 1962],
p. 135).

1799, Blyma was music director at the Petrovsky Theater, Moscow, where he led the first performance of *The Old-Time Yuletide* on 3 February, 1800. Wildly successful, it remained in repertory through the 1830s, epitomizing the sentimental approach to national subject matter that characterized the early romantic style in Russia. Its plot was simple to the point of virtual nonexistence; the essence of the libretto, by A. F. Malinovsky, a famous historian and connoisseur of antiquities, lay in its pageantry of old ceremonies, costumes, song, and dance. Some maidens are seen telling fortunes according to the old Yuletide custom. Their young men unexpectedly intrude, to the consternation of the old folks; but the latter are eventually mollifed, the couples are blessed, and their betrothal is celebrated.

One of the divining songs the maidens sing, led by the ingenue Nastasya, is the famous *Slava!* In *The Old-Time Yuletide* it is heard (for the first time on the stage) in its original context, accompanying a domestic ritual. Yet it quickly took on a state ceremonial character owing to the conditions of the Russian theater, from 1803 a state bureaucratic monopoly under direct control of the crown. First, the name of the sitting tsar (Alexander I) was introduced in place of the heavenly and earthly lords referred to in the original song (Figure 3). Later, during the Patriotic War against Napoleon, it became customary to insert long lists of valorous officers into the *Slava!* turning it into a civic celebration. This direction was continued by another forgotten composer, Alexey Nikolayevich Titov (1769–1827) in his patriotic historical opera of 1817, *The Courage of a Kievan; or, That's What Russians Are Like* (*Muzhestvo kievlyanina, ili Vot kakovïye russkiye*), where the *Slava!* serves as a climactic chorus in praise of the great Prince Svyatoslav. Thanks to these popular spectacles the *Slava!* was indeed turned into a standard civic ode. But its history as such went back only as far as the early nineteenth century, not to the time of Boris Godunov (let alone the tenth-century Svyatoslav).

Musorgsky's use of the song to epitomize a tsar's coronation continued this line of transformation. It stemmed not from the tradition of idealized folklore as represented by the Lvov-Pratsch collection, in light of which it could only seem incongruous and anachronistic, but from the equally significant tradition of theatrical civic celebration as represented by Blyma and Titov. Considering, moreover, that Blyma and Titov had used the song to extol the legitimacy of the Russian crown in one of its official sanctuaries, Musorgsky's appropriation of

FIGURE 3. Nastya's song, from Franz Xavier Blyma's *Old-Time Yuletide* (1800), as sung during the Napoleonic wars. The text now reads, "Glory, glory to Tsar Alexander throughout the world . . ." Source: Nikolai Findeizen, *Ocherki po istorii muzïki v Rossii*, vol. 2 (Moscow and Leningrad: Muzgiz, 1929), musical supplement, p. xci

it in an opera that is all about the tragic consequences of illegitimate rule can be read as a stroke of ironizing genius.

Boris Godunov did not mark the end of the *Slava*'s career on the Russian stage. In 1877, before Musorgsky's work had completed its first run, Anton Rubinstein undertook an opera based on the subject of Mikhaíl Lermontov's 1838 poem, "Song about Tsar Ivan Vasil'-yevich, the Young Oprichnik and the Brave Merchant Kalashnikov." It relates a typical romantic horror story about Ivan the Terrible: Kalashnikov, a Moscow merchant, with his bare fists kills a young *oprichnik*, a member of the tsar's personal guard, who has abducted his wife, and is then unjustly condemned by the bloodthirsty sovereign. Lermontov's poem is famous for its adoption of the diction and meter of the old Russian epic songs contemporary with its subject. Following suit, Rubinstein's *The Merchant Kalashnikov* (*Kupets Kalashnikov*), completed in 1879 and first performed in 1880, conserves many of the poet's original verses, and is composed in what seems an unusually nationalistic idiom for the cosmopolitan supreme of Russian music. (For this reason alone the rather scrappy score has gone down in biased history as one of Rubinstein's best works.)

He did not manage the task without help. A curious letter to Stasov survives in which Rubinstein copied out the *Slava!* exactly as it was printed by Rimsky-Korsakov in his anthology of 1877, with a query: "I need to know under what circumstances the people sang this song in ancient times . . . and whether it may be used in the guise of a *hymn* from those days."[11] Stasov may have answered, "No, but go right ahead"; for the famous song indeed appears in Rubinstein's opera, as in Musorgsky's, in the guise of a hymn, when in act 3 the populace greets Ivan the Terrible's procession before Kalashnikov's trial. (The melody, in Rubinstein's adaptation, follows the version in Lvov-Pratsch, while the text follows that given by Rimsky-Korsakov—who had cribbed it in turn from the work of the great folklorist Ivan Sakharov).

What is so curious about Rubinstein's letter—indeed, about his whole plan to employ the song—is his evident ignorance of Musorgsky's prior use of it. Had he seen *Boris Godunov* he would not have had to ask Stasov his question; the opera itself, by a composer with whom Stasov was so closely associated, would have provided an implicit answer. (But in that case would he have allowed himself such a skimpy strophic setting of the *Slava!* as he finally composed?—see Figure 4, overleaf.) Rubinstein had in fact been boycotting Musorgsky's work, along with that of the other composers of "The Five," since they had given his opera *The Demon* a dismal reception in 1871. His alliance was with his former pupil, Chaikovsky.

And Chaikovsky, as it happened, was next in line to appropriate the *Slava!* With him it symbolized the Russian triumph over Polish-backed Ukrainian separatists at the Battle of Poltava (1709), as depicted in the stormy *Tableau symphonique* before the third act of his opera *Mazepa* (1884)— a sort of "1812 Overture" in miniature. The little *podblyudnaya*, having passed by now through a stage of patriotic appropriation, was being pressed into service in the name of a truly aggressive nationalism.

The last opera to quote the *Slava!* was Rimsky-Korsakov's *The Tsar's Bride*, first performed in 1899. Like *The Merchant Kalashnikov*, this was a pseudohistorical opera about Ivan the Terrible, and the famous song provided one of the tsar's leitmotifs, first sung in his honor near the beginning of the opera by a troupe of minstrels entertaining a noble feast. (It is labeled *Podblyudnaya* in the score, which means that even Rimsky-Korsakov was confused as to the actual purpose of such a song; he evidently thought it was a toast or table prayer.) Once associated with Ivan in this way, it continues to refer to him through-

---

[11] Letter of 7 May 1879; see A. G. Rubinstein, *Selected Letters* (*Izbrannïye pis'ma*), ed. Lev Aronovich Barenboim (Moscow: Muzgiz, 1954), p. 81.

out the opera. It accompanies his one (mute) appearance, in which he crosses the stage on horseback and spies Marfa, the title character, whose life he will ruin by claiming her for his bride. And it sounds ominously in the orchestral introduction to act 3, the act in which Marfa's betrothal to her intended suitor is celebrated before the tragic reversal takes place.

Two instrumental pieces round out the history of the *Slava*'s career in Russian art music. One of them, the last in a set of six little pieces for piano four-hands that the twenty-one-year-old Rachmaninoff tossed off in 1894 at the request of Karl Alexandrovich Gutheil, his publisher, need not detain us. The other is an interesting aberration. Anton Arensky's three-movement Quartet no. 2 in A minor, op. 35, was written in the same year, 1894, as a memorial to Chaikovsky. Its middle movement, a set of variations on one of the deceased composer's songs, has achieved independent fame in an arrangement for string orchestra. The *Slava!* appears in the finale, where its fugal treatment recalls both Beethoven's quartet and Musorgsky's chorus, and where it is contrapuntally juxtaposed with the *Vechnaya pamyat'* [Eternal remembrance], the concluding chant of the Russian Orthodox funeral service. The relevance of the latter to a memorial piece is obvious; that of the *Slava!* less so. Arensky's program note explains: under the influence of *Boris Godunov* he had accepted the melody as an authentic coronation hymn, and had meant through it to crown Chaikovsky king of Russian music. The composer of *Boris Godunov*, no admirer of Chaikovsky, would certainly have found that bizarre.

The story of the *Slava!* is an absorbing study in cultural appropriation. What had started life as a girls' game was transformed by degrees into a potent symbol of the Russian monarchy, an ersatz national (read: dynastic) anthem to place alongside the concluding chorus of Glinka's *A Life for the Tsar*, whose much-repeated initial word—*Slav'sya!* [Be glorified!]—may have functioned as a subtext to the transformation. The final chapter was written in Soviet times. Just as Glinka's opera was sanitized for Soviet consumption under the title *Ivan Susanin*, with a new libretto by Sergey Gorodetsky that banished all mention of the tsar, so Soviet editions of the Lvov-Pratsch and Rimsky-Korsakov folk song collections banished the original words of the *Slava!* which had invoked the heavenly and earthly kings, in favor of another obscure but happy divination text from Sakharov's venerable collection:

ШЕСТВІЕ

Два бирюча съ жезлами въ рукахъ, въ блестящихъ нарядахъ, на лошадяхъ украшенныхъ страусовыми перьями, войско, большія позолоченныя сани въ которыхъ сидятъ Царь Іоаннъ и Князь Черкасскій, а на противъ ихъ Никитка въ колпакѣ и боярской шубѣ, опричники на лошадяхъ въ богатыхъ нарядахъ и шапкахъ, съ накинутыми на плечахъ шубами, въ переди ихъ ѣдутъ Малюта и Кирибѣевичъ, во время шествія съ правой стороны въходятъ земскіе бояре и встрѣчаи поклонами Царя становятся у подмостковъ; при выходѣ Царя изъ саней, Князь Черкасскій и Малюта ведутъ его подъ руки на эстраду, Іоаннъ войди и поклонившись народу садится, съ нимъ тоже на табуретку садится Черкасскій, а Никитка садится на нижней ступени подмостковъ, опричники окружаютъ съ обѣихъ сторонъ эстраду.

FIGURE 4. Anton Rubinstein, *The Merchant Kalashnikov* (1879), Ivan the Terrible's procession, act 3

FIGURE 4, *continued*

Katilosya zerno po barkhatu. Slava!
Prikatilosya zerno ko yakhontu. Slava!
Krupen zhemchug so yakhontom. Slava!
Khorosh zhenikh so nevestoyu! Slava!
Da komu mï speli, tomu dobro. Slava!
Komu vïnetsya, tomu sbudetsya. Slava!
Tomu sbudetsya, ne minuyetsya. Slava!

[A grain of corn was rolling along the velvet. Glory!
The grain rolled up to a ruby. Glory!
A great pearl was with the ruby. Glory!
A fine groom was with the bride. Glory!
To whomever we've sung we wish the best. Glory!
Whoever draws [her trinket] out, for her will it come true. Glory!
It will come true for her, there's no escaping it. Glory![12]]

This is a fine, authentic peasant verse, no less so than the one it replaced. But if it had actually appeared in the Lvov-Pratsch collection of 1790, a hundred years of Russian musical history would have been altogether a different story.

[12] N. A. Rimsky-Korsakov, *Polnoye sobraniye sochineniy* (Complete Works), vol. 47 (Moscow: Muzgiz, 1952), p. 97.

7

THE POWER OF THE
BLACK EARTH

Notes on *Khovanshchina*

IMAGINE, if you will, that Nicolae Ceauşescu, the former dictator of Romania, had lived three hundred years ago, and that his plan of construction and forced resettlement known as "systematization" had succeeded. The modern map of Romania, as well as the country's present-day demographics, would date from the upheaval he set in motion. He would now loom as the one-man boundary separating the modern era of Romanian history from the ancient, and the human costs would have long since ceased being (officially) reckoned. His successors would exploit him as a demiurge and derive their legitimacy from his legacy. His person would be so ineluctably bound up with the national identity that taking a stand on the one would inevitably mean taking a stand on the other.

You have just imagined Tsar Peter I of Russia, his accomplishment, his image, and some of the reasons why he has been such a focus of moral controversy. The reforms through which "Peter the Great" created the modern Russian imperial state after Western European bureaucratic models around the turn of the eighteenth century have been regarded by a divided posterity as either the very best thing that ever happened to Russia or the very worst. "With an autocratic hand / He daringly sowed enlightenment," wrote the poet Pushkin, at one extreme. "Peter the Great killed our native Russian life," wrote the composer Balakirev, at the other. To the conservative religious communities of his day, above all, Peter was unmitigated evil, the very

THIS chapter is specially dedicated to the memory of Gregory Salmon, a graduate student at the University of California at Berkeley, who died on 29 October 1991 in an automobile accident in St. Petersburg, Russia, where he was conducting research for a dissertation on *Khovanshchina* and Musorgsky's idea of history.

Antichrist, because he co-opted a schism among the Russian Orthodox, commandeered the established Church, and made it, even more
than it had traditionally been, an arm of the state bureaucracy. The
"Old Believers"—descendants of the recusants or Schismatics of Peter's time, persecuted under all his successors down to the time of
Stalin and beyond—revile his memory to this day.

Official veneration of the first Russian emperor reached a peak in
June 1872, the bicentenary of his birth. Vast celebrations were organized in the Russian capital, St. Petersburg, the Italianate city Peter
had built on the Neva marshes at the cost of untold thousands of
indentured Russian lives and named after his patron saint. Not only
politicians but academics joined their voices in praise of the "Enlight-
ener of Russia," acclaiming (in the words of an oration by "statist"
historian Sergey Solovyov) "the great state aim [that] could serve as
the justification of the forced perishing of whole masses of people."
Two weeks into this orgy of affirmation of national progress and historical optimism, an obscure thirty-three-year-old St. Petersburg
composer, whose one completed opera had yet to be performed,
wrote the following extraordinary passage in a letter to his closest
friend:

> The power of the black earth will make itself manifest when you plow
> it to the very bottom. It is possible to plow the black earth with tools
> wrought of alien materials. And at the end of the seventeenth century
> they plowed Mother Russia with just *such* tools, so that she did not im-
> mediately realize what they were plowing with, and, like the black
> earth, she *opened up* and began to *breathe*. And she, our beloved, re-
> ceived the various state bureaucrats, who never gave her, the long-suf-
> fering one, time to collect herself and to think, *"Where are you pushing
> me?"* The ignorant and confused were executed: *force!* . . . But the times
> are out of joint: the state bureaucrats are not letting the black earth
> *breathe*.
>
> *"We've gone forward"*—you lie. *"We haven't moved!"* Paper, books have
> gone forward—we *haven't moved*. So long as the people cannot verify
> *with their own eyes* what is being cooked out of them, as long as they do
> not *themselves* will what is or is not to be *cooked out of them*—until then,
> *we haven't moved!* Public benefactors of every kind will seek to glorify
> themselves, will buttress their glory with documents, but the people
> groan, and so as not to groan they drink like the devil, and groan worse
> than ever: *haven't moved!*

The composer was Musorgsky, who prefaced the letter with the cryptic remark that "I'm pregnant with something, I'm giving birth." It was the first inkling of *Khovanshchina*. The recipient of the letter was Vladimir Vasilyevich Stasov. Before long the two of them would be up to their ears in the unprecedented task of fashioning an opera directly out of historical documents. For this was to be no mere "historical opera"; it would be nothing less than an operatic meditation on history. Motivated by protest, it would be a contribution in its own right to the most pressing historiographical disputes of the day, debates that had an enormous contemporary significance in a country that brooked no open political dissent. "The past in the present— that's my task," wrote Musorgsky in the same letter. The phrase became his slogan.

But he never managed to make his point. He died before the opera was finished, and without asserting a point of view on the events he had portrayed. That was left to others.

LIKE the reign of Nikolai I, the strongman tsar of Musorgsky's youth, the reign of Peter the Great had begun amid uprisings and executions. A crisis of succession was created in 1682 by the death of Tsar Fyodor Alexeyevich at age twenty, leaving a sickly and half-witted sixteen-year-old brother Ivan, and also a half-brother Peter, not quite ten. The families of the two royal mothers competed viciously for the throne. After a Church-supported attempt to set the more promising Peter on the throne with his mother as regent, the rival family, assisted by the crack infantry militia known as the Streltsy (Musketeers), secured the installation of the two young heirs as joint sovereigns, with Ivan's sister Sophia as regent. Peter and his mother were settled in the Preobrazhensky Monastery near Moscow, but not before Peter had seen his near relations lynched by the Streltsy; in later years the tsar would give the name of the monastery to the personal guards regiment he organized to replace the Streltsy. (Musorgsky, a former Preobrazhensky Guards officer himself, would jump at the chance to introduce a regimental march into his opera.)

The commander of the Streltsy was Prince Ivan Khovansky, head of an old noble family and probably, like many of the Streltsy, an Old Believer himself. After leading the successful coup he tried to use his troops to force the new regime to abrogate the recent Church reforms; some thought he coveted the throne either for himself or for his son Andrey. This threatened mutiny was the "Khovansky to-do" (*Khovanshchina*). Sophia, formerly the Streltsy's protégée, now turned around and had both Khovansky and his son beheaded. Her agent in this perfidy was a boyar named Fyodor Shaklovitïy, who lured Khovansky into a trap and denounced him. The Streltsy now rose up against Sophia. Fearing their combined might, she ceased her reprisals and pardoned them, placing Shaklovitïy at their head. This series of events became known as the first Streltsy Revolt (*streletskiy bunt*).

For the next seven years Sophia reigned as autocrat, supported by the Streltsy under their new and loyal chief, and assisted by her chief minister, the urbane if superstitious Prince Vasiliy Golitsïn, scion of a Westernized noble house well known to music lovers since a later Prince Golitsïn, keeping up family traditions, became Beethoven's patron. He was an eager reformer who envisioned the abolition of serfdom and mass educational programs.

These plans were doomed in 1689 when a second Streltsy Revolt, organized by Shaklovitïy at Sophia's behest to murder Peter and his family and install the regent as actual hereditary ruler, failed. As a result of this offensive against the seventeen-year-old tsar, Sophia was sent off to a convent, Shaklovitïy was executed, and Golitsïn was exiled. Effective power reverted once more to Peter's mother; but after her death in 1694, followed two years later by that of his feeble half-brother, Peter I assumed his full responsibilities as head of the Russian church and state.

There was one more Streltsy Revolt to be weathered, for Sophia continued to plot. In the fall of 1698, Peter was summoned back from one of his fact-finding tours of the West to quell a rebellion that would have reinstated his rival half-sister on the throne. This time the sovereign showed no mercy to the conspirators or their army. Sophia was forced to become a nun along with Peter's first wife, who had sympathized with the revolts. The Streltsy were punished with unprecedented severity: after an inquest involving prolonged torture, more than a thousand of them were executed, their bodies gruesomely displayed in Red Square as an admonition. The survivors were disbanded.

Meanwhile, the Old Believers, persecuted from the time of Peter's father Alexey, and even more intensely under Sophia as a result of the Khovanshchina, responded to the events herein recounted with an epidemic of mass suicides, chiefly by burning. Between 1672 and 1690 some twenty thousand souls are reported to have gathered in churches and chapels in various far-northern localities and immolated themselves by igniting their shelters.

It was inevitable that Musorgsky, in writing an opera that would contain a judgment of Peter, should have concentrated on the period of the Streltsy Revolts, the convulsions out of which the modern Russian state emerged. It was in any case inconceivable to base a libretto on the life and actions of the tsar himself; the Russian censorship prohibited the representation of any member of the Romanov dynasty on the dramatic stage. He had to remain an offstage presence. His opponents (excepting Sophia) could be shown in action, however, and it was on them that Musorgsky fastened.

The composer began his work as librettist by assembling a notebook of citations culled from historical documents, chiefly memoirs of the Petrine period, but also the autobiography of the archpriest Avvákum (1621–82), the great preacher of Old Belief, who had been burned at the stake by Sophia's government. From this material he and Stasov pieced together an epic or panoramic scenario that compressed episodes from all three revolts into one somewhat ill-defined sequence of events, ostensibly set around the time of the second revolt, when Peter was of an age to act independently (and Khovansky—historically seven years dead—could refer to him as "formidable"), even though the actual Khovanshchina pertained to the first. The conflation technique can be seen most clearly by looking at the opera's fifth scene. It directly juxtaposes the exile of Golitsïn (1689) with the pardon of the Streltsy (1682), the latter taking place on Red Square at the last minute before their scheduled public execution (1698).

The composer's chief concern seems to have been not narration but portrayal. Each of the contending factions in the chaotic period preceding the consolidation of Petrine power is given a chief representative in the libretto. The Streltsy, of course, are represented by their chief, Prince Khovansky. Sophia and her entourage are represented by Prince Golitsïn, who at the beginning of act 2 sings an actual historical document testifying to his intimacy with the regent. For the Old Believers, who did not have an organized clergy, a representative had to be invented. This was Dosifey, whom Stasov and Musorgsky somewhat ironically named after Dositheus, the Greek patriarch of Jerusalem (1669–1707), who authored the last official doctrinal letters of the united Orthodox Church. The libretto identifies Dosifey with Prince Mïshetsky, an Old Believer of noble birth whose narrative "The Depths" (*Glïb'*) explicitly identified Peter as Antichrist. The character's apocalyptic rhetoric was compounded out of that source, as well as the writings of the martyrs Avvákum and Nikita the Lipserver (*Pustosvyat*).

The historical Shaklovitïy, though deprived of his historical office as post-Khovansky head of the Streltsy, is nonetheless recognizable in the opera as the one who engineers Khovansky's downfall, first through denunciation (here Musorgsky again condensed the relevant historical document) and then through actual murder. The operatic Shaklovitïy acts however not on behalf of Sophia, but seemingly as the unseen Peter's emissary. If this mangles history it is nevertheless true to the overriding epic theme, since the murder (as well as Shaklovitïy's superficially puzzling act 3 aria) underscores the violent passing of the old order on the eve of Peter's ascendency.

Two major characters remain to be accounted for, one quasi-historical, the other invented. In order to make their assemblage of historical portraits jell into some semblance of a plot, Stasov and Musorgsky fell back on romantic love—the most conventional, and in this case blatantly anachronistic, operatic glue. Andrey Khovansky exists in the opera only as a skirt-chaser. His main love interest (though he is chiefly seen betraying her with an unwilling Lutheran girl) is his fiancée, Marfa, a figment of the libretto, but one of its most important props. She is an Old Believer, a specially favored member of Dosifey's spiritual community (like him, she was originally conceived as a renegade noble—in one letter Musorgsky refers to her as the "Princess Sitskaya"); she is linked by amorous bonds to the doomed Streltsy (Andrey finally plights his troth truly when he follows her onto the pyre); and she is a soothsayer with a fatal influence on Prince Golitsïn (fatal, that is, to her, for he tries to wriggle free by having her killed) to whom she foretells Sophia's downfall, and his own. Marfa alone, in other words, inhabits all the worlds of the opera, and links them. Her constant tone of keening lamentation symbolizes the doom that overhangs everything and everyone, the doom that is the core and essential message of this most pessimistic of operas.

CONCEIVED in the summer of 1872, *Khovanshchina* was left a torso at Musorgsky's untimely death from alcoholism in March 1881. Not until a very late stage of work was there even a semblance of a libretto, strictly speaking. Beginning with the colloquy between Marfa and Susanna (act 3), composed in the late summer of 1873, scenes gradually accumulated in piano-vocal score in a seemingly random order (see the Appendix to this chapter). Only two tiny excerpts of what eventually became act 3—Marfa's folk song and the waking-up chorus of the Streltsy—were ever orchestrated by the composer. When the scenes he left were finally assembled in order after the composer's death, making use of the draft libretto he had finally written out two years earlier to guide him toward completion, it was found that two acts remained unfinished: act 2 lacked a conclusion, and act 5 (though Musorgsky had described parts of it in detail very early on in letters to Stasov and others) was little more than a sheaf of sketches.

No wonder the action has seemed to exude an air of pointless confusion and ambiguity, and the composer's purpose has proved so susceptible to contradictory readings, though one interpretation has been gradually built into *Khovanshchina* by its various editors. That process is worth recounting in some detail, both for the story's intrinsic interest and for its irony, the standard interpretation being demonstrably at variance with Musorgsky's original conception.

This standard interpretation is the one prevalent in nineteenth-century Russia (and in the Soviet Union), which casts with one fine optimistic gesture all of the variously contending political and social factions portrayed in the opera—the regency, the Streltsy, the Old Believers—into the dustbin of history. All of them, but particularly the Old Believers, were viewed as the symbol of everything that was outmoded and antiquated—everything, in short, that was wrong with Russia. They were Moscow, forced to make way for the new spirit of Russia that would be born in St. Petersburg. They were Asia, withering away in the wake of triumphant Europe. In short, they were *Rus'*, the ancient Russian insular state, perishing in flames out of which modern *Rossiya*, the modern cosmopolitan empire, would take wing. They were for dramaturgical purposes not a religious group at all, only a superstitious foil to the forces of Petrine modernization.

That made them palatable to the state censorship, too, which stringently prohibited the portrayal of Orthodox clergy on the secular stage. From the vantage point of the established Church the Old Believers were not Orthodox, nor did they possess any organized clerical hierarchy. Their ecclesiastical opponents, with the Patriarch

Nikon at their head, were inevitably excluded from the libretto, for the same reason that the young Tsar Peter and the regent Sophia had to be kept offstage. But whereas the temporal authorities could be represented by stand-ins—Golitsyn, Shaklovitïy—the Old Believers had to function as a historically disembodied force. Never once does anyone refer, in the course of the libretto, to the doctrinal and ritual disputes that had led to their defection from the Church. In *Khovanshchina* the Old Believers are schismatics without a cause save opposition to all that was new.

Now owing to the two critical lacunae in the score as he left it, we will never know for sure whether this interpretation, and the melioristic view of Russian history it implies, represented Musorgsky's attitude; though one cannot help having doubts in view of the sentiments expressed in the original letter to Stasov proposing the project. We do know that the "standard interpretation" was Stasov's, enthusiastic anticlericalist that he was. Much of what we know of Stasov's attitudes toward the events of the libretto comes from his letters to Musorgsky, in which he carped constantly at the composer's muddled treatment of themes Stasov saw as clear-cut. He tried to get Musorgsky to expand the role of the Old Believer crone Susanna in act 3, for one thing, so that the Old Believers would be unmistakably identified with that "side of ancient Russia" that was "petty, wretched, dull-brained, envious, evil and malicious."

The melioristic view was fixed once and for all by Rimsky-Korsakov, who had to fill the gaps in *Khovanshchina* as well as orchestrate (and "correct," and cut) it. Act 2, as Musorgsky left it, ends with Shaklovitïy bursting in on a heated political conference at Golitsïn's, in which representatives of all three contending forces—the regency, the Streltsy, the Old Believers—exchange self-interested notions about the future of Russia. When Shaklovitïy announces that a denunciation (his own) against the Khovanskys has been received and that it has aroused Tsar Peter's wrath, Dosifey exclaims, "Leave off your idle scheming!" In an early letter to Stasov, Musorgsky indicated an intention to follow this brusque turn with only a single menacing chord, pianissimo. Later, prompted by his friends, he decided that such a moment needed capping with an ensemble in which each character on stage could react to the electrifying news; he even vowed (in another letter to Stasov) to get Rimsky-Korsakov's advice on handling the "mischievous" distribution of parts (three basses, tenor, and contralto). It seems inconceivable, then, that Rimsky-Korsakov would not have known of this intention. Yet, when it fell to him to complete the scene, Musorgsky's first editor followed neither of the composer's plans, but substituted an idea of his own.

Possibly taking a cue from a line of Marfa's—"Thank God, Peter's people arrived in the nick of time"—which she sings shortly before the end of the act to a fleeting reminiscence of the opera's prelude ("Dawn over the Moskva River"), Rimsky decided to reprise the prelude melody again and develop it into an impressive postlude. At a stroke all ambiguities were resolved: Peter is "day"; the Muscovite opposition, in all its manifestations, "night." This simplified view is driven home again at the very end of the opera. The final chorus—composed on a melismatic Old Believers' melody Musorgsky had taken down from the singing of a friend and designated for the conclusion of the opera—is followed and trumped by a brassy reprise of the Preobrazhensky march that had represented the unseen Peter in the act 4 finale.

That this was Musorgsky's plan may be doubted, interested though he may have been (according to one of his letters to Stasov, where he probably had the second scene of act 4 in mind) in exploiting musical contrasts between the "archaic" singing of the Old Believers and the "European" marching tunes associated with Peter. All these reprises, however, were entirely consistent with the progressive, "statist" historiography associated with the name of Sergey Solovyov, the influential liberal historian whose point of view Rimsky himself had previously embodied in his only historical opera, *The Maid of Pskov* (1872), and whose rabidly pro-Petrine sentiments we have already had occasion to sample.

Dmitry Shostakovich, brought up to accept the Soviet view of Russian history, in which Peter's reforms were portrayed even more unambiguously as positive than they had been by the nineteenth-century "statists" on whom Stasov and Rimsky-Korsakov relied for their ideology, saw no reason, when it came his turn to revise *Khovanshchina* in the 1950s, to reject Rimsky's final chorus, even though he worked ostensibly from Musorgsky's original vocal score as recovered by the Soviet musicologist Pavel Lamm. In addition, he replaced Rimsky's ending for act 2 with a foreshadowing of the act 4 Preobrazhensky march—although unauthorized, this does makes sense, since Marfa mentions that Peter's entourage is in the vicinity—but then transferred Rimsky's reprise of the Dawn theme to the very end of the opera, where it casts an even more conclusive judgment on the whole of the opera's action, and completes the equation of the Old Believers with Ivan Khovansky's Streltsy as representatives of benightedness.

Without all these reprises, first of Peter's march and then of the Dawn, the Old Believers would have the fifth act of *Khovanshchina* all to themselves; and, as they trudge off to their mass suicide, accompanied by the sober strains of their psalm, the opera would end on a note of quiet pessimism, a sense of loss. Loss of what? Of the only characters in the drama who have displayed any redeeming humane characteristics whatever; who have not engaged in denunciations, betrayals, acts of violence or depravity; who have on occasion shown forgiveness, tolerance, resignation, selfless love; who have acted, in short, like Christians.

The fifth act, as Musorgsky evidently intended it (and as realized uniquely in the version of the opera Sergey Diaghilev presented to Paris in 1913 with the help of Ravel and Stravinsky), acts as a gloss on the rest of the drama—a Christian judgment that calls the necessity of the political events portrayed in the other four acts severely into question. More than that, it implies that what for some may have been a dawn was for others the veritable end of the world.

To say this much is by no means to impute a Christian viewpoint to Musorgsky himself. He had his own reasons for a pessimistic, skeptical view of Russian history. It was a view already quite explicitly embodied in the final scene of the revised *Boris Godunov*, which ends pianissimo, with the lonely Simpleton keening a dirge for his unhappy motherland on a stage littered with destruction. And it is a view that is entirely glossed over in our conventional image of the composer, deriving ultimately from Stasov, which casts him, very questionably, in the role of a musical *narodnik*, a radical populist.

THE Russian word *narodnaya* (from *narod*, literally "folk" or "people") has undergone a considerable restriction in meaning since the 1917 Revolution. Nowadays it is commonly used in such connections as "folk song" (*narodnaya pesnya*) or "people's republic" (*narodnaya respublika*), and is distinguished from the loan word *natsional'naya*, which refers to nations as political entities. In the nineteenth century the distinction was by no means so finely drawn. The word *narodnost'*, for example, rather than the then-rare *natsional'nost'*, was used to denote "nationality" (as in the patriotic trinity to which Russians were expected to subscribe under Nikolai I: Orthodoxy, Autocracy,

Nationality). So when Musorgsky subtitled *Khovanshchina* a *narodnaya muzïkal'naya drama*, he did not necessarily mean a "musical folk drama" as most sources now translate it. It is more likely that he meant, simply, a "national drama," or better, a "drama of the national history."

The distinction is worth insisting upon, because otherwise it is hard to understand either the composer's treatment of the chorus (which is in no sense a "protagonist," the way it is said to be in *Boris Godunov*), or his insistence on drawing his dramatis personae almost entirely from the ranks of the nobility. The latter point is one that greatly disturbed Stasov at the time. "A chronicle of princely *spawn*!!" he raged in one letter. "What is this finally to be, *an opera of princes*, while I thought you were planning an opera of *the people*. After all, who among your characters will not be a *prince* or an *aristocrat*, who will come directly *from the people*?"

The answer, excluding the minor roles, is nobody. And the *"real people from the soil"* in *Khovanshchina* (to use another phrase of Stasov's) are treated with unremitting contempt. The choristers representing the rank-and-file Streltsy do nothing but carouse and sleep it off (at noonday); their wives are so exasperated with them that they actually plead with Peter *not* to pardon their husbands. The behavior of the mixed chorus representing the "crowd" (*narod*) in the first act is worst of all. Like the crowd in the opening scene of *Boris Godunov*, it looks on uncomprehendingly; but unlike its predecessor it takes violent and wantonly destructive action, brutalizing the poor scribe and smashing his booth.

No, *Khovanshchina* is an aristocratic tragedy; and this is reflected, too, in the musical style, full of "noble" melody in place of the radically realistic speech-song one finds in Musorgsky's songs or in the earlier version of *Boris*. In part this is a continuation of a tendency, already noticeable in the revised *Boris*, toward a more heroic scale and a more authentically tragic tone—in short, toward a more traditionally operatic style. But Musorgsky refused to call it a retrenchment; on the contrary, in one of his late letters to Stasov he pointed with pride to his *advancement* toward what he called "thought-through and justified melody" (*osmïslennaya/opravdannaya melodiya*), meaning a kind of melody that would embody all the expressive potential of speech. "If I achieve this I will consider it a conquest for art," he wrote, and pointed with pride to certain scenes in *Khovanshchina* in which he felt he had come close to his new ideal. Yet these sinuous melodies, unlike the idiosyncratic recitatives of his earlier manner, are curiously impersonal. The characters who sing them (Marfa throughout, Shaklovitïy in act 3, Dosifey in acts 3 and 5) do not speak, it seems; rather, something is speaking through them. And this is perhaps the central message of an opera in which personal volition is everywhere set at nought; in which everyone plots and strives and everyone loses; in which the final stage picture is one in which the last survivors of the old order, the opera's only morally undefiled characters, are seen resolutely stepping out of history and into eternity, where Peter cannot touch them.

What is speaking? Tolstoy knew. *War and Peace*, another aristocratic tragedy, was a new book when Musorgsky embarked on *Khovanshchina*. The composer must have read it, along with all the rest of educated Russia. And when at length he came to the very end of the whole fifteen-hundred-page narrative, he encountered this famous (and amply foreshadowed) peroration in which the novelist stepped out of his role to lecture the reader directly on the impassive shaping forces of history—what Musorgsky called "the power of the black earth":

> As, with astronomy, the difficulty of recognizing the motion of the earth lay in renouncing the immediate sensation of a stationary earth and moving planets, so in history the difficulty of recognizing the subjection of the individual to the laws of space, time and cause lies in renouncing the spontaneous feeling of independence of one's own personality.
>
> But as in astronomy the new view said: "It is true that we do not feel the motion of the earth, but by admitting its immobility we arrive at an absurdity, while by admitting its motion (which we do not feel) we arrive at laws," so in history the new view says: "It is true that we do not feel our dependence, but by admitting our free will we arrive at an absurdity, while by admitting our dependence on the external world, on time, on [unfathomable] cause, we arrive at laws."
>
> In the first case it was necessary to renounce the consciousness of an unreal immobility in space and to recognize a motion we did not feel; in the present case it is similarly necessary to renounce a freedom that does not exist, and to recognize a dependence of which we are not conscious.

Perhaps it is a mark of the advantage a writer of music enjoys over a writer of words that Musorgsky could "say" all this without intruding his person.

APPENDIX

The *Khovanshchina* Manuscripts

———————————————

NOTE: Mussorgsky's manuscript libretto (the so-called Blue Note-book) contains six scenes, but no indication of how they are to be grouped into acts. The present listing follows the customary division established by Rimsky-Korsakov; a Soviet researcher has recently proposed an alternative grouping as follows: scene 1 = act 1; scenes 2 and 3 = act 2; scenes 4–6 = act 3. The division is attractive: both intermissions (and the final curtain) follow choruses, and the three scenes of the last act show Peter's three opponents (Khovansky, Go-litsïn, Dosifey/Old Believers) eliminated one by one. All dates below are according to the Old Style (Julian) calendar. Unless otherwise noted, all manuscripts are piano or piano-vocal scores.

Action	Manuscript date (when known)	Remarks
PRELUDE Dawn over the Moscow River	4 September 1874	First mentioned in a letter to Dmitry Stasov, 2 August 1873.
ACT 1		Whole act described as finished in letter to Vladimir Stasov, 18 May 1876.
1. Streltsy watch; Kuzka awakes.		Mentioned in letter to Stasov, 2 August 1873.
2. Scribe arrives; Shaklovitïy dictates the denunciation.		First mentioned in a letter to Stasov, 23 July 1873.
3. Scribe and the recent settlers (*prishlïye lyudi*)	2 January 1875	The offstage chorus is based on a folk song from the Villebois collection, 1860. Whole scene omitted in Rimsky-Korsakov version.
4. Ivan Khovansky arrives, addresses Streltsy.		
5. Emma, Andrey, Marfa		
6. Ivan Khovansky returns, demands Emma; Dosifey enters and puts an end to the quarrel.		Much cut in Rimsky-Korsakov version.
7. Dosifey's lament with chorus	30 July 1875	

Action	Manuscript date (when known)	Remarks

ACT 2

1. Golitsïn reads Sophia's love letter.
2. Golitsïn reads letter from his mother. — *Dated by letters, August–December 1875* — Omitted in Rimsky-Korsakov version.
3. Lutheran Pastor arrives, pleads for Emma and for a Lutheran church. — Omitted by Rimsky-Korsakov and also from the Blue Notebook (i.e., dropped from Musorgsky's final plan).

4. Marfa's divination. — *20 August 1870* — Originally intended for an unwritten opera, *Bobïl'* [The lonely Bachelor]. Final version dated 24 July 1878.

5. Ivan Khovansky arrives; quarrel over the abolition of *mestnichestvo* (right of princely succession). — Much abbreviated in Rimsky-Korsakov version.
6. Dosifey arrives, reveals his past identity. — *Dated by letters, August 1876* — Offstage chorus based on folk song from Balakirev's collection of 1866.
7. Marfa returns in fright; Shaklovitïy announces that the denunciation has been received and acted on.
[8. Unwritten conclusion] — Rimsky-Korsakov reprised Dawn theme; Shostakovich foreshadows Peter's march.

ACT 3

1. Old Believers' chorus — *31 December 1875*
2. Marfa's song — *18 August 1873 (vocal score); 24–25 November 1879 (orchestral score)* — Based on a folk song Musorgsky had learned from his friend, the actor Ivan Fyodorovich Gorbunov.
3. Her confrontation with Susanna — *5 September 1873*
4. Dosifey intervenes; Marfa's confession. — *1 February 1876*
5. Shaklovitïy's aria — *6 January 1876*
6. Streltsy awaken. — Orchestral score undated. Abbreviated by Rimsky-Korsakov.
7. Their wives nag them about their drinking.
8. Kuzka's song with chorus. — Omitted in Rimsky-Korsakov's version.
9. Scribe arrives with news of mercenary attacks on Streltsy. — *29 May 1880*
10. Appeal to Khovansky, who declines to fight Peter; Streltsy pray.

Action	Manuscript date (when known)	Remarks
ACT 4, SCENE 1		
1. Khovansky at home; chorus of immured maidens (*sennïye devushki*)	5 August 1880	Based on folk songs from Melgunov collection of 1879.
2. Dances of the Persian Slave Girls	3 April 1876	Orchestrated during Musorgsky's lifetime, and with his approval, by Rimsky-Korsakov.
3. Shaklovitïy's arrival; song in praise of Khovansky; the murder	5 August 1880	Song based on a folk song Musorgsky learned from Makar Fedoseyevich Shishko, the lighting director of the Mariyinsky Theater, published in Rimsky-Korsakov's collection of 1877.
ACT 4, SCENE 2		
1. Golitsïn's exile mourned by Moscow settlers.		
2. Dosifey's aria; he and Marfa decide upon immolation.	25–26 June 1879	First mentioned in a letter to Stasov, 25 December 1876.
3. Andrey confronts Marfa over Emma.		Mentioned in a letter from Stasov to Musorgsky, 15 August 1873.
4. Streltsy enter with execution blocks.		
5. Streltsy wives plead against their husbands' pardon.		
6. Peter's pardon announced.		
ACT 5		
1. Dosifey's lament and appeal	2 April 1880	Expanded in Rimsky-Korsakov version.
2. Andrey in search of Emma; Marfa lovingly leads him to the fire (Love Requiem [*Lyubovnoye otpevaniye*]).		Mentioned in letters as early as 23 July 1873; manuscript lost (partially reconstructed by Rimsky-Korsakov to his own text). A copy of Andrey Khovansky's part, recently discovered in the Glinka Museum (Moscow), was published in 1976.
3. Dosifey leads the faithful into the hermitage.	August 1880	
[4. Unwritten final chorus]		To have been based on an Old Believer melody Musorgsky had taken down from the singing of his friend Lyubov Karmalina. Rimsky-Korsakov adds orchestral figure representing flames to the designated tune, and reprises Preobrazhensky march; Shostakovich keeps Rimsky's chorus and adds a reminiscence of the Dawn to it; Stravinsky bases his chorus on the designated tune plus two other themes associated with the Old Believers.

SOROCHINTSÏ FAIR
REVISITED

―■―

AS LONG as Russian music history is understood in terms that equate "nationalism" with whatever is authentic and progressive, as long as nationalism is construed as folklorism, and as long as folklorism is sentimentally identified with political liberalism, the fact that the three most eminent Russian composers of opera in the latter part of the nineteenth century should all have found themselves at work during the 1870s on operas based on stories from Gogol's early collection, *Evenings on a Farm Near Dikanka*, will seem entirely normal (or, as the Russians say, *zakonomerno*, "by the rules"). Their products will likewise seem entirely "typical," in need neither of any particular explanation nor of any evaluation save a pro forma stamp of approval.

An account of these operas from such a viewpoint would naturally begin with Gogol himself, and with his "St. Petersburg Notes" (*Peterburgskiye zapiski*), published in Pushkin's journal *Sovremennik* [The contemporary] in 1836. That was of course the year of *A Life for the Tsar*, the opera that lives in history as the cornerstone of the Russian nationalist school. Gogol gave it a fervent welcome, and went on from there into one of his characteristic "lyrical interpolations," compounded, as Nabokov put it, of "landscape, expanded metaphor, [and] conjuror's patter":[1]

What an opera one could make out of our national motifs! Show me a people that has more songs. Our Ukraine rings with song. Along the Volga, from source to sea, on all the drifting trains of barges the boatmen's songs pour forth. To the strains of song huts are carved from pine logs all over Russia. To the strains of song bricks are thrown from hand to hand and towns spring up like mushrooms. To the sound of women

[1] Vladimir Nabokov, *Gogol* (Norfolk, Conn.: New Directions, 1944), p. 161.

singing Russian man is swaddled, married, and interred. All traffic on the road, whether noble or commoner, flies along to the strains of the coachman's song. By the Black Sea the beardless, swarthy Cossack with resined moustaches sings an ancient song as he loads his pistol; and over there, at the other end of Russia, out among the ice floes, the Russian entrepreneur drawls a song as he harpoons the whale. Do we not have the makings of an opera of our own? Glinka's opera is but a beautiful beginning.[2]

Gogol's refrain was taken up almost half a century later by Vladimir Stasov, who lacked Gogol's literary gift but not his fervor, as part of his long definitive four-point characterization of what he called the "New Russian School" (roughly corresponding to the mighty kuchka). Along with "the absence of preconception and blind faith," the "Oriental element," and "an extreme inclination toward program music," the school was marked by "its striving for national character." Such a striving, Stasov, insisted,

> cannot be found in any other European school. The historical and cultural conditions of other nations have been such that folk song—the expression of the spontaneous, unaffected musicality of the people—has long since all but vanished in most civilized countries. Who in the nineteenth century knows or hears French, German, Italian, or English folk songs? They of course once existed and were at one time in general use, but over them passed the leveling scythe of European culture, so inimical to all that is at the root of popular life, so that now it takes the efforts of musical archeologists or inquisitive travelers to seek out the remnants of old folk songs in remote provincial nooks. In our country it is an altogether different story. Folk songs fill the air everywhere to this day. Every peasant, every carpenter, every stonemason, janitor and driver; every peasant woman, every washerwoman and cook, every nurse and wetnurse—they all bring folk songs from their native villages to St. Petersburg, to Moscow, or any other city, and you hear them the whole year round. They surround us everywhere, all the time. A working man or woman in Russia today, just as it was a thousand years ago, never does his or her work except while singing a whole collection of songs. Nor does the Russian soldier ever go into battle except with a folk song on his lips. These songs are our birthright: we need no archeologist's help to learn them and love them. And therefore every Russian born with a creative musical spirit is brought up from his first days in a profoundly national musical environment. . . . No sooner had talk

[2] *Sochineniya i pis'ma N. V. Gologya*, ed. V. V. Kallash (St. Petersburg: tip. Prosveshcheniye, 1896), vol. 7, 339–40.

of native things arisen in [Russian] life and literature, . . . then talented individuals immediately appeared on the scene, ready to create music in the idioms most congenial and most dear to them, that is, in Russian folk idioms.[3]

Stasov asserts a direct link between the art and artists of Gogol's time, when "talk of native things arose in life and literature," and those of his own time; later writers have mostly followed him. As for Gogol, what he preached as journalist he practiced in his fiction, creating even in his prose, and seemingly deliberately, "the makings of an opera of our own." Simon Karlinsky, among others, has shown how operatic many of the plots of Gogol's early stories are; nor were his sources confined to "national motifs." "St. Johns Eve" (*Vecher nakanune Ivana Kupala*) is heavily indebted to *Der Freischütz*, while the third of the Dikanka stories, "A May Night; or, The Drowned Maiden" (*Maiskaya noch', ili Utoplennitsa*) embodies a theme that, though indigenous not to Russian or Ukrainian but to German folklore, was well known to early nineteenth-century urbanized Russians. It had come in the form of a singspiel, Ferdinand Kauer's *Das Donauweibchen*, as Russified—or "Little-Russianized"—by Stepan Davïdov (1777–1825) under the title *Lesta, ili dneprovskaya rusalka* [Lesta; or, the Dnepr mermaid], which played the Moscow and St. Petersburg theaters in various versions between 1803 and 1854, and which reached the height of its popularity in the early 1830s, exactly when Gogol wrote his story. The way the tale begins leaves no doubt that reminiscences of operas and singspiels were guiding its author's pen:

> A ringing song flowed like a river down the streets of the village. It was the hour when, weary from the cares and labors of the day, the lads and girls gather together in the glow of the clear evening to pour out their gaiety in strains never far removed from melancholy. The brooding evening dreamily embraced the dark blue sky, transforming everything into vagueness and distance. It was already dusk, but the singing did not cease. Levko, a young Cossack, the son of the village Head, slipped away from the singers with a bandura in his hands. He was wearing an astrakhan cap. He walked down the street thrumming on the strings and dancing to it. At last he stopped quietly before the door of a cottage surrounded with low-growing cherry trees. Whose cottage was it? Whose door was it? After a few moments of silence, he began playing and singing:

[3] "Dvadtsat' pyat' let russkogo isskustva: Nasha muzïka," StasIS 2.526–27.

Solntse nizen'ko, vechir bli-	The sun is low, the evening's
zen'ko,	nigh,
Viidi do mene, moye ser-	Come out to me, my little
den'ko![4]	heart[5]

In the space of a paragraph we have a chorus, a dance to the bandura, and a solo song. No wonder, as Rimsky-Korsakov tells us in his memoirs, his wife kept after him to compose an opera on this subject until in 1877 he finally gave in.[6] It was already an opera in search of a composer. Rimsky allowed Gogol for the most part to dictate the succession of musical numbers, and wherever possible he drew upon authentic folk materials, particularly the then-recent Ukrainian collection of Alexander Rubets, from which he chose no fewer than eight songs.[7] *May Night*, then, with its feast of folk song, was not only a faithful rendering of its literary prototype. It was also a fulfillment of Gogol's prophecy of 1836: an opera made out of "our national motifs."

Rimsky's total of ten authenticated folk songs[8] was considerably outstripped by Musorgsky in the opera he fashioned—or worked at fashioning—out of *Sorochintsï Fair* (*Sorochinskaya yarmarka*), the opening tale in Gogol's *Evenings*, set in the author's birthplace. Musorgsky lived to complete only a little over half of it, to judge by the plan he drew up in 1877. That half, however, already contained fourteen verifiable folk tunes. Of these, just three were from Rubets, the remainder having been collected by the composer directly from his friends and acquaintances, and possibly, in a couple of cases, "in the field." A total of twenty-seven Ukrainian folk songs survive in Musorgsky's transcription: many more of them would doubtless have gone into the opera had he managed to finish it.

Even "Westernized" Chaikovsky saw fit to authenticate the music of his Gogol opera—*Vakula the Smith* (*Kuznets Vakula*, 1874), after "Christmas Eve" (*Noch' pered Rozhdestvom*)—with a sprinkling of gen-

---

[4] N. V. Gogol, *Izbrannïye proizvedeniya* (Moscow: Detlit, 1963), p. 79.

[5] Nikolai Gogol, *Evenings near the Village of Dikanka*, trans. Ovid Gorchakov (New York: Frederick Ungar, 1960), pp. 69–70.

[6] R-KMusL, 188.

[7] Unaccountably, Simon Karlinsky writes that Rimsky-Korsakov "unaccountably failed to utilize the operatic potential of the story's beginning" (*The Sexual Labyrinth of Nikolai Gogol* [Cambridge: Harvard University Press, 1976], p. 34).

[8] See Nina Bachinskaya, *Narodnïye pesni v tvorchestve russkikh kompozitorov* (Moscow: Muzgiz, 1962), pp. 162–63.

uine folk tunes, two of them from Rubets.[9] For this reason, among others, *Vakula* is often cited as evidence of Chaikovsky's flirtation with what is sometimes called "High Nationalism,"[10] under the influence of Balakirev and the mighty kuchka.

By applying the traditional "nationalist" yardstick to this trio of Gogol operas, measuring the degree to which their composers respectively relied on received folklore, we find that Musorgsky comes out the most national, Chaikovsky the least, and Rimsky in the middle of the road. No surprises there. Such are their conventional reputations.

Yet if we look more closely at this Gogol genre, attentive to specifics and to actual circumstances, virtually the whole historiographical scaffolding we have erected will collapse. We will find that there was no continuous tradition linking Gogol and the ideas he espoused about things native and national with the composers of the 1870s; that only for Chaikovsky—who did not actually choose to write a Gogol opera but seized an opportunity—did the project maintain the natural rhythm of his career; that for Rimsky-Korsakov and especially for Musorgsky the project represented an about-face, the explanation for which can only come with difficulty, after opening a whole Pandora's box of considerations, many of them extramusical, extra-artistic, and downright unpleasant. In particular, we shall find that the folklorism embodied in these operas was not a progressive but a retrograde tendency, whether viewed from the aesthetic and artistic standpoint or from that of politics and social attitudes.

I

To begin with, let us return to Gogol himself and fill in the picture just a bit. The somewhat jejune extract quoted above from his "St. Petersburg Notes" was lifted, as it usually is by those who quote it, out of a rather more interesting context. Let us have a look now at the two paragraphs that precede it: they do not pertain to the theme of nationalism or folklore directly but go deeper, to the level of what in Russian is called *narodnost'*, a word our English "nationality" or

[9] David Brown, *Tchaikovsky: The Early Years 1840–1874* (New York: W. W. Norton, 1978), p. 324. One of the Rubets tunes was added when Chaikovsky revised the opera (as *Cherevichki*) in 1885.
[10] Cf. Ibid., chapters 8 and 10.

"nationhood" can only imperfectly analogize ("peoplehood," if it existed, would come closer):

> Opera is received here with special zeal. The enthusiasm with which all St. Petersburg went after the bright lively music of *Fenella* [Auber's *La muette de Portici*] or the wild, hellishly delightful music of *Robert le Diable*, has not abated even now. *Semiramide*, at which the public gazed indifferently for five straight years, all at once completely captivates that very public now that Rossini's music has become a virtual anachronism. There is no need to speak of the enthusiasms generated by *A Life for the Tsar*; by now all Russia knows about it and understands it full well. About this opera one must either say much or nothing at all.
>
> Whereas I do not like to speak of music or of singing. It seems to me that all musical treatises and reviews must bore even musicians. In music the overwhelming part is inexpressible and unaccountable. Musical passions are not everyday passions. Music sometimes merely expresses, or, better yet, simulates the voice of our passions so that, guided by them, it can rush in a splashing, singing fountain of other passions into another sphere. I will note only that melomania is spreading more and more. People, the likes of whom no one would ever suspect of being the least bit musical, sit transfixed through *A Life for the Tsar*, *Robert*, *Norma*, *Fenella* and *Semiramide*. Operas are given nearly twice [apiece] each week; they go through a countless multitude of performances, and still it can be hard to get a ticket. Is this anything but the workings of our Slavic singing nature? Is this anything but a return to our ancient heritage after journeying through the alien terrain of European enlightenment, where all around us everyone spoke an unintelligible language and where all kinds of unfamiliar persons flashed by? It's a return upon a Russian troika with bells a-ringing, and with us standing up on the run, waving our hats, and saying, "There's no place like home!" [*V gostyakh khorosho, a doma luchshe!*].[11]

Again, Gogol has caught us up in one of his lyrical conjuror's tricks, but if we read behind the closing metaphor, we discover that "home" for his Russian melomanes—in fact, for himself—is not Russia, not folk song. It is that "other sphere" into which music draws us, away from "enlightened" Europe. Music—be it Russian, French, or Italian—is celebrated for its irrationality, its inexpressibility and unaccountability. For Gogol music was what it was for other romantics (say Hoffmann), a mysterious element that "discloses to man an unknown realm, a world that has nothing in common with the exter-

---

[11] *Sochineniya i pis'ma*, vol. 7, 338–39.

nal sensual world that surrounds him."[12] Or take the "Russian Hoffmann," Prince Vladimir Odoyevsky, for whom music's chiefest virtue was "its limitless, indefinite form," through which the listener is "able to immerse himself in his own inner, secret world and forget for a time all surrounding reality."[13]

What is both ironic and ultimately revealing is that Gogol applied this romantic paradigm precisely to the repertoire—Franco-Italian opera and its incipient Russian offshoot—which the more typical romantic idealist traditionally set against the Austro-German culture of "pure" instrumental music. For the more conventional romantic, it was "absolute" music that opened the door to the infinite, leaving behind all music that consorted with the "external sensual world." Music that trafficked in folk or popular tunes—musical artifacts of the sensual world if ever there was such a thing—was forever barred from a Hoffmann's or an Odoyevsky's magic inner realm. For Gogol, however, with his "Slavic singing nature," music was a capacious element that enfolded all within its transforming embrace. All music was on the other side of "enlightenment" for Gogol, and his "national motifs," along with the moustachioed Cossacks and bargehaulers who sang them, were located not on Russian terra firma, but in the same aerial space as his mental troikas, from which all ends of Russia were visible at once, and from which her songs, merging in one vast chorus, drowned out all unintelligible "enlightened" voices.

The folk songs that resound through the Dikanka stories were magic conveyances to the "other sphere," which is where these stories—"dealing," as Nabokov puts it, "with ghosts and Ukrainians"[14]—actually take place. The music that for Gogol symbolized the ancient Slavonic heritage of his imagination, moreover, symbolized and idealized the social order as well. The *narodnost'* he hymned was no spontaneous movement of popular liberation; still less did it imply any indictment of social injustice, as Soviet (and not only Soviet) writers would have it. Rather, it was one of that weird troika of concepts—the others being Orthodoxy (*pravoslaviye*) and Autocracy (*samoderzhaviye*)—which together constituted the underpinnings of Official Nationality, the rigid cultural doctrine of the first Nikolai's

[12] E.T.A. Hoffmann, "Beethoven's Instrumental Music," in Oliver Strunk, *Source Readings in Music History* (New York: W. W. Norton, 1950), pp. 775–76.

[13] "Zapiski dlya moyego pravnuka o literature nashego vremeni i o prochem," in V. F. Odoyevsky, *Muzïkal'no-literaturnoye naslediye* (Moscow: Muzgiz, 1956), p. 211.

[14] *Gogol*, p. 157.

reign, to which Gogol subscribed more ardently than any other major writer.[15]

Gogol believed implicitly that his country's social order came from God, and his work celebrated it. In the Dikanka tales (excepting the horror stories) the celebration was benign, the characters inhabiting what has been aptly called a "Little-Russian Abbey of Thélème,"[16] full (in Pushkin's words) of "authentic fun."[17] A dozen or so years later the celebration took a serious, didactic, and quite horrible turn with the publication of Gogol's *Selected Passages from Correspondence with Friends*, in which the institution of serfdom was glorified, in which—according to the outraged Vissarion Belinsky, speaking on behalf of the "enlightened" intelligentsia—"under the cloak of religion and the protection of the knout, falsehood and immorality [were] preached as truth and virtue,"[18] and in which Gogol's romantic, musicalized view of the world, together with his hostility to "enlightenment," reached the point of sinister obscurantism.

The mind and work of Gogol, in short, seem worlds removed from the mind and work of an artist like Musorgsky, the "thinking realist in Russian opera."[19] The sentimental idealization of the peasantry or of its music was no part of Musorgsky's artistic program—not, at least, since he had been free of Balakirev's direct tutelage. By the time he completed the first version of *Boris Godunov*, Musorgsky had appropriated only two authentic Russian folk themes (fewer, that is, than Beethoven), and he had treated them in a manner as far from the Gogolian as it was from the Glinkaesque.

II

Gogol's final comment on *A Life for the Tsar* defined the terms of this distance very precisely. "He has happily succeeded in fusing two Slavic musics in his work," he wrote of Glinka. "You can hear where the Russian speaks and where the Pole: the one is suffused with the

[15] See the standard account by Nichlas Riasanovsky, *Nicholas I and Official Nationality in Russia, 1825–1855* (Berkeley and Los Angeles: University of California Press, 1959), esp. pp. 73–78.

[16] Gennady Gukovsky, *Realizm Gogolya* (Moscow: Goslitizdat, 1959), p. 35.

[17] Quoted in Nabokov, *Gogol*, p. 30.

[18] "Letter to N. V. Gogol," trans. Valentine Snow, in Marc Raeff, ed., *Russian Intellectual History* (New York: Harcourt, Brace, and World, 1966), p. 253.

[19] Cf. Herman Laroche's review of *Boris Godunov* in the newspaper *Golos* (13 February 1874) under the title "Mïslyashchiy realist v russkoy opere."

expansive motifs of Russian song, the other with the headlong motifs of the Polish mazurka."[20] This was indeed a perceptive remark, for we now know from Glinka's memoirs that the possibility of drama through "the opposition of Polish music to Russian" had been one of the main attractions for him of the Ivan Susanin story.[21] He realized the opposition in a typically atmospheric way, as befitted an opera that breathed the spirit of Official Nationality as deeply as Gogol ever did, by casting the speeches of the principal characters (the division of Poles singing in unison as one collective personage) in identifiable folkloristic idioms, occasionally even drawing on authentic tunes for this purpose.

Thus Ivan Susanin's first replique in the opera, which adheres to him thereafter as a leitmotif, was based on a song Glinka had taken down himself from the singing of a coachman in the town of Luga; and the venerable folk song "Downstream on the Mother Volga" (*Vniz po matushke po Volge*) was turned into an ostinato to accompany the dramatic climax, Susanin's self-sacrifice in act 4. These usages were meant not so much to characterize Susanin as to underscore his mystic identification with Russia—his *narodnost'*—thus allegorizing his great civic deed, the laying down of his life for the sake of the Autocracy. The meaning of it all was that the individual Russian life was indissolubly wedded to that of the Russian nation, which in turn was mystically embodied in the Autocracy.

By casting his role in the folk idiom, it could even be said, Glinka had effectively obliterated Susanin as a character. The preachers and practitioners of operatic realism in Musorgsky's time would become exceedingly sensitive to this lapse, as they saw it, for aesthetic and ideological reasons alike. Some rather hard and fast rules grew up around the use of folk songs in the early kuchkist period. They were no longer regarded as instruments of mystical identification with the folk, but as hard objects, positive musical data, to be used only for the purpose of specifying time and place and lending verisimilitude to an action. A folk song could only represent itself: it could be sung on stage only by a character or characters who are actually singing a folk song in the course of the action. Both of the authentic songs in the first version of *Boris Godunov*—the *Slava!* and Varlaam's song—followed this prescription.

[20] *Sochineniya i pis'ma*, vol. 7, 340.
[21] M. I. Glinka, *Zapiski* (Leningrad: Muzgiz, 1953), p. 105.

The kuchkist rules governing the use of folk song were an unwritten canon in the main, but when breached they could be enunciated explicitly. César Cui, writing as critic for the *Sanktpeterburgskiye vedomosti* in 1873, reproached his brother kuchkist Rimsky-Korsakov for misusing a folk song in a love duet from his first opera, *The Maid of Pskov (Pskovityanka)*:

> Why not use folk songs as a rich material, you ask. Why not develop it—it lends such a marvelous local color? That is true. At the same time, though, one must note that one can give a folk song to a chorus representing the folk; one can give it also to individuals who are singing a song; but individual feelings cannot be poured forth in the sounds of a folk song. Here Olga and Tucha are speaking of their own love, of their own feelings; in such a spot the sounds of a folk song are altogether out of place on their lips. And besides, Rimsky-Korsakov develops it badly . . .[22]

To the extent, then, that a composer was interested in individualized characters, the less he was likely to be attracted to folklore. That certainly seems to hold for Musorgsky, for whom the very subject matter and genre of Gogol's Dikanka tales would seem profoundly alien and uncongenial. True, he was interested in Gogol as a humorist, and even began an opera based on Gogol's farce *Marriage*—but that was another Gogol, a satirist of urban mores who portrayed a grotesque cast of characters through unprecedentedly prosaic and laconic dialogue. *That* Gogol, though to us he looks surrealistic, appealed to the realist extremist in Musorgsky, and the resulting "experiment in dramatic music in prose" was aggressively antioperatic. As he put it to Rimsky-Korsakov, "only if one completely renounces opera traditions and can without flinching visualize musical dialogue on the stage as plain ordinary conversation, only then is *Marriage* an opera."[23]

By contrast, no one seems able to do without the word "operatic" when describing the Dikanka tales. Coming from a literary critic it is no more flattering a word than it is when coming from a Musorgsky. It conjures up the artificial, the rhetorically inflated, the inauthentic. Nabokov, having used it, adds, "When I want a good nightmare, I

---

[22] *Sanktpeterburgskiye vedomosti*, no. 9 (9 January 1873); reprint, CuiIS, 220. The editor of the latter collection, I. L. Gusin, considered it necessary to instruct his Soviet readers that "Cui's viewpoint on the problem of using folk song, which in its origin also expresses individual feelings, is incorrect" (Ibid., p. 590).

[23] Letter of 30 July 1868. MusLN 1.101.

imagine Gogol penning in Little-Russian dialect volume after volume of *Dikanka* stuff about ghosts haunting the banks of the Dnieper, burlesque Jews and dashing Cossacks,"[24] while Janko Lavrin connects the word with "hyperbolism," with "technicolor," and—most to the point—with an "infantile mythology."[25] Musorgsky knew this last only too well. "It's shameful to take pen in hand to depict nonsense words like 'Sagana, chukh!' and suchlike folderol," he complained to Stasov in March 1872, while laboring over his contribution to *Mlada*, an abortive "folk-mythological" opera-ballet commissioned from the whole mighty kuchka by the Imperial Theaters.[26] (A few years later he would contrive to insert the whole *Mlada* folderol, Sagana, chukh, and all, into *Sorochintsï Fair*.) And he might as well have had Gogol's "operatic" landscapes in mind when he wrote, also to Stasov in 1872, that "the artistic depiction of beauty alone, in the material sense of the word, is coarse childishness, art in its infancy. *The subtlest aspects of human nature* and of humanity as a whole, the persistent exploration of these uncharted regions and their conquest—that is the true mission of the artist."[27]

That is a task the Dikanka tales simply do not set. They are horror stories and situation comedies, peopled by stock characters without psyches—puppets in the literal sense of the word, adapted in many instances directly from the *vertep*, the Ukrainian itinerant theater in a box, which featured the same petty devils and demons, the same simpleminded peasants with shrewish wives, the same swaggering Poles and Cossacks, wily Gypsies and comical Jews as the Dikanka tales.[28] To speak of *Sorochintsï Fair* in particular, it is a story of boy getting girl by playing her parents outlandishly one against the other with the help of a clever Gypsy. The sottish, superstitious father, his *kum* (Nabokov translates this word as "Ukrainian good companion"), the vain and nagging mother, her paramour the priest's son (compounded out of every cliché of the folk imagination that regarded the rural clergy as "a symbol of gluttony, avarice, sycophancy, bawdi-

[24] *Gogol*, p. 32.
[25] *Nikolai Gogol: A Centenary Survey* (New York: Russell and Russell, 1952), pp. 37–38.
[26] MusLN 1.129.
[27] Ibid., p. 141.
[28] See Lavrin, *Nikolai Gogol*, p. 33; also Faith Wizgell, "Gogol and Vaudeville," in Jane Grayson and Faith Wizgell, ed., *Nikolay Gogol: Text and Context* (London: Macmillan, 1989), pp. 1–18.

ness;" to quote Belinsky's 1847 letter to Gogol),[29] not to mention the conventional young couple, drawn virtually without qualities—what could such stick figures offer "a musician, or rather a nonmusician" bent on "producing a living man in living music," which is how Musorgsky characterized himself when inscribing the manuscript of *Marriage* to Stasov in 1873?

III

We have, in short, some historical and stylistic "problems" on our hands. They begin with what is so often taken for granted—the *zakonomernost'*, the "natural orderliness" of the development that led to the establishment of the Little-Russian peasant comedy as a genre in Russian opera, to say nothing yet of what led Musorgsky to it. The composer himself pointed obliquely to the problem when he wrote to his friend Golenishchev-Kutuzov that *"Sorochintsï* is no bouffonade, but a genuine comic opera based on Russian music and is, chronologically, the first of its kind."[30] This was not quite candid, but correct enough to illustrate how slow the genre, so confidently predicted by Gogol himself forty years earlier, had been to get off the ground.

The earliest genuine forerunner to Musorgsky's opera—*Zaporozhets za Dunayem* [The Dnepr Cossack across the Danube], a singspiel in Little-Russian dialect by Semyon Stepanovich Gulak-Artemovsky (1813–73)—was fourteen years old when Musorgsky claimed primacy in the genre. The Ukrainian-born Artemovsky was a star of the St. Petersburg opera, an Italian-trained bass-baritone who was one of the few to cross over regularly between the Italian and Russian troupes in the capital. His portrayal of the male lead in Glinka's *Ruslan and Lyudmila* was famous. His popularity with St. Petersburg audiences vouchsafed his singspiel a production at the Mariyinsky Theater, despite its musical skimpiness and its superannuated genre. The première took place in April 1863, and by the end of the next season had received a total of fourteen performances.[31] There is no

---

[29] *Russian Intellectual History*, p. 256.

[30] 10 November 1877; MusLN 1.235.

[31] GozROTII, 61–62. In Soviet times the opera was elevated to the status of a Ukrainian national classic, the author to that of a Little-Russian Glinka, and it became the official season opener and closer at the Kiev Opera House, where it was never performed during the author's lifetime. To achieve this standing, the libretto had to be translated into Ukrainian.

way Musorgsky could have missed it. Alongside the usual ditties and dances, *Zaporozhets za Dunayem* contains a scene of marital bickering in a sort of Little-Russian buffa style, a big hit with the public, between Ivan Karas (the title character, played by the composer) and his wife Odarka. It is hard to listen to this scene and not be reminded of Solopiy Cherevik and Khivrya, the bickering couple in *Sorochintsï Fair*.

More significant perhaps than the singspiel itself were the circumstances that inspired it and led to its performance in the capital. These had to do with the so-called *velika vikhidka*, the Great Exodus or repatriation of Ukrainians from the newly created principality of Romania (located "across the Danube," or rather its tributary the Prut, on what had been Ottoman territory) in the aftermath of the Crimean War and the abolition of serfdom (many of the Ukrainian colonists having been runaway serfs).[32] Artemovsky's singspiel was thus an implicit celebration of *narodnost'*. Moreover, the fictionalized repatriation depicted in the singspiel was brought about by the intervention of a beneficent autocrat (the Turkish sultan), to whom lavish and submissive thanks are tendered in the finale. So the opera celebrated a displaced but still recognizable *samoderzhaviye*, too. It was a sort of remnant of Nikolaian Official Nationality, and this surely paved the way for its production in a country where theaters were a state monopoly—indeed, the legal property of the crown.

From our vantage point *Zaporozhets za Dunayem* is as much a harbinger as a remnant, heralding an upsurge in romantic nationalism that followed the humiliations of the Crimean War and reached a peak with the Balkan adventures of the 1870s. It was a movement in which both liberals and conservatives participated for their various reasons.[33] On the official stage, of course, it was the conservative viewpoint that dominated. The important musical name in this connection is that of Alexander Serov. His opera *Rogneda*, which scored a huge success in 1865, was a historical opera in form but a romantic legend in actual content. It glorified the tenth-century Christianization of Russia from a patently nationalistic standpoint. By adding the religious theme to those of nationality and statism, the opera brought

[32] Ibid., p. 54.

[33] For a discussion of resurgent Russian nationalism in the 1870s and its impact on art, see Elizabeth K. Valkenier, *Russian Realist Art* (Ann Arbor: Ardis, 1977), pp. 68–73.

the full trinity of Offical Nationality into explicit conjunction, as witness the culminating chorus:

> Pokoris' krestu, prosvyati narod,
> Veru pravuyu utverdiv zemle.
> I vragam grozna, i na vek slavna
> Svyatorusskaya budet zhit' zemlya.

> [Submit to the cross, consecrate thy people,
> Affirming the true faith to all the land.
> And awesome to her foes, and in eternal glory,
> The holy Russian land will ever live.]

The conservative press received *Rogneda* deliriously; the reaction of an old acquaintance of Gogol was typical:

> Serov's new opera, besides being a remarkable musical work, is a civic deed deserving of everyone's gratitude. We live in an era of doubts and hesitation [and so] one cannot help thanking Serov . . . for the underlying theme of his musical drama. A more felicitous theme we have never seen for opera. . . . The young Varangian, who has sworn to kill the Kievan prince . . . saves his enemy from certain death and dies for him. Who brought about such a miracle? God! What God? The Christian God! The God of love and forgiveness. The God of the future Orthodoxy. . . . This scene will always remain an ornament of the Russian theater. In it there is so much religious faith, so much submission, and withal, so much compelling force. . . . This scene, we repeat, is a civic deed. . . . Nowadays it is a great merit to have stirred up in the spectators such feelings of love, reconciliation and self-sacrifice.[34]

For perpetrating this civic deed, this Orthodox "life for the tsar," Serov was awarded by the crown a lifetime pension of one thousand rubles per annum. The last creative artist to be so honored in Russia, twenty years before, had been Gogol.

Serov's next opera was a different sort of deed. *The Power of the Fiend (Vrazhya sila)* was a dark realistic drama of domestic murder after one of Ostrovsky's grim "comedies" of the 1850s. Its signal musical contribution was the raising of folk song saturation to a new plane. Taking his cue from the attitudes of a romantic conservative faction known as *pochvenniki*, many members of which were his personal friends, Serov made sure that all levels of dramatic and musical structure in his opera were permeated with the "intonations," and as

---

[34] Count V. A. Sollogub in *Vest'*; for a fuller citation see TarODR, 125.

often as not the actual melodies, of what he was now pleased to call *pochvennaya muzïka*, "music of the soil." Folk song undergirded everything from recitative to perorative ensemble, and the characters expressed the full gamut of their personal feelings to its strains. *Rogneda* and *The Power of the Fiend* seem on their face to be the work of two different composers. Serov's next opera would have bridged the gap in a novel fashion.

Rogneda having made him the uncrowned composer laureate of Russia, Serov was the recipient in 1870 of a signal honor. The Grand Duchess Yelena Pavlovna—the German-born aunt of Tsar Alexander II, and patroness extraordinaire of Russia's burgeoning musical establishment—personally commissioned an opera from Serov, to a libretto she had previously commissioned (in 1866) from the prominent poet Yakov Polonsky (1819–98). This was the first time since *A Life for the Tsar* that the imperial family had participated directly in the creation of an opera. The opera envisioned this time, however, seemed as far from Glinka's grand, patriotic offering as could be imagined: it was to be an adaptation of "Christmas Eve" from Gogol's Dikanka tales, a story of witches and demons, of merry Christmas caroling, of drunken muzhiks and "good companions," the whole centering around the caprices of a village coquette wooed by a steadfast if dim-witted village blacksmith. In what way would setting such a tale to music be a "civic deed" worthy of imperial sponsorship?

In this way: "Christmas Eve" contained one additional ingredient. As a way of getting rid of Vakula (the blacksmith), Oksana (the coquette) humiliates him in front of her girlfriends by promising to marry him only if he brings her the tsaritsa's holiday boots (*cherevichki*). Vakula accomplishes this task by jumping on a devil's back and compelling said devil to fly him to St. Petersburg. There he falls in with some Zaporozhian Cossacks (as in Artemovsky's singspiel) who are on their way to an audience with the Empress Catherine. They protest to her their undying loyalty to the Russian crown, a quality Zaporozhian Cossacks possessed only in Gogol's imagination:

> "Be gracious, *Mamo*! Why do you punish your faithful people? How have we angered you? Have we taken the hand of the vile Tatar? Have we come to agreement with the Turk? Have we been false to you in deed or in thought? Why have we lost your favor? First we heard that

you were commanding fortresses to be built everywhere against us; then we heard you meant to make us into regular soldiers; now we hear of new misfortunes coming. Wherein are the Zaporozhian troops in fault? In having helped your generals to beat the Crimeans?"

Potemkin [Catherine's minister] carelessly rubbed with a little brush the diamonds with which his hands were studded, and said nothing.

"What is it you want?" Catherine asked solicitously.

The Zaporozhians looked meaningly at one another.

"Now is the time! The Tsarina asks what we want!" the blacksmith said to himself, and he suddenly flopped down on the floor.

"Your Royal Majesty, do not command me to be punished! Show me mercy! Of what, be it said without offense to your Royal Grace, are the little boots made that are on your feet? I fancy there is no shoemaker in any kingdom in the world can make them like that. Merciful heavens, if only my wife could wear boots like that!"

The Empress laughed. The courtiers laughed too. Potemkin frowned and smiled all at once. The Zaporozhians nudged the blacksmith near the arm, wondering whether he had not gone mad.

"Rise!" the Empress said graciously. "If you wish to have boots like these, it is very easy to arrange it. Bring him at once the very best boots with gold on them! Indeed, this simple-heartedness greatly pleases me . . ."[35]

"Christmas Eve," then, was a story that could be read only too easily as an allegory in praise of the beneficent Autocracy, Vakula standing among the Zaporozhtsï for the suppliant Ukraine, unable to subsist without Russian mercy. Meanwhile, it was under Catherine, as the story even hints, that the final steps were taken in the liquidation of Ukrainian—and specifically Cossack—autonomy. The Ukrainian lands west of the Dnepr—the so-called Zaporozhye—were acquired, cut up into separate administrative units (*guberniyas*), their peasants were enserfed, and thus they were incorporated into the Russian Empire. This had led inevitably to the rise of Ukrainian nationalism and separatism in the wake of the Napoleonic Wars and the advent of romantic literary movements. In the period of liberalism following the Emancipation in 1861 the romantic nationalist movement in the Ukraine reached what for the Autocracy became crisis proportions, and harsh repressions followed in the seventies, including a ban on publications in the Ukrainian language (1876). There can hardly be a doubt that the imperial government, by commissioning

---

[35] *Evenings near the Village of Dikanka*, trans. Gorchakov, pp. 174–75. The common mistranslation of *cherevichki* as "slippers" is corrected to "boots" throughout.

an opera based on Gogol's "Christmas Eve," sought to exploit as propaganda a story by the most ardent Ukrainian apologist Catherine's grandson Nikolai ever had. Another civic deed was being requisitioned from the author of *Rogneda*, the favorite composer and stipendiary of Catherine's great grandson Alexander.

Polonsky, in fashioning his libretto, had to submit to an old statute forbidding the portrayal of a ruler of the Romanov dynasty on the operatic stage, so the Empress Catherine had to be replaced by an unnamed "excellency" (*Svetleyshiy*), commonly assumed to be a stand-in for Potemkin. The empress's absence in person, however, is more than compensated by the fulsome choruses of praise the poet concocted in her honor:

Ura! Da zravstvuyte Tsaritsa!	Hurrah! Long live the Tsaritsa!
Gryant'te strunï, poy tsevnitsa,	Let the strings burst forth, the pipes resound;
se zhena gradyot na tron;	Behold, she approaches the throne.
oblekayet bagryanitsa	Her purple robe instills
mudrost' v silu i v zakon.	wisdom into the might and law of the land.
Slavu dney tvoikh, Tsaritsa,	The glory of thy days, Tsaritsa,
obessmertit lirï zvon.	will the lyre immortalize.
Gorï, stepi i dubravï,	Mountains, steppes, and leafy oaks,
pleski vsekh semi morey,	the waves of all the seven seas,
zvuchno vtoryat pesnya slavï	loudly echo songs of glory
v chest' tvoikh bogatïrey!	in honor of thy warriors!
Slav'sya, mudraya Tsaritsa,	Glory, wise Tsaritsa,
slav'sya do skonchan'ya dney!	Glory to the end of thy days!
I vselennaya ne dremlet,	The universe is wide awake,
smotrit zapad na vostok,	the west looks eastward,
sever yugu chutko vnemlet,	the north hearkens keenly to the south;
mir zhelannïy nedalyok!	the much-desired peace is at hand!
Pal'mï vetv' voz'mi, Tsaritsa,	Take up the palm branch, Tsaritsa!
lavrï polozhi u nog,	Place laurels at her feet.
slav'sya tï vo vek vekov!	Glory to thee for evermore!
[Salvoes are heard from the fortress.]	
Nashim vnukam budut gromki	To our grandchildren will come loud reports
trud i doblesti ottsov,	of their forefathers' works and deeds,

no dela tvoyí potomki	but thy deeds will our progeny
soprichtut k delam bogov;	compare with those of the gods;
slav'sya tï vo vek vekov!	Glory to thee for evermore![36]

Polonsky had in effect donned the robe of a court poet and penned a thundering neoclassical ode in honor of the autocrat in the manner of his eighteenth-century forebears Lomonosov and Sumarokov. Following the chorus, and after a minuet to the strains of which Vakula makes his request, the excellency announces, in a paraphrase of Gogol's tsaritsa: "This simple-heartedness pleases me! Show [the Zaporozhtsï] a good time while they are here. Get someone . . . to do a Russian dance for them, and they in turn shall dance us a Kazachok." For this scene Serov composed a hopak, subtitled in its separate publication "Ukrainian Dance on Ukrainian Motives Transcribed *in Situ*." To its strains Gogol's Cossacks are set to entertaining the assembled Great-Russian nobility in a manner again calling to mind the conventions of the old court opera.

In the days before Soviet arts policy demanded immoderate reverence for what was known in the USSR as *russkaya klassika*, the Russian classical tradition, this scene evoked some healthy indignation from critics who saw it for what it was. Ivan Sollertinsky, for example, wrote about it in this vein for the journal *Worker and Theater* in 1934:

> In Gogol . . . the description of Catherine's palace is reduced to the level of the blacksmith's naive apperceptions. . . . Instead of this magnificently artless and humorous description [we now get] a pompous decorative portrait in the manner of [eighteenth-century court odes like] "Let the Thunder of Victory Resound," or "Glory in This, O Catherine," with an opera-ballet apotheosis. And Potemkin, who is described by Gogol in terms of tousled hair, a crooked eye, an affected grandiosity, and so on, [is now] characterized as some kind of Adonis or Apollo in an embroidered uniform with stars and regalia, in a powdered wig . . . in short a *svetleyshiy*, who could be taken for a double of Prince Yeletsky in *Pique Dame*. . . . Neither Gogolian characterization nor the Gogolian manner of tale spinning do we find.[37]

Uncommitted to the Soviet image of Gogol the realist, we may not be inclined to distance story from libretto quite so radically as this.

[36] Translation adapted from Philip Taylor, *Gogolian Interludes* (London and Wellingborough: Collets, 1984), pp. 108–10.

[37] "Gogol v russkoy opere," *Rabochiy i teatr* 10 (1934); quoted in Sergey Danilov, *Gogol i teatr* (Moscow: Goslitizdat, 1936), p. 277.

Yet one could hardly deny that the courtly and panegyric aspects of "Christmas Eve" were blown far out of proportion in the process of adaptation for the imperial stage, or that the librettist's explicit provision for the insertion of Russian and Ukrainian folk dances are a throwback to a preromantic conception of the folk as the peasantry, not the "nation." What this libretto glorified was not an ethnic but a political entity, the tsarist state.

The opera composed to Polonsky's libretto was given its première at the Mariyinsky Theater precisely in the year of the most stringent anti-Ukrainian repressions, 1876—only the composer was not Serov. Serov had died suddenly at the beginning of the year 1871, having composed only a few scattered items for the score.[38] Determined to get Polonsky's libretto set by hook or crook (and this determination testifies to the political nature of the work), the grand duchess announced a competition in memory of the deceased composer, the winner to be rewarded with a cash prize and a production at the Mariyinsky. The winner, as is well known, was Chaikovsky, and *his* "genuine comic opera based on Russian music," not Musorgsky's, was thus "chronologically the first of its kind."[39] Quite obviously, though, Chaikovsky cannot be counted the founder of the genre to which his opera belonged: that distinction belonged to the grand duchess and Polonsky.

The Russian comic opera after Gogol was thus in its origins an "official" genre, established—even imposed—as part of the resurgence of romantic nationa'sm that went hand in hand with political reaction. That suited Chaikovsky perfectly well. He was intensely conservative and monarchist in his political convictions, and it was this as much as anything that conditioned his mania for old-regime stylization that reached a peak in his music of the 1890s. Sollertinsky's critique, which made such pointed comparison with *Pique Dame*, was written, of course, with reference to Chaikovsky's setting of the Po-

---

[38] Published posthumously, they included the "Hopak" and a setting of a dance tune for the "good companions" entitled *Grechaniki* [Buckwheat cakes]. Serov's widow, herself a composer, arranged a few other items into a piano suite: 1) "Oxana, Vakula, and the Girls"; 2) "The Tsaritsa's Ball: Minuet"; 3) "Mazurka"; and 4) "Arietta: Oxana's Sorrow (in the Absence of Vakula)." See Nikolai Findeyzen, *Aleksandr Nikolayevich Serov: Yego zhizn' i muzïkal'naya deyatel'nost'*, 2d ed. (Moscow: Jurgenson, 1904), p. 141.

[39] Details of the contest may be found in David Brown, *Tchaikovsky: The Early Years*, pp. 306–11, and Taylor, *Gogolian Interludes*, pp. 19–23.

lonsky libretto, in which his "rococoizing" tendency received its first major outlet.

The rococo element was only strengthened, by the way, in the revised version of the opera—the one Sollertinsky knew—entitled *Cherevichki*, which was composed in 1885 in the early part of Alexander III's reign, and first performed two years later. Chaikovsky interpolated an extra number in the St. Petersburg scene ("His Excellency's Couplets"), an even more unctuous panegyric to the empress, and one, moreover, that was actually set to music in a style evocative of the period.

Another interpolation made in 1885, even more telling, consisted of an extended aria for the lovelorn Vakula in which he gives poignant expression to his personal suffering, and does it to the strains of an actual folk song from the Rubets anthology.[40] The old Glinka-esque stylization of folklore thus went hand in hand with the sentimental idealization of the autocracy. On the level of musical style the political and cultural tendencies of the opera were confirmed.

So Musorgsky did not quite tell the truth in his letter to Golenishchev-Kutuzov. By the time he wrote *Sorochintsï Fair*, he was familiar with all the works we have been recalling—by Artemovsky, by Serov, and by Chaikovsky (the last, of course, only in its original version). A careful chronology of Musorgsky's work on the opera suggests that Chaikovsky's work gave Musorgsky's a crucial impetus, that Serov's work exercised a transforming influence on Musorgsky's attitude toward folklore, and that both profoundly affected his handling of operatic form. Finally we shall ask the larger question: how were the political and cultural ramifications of the new genre reflected in Musorgsky's contribution to it?

IV

After abandoning work on *Marriage*, Musorgsky continued to flirt with Gogol. The tantalizing final entry in a work list he put together at Lyudmila Shestakova's request in the summer of 1871, when he was in the midst of revising *Boris Godunov*, reads as follows:

---

[40] The song is no. 66, *Oy, ne pugai, pugachen'ku*. For the opera, words were supplied by Nikolai Alexandrovich Chayev (1824–1914), a minor playwright on the staff of the Imperial Theaters in Moscow.

1871   New version of *Boris Godunov*.
       Comic opera planned on a subject from Gogol.
       Plans served as the basis of a national historical musical drama
       involving the Volga Cossacks.[41]

It is unclear from this even whether Musorgsky was planning one opera or two. If one, some speculation has centered on *Taras Bulba* as the Gogol subject, even though the Cossacks in that story were not from the Volga but the Dnepr. If two, there is no reason why the subject could not already have been *Sorochintsï Fair*. Some circumstantial evidence would seem to implicate that story rather than *Taras Bulba*. It centers on the Purgold sisters, Alexandra and Nadezhda, the musically gifted daughters of a prominent civil-service family, who through Dargomïzhsky had become acquainted with the young kuchkists around 1868. They were especially close to Musorgsky and Rimsky-Korsakov. Nadezhda became the latter's wife, while Alexandra chased the unresponsive Musorgsky for no little time.[42] The four of them were at their closest in the fall and winter of 1871–72, when Musorgsky and Rimsky were roommates. As we have seen, Rimsky-Korsakov traced the origins of his opera on *May Night* to the urgings of his bride during this idyllic period.[43] In an intriguing letter dating from the month of their engagement, December 1871, Nadezhda wrote to her future husband about her favorite Dikanka tales: "Today I have read another of Gogol's stories, *Sorochintsï Fair*. This one, too, is good, and is even possibly suitable for an opera, but not for you, and, in general, it is not what *May Night* is, for example. But what can I do? It has so lodged in my head that nothing can drive it out."[44]

The difference between the tender *May Night* and the uproarious *Sorochintsï Fair* is very much like the difference between Rimsky-Korsakov and Musorgsky as the Purgold sisters viewed them: their private names for the two young men were "Sincerity" and "Humor," respectively. So it would not surprise us to learn that Nadezhda had tried to sell the story with which she found herself momentarily obsessed to Musorgsky. This she evidently did through her sister. Within a couple of weeks of the letter just quoted, Musorgsky wrote to Alexandra (3 January 1872) that "I am well acquainted with the

[41] MusLN 1.264.
[42] See Nadezhda Purgold's diary, excerpted in MR, 154–55.
[43] R-KMusL, 188.
[44] Ibid.; Alexandra Orlova (OrTD, 233) dates the letter 20 December.

Gogol subject. I gave it some thought two years or so ago, but it doesn't go well with the path I have chosen—it takes in too little of Russia in all her openhearted breadth."[45] When the letters are put together, it seems pretty clear that he had *Sorochintsï Fair* in mind.

The path to which Musorgsky alluded was the one that led through the revised *Boris*, with its Kromy Forest scene, to *Khovanshchina*, first mentioned in Musorgsky's correspondence in a letter to Stasov dated 22 June 1872.[46] A "national historical musical drama" is precisely what Gogol could not provide; and so it is not surprising that all mention of him, or of plans for setting him, disappears from Musorgsky's correspondence for a period of more than two years, while (as Musorgsky put it in one of his letters) he "lived in *Khovanshchina* as I lived in *Boris*,"[47] and got ready for the greatest moment of his life, the triumphant production of this first and only finished opera in January 1874. His ebullience afterward found an outlet in the *Pictures at an Exhibition*, composed in a great rush of inspiration and completed on 26 June. Stasov announced the news to Rimsky-Korsakov in a letter of 1 July, and added the delighted comment that "all of a sudden there has awakened in him such a thirst for composition that apparently not one day passes without it. He's beginning a new opera."[48] The name of the new opera is revealed for the first time in a letter of 23 July to Lyubov Karmalina, in which Musorgsky thanked her for supplying the Old Believers' melody he planned to use in the final chorus of *Khovanshchina* (the one that would be composed after his death, first by Rimsky-Korsakov and then by Stravinsky). The reason for what would turn out to be a fatal delay on *Khovanshchina* follows: "But the air carries the clear command, 'Whoa!' and *Khovanshchina* will appear (God willing) a little later; first there will be a comic opera, *Sorochintsï Fair*, after Gogol."[49]

Karmalina must have wondered why, and so must we. Why interrupt *Khovanshchina*, and why return to a subject previously rejected? The reasons Musorgsky offered at the time were patent rationalizations: "It's a good way of economizing my creative powers. Two heavyweights, *Boris* and *Khovanshchina*, in a row might crush them; and besides, the comic opera possesses the real advantage that the

[45] MusLN 1.126.
[46] Ibid., p. 133.
[47] To Polixena Stasova, 23 July 1873; ibid., p. 153.
[48] MR, 275.
[49] MusLN 1.180.

characters and the setting are of a different locale, a different historical period and a nationality that is new to me."

This simply does not sound like Musorgsky, and neither do the
remarks that follow, full of enthusiasm for "Little-Russian tunes, so
little known that self-styled experts pronounce them forgeries (of
what?)," and satisfaction in the fact that "a fair number of them have
been collected."[50] The kuchkists, himself included, had been just the
sort of carking purists he now derides, scorning "Little-Russian"
tunes—as opposed to the kind of archaic melismatic Russian song he
had just received from Karmalina—for their admixture of Polish
(doubly damned as "Catholic" and "Western") as well as Gypsy elements. The letter to Karmalina sounds as though it were parroting
someone else's words. It will not be hard to guess whose.

The great thing the *Boris* production accomplished for Musorgsky
was to bring him for the first time a modicum of precious professional recognition—not from the critics or from the faculty of the
Conservatory, to be sure, but from a group whose esteem may have
meant even more to him: the singers of the Russian Opera. It had
been a pair of singers—Gennadiy Kondratyev and Yulya Platonova—
who by exploiting the system of *bénéfices* had exerted the pressure it
took to get *Boris* its first (fragmentary) hearing in 1873.[51] They had
gotten to know Musorgsky through Shestakova, who as Glinka's
long-surviving sister had become an object of veneration, and whose
musical soirées were among the few meeting grounds between members of the musical establishment and the mavericks of the old Balakirev circle.

The singer with the most venerable Glinka credentials was the
basso Osip Afanasyevich Petrov (1806–78), the incredibly durable
artist who had created the role of Ivan Susanin in *A Life for the Tsar*
and who, four decades later, was still going strong. He had met Musorgsky at Shestakova's in 1870,[52] but the two became really close in
1873 when Petrov created the role of Varlaam at the preliminary per-

[50] Ibid.

[51] Three scenes (the Inn and the whole Polish act) were performed on 5 February at
a bénéfice for Kondratyev, a leading baritone and chief régisseur of the Mariyinsky
Theater, who did not actually appear in the performance of these scenes (his vehicles
came later in the program: the second act of *Lohengrin* and act 2, scene 1 of *Der Freischütz*). The première of the whole opera took place at the *bénéfice* of Platonova, the
company prima donna, who played Marina. According to a letter from Stasov to Nikolai Findeyzen (15 February 1900), Platonova had been the driving force behind both
occasions. See OrTD, 277.

[52] Shestakova to Vladimir Nikolsky (1 June 1870); MR, 136.

formance of three scenes from *Boris*.[53] Musorgsky, who took to calling Petrov "Grandpa," appeared very often as his accompanist, and
began spending lots of time at home with the basso and his wife, the
distinguished contralto Anna Yakovlevna Vorobyova-Petrova (1816–
1901), who had been the first Vanya in Glinka's epochal opera. Petrov, born in Yelizavetgrad (now Kirovograd) in south-central
Ukraine, was of Little-Russian and Gypsy extraction. Stasov, in his
lengthy Musorgsky obituary of 1881, associates the origins of *Sorochintsï Fair* with the composer's "wish to create a Little-Russian rôle"
for Petrov, "whose uncommon talent he worshiped passionately."[54]
We may believe him, for Stasov's private correspondence confirms
the report in a rather surprising way. Furious over Musorgsky's apparent inconstancy with regard to his beloved *Khovanshchina* project,
Stasov had railed in a letter to Golenishchev-Kutuzov (22 August
1877) at "this whole unfortunate Little-Russian undertaking, incited
by the foolishness of Anna and Osip," whom he further insulted by
calling them "Russia's Rosciuses," after the fabled Roman clown.[55]

Whatever one makes of the source of Musorgsky's inspiration, it
was not the usual quixotic idealism of the kuchka that had motivated
him this time, but a sort of professional commission no kuchkist had
ever rated before. It must have been a tremendous thing for him, and
it could only have transformed his self-image, and along with that
his creative attitudes, aims, and, ultimately, his style.

Which is not to say that he submitted to the Petrovs' blandish-
ments without wavering. In April 1875 he wrote to Karmalina, whom
he had disappointed the year before, that "for the sake of discoveries
I have firmly settled back on *Khovanshchina*," and, more to the point,
that

> I have given up the Little-Russian opera. The reason for this renuncia-
> tion is the futility of a Great-Russian trying to pretend he's a Little-Rus-
> sian, and consequently, the futility of trying to master Little-Russian
> recitative—that is, all the shades and peculiarities of the musical contour

[53] Their special relationship was touchingly demonstrated that night on the very
stage of the Mariyinsky. According to the unsigned review in the newspaper *Birzheviye
vedomosti* 36 (8 February 1873), when Musorgsky appeared on stage for the first time,
after the Inn scene, "Mr. Petrov turned to him and started to applaud. The young
composer was so moved by the sign of sponsorship shown him by the veteran of the
Russian opera troupe, that he fell upon his neck. This impromptu scene was very
sweet."

[54] StasIS 2.211.

[55] MR, 362.

of Little-Russian speech. I prefer to lie as little as possible, and to speak the truth as much as I can. In an opera of everyday life one must be even more attentive to recitative than in a historical one, since there are no grand historical events in the former to act as a screen to cover any kind of negligence or slovenliness. Therefore a master with a weak grip on recitative will avoid genre scenes in his historical operas. The Great-Russian I know to some extent, and his sleepy roguishness beneath a smoke screen of good nature is not foreign to me, likewise, the sorrow that in point of fact oppresses him.[56]

Spoken like a card-carrying realist, this—like the composer of *Marriage*, in fact. Such a deliberate, self-conscious *profession de foi* bespeaks a creative crisis; and indeed, something was coming to a head in Musorgsky that had been brewing since the *Boris* revision. It came to this: what was it going to be, romantic folk song or realist recitative? The composer was only too well aware of the stakes, and one can imagine the kind of interior dialogues that tormented him at the time—even exterior ones, Stasov and Petrov exhorting him by turns.

For the time being it was back to work on *Khovanshchina*, and the Petrovs were given what looks like a consolation prize: each became the dedicatee of one of the *Songs and Dances of Death*. The "Trepak," dated 17 February 1875, went to Osip Petrov, and the "Cradle Song," dated 14 April, went to his wife. But if Stasov seemed at this point to have won a round in the battle for Musorgsky's soul, events during the next year drew Musorgsky closer than ever to the Petrovs, and work on *Sorochintsï Fair* not only revived but gained the upper hand.

The year 1876 marked Petrov's golden anniversary as a singer. Celebrations culminated in a jubilee performance of *A Life for the Tsar* at the Mariyinsky, with the hoary basso in the role he had created forty years before. Musorgsky acted as Shestakova's factotum in arranging this event: he picked out the piano she presented to Petrov and arranged the wording for a commemorative plaque to be placed within it; he bought the wreaths, wrote a commemorative article for the *Vsemirnaya illyustratsiya*, St. Petersburg's illustrated weekly, even devised a fireworks display.[57] This frenzy of Petrovian activity seems to have spurred him back to work on the *Fair* project. But he remained circumspect and chary of "Little-Russian recitative," and avoided confronting the issue as long as he could.

He eased back into his Gogol opera through the rear door of *A*

[56] 20 April 1875; MusLN 1.189.
[57] See OrTD, 460–62.

Night on Bald Mountain, as previously adapted for *Mlada*. "He wants to insert this number into his future opera *Sorochintsï Fair*," wrote Stasov to a relative in June 1876, for which purpose he fitted it out with "a new beginning and end," turning it into "one of the most wonderful things he's ever done."[58] The motivation for this arrangement has always been a problem. There is nothing in Gogol's story to justify it—indeed *Sorochintsï Fair* is one of the few Dikanka tales in which "real" demons and witches play no part. The only way Musorgsky could work his old "witches' " music back into the opera was to have one of his characters dream them (he chose Gritsko, the peasant lad).[59]

This was a strange way of getting back into the Gogol opera. It had its advantages: it was a reasonable good-faith offering to Petrov, who would sing the bass solo for the "Black God," Chernobog. It was a way of rescuing (for the second time) a beloved old score from oblivion. Not least, it was a way of staving off the inevitable confrontation with "Little-Russian recitative." Yet at the same time it shows how aimless work on the opera had become: Musorgsky was accumulating accessories and trappings for his opera before the main parts had been written or even planned in detail.

The situation is reminiscent of the way Serov's operas tended to take shape; and mention of that name suggests an additional explanation for Musorgsky's strange course of action. On the very day he died, 20 January 1871, Serov enthusiastically described Polonsky's "Christmas Eve" libretto to a young admirer, Mitrofan Yevstafiyevich Slavinsky (1844–1915): "What deviltries there'll be, really special!" he exclaimed, "What fantastic effects I'm going to put in here. Purely ours [that is, Russian]!" After a few more remarks in this vein, Serov dropped dead of a sudden heart attack. Slavinsky's report of this sensational turn of events, entitled "The Last Three Hours in the Life of A. N. Serov," appeared a few weeks later in the newspaper *Golos* and was snapped up by countless other papers and music journals.[60] As we know from his work list and his subsequent letter to Alexandra Purgold, this story broke just as Musorgsky was first considering his

---

[58] To Polixena Stasova, 19 June 1876; StasPR 1/2.285.

[59] The supposition that the original "witches' " tone poem was inspired by another Dikanka tale, the horror story "St. John's Eve" (*Noch' na Ivanov den'*), rests on an ambiguous report of a scenario-planning meeting that took place in December 1858, when the nineteen-year-old Musorgsky was very much under Balakirev's sway (see OrTD, 73). The libretto seems more likely to have been planned for Balakirev, not Musorgsky.

[60] M. E. Slavinsky, "Posledniye tri chasa zhizni A. N. Serova," *Golos*, no. 40 (1871).

"comic opera on a subject by N. V. Gogol." Furthermore, it was included intact in the most substantial and "permanent" memorial article on Serov to appear in the Russian press, Feofil Tolstoy's memoirs, published in the journal *Russkaya starina* near the end of 1874, that is, just as Musorgsky was getting serious about the project.[61]

Now the first word Serov used in describing the music he would write was a very colorful one: *chertovshchina* [deviltry]. And the line of recitative Musorgsky concocted for the waking Gritsko, so as to connect the *Night on Bald Mountain* cantata to the plot of *Sorochintsï Fair* was this: "Gospodi! Kakaya chertovshchina prisnilas'!" [Good Lord, what a deviltry I dreamed up]. Serov's reminder from beyond the grave that Gogol's tales were full of deviltries may have impelled Musorgsky to write a Gogol opera in which he could salvage his old "witches' " music, and his choice may have landed on *Sorochintsï Fair* because his discarded *Mlada* music also contained a market scene that could be salvaged in the same way.

Some more desultory jottings relating to the Gogol opera are mentioned in the composer's correspondence during the summer of 1876. To Shestakova he wrote on 24 July that he had "acquired a little chorus of girls for *Sorochintsï*,"[62] and at the end of August he notified her that he had "composed a Gypsy for *Sorochintsï Fair*—I have the honor of reporting to you that this Gypsy is a dashing rascal."[63] But these were just notations of themes and leitmotifs, not scenes or numbers.[64] They contain no voice parts, as indeed they could not. For until Musorgsky resolved the aesthetic and technical dilemmas his letters ponder, there could be no real progress on his Ukrainian opera qua opera—that is, as a matching of music to words and scenic or dramatic situations. Indeed, at this point Musorgsky did not even have a scenario in hand, let alone a libretto. Nor could he think of fashioning one until he knew what kind of music he wanted to write. He was effectively stymied.

V

It was at this critical juncture, with Musorgsky at sixes and sevens about the style and idea of opera in general, and about his Ukrainian

---

[61] See Feofil Matveyevich Tolstoy [Rostislav], "A. N. Serov, Vospominaniya," *Russkaya starina* 17 (1874): 370–99.

[62] MusLN 1.221.

[63] Ibid., p. 224.

[64] They may be seen in MusPSS 5/10 (MusCW 20), pp. 38–40.

comic opera in particular, that Chaikovsky's prizewinning setting of Polonsky's libretto reached the stage. The première of *Vakula the Smith* took place at the Mariyinsky Theater on 24 November 1876. The opera had a very curious reception, falling as it did right between the stools of tradition and reform. As a result, all the camps in the highly polarized world of St. Petersburg musical politics claimed it not for themselves but for their antagonists. Chaikovsky's Conservatory classmate Herman Laroche saw the composer as dangerously close to contamination by "that noxious substance known as 'dramatic truth in tones' "—the phrase being a quote from Serov's notorious preface to *Rogneda*—with its attendant symptoms of overly weighty and too-richly harmonized accompaniment, avoidance of "natural" lyricism in favor of a dutiful submission to pedantic rules of correct declamation, and an excessive, inefficient, and wearying burden of detail. "The latest realism," Laroche complained, "possesses the trait of not being able to say two words simply, of needing a massive artillery and an endless wagon train for the most insignificant errands, of sending whole armies into battle where previous commanders had been content with mere battalions. It wages perpetual all-out war with results somewhat less impressive than Moltke's but just as costly."

All this added up, in a word, to "kuchkism," and, consequently, to a betrayal of Conservatory traditions; but Laroche was quick to note with satisfaction that Chaikovsky's sense of moderation kept him from the excesses of Rimsky-Korsakov (in *Pskovityanka*) or Cui (in *William Ratcliff* and the very recent *Angelo*), and that as a result his opera had been received less than fervidly by "the Serovians and the kuchkist . . . fanatics of 'dramatic truth,' who denounce musical form on principle, because their primitive technique cannot cope with it, and who arrogantly affect to despise that temple of beauty from which their failings have debarred them."[65]

Meanwhile, the fanatics of dramatic truth, represented in print by César Cui, regarded Chaikovsky's opera as all too obviously the product of the composer's Conservatory schooling. It was "absolute music," composed "not to a text, but in and of itself; only later did the text come to be adapted to these symphonic *Mittelsätze*." Cui calls this the Wagnerian method:

[65] *Golos*, no. 333 (2 December 1876); reprint, G. A. Larosh, *Sobraniye muzĭkal'no-kriticheskikh statey*, vol. 2 (Moscow, 1922), pp. 130–32.

Mr. Chaikovsky does it like this: he takes some musical phrase, often a beautiful one, almost always a short one, and begins torturing it harmonically and contrapuntally, leading it on a parade through the entire orchestra, modulating constantly, and over this endless, unabating cantilena, the characters carry on their dialogue on any old harmonizing notes. The result of this is that you hear neither orchestra (for the singers are in the way) nor the singers (for the orchestra is in the way); instead of a union, instead of a unity of purpose, there is a complete dissension, antagonism, schism.

The critic explains:

Chaikovsky resorted to these *Mittelsätze* out of a desire that his opera have uninterrupted music. But music consists not only of modulations and contrapuntal developments. It consists mainly and above all of themes. What is there to prevent each phrase of recitative from being a theme, and a good theme at that?[66]

As a description of Chaikovsky's opera this may have been absurdly one-sided, the remarks on Wagnerian style may be naive, yet the last quoted comment is substantial and important, as it contains the pithiest and clearest definition Cui ever gave of what he called "melodic recitative," the style of vocal writing Dargomïzhsky had brought to its peak of development in *The Stone Guest*, and the one Cui held up as a critical yardstick forever after.

In Cui's eyes Musorgsky had never quite measured up as a recitative writer to the Dargomïzhskian ideal. His recitatives were too *parlando*, too strictly modeled on speech; they aspired too little to songfulness. Cui despised *Marriage*, and had complained in his notorious review of *Boris* that when Musorgsky wrote his recitatives to a poetic text (as in the Cell scene) rather than to one in prose (as in the Inn scene), the results were "choppy" (*rublyonnïy*).[67] The friendship between Cui and Musorgsky had been dealt a heavy blow by that review; indeed, even a year later Musorgsky was railing at it, calling Cui (along with Rimsky-Korsakov, lately of the Conservatory) a "soulless traitor."[68] Yet it was an inescapable fact that Cui had been Musorgsky's elder within the old Balakirev circle, and however much he railed, Musorgsky was always afraid of Cui, always deferential in

[66] César Cui ["****"], "Muzïkal'nïye zametki," *Sankt-peterburgskiye vedomosti*, no. 332 (30 November 1876).

[67] On Cui's reaction to *Marriage* see R-KMusL, 100; the relevant passage from the *Boris* review may be found in OrTD, 357.

[68] Letter to Stasov, 19 October 1875; MusLN 1.203.

his presence, and always attentive to his criticism. A rather startling insight into the inner dynamics of the mighty kuchka even as late as November 1880, only months before Musorgsky's death, is found in a memoir by Mikhail Berman, a choir director on the staff of Balakirev's Free Music School, describing an evening gathering at which Musorgsky played through *Khovanshchina* for his old comrades:

> It was pitiful to observe the way those present (especially Cui) would incessantly pester [Musorgsky] with demands for all kinds of cuts, changes, abbreviations, and so on. (Balakirev, strange though it seems in view of his well-meaning but despotic personality, behaved more modestly than the others.) To worry and poke at a newborn piece like that, and not just face to face but in public, is not only the height of tactlessness, but an out-and-out act of cruelty. But the poor, modest composer keeps still, assents, makes the cuts . . .[69]

Having established that Musorgsky was in the habit, perhaps despite himself, of paying attention to Cui, it is reasonable to assume further that he would have been most susceptible to Cui's direction at a time when he was particularly unsure of his creative path. Facing the task of writing a Gogol opera but not knowing how to proceed, Musorgsky would have been keenly interested in what his big brother kuchkist would have to say about Chaikovsky's handling of the same task. And that is why it is so striking to set Cui's review of *Vakula the Smith* alongside a letter Musorgsky wrote Stasov later the same month, one of the most famous—and one of the most difficult—of all Musorgskian texts.

This is the letter of 25 December 1876, in which the composer ostensibly described a creative breakthrough and outlined a new creative ideal. The pertinent passage, in a deliberately literal and therefore somewhat stilted translation, runs as follows:

> You know that before *Boris* I did some folk pictures [*narodnïye kartinki*]. My present desire—to make a *pronostic*, and here it is—is lifelike, nonclassical melody. Through my work on human speech I have arrived at a melody created by that speech; I have arrived at an embodiment of recitative in melody (except for dramatic turning points, *bien entendu*, when [recitative] can go all the way to interjections). I would like to call this rationally justified melody [*osmïslennaya/opravdannaya melodiya*, literally, "thought-through/justified melody"]. And this work gratifies me; all at once, unexpectedly and inexplicably, something inimical to

[69] OrTD, 588.

classical melody (the old favorite), yet immediately intelligible to one and all, will be sung forth. If I attain it I will consider it a breakthrough in art, and attain it I must. I'd like to do some pictures as a trial. In fact *Khovanshchina* already contains the makings of them.[70]

Most discussions of "rationally justified melody" have placed the emphasis on the modifiers, and have followed Musorgsky in comparing it with "classical" melody, whatever a Russian composer in 1876 might have meant by that.[71] Perhaps, though, the emphasis ought to be placed on the noun; the melody of which Musorgsky speaks might then be compared not with other composer's melodies, but with his own recitative—that is, his previous "work on human speech." He invites such a comparison when he tells Stasov that he "would like to do some pictures as a trial."[72] If we assume that the "folk pictures before *Boris*" to which Musorgsky refers at the beginning of the quoted passage are his songs of the mid-to-late 1860s— say, from *Otverzhennaya* [The outcast], an "experiment in recitative" written in 1865, through *S nyaney* [With Nanny], the first song in the *Nursery* cycle—and that the "trial pictures" (no longer "folk") proposed at the end of the passage are the songs to words of Alexey Tolstoy composed in the early spring of 1877, the interpretation advanced here leads to interesting results.

The sentimental *Gornimi tikho letela dusha nebesami* ["Spirit so gentle is roaming through fair fields of Heaven," in Edward Agate's singing translation] offers itself as the obvious test case because of its rather programmatic performance direction: *Quasi recitando, ma cantando.* It retains demonstrably Musorgskian *recitando* features, especially by comparison with the somewhat later, more conventional settings of the same poem by Chaikovsky and Rimsky-Korsakov (Example 1).[73] Particularly telling is the directness with which Musorgsky handled the unusual meter of the poem. Tolstoy's long lines of dactylic pentameter are set with characteristic speechlike isochrony in what amounts to a musical meter of $\frac{15}{4}$. This is at once more simple and

[70] MusLN 1.227.
[71] The most extensive discussion is in FridMPM, 116–24.
[72] MusLN 1.277.
[73] Cf. Gerald Abraham's comparison of the three settings in his article "Russia" for *A History of Song*, ed. Denis Stevens (New York: W. W. Norton, 1970), p. 365 (reprinted as "Russian Song" in G. Abraham, *Essays on Russian and East European Music* [Oxford: Clarendon Press, 1985], p. 27), where, proceeding from very different premises than those proposed here, he found Musorgsky "in the—for him—very unusual position of inferiority to both" the other composers.

EXAMPLE 1.

a. Musorgsky (1877)

A soul flew serenely through celestial skies, its sorrowing lashes cast downward; tears falling from them like stars through space, curled behind it in a long bright train.

b. Chaikovsky, op. 47, no. 2 (1880)

A soul flew serenely through celestial skies, its sorrowing lashes cast downward; tears falling from them like stars through space, curled behind it in a long bright train.

EXAMPLE 1, *continued*

c. Rimsky-Korsakov, op. 27, no. 1 (1883)

Gor - ni - mi ti - kho le - te - la du-sha ne-be-sa - mi,

grust - nï-ye do-lu o-na o-pu-ska - la res-ni - tsï;

Slyo - zï v pro-stran-stvo iz nikh u-pa-da - ya zvez-da - mi,

Svet - loy___ i dlin - noy___ za ne-yu vi-lis' ve-re-ni-tsey.

A soul flew serenely through celestial skies, its sorrowing lashes cast downward; tears falling from them like stars through space, curled behind it in a long bright train.

more original—that is, more "primitive"—than the teasing to which Rimsky and Chaikovsky subjected the scansion in order to preserve conventional symmetry in the musical rhythm. Musorgsky sets—or rather, transcribes—the poem "as read"; and that, one may suppose, is what is "inimical to classical melody" in his new approach.

At the same time the melodic contour has lost the intimate association with the tonic accent that had characterized Musorgsky's earlier manner. The accented notes are no longer pitched as they would be in spoken Russian, and this lends the melody a more abstractly lyrical—that is, *cantando*—quality than had formerly been typical of Musorgskian vocal lines. It can no longer be said that this song is a "representation of . . . the peculiar speech of sharply realized individuals," in Gerald Abraham's shrewd phrase.[74] The voice has been generalized; the singer/speaker has become anonymous, transparent. Add to that the clear three-part sectionalization by means of fermatas and the da capo return of the opening melody (set, however, to different words), and it is clear that Musorgsky's new manner is not really as inimical to classical melody as all that. In particular, since themes are by definition recurrent, it is evident that Musorgsky is

[74] The *New Grove Dictionary* 12.871.

following Cui's prescription for "melodic recitative." He is no longer "preventing the phrases of his recitative from being a theme."

Commentary on Musorgsky's late songs in light of "rationally justified melody" is necessarily speculative; the composer never explicitly identified any existing song as a "trial picture" for applying the practice. More positive evidence can be found that Musorgsky's idea of "rationally justified melody" was congruent with Cui's idea of "melodic recitative" (hence that it was as much a retreat as a breakthrough). The last sentence in the paragraph from Musorgsky's letter to Stasov in which the term is introduced announces that "the makings are already there" in both the post-*Boris* operas. Musorgsky even identifies a spot: "Marfa's grieving before Dosifey" in *Khovanshchina*.

There are two scenes in *Khovanshchina* that might be so described. For some reason Lamm assumed that Musorgsky was referring to the brief exchange between Marfa and the leader of the Old Believers in the second scene of act 4,[75] where between her entrance and his exit she sings only one seven-bar phrase.[76] It is a grieving phrase, all right, but it is no more than a reprise of a phrase she sings in act 3, in the course of a much richer, more extended scene of "grieving before Dosifey." If we assume that it was this much more varied scene, composed in September 1876, that Musorgsky had in mind when he wrote to Stasov in December, then we have four "rationally justified" themes by which to take the measure of Musorgsky's new style (Example 2).

What is especially striking about these melodies is that they are far less recitativelike than the 1877 songs, even though they are written not to Alexey Tolstoy's elegant verses but to Musorgsky's own prose dialogue. The first of them is a downright "classical" parallel period; the second—in which Dosifey's replique is given along with Marfa's to show that the two, thematically linked by the orchestra, form a single melodic entity—is the one reprised in the later scene. The fourth melody is a thematic reprise of a melody Marfa sings earlier in the same act during her exchange with Susanna. Its periodic structure and its "neumatic" prosody, with melodic turns appropriated from the idiom of the Russian melismatic peasant song (the so-called *protyazhnaya*—see Chapter 1), show how far into the domain of the

---

[75] See his chronological table on p. xi (Russian) and xvii (German) in the critical vocal score (MusPSS 2/1; MusCW 4).

[76] Fig. ⬚13; Lamm score, p. 293.

EXAMPLE 2. *Khovanshchina,* act 2: four vocal "themes"
a. Fig. 29

Ma - ti Su - san - na   gne-vom vos - pï - la - la na

rech'   na mo - yu,   bez   le - sti i ob - ma - na

Mother Susanna flared up in a rage at my words, [which were] guileless and sincere

lyric arioso Musorgsky's "rationally justified melody" was prepared to go.

The third melody (Ex. 2c, p. 364) is the most momentous, both as an indicator of Musorgsky's new/old aesthetic and as a harbinger of his methods in *Sorochintsï Fair.* For this melody, to which Marfa sings what is just another dialogue replique in the context of her scene with Dosifey, is in fact a reprise of the song she had sung at the beginning of the act: *Iskhodila mladyoshen'ka vse luga i bolota* [The young girl went walking through all the meadows and bogs], an actual folk melody Musorgsky had transcribed in July 1873 from the singing of his friend, the actor and theatrical historian Ivan Fyodorovich Gorbunov (1831–95).[77] To allow a character to sing "her own" words—that is, to express her own thought—through the medium of a folk song, was, as we know, altogether at variance with prior kuchkist thinking and practice. It was an abandonment of his former "enlightened" realism and a return to the romantic *narodnost'* of the Official Nationalists and (latterly) the *pochvenniki,* an ideal that had most recently found a prominent and serious musical embodiment in the operas of Serov.

Musorgsky's unacknowledged aesthetic kinship with Serov, amply discussed elsewhere in this volume, was a facet of a long-standing ambivalence between notions of realism and *narodnost',* an ambivalence that reached its crisis when Musorgsky had to find an entrée into *Sorochintsï Fair.* "Rationally justified melody" was Musorgsky's way of rationalizing an end to resistance. It justified his embracing

[77] Compare Musorgsky's letter to Golenishchev-Kutuzov, 22 July 1873 (MusLN 1.151) with Rimsky-Korsakov's citation of the source of the song, which he included as no. 11 in his collection, *One Hundred Russian Folk Songs* (1877).

EXAMPLE 2, *continued*

b. Fig. 39

the viewpoint of the *pochvenniki* and abandoning his commitment to positivistic realism. Folk motives ("intonations," as Asafyev would later call them) and folk songs could now *replace* speech patterns as the primary agents of dramatic characterization, since in the new view characters were no longer alienated individuals (such as Pod-kolyosin, the antihero of *Marriage,* or, on a more exalted plane, Boris Godunov himself) but types who took their identity from their mem-

EXAMPLE 2, *continued*

—Ah, little swallow mine, endure a little longer and you will stoutly serve all ancient holy Russia, the very one we seek.
—O it aches, my heart it aches, Father, it seems a bitter sorrow is foretold!

c. Fig. 41

Like godly candles he and I will soon take warmth. Our brethren all around us in flames, he and I fly up in fire and smoke!

bership in groups. That is precisely the difference between *Boris Godunov* and *Khovanshchina*, and it spelled the difference between tragedy and chronicle. Romantic *narodnost'*, it could even be said, made personal tragedy impossible.

All of this was in its way a profound return to Gogol from the clutches of "Enlightenment." It was a return on levels far deeper than the composer was probably aware. But in ways of which he was very much aware it removed the impediments to his composing *Sorochintsï Fair*. Folk song had beaten recitative. Now he could proceed.

EXAMPLE 2, *continued*

d. Fig. 43

Strash - na - ya pït - ka lyu - bov'___ mo - ya, den' i

noch' du - she___ po - ko - ya___ net. Mnit - sya,

gos - po - da___ za - vet ne bre - gu i gre -

khov - na, pre - stup - na___ lyu - bov'___ mo - ya.___

My love is a terrible torment, day and night my soul knows no peace. I feel I have not heeded the Lord's commandments and my love is sinful, wicked.

VI

On 19 May 1877 Musorgsky finally got down to work in earnest on *Sorochintsï Fair*. At the Petrovs' apartment, and with the active participation of his hosts (especially Mme Vorobyova-Petrova), he drew up a detailed scenario in three acts, containing seventeen numbers.[78] Over the three and a half years remaining to him he managed to compose eight items, roughly corresponding to this plan, as follows:

    1. An orchestral prelude in full score, inspired by the famous opening paragraph of Gogol's story ("How intoxicating, how magnificent is a summer day in Little Russia!"), an "invariable item in all Russian anthologies."[79]

    2. A vocal score of the Fair scene in act 1, corresponding approxi-

[78] The autograph is in the Saltykov-Shchedrin State Public Library, Leningrad. It is reproduced in full in Lamm's preface to the Academy edition of the full score (MusPSS 3/2; MusCW 4), in the separate publication of the Lamm-Shebalin vocal score (Moscow: Muzïka, 1970), and in MusLN 2.153–54. English translations may be found in MR, 354–55, less reliably in M. D. Calvocoressi (with Gerald Abraham), *Mussorgsky* (Master Musicians series, London: J. M. Dent, 1946), pp. 187–88, and still less reliably in Oskar von Riesemann, *Moussorgsky*, trans. Paul Englund (New York: Alfred A. Knopf, 1929), pp. 300–301.

[79] Lavrin, *Nikolai Gogol*, p. 36.

mately to act 1, nos. 1, 3, 4, and 5 in the 1877 scenario, all framed with choruses (the first borrowed from the *Mlada* music of 1872).

3. A drunk scene in vocal score for Cherevik and his "good companion" (Kum), perhaps related to act 1, no. 3 in the scenario.

4. "Hopak of the Merry Peasant Lads" (*Gopak vesyolikh parobkov*) in piano score, corresponding to act 1, no. 8 in the scenario.

5. Act 2 in vocal score, up to but not including the middle item of the last scene planned in 1877 ("Narrative about the Red Jacket").

6. The "Peasant Lad's Dumka" (*Dumka parobka*), corresponding to act 3, no. 2 in the scenario.

7. "Parasya's Dumka," in vocal score (partly orchestrated), corresponding to act 3, no. 3 in the scenario.

8. The old *Night on Bald Mountain* cantata from *Mlada*, fitted out with a reprise of the "Peasant Lad's Dumka" and a concluding replique for the awakening Gritsko. This corresponds to the Intermezzo marked with a "nota bene" preceding act 2 in the 1877 scenario.[80]

The act that exists in closest to its complete projected form is the second. Not surprisingly, that was the act with which a greatly exhilarated Musorgsky began serious composition. By the middle of August he was able to announce to Golenishchev-Kutuzov that

> I have pretty well embarked on *Sorochintsï*, so that if the Lord would help me carry on in the same way, we might expect to be able to decide the season after next whether this *Sorochintsï Fair* is a good opera or a bad one. I did not set to work immediately with the first act, whose scenic complexity would require very concentrated work and lots of free time (I'm not on vacation yet), but rather with the second, that is, the nucleus of the whole opera. This act (the second), as you will recall, follows immediately after the intermezzo (Witches Sabbath on the Bald Mountain;—it will be called the "Parabok's Dream"). The scene of Khivrya and Cherevik, plus the one of Khivrya again with the priest's son I have finished already and I have even managed to get Cherevik and Kum and their guests on stage: all that is finished. Now I am starting on the nucleus: the "Tale of the Red Jacket." It's a terribly difficult assignment. . . . I further add that in *Sorochintsï Fair* the "Tale of the Red Jacket" is the finale of the second act, so that very soon, with God's help, one act of *Sorochintsï* will already be done.[81]

[80] The list of completed items has been compiled by comparing Lamm's discussion of the sources in the critical edition of the vocal score (MusPSS 3/1 [MusCW 5], pp. x–xv) with information in OrTD, 673, 683–85.

[81] 15 August 1877; MusLN 1.231, 233.

God did not help. The whole tragic story of the end of Musorgsky's career is adumbrated in this letter. The "Tale of the Red Jacket" (for which Golenishchev-Kutuzov had adapted the text) never got written, though Musorgsky continued to work fitfully on the opera for the rest of his life.

Now why did he consider the second act to be the nucleus of the opera? Not because of its dramatic significance (for it is mostly given over to subplots) but because of its form. It was the only act to be cast practically throughout in uninterrupted dialogue. From this point of view the task of setting it was just the same as the task of setting *Marriage* or the Inn scene, and Musorgsky was accustomed to regard such a task as a composer's highest calling. The same letter to Golenishchev-Kutuzov contains a sententious little disquisition on this familiar theme—so familiar that it would be tedious to cite it in full. What is most significant are the differences, as Musorgsky saw them, between the task he now faced and the one he had faced nine years before:

> *Marriage* was the strengthening exercise of a musician, or rather, a non-musician, who wished to study and at last to comprehend the twists of human speech in all the immediacy and truthfulness with which it was captured and set forth by Gogol's genius. . . . From a large stage it is necessary that the speeches of the characters—each according to his own endemic nature, habits, and "dramatic inevitability"—reach the audience in bold relief. . . . What you read in the speeches of Gogol's *characters*, my *characters* must convey to us in musical speech, *without any distortions* of Gogol. . . . One wants so very much to reveal truth to people—if one could only manage to get across the tiniest scrap of that truth! . . . Pushkin wrote *Boris* in dramatic form but not for the stage. Gogol wrote *Sorochintsï Fair* in the form of a story—needless to say, not for the stage. But both giants charted the outlines of a scenic action so subtly, thanks to their creative powers, that all one has to do is to tip in the colors.[82]

The one scene in which Musorgsky took his scenic outlines, as he put it, directly from Gogol, *Marriage*-fashion, was the scene of Khivrya and the priest's son, which was adapted virtually in toto from Gogol's original dialogue. Some of the declamation in this scene does indeed resemble that of *Marriage*, particularly the lines in which the

[82] Ibid., p. 232.

EXAMPLE 3. *Sorochintsï Fair*, act 2

a. Fig. 67

Greetings, Afanasy Ivanovich. Good evening!

b. Fig. 76

Wonderful, incomparable Khavronya Nikiforovna!

c. Fig. 87

God knows what you'll think up next, Afanasy Ivanovich!

two characters, addressing each other with clumsy peasant *politesse*, hurry through one another's unwieldy full Christian name–plus–patronymics: Afanásiy Ivánovich (or Ivánïch) and Khavrónya Nikíforovna (Examples 3a and 3b). Musorgsky seems at times more to be lampooning his old manner than reactivating it. Whether intended

EXAMPLE 3, *continued*

d. Fig. 80

There is one thing I have yet to receive from you, Khavronya Nikiforovna!

as parody or in earnest, this scene, composed at the age of thirty-eight, was Musorgsky's farewell to realistic speech-song.

More than through their speech patterns, the characters in it are delineated by a sort of musical typecasting. Khivrya has a folkish signature tune associated throughout act 2 with her cooking. In the scene with the priest's son, when the dainties she has prepared for him are served and consumed, the tune not only furnishes orchestral continuity but also rises at times to the vocal surface, producing what amounts to a parody of "rationally justified melody," superseding the niceties of realistic declamation. Particularly telling is the way the name "Afanasiy Ivanovich" gets stretched out on a Procrustean frame (Example 3c). As for Afanasiy Ivanovich himself, his speeches are mainly set to a witty parody of hackneyed ecclesiastical formulas of a kind, it should be noted immediately, that were part of the everyday churchgoing experience of Musorgsky's intended St. Petersburg audience, not that of his characters. The name "Khavroniya Nikiforovna," treated as a special joke, is regularly set to cadences from Bakhmetev's *Obikhod notnago peniya*, the standard book of harmonized chants (Example 3d).[83] The result is a virtual lampoon of Pimen's music in *Boris*.

---

[83] See Vladimir Morosan, "Musorgsky's Choral Style," MusIM, 129. It is by the way

EXAMPLE 4. *Sorochintsï Fair*, act 2, fig. 15

A young sir, a youth, came up to me and asked, What have you got for sale?

The first scene in act 2, between Khivrya and Cherevik (text by Musorgsky), is sewn together out of a patchwork of folk tunes both real and artificial. Khivrya's cooking leitmotif is a good example of the artificial type. Cherevik has a folkish leitmotif too: the little strophic tune to which he sings his story (to a text partly adapted from Gogol's dialogue) of how he almost sold his mare (Example 4).

Out of three real folk tunes taken down from an office acquaintance named Alexander Vasilyevich Morozov, Musorgsky fashioned the heart of the scene, the bickering duet. This kind of thing, with its precedent in *Zaporozhets za Dunayem*, was standard singspiel fare; but for its level of musical invention, Musorgsky's piece could have fit right into Artemovsky's (Example 5). It shows how stereotyped and romanticized his musico-dramatic conceptions were becoming.[84]

The real showpiece of act 2 was neither of the scenes so far discussed, nor in fact any item listed in the 1877 scenario. For nowhere in that document did Musorgsky mention "Khivrya's Song," which he wrote less than two months after the scenario was drawn up. Completed on 10 July 1877 and dedicated to Alexandra Molas (*née* Purgold), an accomplished amateur singer, it was the very first major item from *Sorochintsï Fair* to be composed, not counting the parts adapted from abandoned works. This effective concert item, which

typical of doctrinaire Soviet commentators—the kind who find the Musorgsky of *Sorochintsï Fair* to be close to "Gogolian realism" by virtue of his "raznochinets-democratic tendencies"—to congratulate the composer for the "grotesquerie" and the "antireligious satire" in his portrayal of the priest's son, as if Pimen and Dosifey did not exist. See Danilov, *Gogol i teatr*, p. 281 (including a quotation from Sergey Bugoslavsky).

[84] It is moreover noteworthy that the line leading into this number is one that an exasperated Khivrya addresses to the audience ("No, take pity on me, good people; I'm simply worn out by this [pointing to Cherevik] 'divine punishment.' "). Violation of the "fourth wall," unthinkable in realist theater, is of course a standard comic opera ploy.

EXAMPLE 5. Quarrel duets

a. *Zaporozhets za Dunayem*, no. 6 (Urainian version [Kiev: Mistetstvo, 1954])

—Oh, if only I had known before what kind of man I was living with, quicker than a wink I'd have been off, I wouldn't be shedding tears now.
—Hey, Odarka, hold on, stop yelling your head off!
—No, let people hear! I have no intention of shutting up!

Darya Leonova would sing with great success to Musorgsky's accompaniment on their tour of the Crimea and the Ukraine in 1879, was patently an insert, a "sung song" based on three Ukrainian folk tunes, two of them taken down from the singing of the writer Vsevolod Krestovsky in November 1876.[85] They are linked by a few

[85] A hint of lingering realist *pudeur* can be detected in the way Musorgsky "excuses" Khivrya's song by invoking a dodge Laroche had memorably mocked with reference to Laura's songs in the second scene of *The Stone Guest*. Laroche called it the "invitation to sing" (*priglasheniye pet'*), and looked forward to the day when one of the chief tasks of realist librettists "will be creating situations and inventing characters to ask one another to sing, whereupon the one asked takes up his guitar and charms the world with his art." He added, prophetically, "As long as this cunning idea is new it will be bearable, but when it becomes a stock situation it will become funny and then begin to pall" (*Vestnik Yevropï*, no. 4 [1872]: 895). And funny it is when Musorgsky's Khivrya all at once invites herself to sing: "Enough, Khivrya, no point scolding; come, be merry, sing a song!" One even suspects that Musorgsky was in on the joke, that he was actually lampooning his earlier realist commitment.

EXAMPLE 5, *continued*

b. *Sorochintsï Fair*, act 2, fig. ⟨23⟩

—*So you won't listen to me, you're going to put on airs before me! Who ever saw such a thing, who ever heard of such a thing, that a man all of a sudden stopped listening to his wife and sat around before her like some kind of lord!*
—*That's enough, Khivrya, stop ranting, you'll just wreck your health; your Cherevik knows his Khivrya better than Khivrya*

snatches of "rationally justified melody" in *protyazhnaya* style. The songs proceed Gypsy-fashion (or, alternatively, as per the Italian convention) from slow to fast, ending with a melismatic flourish and a shout, plagiarized (whether unconsciously or parodistically one can never be sure) from the title character's "Varangian Ballad" in the fourth act of Serov's *Rogneda*.

The fast song, *Otkoli ya Brudèusa vstretila* [Ever since meeting Brudeus], the main body of the number, is a strophic concoction—the first stanza adapted from the original folk words, the remaining three set to ersatz folk poetry—with contrasting tempi, harmonization, and figuration on the order of Varlaam's song from *Boris*. What is partic-

EXAMPLE 6. End of Khivrya's song

Tut u - zhe ne di - vo - va - las', s Bru - dè - u - som ras - kvi - ta - las'!

Tut u - zhe ne di - vo - va - las', s Bru - dè - u - som ras - ta - va - las'!

Akh!_____ Ras - ta - va - *3* las!_____ O, gey!

There's nothing to marvel at here. I settled with Brudeus, I left him flat! So there!

ularly interesting is the style of the folk model. It is of the "adulterated" genre Musorgsky had written about to Karmalina, replete with conventional harmonic-minor cadences at the end of each stanza. Musorgsky not only retained these cadences, leading tones and all, he actually enhanced their urban sentimentality by introducing typical Gypsy-style diminished fourths. Moreover, in the earliest version of the song, published as a separate number by the firm of Bernard just after the composer's death, the cadences are adapted even more overtly to Gypsy performance practice by transposition to the chest register (Example 6).

The really startling thing about Khivrya's song is that it was inserted into the opera at the precise point where the 1877 scenario reads "Khivrya's recitatives." Romanticized, popularized *narodnost'* was replacing realist speech-song in the most literal, hence symbolic, way. One could easily imagine Stasov's reaction to all of this if one had to, but one doesn't have to: Stasov recorded his reaction in a couple of letters to Golenishchev-Kutuzov. In one, dated 22 August 1877, he reports that Musorgsky had written "some scene for Khivrya," and that it was *"terribly mediocre and pale."* In another, dated 7 November, he writes that Musorgsky "has written a lot of *rubbish* for *Sorochintsï Fair* this summer, but after everyone's attacks (especially mine), has now decided to throw it all away."[86]

There is no evidence that Musorgsky did any such thing. Everything that he mentioned in his letter to Golenishchev-Kutuzov about

[86] Both letters in MR, 362.

act 2 survives. In the fall of 1877 Musorgsky seems to have embarked on the Fair scene in act 1, adding a couple of Gypsy choruses and the chorus of young girls to the earlier market scene from *Mlada*.[87] Of this music, which quotes a more authentic-sounding variety of folk song, given more properly (from a traditional kuchkist perspective) to a collective body rather than an individual, Stasov had better things to say. Nevertheless, owing perhaps to the less than ecstatic reception his music received from trusted friends, but surely to the sudden death of Osip Petrov in March 1878, Musorgsky lost his momentum, and work on *Sorochintsï Fair* languished for more than a year.

It was his concert tour of South Russia, the Crimea, and the Ukraine as accompanist to Darya Leonova (a trip Stasov had strenuously opposed) that revived Musorgsky's inspiration. He wrote back to Stasov from Yalta with not only a sense of vindication but also a touch of bravado, that "Ukrainian men and women have recognized the character of the music in *Sorochintsï* as completely national [*narodnïm*], as I myself have become convinced having verified it on Ukrainian soil."[88] It must have been under the spell of rehearsing Khivrya's song with Leonova that Musorgsky broke his creative impasse by composing "Parasya's Dumka" for act 3 of the *Fair*, completed (according to the signature on the manuscript fair copy) on 3 July 1879 at Leonova's dacha in Peterhof. In form the Dumka is a veritable remake of Khivrya's song (sans linking recits); in expression it is even more conventionally sentimental; in style it is virtually anonymous. No source melodies have been discovered in it, though some characteristically Polonian Little-Russianisms ("Lombard" rhythms and the like) suggest they lurk. If Musorgsky did compose the tune as well as the saccharine accompaniment, the same must be said of him as Lavrin has said of Gogol: "Matchless in his portraits of the old and the ugly, he was strangely weak as a painter of normal [!] beautiful women."[89]

The rest of the extant *Sorochintsï* manuscripts belong to the last penurious year of their creator's life. The vocal score of the Fair scene, including several dramatic episodes interspersed among choruses, was completed, according to a letter from Musorgsky to Stasov, during the night between 27 and 28 August 1880. The scene is distin-

[87] See the Lamm critical score, act I, figs. 20–23 and 26–30.
[88] 10 September 1879; MusLN 1.254.
[89] *Nikolai Gogol*, p. 54.

EXAMPLE 7. *Sorochintsï Fair*, act 1, three bars after fig. 24

—*What a delight, what a marvel! Oh Daddy, Daddy, get it for me, will you. Ah, a necklace! Look at that necklace! Look how rich it is, just like a lady's!*
—*First let's sell the wheat and the mare.*

guished at last by the total eschewal of anything that could be described as recitative, even in contexts that would normally have called it forth even from the most depraved routinier, let alone one nourished in his formative years at the pure spring of "dramatic truth." At times recitative is replaced by "rationally justified melody," as for example the passage corresponding to no. 3 in the 1877 scenario: "Chumak [i.e., Cherevik] with Parasya (their individualities—wheat—beads)." In the end it turned into a sort of cavatina for Parasya, Cherevik's part shrinking to a single replique—"But first we'll sell the wheat and the mare"—interjected while Parasya, admiring the beads, soars in midphrase (Example 7).

The same could be said of the Gypsy's solo (unmentioned in the 1877 scenario) as of Parasya's: it is a cavatina. The delightful little trio formed by Gritsko's flirtation with Parasya while the Gypsy continues his song has an obvious precedent in *Boris Godunov*: Grishka interrogating the Innkeeper while Varlaam sings his boozy song. But whereas in *Boris* a striking contrast was maintained between the realistic *parlando* of the "speaking" characters as against the drawling cantilena of the "singing" one, here all three characters speak through song. This sixteen-bar passage has the distinction of being the only "normal" beautiful operatic ensemble Musorgsky ever wrote.

In the passage following the trio, the development we have been tracing throughout this discussion of form and expression in *Sorochintsï Fair* reaches a logical conclusion. The scenario at this point reads "Recitative scene of recognition between the Peasant Lad and Chevrik [Cherevik]." What Musorgsky actually composed for this spot is an exchange of repliques sung to the strains of a Ukrainian folk song in mazurka style. (It has already been cited in part in Chapter 3 for its Serovian resonance; much later, perhaps in memoriam, Rimsky-Korsakov would quote it in his own operatic version of "Christmas Eve.") Cherevik's challenge and Gritsko's response form a parallel period. There can be no question here of "rationally justified melody": the tune fits the words poorly, Musorgsky even admitting an occasional distortion of declamation to accommodate the folk melody (e.g., "*s móyey dochkoy*"). Since, moreover, the same tune is sung by both antagonists in turn, it obviously characterizes neither. Not even Serov's folk song recitatives, the evident model here, had ever been so purely folkish or so unrecitativelike (Example 8).[90]

[90] Another striking instance of folk song (this time an imitation *protyazhnaya*) functioning in a manner hitherto reserved for recitative is the "Parabok's Dumka," found only in an undated autograph that prevents its being cited as part of the chronological discussion of the composer's progress through the opera. Most writers (e.g., OrTD, 577) have assumed it to have been one of the numbers Musorgsky is known to have been working on in March and April 1880 (the basis for this supposition being a letter dated 1 May 1880 from Musorgsky to the publisher Bernard, asking that the latter speed the "publication of excerpts," which he had just submitted). Although the only provision made for the item in the 1877 scenario would place it in act 3, all of the arranger/completers of the opera (Cui, Cherepnin, Shebalin) have concluded that the piece as finally written was meant to precede the *Night on Bald Mountain* insert, which quotes its ritornello as a reminiscence. This seems reasonable. Less reasonable is Lamm's and Shebalin's assumption that the "Hopak," which Musorgsky left only in the form of a piano piece, should be the finale of the whole opera rather than that of act 1 (as per the 1877 scenario). Its theme is reprised in act 2, which means it has to be heard before that occurrence. The "Hopak," too, is usually listed among the March–April 1880 manuscripts, but Musorgsky is known to have played it on tour with Leonova (possibly before notating it) in the summer of 1879.

EXAMPLE 8.

a. *Yak pishov ya do divchïnï* (Rubets, *Dvesti shestnadtsat' narodnïkh ukrain-skikh napevov* [1872], transcribed by Musorgsky)

b. *Sorochintsï Fair*, act 1, fig. 37

—*Do you think you can approach my daughter just like that? You think that's okay?*
—*Bah, it's Solopy himself! Greetings, friend! Greetings, Mr. Cherevik.*
—*Wait a minute, pal! How come you know my name is Solopy?*
—*You mean you haven't recognized old Cossack Okhrim's son? Golopupenko's son?*

c. Rimsky-Korsakov, *Christmas Eve*, act 2, scene 2

Hello, dear Solokha, how are you?

VII

Yet none of this talk of retrenchment implies the slightest endorsement of the familiar judgment that (as the *New Grove* would have it) "after 1874 a gradual falling-off in quality is perceptible in all Musorgsky's work."[91] This is the old Stasovian viewpoint that puts an automatic premium on extremism or realism, privileging without warrant a certain category of authorial intention. On the other hand, there can be no gainsaying the fact that Musorgsky's intentions became far more moderate and conventional—which, to a critic, means less interesting—during the years he spent working on his late, unfinished operas. The retreat began earlier than 1874. It had ruled the revision of *Boris*, and emerges just as clearly from a comparison, say, of the *Songs and Dances of Death* (1875–77) with *Nursery* (1868–72) as it does from study of the operas. (But would anyone claim that the later song cycle represented a "falling-off in quality"?) The interesting question is whether the conservative turn in Musorgsky's musical thinking reflected a more general conservatism, the way it did in the case of Chaikovsky.

This is an exceedingly difficult problem to research. Soviet musicography, until very recently, resolutely depicted not only Musorgsky but every great creative artist in nineteenth-century Russia as a "militant realist" and a "liberal democrat" if not a downright "populist" (*narodnik*) at heart.[92] The Soviet model of the Russian intellectual in the nineteenth century is a composite portrait of the so-called *shestidesyatniki* [sixties men] like Chernïshevsky, the apostle of civic and utilitarian aesthetics, or the even more clamorous writer to whose name Nabokov, among others, insists on adding an extra *s*, as if to suggest the nature of his contribution to Russian culture: "Pissarev."[93] In the case of Musorgsky it has meant establishing fac-

---

[91] S.v. "Musorgsky," 12.872.

[92] See, for example, Georgiy Khubov's introductory essay, "Aleksandr Serov, voinstvuyushchiy realist," in SerIS 1.5–66; or Izrail Gusin's introductory essay, "Ts. A. Kyui v bor'be za russkuyu muzïku," in CuiIS. These two articles have been singled out not only as examples of high-Stalinist musicography but because their subjects were confirmed political reactionaries in life.

[93] Nabokov, *Gogol*, p. 128; also Stravinsky, in *La Poétique musicale*, where he speaks of "the dark period of the years 1860 to 1880, the period of the Chernyshevskys, the Dobrolyubovs, the Pissarevs, when a perfidious wave that defiled the true foundations of culture and the state welled up from the milieu of false intellectuals, morally disinherited and socially uprooted, and from the centers of atheistic seminarists and flunked-out students" (*Poetics of Music in the Form of Six Lessons*, trans. Arthur Knodel

titious connections with radical historians like Afanasiy Shchapov or with out-and-out revolutionaries like Ivan Khudyakov.[94] It has also meant sanitizing his epistolary legacy, which has had "complete" bowdlerized editions only in Soviet times.

Of course Musorgsky is not the only famous Russian musician whose image has been retouched by the Soviets. One of the main tasks has been to rid everyone's published correspondence of all trace of "normal" Russian anti-Semitism. Robert Ridenour has shown that the offensive epithet *zhid*, for Jew, has been purged from the published letters of Glinka, Balakirev, and Borodin, besides Musorgsky.[95] It is often pointed out in extenuation that use of that word was too widespread and accepted among Russians at the time to count as a mark of anti-Semitism; yet it does not occur in everyone's correspondence. Rimsky-Korsakov's, for example, seems free of it— and Musorgsky's oft-maligned arranger gave the best possible evidence of his tolerance for Jews by encouraging his daughter to marry his pupil Maximilian Steinberg.[96] Rimsky's behavior in 1905, when he got into some real trouble for his support of political activism among the students at the St. Petersburg Conservatory, also testifies to his liberalism, as does his openly professed agnosticism (of which we have been informed chiefly by Stravinsky, who indignantly disapproved). In all of these traits he seems to have been quite alone among the members of the mighty kuchka.

By contrast, Musorgsky went far beyond the mere use of the word *zhid* in professing his anti-Semitism. A letter of consolation he wrote to Balakirev (a really violent anti-Semite) during the latter's trying stay in Prague during the 1867 opera season, is peppered with tidbits like these: "I am seized with the impulse to bar Germans, Italians, or (what's the difference?) our own Russian *zhidy* from coming to swindle good-natured Russians"; "force me to sing one of Mendel's lieds, and I will turn from a gentle, polished soul into an uncouth boor";

---

and Ingolf Dahl [Cambridge: Harvard University Press, 1970], p. 131). Stravinsky is describing the class known as *raznochintsï*, to which Musorgsky, a hereditary aristocrat, is often quite incorrectly assigned.

[94] See Marina Rakhmaninova, "Musorgskiy i ego vremya," SovM, no. 9 (1980): 101–10; Mikhail Pekelis, "Musorgskiy—Pisatel'-dramaturg," introductory article to MusLN 2.5–34, especially pp. 26–30. The tendentious thesis of the latter article is disseminated in English by Richard Hoops in "Musorgsky and the Populist Age," MusIM, 288–89.

[95] *Nationalism, Modernism, and Personal Rivalry in Nineteenth-Century Russian Music* (Ann Arbor: UMI Research Press, 1981), pp. 83–84, 104n.135, etc.

[96] His son Andrey also married a Jew, the composer Julia Weisberg.

and finally, something downright sinister about folk songs and nationalism:

> A people or a society insensitive to sounds that—like memories of one's mother or of one's closest friend—ought to set all a person's vital strings aquiver, awaken him from the deepest sleep, make him realize both his uniqueness and the oppression that lies upon him and gradually saps that uniqueness—such a society, such a people is a *corpse*, and its chosen ones are doctors who by means of an electrogalvanic shock force that corpse-nation's limbs to jerk, so long as it has not gone over into utter chemical decomposition. The *zhidy* leap up at the sound of their songs, handed down from generation to generation. Their eyes blaze with an honest, not a mercenary, fire, and their loathsome mugs straighten out into something almost human—I've seen this happen more than once. The *zhidy* are better than the Czechs—our own Bialystok, Lutsk, and Nevel *zhidy*, who live in filth in their stinking shacks.[97]

Like many anti-Semites, Musorgsky drew a fundamental distinction between the *yevrei*, the biblical Hebrews or Israelites, who symbolized proud archaic manliness and nationhood, and the *zhid*, the contemptible diaspora Jew encountered in everyday life, who embodied nothing more than petulance, rootlessness, and greed.[98] Serov, whose letters were as replete as Musorgsky's with fulminations against *zhidy*, wrote an entire opera glorifying the *yevrei*. Musorgsky, in a letter to Balakirev concerning that opera, *Judith*, carefully uses the word *yevrey* to refer to Serov's characters, reverting to *zhid* for the likes of Leschetizky, Rubinstein, and so on.[99] In the same year as the letter about the *zhidy* of Bialystok, Lutsk, and Nevel, Musorgsky wrote his *Yevreyskaya pesnya*, his "Hebrew Song," to words from the Song of Solomon as translated by Lev Mey. (As late as 1879, on tour with Leonova, Musorgsky would drop in on synagogue services in Odessa to enjoy the ancient "Israelite" [*izraíl'skikh*] melodies.)[100] Stasov extolled the Hebrew song for its "profound Oriental shading," one of the prime attributes, for Stasov, of true "Russian"

---

[97] 26 January 1867; MusLN 1.84–85. In all cases the Soviet editors have suppressed the word *zhidy*, substituting the more proper Russian word *yevrei*. Beginning with MusLN the substitution has been signaled by the use of brackets, permitting the reconstruction of the original text.

[98] For an interesting parallel, see the discussion of the American "Brahmins" and their distinction between the "noble ancient Hebrew" and the "repugnant modern Jew," in Macdonald Smith Moore, *Yankee Blues: Musical Culture and American Identity* (Bloomington: Indiana University Press, 1985), pp. 130–35.

[99] 10 June 1863; MusLN 1.69.

[100] Letter to Stasov, 10 September 1879 (MusLN 1.254; MR, 394).

EXAMPLE 9.
a. Musorgsky, *Yevreyskaya pesnya* (1867)

I am the flower of the field; I am the lily of the valley.

b. Rimsky-Korsakov, *Yevreyskaya pesnya*, Op. 7, no. 2 (1867)

I sleep, and yet my tender heart sleeps not. Behind the door I hear my beloved's voice:

c. Balakirev, *Yevreyskaya melodiya* (1859)

My soul is gloomy. Quick, singer, quick! Here is your golden harp:

style. Actually, Stasov might better have been describing not Musorgsky's song but its companion piece, Rimsky-Korsakov's *Yevreyskaya pesnya* (op. 7, no. 2), also to a Mey translation, composed the same year, and dedicated to Musorgsky. The two songs had a common prototype, Balakirev's *Yevreyskaya melodiya* (1859), to a translation by Lermontov of one of Byron's Hebrew Melodies (Example 9).

Of the three, Rimsky's is the most stereotypically "Eastern." It smacks more of the harem than of the temple, deriving directly from the Orientalisms in *Ruslan and Lyudmila* by way of Balakirev's "Geor-

gian Song" of 1863 (to Pushkin's "Leave off thy singing, maiden fair
. . ."), and is stylistically indistinguishable from Rimsky's own "Oriental romance" of 1866, "The Nightingale and the Rose," to words
by Alexey Koltsov. By contrast, Musorgsky's "Hebrew" compositions—which, besides the *Yevreyskaya pesnya*, include "King Saul"
(1861) after Byron, and two choruses: "The Destruction of Sennacherib" (*Porazheniye Sennakheriba*, 1867) and "Joshua" (*Iisus Navin*,
1877), the last actually based on the theme of a wordless Hasidic *ni-
gun* Musorgsky had used first in *Salammbô*[101]—do not revert to the
hackneyed Orientalisms we find in Rimsky's and Balakirev's compositions. In particular, we will scour them practically in vain for an
augmented second, that easiest and most trivial of "Jewish" devices.
Clearly, it was not the picturesqueness of the Hebrews that captured
Musorgsky's imagination but their virility and their aggressive nationalism.

Yet unlike Rimsky and even Balakirev, Musorgsky did not portray
only *yevrei* in his music. Alone among his colleagues, he also portrayed *zhidy*—and here is where we find augmented seconds in car-
toonish abundance. We have only to recall the familiar suite *Pictures
at an Exhibition*, with its distasteful portrayal of two loathsome Jewish
mugs (or is it only one?).[102] And in the opening market scene of *Sorochintsï Fair* there is a pair of whining "burlesque Jews," vying un-
becomingly with the Gypsies (Example 10).

In Lamm's critical edition, the singers of this music are designated
yevrei, but the brackets around the word leave no doubt what was

[101] Boris Schwarz, "Musorgsky's Interest in Judaica," in MusIM, 90–92. Ultimately,
the "Hebraic" line in nineteenth-century Russian music goes back to Glinka and the
Yevreyskaya pesnya from his incidental music to Nestor Kukolnik's drama *Prince Kholm-
sky* (1840). Glinka's song, aggressive and martial, is not at all Orientalist in character.

[102] The title of the piece is rarely if ever correctly transcribed: " 'Samuel' Goldenburg
und 'Schmuÿle.' " The use of quotation marks points up the fact that the two *zhidy*
have the same first name: one Germanized, the other in the original Yiddish. They are
in fact one *zhid*, not two. The portrayal is a brazen insult: no matter how dignified or
sophisticated or Europeanized a *zhid*'s exterior, on the inside he is a jabbering, pester-
ing little "Schmuÿle." The sanitized title by which the piece is generally known, "Two
Jews: Rich and Poor" (*Dva yevreya: bogatïy i bednïy*), originated in Stasov's 1881 obituary
for the composer (see StasIS 2.209n). It was taken over by Lamm in his critical edition
(MusPSS 8; MusCW 17), where Musorgsky's original title was suppressed. There is,
by the way, no extant picture by Victor Gartman that shows two Jews, and none bearing the title of Musorgsky's piano piece. It is usually assumed, on Stasov's say-so, that
the composer conflated two different portraits of Sandomierz Jews. If that is true, the
title and all its implications are Musorgsky's alone. The exact form of the title may be
verified by comparison with the published facsimile of the holograph fair copy: M. P.
Musorgsky, *Kartinki s vïstavki: faksimile* (Moscow: Muzïka, 1975).

EXAMPLE 10. *Sorochintsï Fair*, act 1, fig. ⬚19⬚

Zha - luy - te, pa - no - ve, zha - luy - te, nam v yat - ku!

Sa - mïkh vin luch-shai - shikh vï u nas nai-dyo - te.

Vsyo che - go kho - ti - te, vsyo u nas nai-dyo - te.

Net ta - koy uzh ve - shchi, chto - bï ne na - shla - sya!

Favor us, milords, favor us with a visit to our tent! You'll find the very finest wines here.
You'll find everything you want here. There is nothing you won't find!

written in Musorgsky's "Autograph no. 293" at the Taneyev Library of the Moscow Conservatory. Later on, the "Tale of the Red Jacket" is all about a *zhid* pawnbroker whose greed was his undoing. Musorgsky's setting breaks off after one line, before the *zhid* is mentioned; but as that line is set to Gogol's unaltered text there is no reason to suppose that Musorgsky would have flinched from setting the word. In Lamm's edition, where the music for the narrative was supplied by Shebalin, the *zhid* becomes a *ded* (old man, literally, "grandpa"); but this deprives the story of its point. Pigs' heads appearing at the window are an insult to a *zhid*, not a *ded*.

VIII

From what has been said, it is evident that Musorgsky was Russia's most conspicuously anti-Semitic composer. Even Balakirev's anti-Semitism must be discovered in his personal utterances and biographical impedimenta, not his musical works. But Musorgsky put his into his works, and *Sorochintsï Fair* stands out among its manifestations. This in itself constitutes a link between the opera and official reaction in Russia.

Nor should it surprise us in a man of Musorgsky's social background. Though the fact is often forgotten if not actually repressed, he was a personage of high birth. His lineage derived from the medieval princes of Smolensk, his family being mentioned in the "velvet book" (*barkhatnaya kniga*), the sixteenth-century genealogy of the boyars that more or less defined blue blood in prerevolutionary Russia. By the nineteenth century the Musor(g)skys had lost their princely title, but they were still large landowners in the Pskov and Yaroslavl districts of north central Russia. The composer's father, Pyotr Alexeyevich Musorsky, was the son of an elite guards officer of the Preobrazhensky Regiment, the tsar's own corps of bodyguards that had been created by Peter the Great (and which represents their creator in *Khovanshchina*). Many Musor(g)skys of earlier generations had also been distinguished in arms. The composer's mother also came from a venerable gentry family, the Chirikovs (cf. Gogol's Chichikov, the déclassé hero of *Dead Souls*), who had intermarried extensively with the Golenishchev-Kutuzovs, another old boyar line.[103] As is well known, the composer had been groomed for a life in his grandfather's footsteps, and as late as 1880 referred to himself as "a scion of an ancient Russian family (*boyard*)."[104] Borodin, who chanced to meet Musorgsky as a seventeen-year-old Preobrazhensky cadet, recalled him as being "aristocratic, somewhat foppish, and extraordinarily well-bred."[105] According to Nadezhda Purgold (Rimskaya-Korsakova), he never lost his "elegant, aristocratic" manners or "the air of a well-bred society man."[106]

His eventual poverty was brought about by the abolition of serfdom in 1861. It was the consequent loss of the income from his family estates that forced Musorgsky to seek refuge within the huge Russian civil-service bureaucracy, where he was given a series of sinecures. In all of this the composer's outward career was very typical of the déclassé nobility. His embittered, alcoholic fate, too, was a sadly common lot for members of the suddenly impoverished petty gentry.

Nor is there any reason to assume that he ever betrayed his class interests and attitudes. He was not a "civic" artist. The voice that

---

[103] See Vyacheslav Karatïgin, "Rodoslovnaya M. P. Musorgskogo po muzhskoy i zhenskoy liniyam," *Muzïkal'nïy sovremennik* 5–6 (1917): 15–16.

[104] "Avtobiograficheskaya zapiska," MusLN 1.267. This note was prepared for the Riemann Lexicon; the word *boyard* appears only in the French version, which was not collated with the Russian text translated in MR, 416.

[105] MR, 3.

[106] N. N. Rimskaya-Korsakova, "Iz moikh vospominaniyakh ob A. S. Dargomïzhskom," *Russkaya molva*, no. 53 (2 February 1913); trans. MR, 106.

speaks from the *Sunless* cycle is that of a neurotically self-absorbed, broken-down aristocrat. That was Musorgsky by 1874. The voice that speaks from *The Nursery* is that of a pampered gentry brat. That, too, was a self-portrait, and a very nostalgic one. The peasant types that abound in his songs and operas of the 1860s are objectively drawn life-portraits motivated by Musorgsky's peculiar scientistic views of the period, not by any hint of sentimental identification. The portrayal of the crowd in *Boris* and (especially) *Khovanshchina* is unflattering. His reputation as a *narodnik* or radical democrat notwithstanding, the composer's correspondence gives no hint of any such involvement. Belinsky, Chernïshevsky, Pisarev—these names will be absent from the index to any collection of Musorgsky's letters (save, of course, the editorial commentary). His one epistolary reference to Dobrolyubov, the most ardent radical of all, is ironic.[107]

Musorgsky's reputation as a populist outside of Russia is bolstered by a great deal of faulty translation. Loose articles have played more havoc with Musorgsky's reputation than anything else. It is true that Musorgsky often described his artistic aims in terms of "communicating with people," or "conversing with sensible people," or even "giving one's whole self to people." But none of this gives evidence of political commitment, for in all cases he used the word *lyudi*—"people" as the plural of "person"—not the word *narod*, which is what translates into English as "the people."[108] To the latter, this composer never spoke, nor wished to.

With whom *did* he speak? Who were his "sensible people"? The only reliable answer would consist in a list of his correspondents, his dedicatees, and persons for whom Musorgsky expressed admiration. If we exclude from the list his fellow musicians and recipients of non-committal or purely business messages, the composer's correspondents during the last six years of his life, the period of *Sorochintsï Fair*, can be narrowed down to half a dozen or so significant names. In addition to lifelong friends and supporters like Stasov and Shestakova they included some interesting new acquaintances.

First, there were the "revolting sots and slime of the crudest, low-

---

[107] MusLN 1.257.

[108] For an example of how much can hinge on the presence or absence of an article, see Hoops, "Musorgsky and the Populist Age," MusIM, 292, where an argument for the composer's commitment to populism is educed from a mistranslation of this kind in Leyda and Bertensson's *Musorgsky Reader*. Musorgsky's *lyudi* is rendered there as "the people," implying *narod*; and this in turn becomes "the masses" in Hoops's discussion.

est sort: all these drinking buddies at the Malïy Yaroslavets," which is how a distraught Stasov described the friends and companions of Musorgsky's last years, notably one Pavel Alexanderovich Naumov, with whom Musorgsky boarded for a while and with whom he was photographed in 1880, a retired naval officer and self-proclaimed "good-for-nothing" to whom Musorgsky sent back some revealing letters from his concert tour in 1879.[109] They show certain of his attitudes to have changed little since his letters to Balakirev in the 1860s: "The other side of the coin here in Poltava," he complained in one of them, "is the *zhidy*; soon the city itself and the whole birthright of the Poltavians will be in *zhid* hands. The Poltavians themselves acknowledge this, and the *zhidy* act just so for the sake of support from you-know-where."[110]

In a second group, there was Ivan Fyodorovich Gorbunov, the actor and raconteur and folk song connoisseur from whom Musorgsky had taken down the melody that would become Marfa's song in *Khovanshchina*. A very interesting letter from Musorgsky to Gorbunov survives from January 1880, in which the composer recalls a toast Gorbunov had made to Tertiy Ivanovich Filippov (1825–99), whom Musorgsky describes as "dear to Russian folk." Not all Russian folk: anyone with even mildly liberal sympathies reviled him. Filippov was one of the most exalted bureaucrats in Russia—the imperial controller, no less, who held the purse strings of the Empire—and a mainstay of what was left of Official Nationality in the reign of Alexander II. Rimsky-Korsakov thought him a fossil, one of the "ancient bulwarks of absolute monarchy, . . . of religion, Orthodox faith, and remnants of Slavophilism."[111] Filippov was also, and not at all by accident, perhaps the most fanatical connoisseur of folk songs in Russia. It was a mania that went back to his days on the editorial board of the journal *Moskvityanin*, where he worked alongside Alexander Ostrovsky, Apollon Grigoryev, and other future *pochvenniki*. Inevitably, his passion for folk song brought him into contact with

[109] MR, 220. Stasov's epithets are from a letter to Balakirev from Paris (18/30 August 1878; BalStasP 1.309).

[110] MusLN 1.245 (the passage had been censored out of all previous editions of Musorgsky's correspondence). The Jewish editors of MusLN intervene at this point to assure the reader that "despite what might seem to be the blatantly anti-Semitic character of these lines, knowing Musorgsky's outlook, as well as his personal friendships and creative inclinations, this sally is to be explained not by the composer's chauvinistic views but by his antipathy toward the bourgeois mercantile element in general" (MusLN 1.354, n. 6 to letter 249).

[111] R-KMusL, 264–65.

the composers of the New Russian School; first with Balakirev, a notorious like-thinker, thence with the others.[112]

Filippov was one of the most important persons in Musorgsky's life during the years when *Sorochintsï Fair* was gestating. From 1878 to 1880 he was Musorgsky's very indulgent nominal boss, having arranged for the composer's transfer to the Office of Government Control when he was on the point of being fired from his job at the Ministry of Forests.[113] Later Filippov was instrumental in arranging a pension for Musorgsky in the guise of a commission to complete *Khovanshchina*.[114] Finally, he became Musorgsky's executor.[115] That a nationalist of the Old Guard like Filippov should have been so drawn to Musorgsky must inevitably color not only our perception of the continuing significance of folk song within Russian art music but also our perception of Musorgsky's return to it as a source of creative inspiration. Obviously, too, Filippov could have seen no radical democrat or populist in Musorgsky, and the way Musorgsky reciprocated the imperial controller's affection suggests that the latter had made no mistake.

Finally, and most important by far, there was Count Golenishchev-Kutuzov, the poet of *Sunless* and the *Songs and Dances of Death*, as well as the memoirs described closely in the Introduction to this book. Over seven years, beginning in 1873, Musorgsky sent him a total of twenty-six surviving letters, making Golenishchev-Kutuzov, in terms of volume, his third-ranking correspondent (after Stasov and Balakirev). There would surely have been more letters had the two men not spent the years 1874–75 as roommates. The letters we have reveal an enormous emotional dependence. Time and again Musorgsky exclaims that only Kutuzov now understood him, forsaken as he was by his old brethren-in-arms. One such letter concerns *Sorochintsï Fair* directly:

---

[112] Filippov actually collaborated with Rimsky-Korsakov on a volume of harmonized folk songs: *40 narodnïkh pesen, sobrannïkh T. I. Filippovïm i garmonizovannïkh N. A. Rimskim Korsakovïm* (Moscow: Jurgenson, 1882). It contained a high proportion of "spiritual verses" (*dukhovnïye stikhi*), some of which found their way into the late operas and choral works of his collaborator (*Sadko, Kitezh*). In his memoirs, Rimsky-Korsakov looked back on his association with Filippov as a sort of martyrdom endured for the sake of art (and possibly money—see R-KMusL, 164).

[113] See the memoir by Nikolai Lavrov in MR, 371–72.

[114] See Stasov to Balakirev, 14 January 1880 (BalStasP 1.334).

[115] See the deed of transfer of rights drawn up and executed two days before Musorgsky's death (14 March 1881), MR, 413–14.

I'll begin with the fact that at the first showing of the second act of *Sorochintsï* I became convinced of the basic lack of understanding of Little-Russian comedy on the part of the *musici* of the disintegrated "kuchka." Such a deep freeze radiated from their views and demands, that "my heart did congeal," as Archpriest Avvakum would say [also Dosifey in the first act of *Khovanshchina*]. . . . It's annoying to have to talk to the *musici* of the disintegrated "kuchka" from across the barrier behind which they have remained. . . . If you'd like as a sample one of the aforementioned *musici*'s many pronouncements, here it is: "The text contains the most commonplace, everyday prose, so insignificant it's laughable, yet in the music all these people are very serious—they invest their utterances with a sort of importance." Curious, no? . . . You, O friend, will see praise in the pronouncement of the "kuchkist" which I have adduced; but believe me, friend, it was uttered as a severe criticism of the opera's fundamental flaws.[116]

Musorgsky introduced Golenishchev-Kutuzov to Stasov in a letter that is somehow overlooked by those who would make a populist of the composer. It takes the form of a sustained invidious comparison between Kutuzov and Nikolai Nekrasov, whose verses Musorgsky had set twice in the mid-sixties and who is so often portrayed as the composer's poetic counterpart.[117]

Since Pushkin and Lermontov I have not encountered what I encountered in Kutuzov: this is no simulated poet like Nekrasov, and without Mey's sense of strain (though I prefer Mey to Nekrasov). . . . It is noteworthy that in his university days (at a time when, etc. [i.e., when students were politically active and protests followed by reprisals were the order of the day]) our youthful poet (and he is *very* youthful) was not carried away by civic themes, that is, he did not submit to fashion and ape Mr. Nekrasov's grimaces, but hammered into verse those thoughts that occupied *him*, and those longings that were inherent in *his own* ar-

[116] 10 November 1877; MusLN 1.234–35. The editors assume the "kuchkist" in question to have been Cui; but it seems virtually certain that Musorgsky had Stasov in mind—first because we know from Stasov's own letter to Golenishchev-Kutuzov, quoted above, what he thought of the work Musorgsky had produced during the summer of 1877, and that he expressed himself forthrightly on the matter to the composer's face; and second, because the person most likely to be ironically identified by Musorgsky as a "kuchkist" would not have been a fellow composer but rather the man who had actually been unwittingly responsible for the unflattering sobriquet *moguchaya kuchka*, coined ten years earlier in a review.

[117] E.g., by Hoops ("Musorgsky and the Populist Age," MusIM, 284). Emiliya Frid, devoting an entire essay to this spurious congruence, goes through some extraordinary contortions to explain this letter away on the basis of Musorgsky's presumed involvement in the sectarian literary politics of the 1860s ("O nekrasovskom nachale v tvorchestve Musorgskogo," FridMPM, 25–47).

tistic nature. This *lordliness of mind* especially pleased me when I glanced at Kutuzov's notebooks (here in pencil, there in pen, there a blank page—a photograph of an artist's mental activity). . . . And how he is drawn to the people, to history! One more thing I'll relate: a poet can treat with complete sincerity what he has found out *at close hand*: and so Kutuzov has done: not a single civic motif, not the slightest Nekrasov-esque *Weltschmerz*.[118]

This curiously formal encomium reads like nothing so much as a job recommendation (in view of the recipient, a strangely maladroit one). As we know, it inspired nothing but suspicion in Stasov. Indeed, to Stasov, the dreamy, decadent Golenishchev-Kutuzov was first, last, and always a threat. Toward the end of his hagiographical necrology for his departed friend, written in the year of Musorgsky's death, one laconic paragraph in a single sentence stands out from the rest of Stasov's fevered prose for its sudden arctic plunge in temperature. "Two series of songs from the last period, one entitled *Sunless* (1874), to words by his friend Count Kutuzov, the other to words by Count Alexey Tolstoy (1877) already contain little by which one might recognize the earlier Musorgsky."[119]

Count this and Count that . . . was Musorgsky really hankering after the nobility in his last years? So it would appear. In a postscript to the very letter in which he unveiled his idea of "rationally justified melody," he informed Stasov that he was moving *"dans les plus hauts rangs,"* and that his "position is hopeful." Nor was this Stasov's first intimation of his friend's burgeoning identification with what was after all his own hereditary class. As early as August 1873, when *Khovanshchina* was still in the planning stage, Stasov sent Musorgsky his frank response to the way the libretto was turning out:

All that you've planned for [Marfa] is *excellent*, but what the devil pushes you to make her—a Princess?!! The entire opera will finally consist so exclusively of princes and princesses that it will be a chronicle of *princely spawn*!! Golitsïn—a Prince, Khovansky senior—a Prince, Khovansky junior—a Prince, you plan Dosifey as the former Prince Mïshetsky, [Marfa] as the Princess Sitskaya. What is this finally to be, an *opera of princes*? I thought you were planning an opera of the *people*.[120]

[118] 19 June 1873; MusLN 1.149. In later life Golenishchev-Kutuzov would amply justify the impression his early works made on Musorgsky (see the Introduction to this book).

[119] StasIS 2.212.

[120] MR, 244.

So much for Musorgsky the populist. It is just as easy to portray him as a bigoted blue-blood, conventionalizing his music in accordance with aristocratic taste; a social climber fawning on highly placed bureaucrats, deriding artists with a social mission in favor of romantic solipsists, and cultivating the folkloristic genre as a way of reasserting the old *narodnost'* that was part of an ancient and rickety troika with *pravoslaviye* and *samoderzhaviye*. It is easier, in fact, to portray him so, for the portrait rests on some solid facts and documents, while the image of Musorgsky as populist or radical democrat depends on a host of perhapses, presumablies, if-thens, and not-impossibles, with Herr Zeitgeist in the lead role.

IX

One of Musorgsky's last finished compositions will furnish a final illustration. In 1880 the twenty-fifth anniversary of the reign of Tsar Alexander II was celebrated. The festivities were to culminate on 19 February in a gala at the St. Petersburg Bolshoy Theater, and were to take the form of a court spectacle reminiscent of eighteenth-century odes or even Renaissance *intermedii*: a series of *tableaux vivants*, each depicting one of the outstanding triumphs, conquests, or military adventures of Alexander's reign. They were to be accompanied by specially commissioned music and linked by a text in the form of a dialogue between the Muse of History and the Spirit (*geniy*) of Russia. Music was commissioned from a dozen prominent Russian composers, including Rimsky-Korsakov (a prefatory *Slava!* on the familiar tune), Borodin (the popular *In Central Asia*, celebrating Russian expansion to the east), and Chaikovsky (a now-lost composition for small orchestra—but very noisy, as the composer confessed—entitled "Montenegro" [*Chernogoriya*], to accompany a tableau depicting Russia's declaration of war on Turkey in the Balkan disturbances of 1877).

For this orgy of reactionary official nationalism Musorgsky was assigned the task of accompanying a tableau depicting the capture of the Turkish fortress of Kars in the Caucasus in 1855—Russia's only important victory during the Crimean War, which happened to take place right after Alexander's accession to the throne, and which enabled him to save some face when, after the disastrous siege of Sevastopol, he finally sued for peace. Musorgsky accepted this commission with alacrity, dusting off the "March of the Princes and Priests" from the old *Mlada* score (his only other quasi-official commission), replacing its trio (contributed at the time by then-roommate Rimsky-Korsakov) with a seat-of-the-pants concoction based on "some Kurdish theme," as Rimsky recalled, which is why the piece is now generally known as Musorgsky's "Turkish March."[121] The main theme of the march, meanwhile, was a Russian khorovod tune from Balakirev's collection,[122] so that when the trio gave way to the reprise of the march da capo, it could be heard as a triumph by the Russians over the Turks.

The use of "national" songs was of course de rigueur in hack work like this: witness *1812*, or even more to the point, the *zhid* Rubinstein's *Ouverture triomphale*, op. 43, composed in 1855 for Alexander's coronation. Even compared with a piece like Chaikovsky's "Festival Coronation March" for Alexander III, composed in a hurry a few years later after the object of the 1880 festivities had been assassinated, Musorgsky's march was a flimsy piece of work. It was a major event in his career, though, and if he had not died unexpectedly so soon after composing it, it would surely look to us now like a turning point.

For by the time of Musorgsky's demise the mighty kuchka was being unmistakably drawn into the establishment, and there is no reason to assume Musorgsky would have resisted. Indeed, the kuchkists were never quite so far outside the pale of official patronage as is popularly believed. Balakirev's Free Music School, the kuchkist forum par excellence, enjoyed the protection of the Crown Prince Nikolai from its second year of existence, and after Nikolai's untimely death, patronage of the school was assumed by his brother, the future Alexander III. Musorgsky benefited from this patronage along with his fellows, and in later life might well have gone the way of his kuchkist brethren Balakirev, who ended up writing hymns to the dowager empress and other members of the imperial family, or Cui, who was given the signal honor of composing the official cantata to mark the Romanov tercentenary in 1913.

As it happened, the Bolshoy gala, like the earlier *Mlada*, did not come off as planned, and *The Capture of Kars* did not accompany a tableau vivant after all. Instead, it was performed under the august aristocratic auspices of the Russian Musical Society—the reputed

---

[121] R-KMusL, 216.
[122] No. 20: *Kak po lugu, lugu* [As we go round the meadow].

archenemy of the mighty kuchka and the Free Music School—where it shared the program with *In Central Asia* under Eduard Nápravník's baton. According to Cui's review, the composer was called out and greeted with a round of applause.[123]

Just on the point of death, Musorgsky was arriving. And if it cannot be said that he was arriving with all his old ideals intact, that is because those ideals were in part a response and a reaction to his outsider's status. The composer of *Sorochintsï Fair* was no longer a cloistered Pimen of music, laboriously penning his scrolls of Truth far from the seats of power. He was now a member of the musical duma at the very least, and at times, as in *The Capture of Kars*, he was even a bit of a pretender. But we need not censure out of hand the conventionalisms in *Sorochintsï Fair*, or the occasional descents into claptrap like the "Turkish March." Both testify to the beginnings of professionalism, something that has its good sides as well as its bad ones. As Rimsky-Korsakov put it a decade and a half after Musorgsky's tragic death, in a letter to his disciple Semyon Kruglikov that contained a report of his summer's crop of compositions (forty romances, two duets, a one-act opera, a cantata, and a piano trio): "You are no doubt amazed? Well, there's nothing to be amazed at; that's the way it ought to be. Already thirty years have passed since the days when Stasov would write that in eighteen-sixty-so-and-so the Russian School displayed a lively activity: Lodïzhensky wrote one romance, Borodin got an idea for something, Balakirev was planning to rework something, and so on. It's time to forget all that and *travel a normal artistic path*."[124]

X

The composer of *Sorochintsï Fair* was beginning to travel that path. A normal artistic path meant working on commission and under a deadline. So it was with *Sorochintsï*: in February 1881 Musorgsky accepted a commission from an old friend from his miliary school days, Fyodor Ardalionovich Vanlyarsky, now a prominent banker,[125] to finish the opera within a year, and as an earnest of his progress to issue

[123] OrTD, 587.

[124] Andrey Nikolayevich Rimsky-Korsakov, *N. A. Rimskiy-Korsakov* (Moscow: Muzgiz, 1937), vol. 4, p. 10.

[125] Musorgsky had dedicated one of the Tolstoy songs of 1877 (*Ne bozhim gromom gorye udarilo*) to Vanlyarsky.

individual numbers through the publishing house of Bernard. "Khivrya's Song," "Parasya's Dumka," the "Hopak," and possibly the "Peasant Lad's Dumka" were submitted to be printed in this way, and the terms of the agreement with Vanlyarsky must have told on the sectional format of the opera. In particular they must account for the rather formal buffo duet of Kum and Cherevik (presumably for act 1, and inserted there by all the opera's completers) that does not correspond to the draft scenario, and does not contribute materially to the action.

A normal artistic path meant collaborating actively with performers and writing with specific executants in mind. So it was with *Sorochintsï*: roles were envisioned for the Petrovs, and after Osip Petrov's death, for Leonova. It was true of *Khovanshchina*, too. Shaklovitïy's act 3 aria, seemingly unmotivated or even at odds with the general portrayal of the character who sings it (and which Stravinsky was certainly not alone in finding "banal"),[126] was inserted as a vehicle for Ivan Melnikov, the creator of the role of Boris Godunov, whom Musorgsky envisioned as Shaklovitïy's creator as well.

A normal artistic path, finally, meant tilting not only with aesthetic windmills but with the practical exigencies of performance and the stage. *Boris* had been conceived without a prima donna role. The second act of *Khovanshchina* was to have ended with an oddly assorted quintet that included three basses. *Sorochintsï Fair* had a normal cast of characters at last, and each of the major roles was to have a solo turn. The numbers format and the character of the melodies, "rationally justified" or not, suggest that Musorgsky was planning, as Borodin once put it in his famous letter to Karmalina, to downplay "small forms, details, niceties," and to "paint in bold strokes, clearly, vividly, and as practicably as possible, from both the vocal and the orchestral standpoint."[127]

Had Musorgsky lived a normal span of years, such that *Boris Godunov* would be regarded as an early work, *Sorochintsï Fair* would very likely look to us like a pivotal one. What we think of as the essential Musorgsky would look like his growth phase, and what we think of as his late "falling-off" would look like his *prise de contact* with the mainstream of Russian artistic and social life as it was lived in his time. That mainstream was not in all ways an attractive or an

---

[126] Igor Stravinsky and Robert Craft, *Conversations with Igor Stravinsky* (Garden City, N.Y.: Doubleday, 1959), p. 67.

[127] 1 June 1876; BorP 2.109.

exalted one. By living longer, Musorgsky could as easily have lost in historical stature as gained.

But it has certainly not been the purpose of this chapter to diminish that stature. On the contrary, I have pushed hard for a more balanced point of view on Musorgsky's achievement precisely because I believe that the reductive categories to which conventional historiography assigns Russian composers have diminished him—as they have certainly diminished Chaikovsky—and, to speak more broadly, that the reductive viewpoint usually adopted on Russian music has diminished it generally. As a great scholar once put it, concluding a masterpiece of musicological revisionism, "I have stated the case as forcefully as I know how, which probably means I have overstated it; if so, the overstatement should be taken as, in all modesty, corrective in intent."[128]

At the very least, it should be apparent what was meant at the outset of this investigation by a Pandora's box. After the evil spirits of Official Nationality, anti-Semitism, aristocratic pretension, and revolutions betrayed have swirled about our heads, beaten their wings, and flown abroad into the world, what hope is left? Just this: that by getting beyond the facile categories and the shopworn propaganda—and by discarding the composer's flawed and unattractive person as finally irrelevant to the import of his greatest works—we may yet overcome the obstacles that have impeded the "human exchange" (*beseda s lyud'mi*) Musorgsky saw as the overriding purpose of his art.

[128] Richard L. Crocker, "The Troping Hypothesis," *Musical Quarterly* 52 (1966): 203.

Epilogue

MUSORGSKY IN THE
AGE OF *GLASNOST'*

"IF *Boris Godunov* and especially *Khovanshchina* had appeared in 1970s rather than the 1870s, . . . they would not have been allowed on stage or in print."[1] Thus did Sergey Slonimsky, the Leningrad composer, assert in a special number of *Sovetskaya muzïka*, issued in March 1989 to mark the sesquicentennial of Musorgsky's birth. The well-timed jubilee became the occasion for the composer's recanonization. So far from the proto-Soviet populist of old, he was now to be consecrated as the grim prophet of the Soviet tyranny. "Musorgsky foresaw and foretold much," Slonimsky declared. "He beheld the past not only in the present but in the future." His dramas of power politics and crazed cowed crowds would continue to point an implacable finger wherever a finger needed pointing.

It is through the "panoramic vision of history," a vision that includes all that was future to Musorgsky but is past to us, that we can now draw sustenance from his dramas, writes Slonimsky. Such a view judges the works as well as the times. It has diminished the figure of Tsar Boris—"operatic, consummately theatrical, actorish"—because we have learned from Stalin, from Beria (more recently from the obscenely long-lived Molotov and Kaganovich), that a tyrant may fear for his own safety but is immune from conscience.

What seizes the imagination now is Musorgsky's divided crowd in all its frightening credulity. In his peasants and mysteriously rootless "new arrivals" (*prishlïye lyudi*) we now see the heros of the Civil and Patriotic Wars who slaughtered the innocent in the name of great causes. We see the beastly malice and childish mass gullibility that enabled Stalin's terror to succeed: "It was easier, don't you see, more comforting to believe the higher-ups rather than one's own sweet suffering acquaintances ('nobody's put away for nothing,' 'if they've

[1] Sergey Slonimsky, "Tragediya razobshchennosti lyudey," SovM, no. 3 (1989): 20.

got you it means you're guilty, it means something must be there')."
We see the strange readiness of the arrested innocent to believe in
the guilt of their fellow sufferers. In short, we see the "tragedy of
human disconnectedness" from which Slonimsky took his title.[2]

We see more timely images as well. Watching a Musorgsky opera,
"you feel you are not in the auditorium or reading a score, but in one
of today's crowds, on the street amid one of the newly awakened
political groups or waiting in one of those enormous inescapable
lines for necessities."[3] Nor is Slonimsky's the only account of a new
sensitivity to Musorgsky's terrible messages on the part of formerly
complacent intellectuals, who now, amid the rubble of political and
economic collapse, stand face to face with a hunger they had formerly known "only in its historical aspect."[4]

Thus, Slonimsky avers, Musorgsky's operas "presuppose the intellectual cooperation of an educated listener, an active *counterpoint*,
a *mutual complementation* of the work's images and life itself."[5] The
reading of art for its truly contemporary relevance—its relevance to
our times—is, of course, precisely what traditional Soviet notions of
realism did not encourage. Musorgsky could be interpreted in relation to the times of which he treated, or in relation to the times in
which he lived, but in either case only from a single (melioristic)
perspective. That is why these preternaturally seditious works of
his could hold the stage during the very periods they now appear to
indict.

To limit interpretation to the historical dimension is sterilizing and
falsifying whether practiced in the East or in the West. This book has

[2] Citations in this paragraph from ibid., p. 23. Though the application to recent or
contemporary events is not usually made so explicitly, it has indeed become fashionable in the age of *glasnost'* to do the formerly unthinkable and indict the crowd—not
only for embracing pretenders but for electing tsar-Herods in the first place. See
Alexey Kandinsky, "K voprosu o tragicheskom v 'Borise Godunove,' " paper delivered at the jubilee conference at Velikiye Luki, 18–21 May 1989, reported in D. Logbas,
"God Musorgskogo prodolzhayetsya: V kontekste XX veka," SovM, no. 11 (1989): 91.
Andrey Tarkovsky's 1983 Covent Garden *Boris*, which came to the Leningrad Kirov
Theater just after the sesquicentennial year in January 1990, made the point most insistently. Much of the action is played before an unheroic onstage crowd of (mostly
inattentive) spectators, and mirrors directed outward from the stage into the house
implicated the theater audience as well. See Marina Kornakova, "Tarkovskiy prodolzhayetsya," MZh, no. 1 (1991): 2–5.

[3] "Tragediya razobshchennosti lyudey," p. 20.

[4] Caryl Emerson, "*Glasnost'* Comes to Russian Music: New Soviet Views on Musorgsky's Historical Operas and the Beginning of the End of the World," typescript, p. 14;
the quotation is from a personal communication.

[5] "Tragediya razobshchennosti lyudey," p. 21.

been marked throughout by a concern with original intention: discovering it, interpreting it, deploying it as a corrective to misunder-
standing, whether "statist" or Soviet or positivist. In the spirit of *glasnost'*, then, let me conclude by forswearing any claim of privilege for
the authorial conceptions and purposes I have tried to tease out of
the scores and documents. In no sense do they set boundaries to legitimate reading, nor can they alone define the meaning of works
that have existed in such a multiplicity of redactions and versions—
author's, editors', directors', performers', critics', scholars'—encompassing contributions by the likes of Stasov, Golenishchev-Kutuzov,
Rimsky-Korsakov, Diaghilev, Debussy, Ravel, Stravinsky, Ippolitov-
Ivanov, Shostakovich, Lunacharsky, Asafyev, Chaliapin, Stanislavsky, Tarkovsky, Dahlhaus, Emerson, and now Slonimsky.

So rich a hermeneutic field will not be denied—least of all right
now, when new kettles are coming to such an exciting boil. The endless stream of meanings is precisely what has given Musorgsky's
work its unique cultural value. "In the real historical space of nine-
teenth- and twentieth-century culture," rather than the cloud-
cuckoo-land of philology, "the ceaseless framing of ad hoc variants
and apocrypha" through which an opera like *Boris Godunov* now exists, "paradoxically unites all the various stages, levels, and layers of
artistic culture: traditional folklore, domestic consumption [*bïtovoye
lyubitel'stvo*], professional (literate, high-style, academic) art." So
writes the critic Sergey Rumyantsev, an exemplary voice of *glasnost'*.[6]
The works are ours now, not Musorgsky's. We experience and appreciate them—inevitably and properly—as they have been handed
down to us, the way tradition hands anything down: "guaranteed
highly adulterated," as the clever peddler's sign once read, encrusted
with meanings that have come from anywhere and everywhere—including the author, a good strong voice from the chorus. It is now for
us to re-encrust them and hand them on in turn.

So the philologist's claim of priority in interpretation is not only
futile, it impoverishes and diminishes. We "historicize" in the most
invidious sense of the word if we insist on identifying the meaning
of the works with the intentions of the author. The historical Musorgsky, the man who had the intentions, is dead. It is the works that live
and continue to affect our lives. There may be stronger claims than
that of historical veracity in the interpretation of any work that re-

[6] "Podlinnost' istinï: Yeshcho raz o 'Borise Godunove,' " SovM, no. 8 (1990): 49.

mains within an open, living tradition; in pursuit of them, anachronism need be no vice.

But simplemindedness, tendentious reduction, dogmatic textualism—these are vices. Historical awareness can mitigate them. Not all interpretations are equally worthy of defense. Authorial intentions, insofar as we can know them, should be among the available options: to be wittingly followed or wittingly departed from. In Musorgsky's case they have often been simply stifled—as often by his champions as by his detractors. Thus my project: to inform choice, not delimit it, thus to facilitate "the intellectual cooperation of an educated listener."

"Let us trust the very unfinishedness of unfinished music," Slonimsky proposed (thinking, of course, of *Khovanshchina*) at the end of his searing essay, "and it will answer our questions with a steadfast, unimprovable confession." Being ineluctably open-ended—in the one case because unfinished and in the other because multiply finished—and dealing with eternal quandaries of moral and social existence, Musorgsky's historical operas are fated to be oracles, forever attracting new questions and yielding new answers. They will never run out of answers so long as we do not run out of questions. And that is why renewed interest in Musorgsky, and new approaches to his work, have (together with debate about the cursed life and legacy of Shostakovich) been the essential musical symptom of the era of *glasnost'*. The present moment is more burdened with unanswered questions in Russia than any since the great emancipation that started the country on its slide to revolution (and incidentally wiped out the Musorgsky family fortune).

UNTIL the 1980s, of course, there was virtually no such thing as an unanswered question in Soviet Russia. The new approach to Musorgsky, consisting in the main of new productions of *Boris Godunov* and critical commentary on them, has therefore been a cultural event of tremendous importance —at once a musical catharsis for the country and the cutting edge, not only of Musorgsky interpretation but of a whole burgeoning field of "free-market" musical hermeneutics.

This complex of dramatic spectacle and exegesis has been going on now for a decade, extending back a bit before the officially proclaimed era of *glasnost'* to 1981, the composer's death-centennial, when the 1869 version of *Boris*, with its concentrated focus on the title character and his crime, was revived (as was then necessary for anything so risky) on the peripheries of the Union. What made this production, by the Estonian State Opera and Ballet Theater in Tallinn, nationally newsworthy was a review by Yevgeniy Levashov, a remarkable scholar who has emerged over the course of the 1980s as the outstanding textologist and historian of Russian classical opera.[7] Finally cleared for publication in *Sovetskaya muzïka* two years later, it produced a furor those of us with Soviet or émigré friends remember well.

While both production and review paid the still-required lip service to the official view of the opera that cast it even in its first version as a "populist" (hence proto-Bolshevik) parable of revenge by an offended historical populace on an illegitimate historical ruler, they both allowed far more complexity and range to the drama of a usurper claiming to enact the people's will than was then considered safe. The director (Arne Mikk) and the designers (Valeriy Levental, on loan from the Moscow Bolshoy, and Marina Sokolova) managed to elevate the "divine" theme of conscience, judgment, and expiation over that of secular legitimacy. The production was saturated in religious imagery. It was played before a backdrop of candle-bearing monks, standing like an army of Pimens in mute witness. Candlelit monastic processions, accompanied by tolling bells, linked the scenes. For the sake of an additional monkish presence, the musical text was slightly adulterated: the offstage service choruses in the Cell scene, added by the composer as part of his 1871–72 revision, were interpolated into the earlier version.[8]

A prescient insinuation of universal complicity was evoked by the use of colored lighting to highlight all allusions to the crime, whether by Pimen (who, in the words of the review, "saw but took no part"), Boris ("who saw not but took part"), Shuisky ("who saw and took part but lied"), the Holy Fool ("who saw not and took no part but

[7] Levashov first came to wide attention in the early seventies with a radical new version of Borodin's *Prince Igor*—prepared in collaboration with the veteran composer Yuriy Fortunatov and Boris Pokrovsky, the chief régisseur of the Moscow Bolshoy Theater—which was first produced in Vilnius in 1974, thereafter at the Deutsche Staatsoper (East Berlin), and published in Berlin in 1978. More recently he was named general editor of the new Academic edition of Musorgsky's complete works, projected in thirty-two volumes. The first volume to appear, edited by Levashov himself, was in fact the first edition of the 1869 *Boris* in full score (Moscow: Muzïka, 1989), presented as a complete and independent entity, not (as in the 1928 Lamm edition or the 1975 Lloyd-Jones edition) in the guise of a preliminary version to be laboriously extracted by the reader from a "supersaturated" editorial text—see Chapter 5.

[8] See Genrikh Isakhanov, "Liki festival'nïkh 'Borisov,' " SovM, no. 12 (1990), 43.

spoke the truth") or the future Pretender ("who profits by the fruit of truth and falsehood"). The narrative was fragmented, Rashomon-fashion, into a morass of unresolved contradiction, in which the people were not spared.

Following suit, the reviewer refused to declare a moral victor. Instead he compared Musorgsky's opera with the epilogue to *Crime and Punishment*, Dostoyevsky's roughly contemporaneous novel, in which the murderer-protagonist Raskolnikov has a ghastly vision of the whole world inflamed with his own moral disease: "Whole villages, whole towns and peoples had caught it and were raving . . . not knowing whom to judge or how, unable to agree on what was evil, what was good. They did not know whom to accuse, whom to exonerate . . . Fires broke out, famine broke out. Everything and everyone perished." Even more boldly, Levashov quoted the concluding lines from Alexey Tolstoy's drama *Tsar Boris* (1869) as a subtext to Musorgsky's exactly contemporaneous opera: "From evil only evil grows—all is one: / Whether we wish to serve ourselves with it or the kingdom— / Neither us nor kingdom will it profit!"[9]

What was so new and noteworthy here, even beyond the possibility of reading an implicit challenge to Soviet legitimacy, was the reading of a Musorgsky work as embodying a pessimistic—or at the very least, an ambivalent—outlook on history, and on the historical role of the Russian people. That was revelation, and it required the death of Brezhnev to see it into print.

A scant six years later came the sesquicentennial jubilee, and with it another revisionist production of the 1869 *Boris*, by the Moscow Musical Theater named after Stanislavsky and Nemirovich-Danchenko, directed by Olga Ivanova and designed by Sergey Barkhin.[10] What a benchmark of change it proved to be—but also of disillusion.

[9] Yevgeniy Levashov, "Drama naroda i drama sovesti v opere 'Boris Godunov,' " ibid., no. 5 (1983): 32–38. The review also included a pointed description of the poster for the Tallinn production, in which St. Basil's cathedral on Red Square, the site of Boris's confrontation with the Holy Fool, and Ivan the Terrible's "symbol of the unification of the Russian lands" is shown aflame and disintegrating.

[10] Moscow saw three "authorial" *Boris*es during the jubilee year (in addition to the venerable Bolshoy production of Rimsky-Korsakov's version as supplemented by Ippolitov-Ivanov, staged by Leonid Vasilyevich Baratov and designed by Fyodor Fyodorovich Fyodorovsky, first mounted in 1946); the Estonian production of the 1869 version, appearing in the capital for the first time, played the Bolshoy, as did a 1986 Leningrad Kirov Theater production, based on the David Lloyd-Jones score and directed by Boris Pokrovsky, which conflated the two authorial versions in a fashion that has become fairly standard. For a composite review, see Isakhanov, "Liki festival'nïkh 'Borisov,' " pp. 39–47.

The musical text this time was unadulterated (Levashov's new score was used) but the staging was radically transformed: the opera was wholly depopulized, in open defiance not only of Soviet tradition with respect to the opera but of Soviet historiography as well.[11]

For Soviet consumption *Boris Godunov* has apparently been redefined as a "purely psychological drama" with "surrealist" trappings. Alexey Kandinsky, the ranking "Rusist" among Soviet musical scholars, described the new slap in the face of civic optimism with great consternation: "The people are portrayed in this production as some kind of vague scenic apparition, at times completely unreal, devoid of any clearly typical social or historical identity." They even disappear at the moment traditionally conceived as their most direct confrontation with the tsar, the scene at St. Basil's.[12] Not only that: the whole production is haunted by a mysterious little fair-haired boy with a candle, who is seen seated on the throne at the beginning of the Coronation scene (at Boris's entrance he gets up from it, candle in hand, and, crossing paths with the tsar, makes a menacing gesture); who rematerializes, shadowing Boris, on the latter's emergence from the ancestral shrine where he is crowned; who comes forth at the moment of Boris's death to lead the dead tsar into the dark recesses of the stage and out of sight. Kandinsky declared himself at a loss to understand this imagery: "What on earth is that boy doing there?!"[13]

Evidently he was not paying attention as he entered the theater, where, in the foyer, two lithographs of fair-haired boys were on display. One showed the Tsarevich Dmitry Ioannovich, slain at the behest of usurpers at Uglich in 1591. The other showed the Tsarevich Alexey Nikolayevich, slain at the behest of usurpers at Yekaterinburg in 1918...[14]

Such didactic editorializing is no more to everyone's taste in the post-Communist East than it is in the postmodern West. One Western commentator has lodged a characteristic protest: "The one thing

---

[11] Hostility toward the populist tradition is apparent even in more traditional stagings, such as Pokrovsky's at the Kirov (see the preceding note). Its policemen are knoutless, and the Kromy scene depicts "not a revolution, not 'the people,' just a bunch of tramps," as Pokrovsky stated explicitly to a reporter ("Narod bezmolvstvuyet?" in *Literaturnaya gazeta* [22 March 1989]: 8). Although such was surely not its motivation, this conception is a clear return to that of the composer, as established in Chapter 4.

[12] "Tsena podlinnika," SovM, no. 8 (1990): 48.

[13] Ibid., p. 47.

[14] Sergey Korobkov, "Venchaniye na tsarstvo," MZh, no. 14 (1990): 9.

that we all wait for from Russian art—the possibility of it being simply art without tendentious political lacquering pro or contra—seems
still as distant as ever. The possibility of a strong but fundamentally
ambivalent artistic production inviting multiple hypotheses from its
audience has not been realized."[15] But as the reviews attest, the audience *has* read this production in a multitude of ways, according to
its perspicacity, its predispositions, and its interests—the way all audiences react to all productions.

Nor can one expect neutrality from artists who are only just now
tasting "the freedom to read Pushkin, Karamzin, Musorgsky outside
the rigid framework of an ideological *diktat*."[16] Extremism has got to
be expected. Musorgsky having so long been "impressed by Soviet
scholarship into pre-Marxist duty as a radical populist" (as Emerson
herself has written), "so the chance to *undo* that false label has
proved irresistible."[17] Hence the zealous partisanship on behalf of the
earlier *Boris* over the revised version, which for now is palpably
tainted not only with Rimsky-Korsakov—and not only with pre-*per-
estroyka* "sloganeering kitsch," the legacy of the Stalin prize–winning
Bolshoy brontosaurus of 1946, still lumbering after forty-six years[18]—
but, most important, with the retrospective self-loathing of the long-
impotent Soviet intelligentsia, a *narod*-within-the-*narod* whose dull
speechlessness had saved skins but numbed souls.

AND hence, too, the determination to find a religious thinker in the
composer, already implicit in the quasi-sacral Estonian rendering of
Boris, which Emerson so aptly compares with a passion play.[19] The
theme was taken up with a vengeance during the jubilee year:

> For me Musorgsky is a deeply believing person. His merit consists in
> his having created in his musical works the image not only of suffering
> Russia but of a Russia transformed by the laws of the spirit and the love
> of Christ. Musorgsky's musical dramas are above all an image of com-

[15] Caryl Emerson, "Musorgsky's *Boris* and the 21st Century," in C. Emerson and
R. W. Oldani, *Modest Musorgsky, Boris Godunov.* Cambridge Opera Handbooks (Cambridge: Cambridge University Press, forthcoming).

[16] Korobkov, "Venchaniye na tsarstvo," p. 9.

[17] In "Musorgsky's *Boris* and the 21st Century."

[18] Korobkov, "Venchaniye na tsarstvo," p. 8.

[19] The same determination can be seen in the ascription to Musorgsky, on slender
evidence, of a church composition, the a cappella chorus *Angel vopiyashe*, first described and printed by Yevgeniy Levashov ("Neizvestnoye sochineniye," SovM, no. 3
[1981]: 111–12) and scheduled for publication in the new Academic edition of the composer's complete works.

mon penance, of common prayer, inner grief at the deeds of men, but then the light that transforms into the image of the Resurrection.[20]

Musorgsky composed as if praying; for him the act of writing music was itself a religious rite, even a sacrament. In contrast to the strictly rationalized logic of symphonic development that predominated in Western European composition schools (the nearer to the twentieth century, the more so), he created his works by submitting to a process of extraordinary inner *epiphany*, whereby the components of musical logic, insofar as they do not altogether disappear, give way to a phenomenon of syncretic Logos that comprehends all existence.[21]

Assertions like these find precious little documentary support.[22] The first of them is a wholly gratuitous interpolation in an article ostensibly devoted to the composer's genealogy. The other—by a Hero of Socialist Labor cum Peoples Artist of the USSR, formerly a reliable apparatchik—is a typical *glasnost'* affectation, laden more with nationalism than with spirituality. It is tempting to write off the Christianization of Musorgsky as another of those lemming-runs at the negative image that have plagued reassessment of the Soviet past (scandalously in the case of Shostakovich), reversing black and white but still omitting grey.

But it raises the temperature of Musorgsky debate in today's Russia the highest, and to that extent it must be regarded as an authentic artifact of *glasnost'*. At an otherwise fairly tame academic conference

[20] Vladimir Sorokin (rector of the St. Petersburg Seminary), quoted in Nikolai Novikov, "Ego rodoslovnaya," SovM, no. 3 (1989): 33–34.

[21] Georgiy Sviridov, "O Musorgskom," NasMPM, 9.

[22] The only letter that deals centrally with religious themes is a very early one to Balakirev (19 October 1859), in which Musorgsky confesses to a bout of "mysticism." Far from embracing it, however, he calls it a "terrible illness," and expresses relief at its passing (MusLN, 1.46; MR, 21). In his third-person autobiographical note of 1880 Musorgsky mentioned frequent visits as a teenager to the religious instructor at the Cadet School of Guards, Father Krupsky, but the only acknowledged purpose of these visits was musical, rather than spiritual, instruction: "He managed, thanks to [Father Krupsky], to penetrate deeply into the very essence of ancient Greek and Catholic [and, he adds in the French version, "luthérienne-protestante"] church music" (MusLN 1.267; MR, 417). Perhaps the closest one can come to the sort of religious commitment recent Soviet commentators have asserted is the closing paragraph in Musorgsky's huge letter to Stasov of 13 July 1872: "I've taken up the cross [*Krest na sebya nalozhil ya*] and with lifted head I shall go forth, boldly and merrily, against *all* [obstacles] toward a bright, strong, righteous goal, toward a genuine art, one that loves mankind, lives its joys and sorrows and sufferings" (MusLN 1.137; MR, 193). Predictably enough, Nikolai Novikov cites this very passage in support of the seminarian's letter (SovM, no. 3 [1989]: 33–34). But is it anything more than an expression of "crusader's" zeal?

held in observance of the 1989 jubilee in Velikiye Luki, the city near-
est the composer's birthplace, the religious theme elicited the one
moment of passion. After several Russian participants had argued
that Musorgsky's entire output must be read as Christian allegory, a
Bulgarian delegate (Ivan Khlebarov) countered, first, that had the
composer been truly religious his Holy Fool would have prayed, not
just lamented; and, second, that the others were in fact practicing a
reverse-Soviet bigotry against atheists ("Why do you strip me, a non-
believer, of the right to the pangs of conscience? Why do you refuse
me, an atheist, the right to be a moral person?"). Still, a point raised
quietly but resolutely by a Polish scholar, Teresa Malecka, deserves
consideration. "It is hard to find traces of religious questions in the
published documents," she conceded, "but, on the other hand, the
composer's works are utterly saturated with them!"[23]

The work that must form the starting point of any such investigation is *Khovanshchina*. It, too, is undergoing reevaluation in the spirit
of *glasnost'*, though not with anything like the zeal lavished on *Boris*.
Its only revisionist staging took place in Novosibirsk in 1987, and
amounted to little more than replacing the Rimsky-Korsakov redaction with the Shostakovich one, which has been in the Leningrad
repertory since 1960, and which still depends in certain crucial respects on Rimsky-Korsakov.[24] The revisionist touch came at the very
end, when Shostakovich's quintessentially Sovietizing reminiscence
of the Dawn prelude—interpolated "so as to underscore Musorgsky's [!] faith in Russia's future, in defiance of 'Khovanshchina' and
'Petrovshchina' alike [i.e., the machinations both of Tsar Peter and
his opponents]"[25]—was excised. On the other hand, the (mute) appearance of Peter on stage at the end of scene 5, explicitly disavowed
by Musorgsky but demanded (so the legend goes) by Stalin himself,
was retained.[26]

[23] Logbas, "God Musorgskogo prodolzhayetsya," pp. 89–91.

[24] Compare Vienna, where the State Opera mounted a "restored" version of the
opera, overseen by Claudio Abbado, in which Rimsky-Korsakov's hand was as far as
possible erased, in which Shostakovich's thematic reminiscences were removed, and
in which Stravinsky's final chorus, composed for Diaghilev in 1913, was revived. A
recording is available: Deutsche Grammophon 429 758–2 (three compact discs).

[25] Yakov Naumovich Fain, "Pravo na 'Khovanshchinu,' " SovM, no. 8 (1987): 78.

[26] The concluding reminiscences were finally removed from the Kirov's high-Stalinist (1952) production in 1989. In a roundtable published in *Sovetskaya muzïka*, the Leningrad critic Yelena Tretyakova interpreted this as a political move, not a religious one
(nor did she try to connect it with the composer's putative intentions): "In the 1952

In a sense the timid neglect of Musorgsky's second historical opera is surprising, since *Khovanshchina* implied a much more direct comment than did *Boris* on its own contemporary world. But the opera does not present a focus of empathy as compelling as its predecessor's suffering protagonist, nor does it pose questions that can have equally satisfying or cathartic answers. Instead one is forced back upon those rather abstract questions dealt with in Chapters 7 and 8— such as what constitutes "the people" (*narod*) in Musorgsky's conception of a *narodnaya muzïkal'naya drama*[27]—and to the comparatively unreassuring realization that, decades of sanguine Stalinist propaganda notwithstanding, the folk are for this composer no "nation," no monolithic moral fount, but a fallible disharmonious motley that can easily turn into a mob.

Only the Old Believers, Soviet observers are at last allowed to admit, possess unity of purpose and dignity among the contending groups in *Khovanshchina*: only the reactionary religious are a folk that can never be a mob. Herein lies the opera's potential religious import, a message that was apparent enough all through the Stalinist period to make the composer's devotees uneasy. "Haven't we known ever since our school days," wrote Anatoliy Volkov, a veteran music journalist, "that Musorgsky is 'inconsistent,' that on the one hand, *Khovanshchina* is a classic, but on the other, that there's something not quite right about it?"[28]

That admission came in a formidable essay entitled "Folk and Mob: The Lessons of *Khovanshchina*," one of the really programmatic musical texts of the *glasnost'* era. But even Volkov, it appeared, had to recoil from so un-Soviet a notion, denying that the moral strength of

---

production the central conflict was the struggle among the leaders of the rebellion, the schismatics, and the state in the person of Peter. The conflict was resolved in favor of the state, and it was no accident that the young soldiers of the tsar were made to rescue an [Old Believer] youth by pulling him out of the fire. The spectacle was all about the state's mercy and compassion, affirming the state as the people's sole constant strength and support. Now the times have changed, and in a 1989 *Khovanshchina* another ending is apropos: the self-destruction of the Old Believers as an act of protest, as an expression of a spirit that no amount of pressure can break" ("Uroki proshedshikh sezonov . . . ," SovM, no. 2 [1991]: 85).

[27] Leningrad's Malïy Theater finessed that one in 1989 by simply presenting *Khovanshchina* as an "opera in two [!] acts" (Ibid., p. 89). That is antipopulism with a vengeance.

[28] "Narod i tolpa: uroki 'Khovanshchinï,' " MZh, no. 23 (1989): 19–21; and 24 (1989): 19–21.

the Old Believers stemmed from their religion, preferring, rather, to locate that strength in the fortuitous strength of personality—Dosifey's and Marfa's in particular. Retreating behind the composer's authority as he chose to construct it, he concluded point blank that "spiritual values for Musorgsky are personal values." Unlike the pantheistic and "organic" Rimsky-Korsakov, he argued, whose fairy-tale *narod* (as in *The Snow Maiden*) embodied idealized virtue and order, Musorgsky was first and last an individualist, for whom virtue and order could not be inherited or merely submitted to, but only won by free choice. As an individualist, Musorgsky could not be a Christian thinker.[29]

That puts a new and hopeful slant on things: resistance to the Christian theme, unwillingness to make a Tolstoy out of Musorgsky, need not be merely inertial or reflexive. In Volkov's case it arises from an abhorrence of collectivism learned over "seventy years of barracks socialism," and represents the best strain of emergent Soviet liberalism. "Shall we have done at last with fetishizing mass consciousness," he asks, "or, remaining true to the myth of the monolith, shall we reduce spiritual renewal to a new set of slogans?" And he concludes: "Will we finally understand, will we feel it in our bones, that a free people can only consist of free persons? That, unlike unfreedom, freedom cannot be collective? That human harmony, unlike the zoological kind, cannot be given and assigned for all time, but forever creates itself anew—for each and for all?"[30]

This is the obverse, the hopeful side, of the "tragedy of human disconnectedness" Slonimsky saw symbolized in Musorgsky's divided crowd. It would be pointless to observe that Musorgsky could not have intended them both; still less would it make sense to object that the historical Rimsky-Korsakov proved himself a true liberal (in 1905), while investigation of the historical Musorgsky's social and political views, as in our Chapter 8, quickly leads in directions deeply offensive to all liberal and democratic thought. To repeat once more: the works, not the man, are still with us, still malleable. And Musorgsky's works, after all these years, are the ones that (with Shostakovich's) fill a *glasnost'*-inspired need.

"We will not wring from this great artist impossible answers," Volkov had already written in another groundbreaking *glasnost'* piece.

[29] Ibid., no. 24 (1989): 20.
[30] *Ibid.*, p. 21.

"Better be grateful to him for all his many questions, so close to us today."[31] Indeed, could there be any better measure of his greatness?

POSTSCRIPT, SEPTEMBER 1991: No sooner had the words above been written, it seemed, than a whole new chapter, possibly a whole new volume, in the history of Musorgsky's motherland suddenly burst open, accompanied by an access of civic optimism that seems unprecedented in all of Russian history. "Never in my life did I expect to hear so much Russian laughter," wrote Tatyana Tolstaya in the wake of the failed hard-line coup.[32] And it was for once a wholly unsardonic laughter, untinged by resentment or self-loathing.

While these will inevitably return, they will do so under changed circumstances, to which, one hopes, the events of the seventeenth-century Time of Troubles will no longer seem so urgently relevant. Tarkovsky's indictment of the passive crowd has been answered on the barricades surrounding the Russian parliament. The dethronement of the Communist Party may put paid to the theme of regicidal guilt so insistently advanced at the Stanislavsky Theater. And Anatoliy Volkov's fears of a new monolith in the form of blind, democracy-threatening mob action have so far been, if not confuted, at least deferred. "This time," wrote Tolstaya, "the crowd was not the mob. This time the crowd was the people. It was one of those rare moments when the crowd is transformed, by truth and by danger, into something higher, not something lower."[33]

So what took place on 19–22 August 1991 was no Musorgsky opera—yet. And if the Russian people do not revert to Musorgskian type—if they remain persons, free and undeceived, and if *vlast'*, the power, remains accountable to *narod*, the people—then it is the operas, ever malleable but ever vigilant, that will eventually change to conform. The best outcome one could desire for Russia is one in which her tragic historical music dramas can at last retire from current events and find a permanent home in the museum. A Russia in which Musorgsky no longer looks like a prophet is the Russia we all long to see.

[31] "Pravo na vïbor," MZh, no. 5 (1989): 20.
[32] "When Putsch Comes to Shove," *New Republic* (16/23 September 1991): 24.
[33] Ibid.

INDEX